Elite White Men

This book examines the "who, what, when, where, and how" of elite-white-male dominance in U.S. and global society. In spite of their domination in the United States and globally that we document herein, elite white men have seldom been called out and analyzed as such. They have received little to no explicit attention with regard to systemic racism issues, as well as associated classism and sexism issues. Almost all public and scholarly discussions of U.S. racism fail to explicitly foreground elite white men or to focus specifically on how their interlocking racial, class, and gender statuses affect their globally powerful decision-making. Some of the power positions of these elite white men might seem obvious, but they are rarely analyzed for their extraordinary significance. While the principal focus of this book is on neglected research and policy questions about the elite-white-male role and dominance in the system of racial oppression in the United States and globally, because of their positioning at the top of several societal hierarchies the authors periodically address their role and dominance in other oppressive (e.g., class, gender) hierarchies.

Joe R. Feagin, Ella McFadden Professor and University Distinguished Professor at Texas A&M University, does research on racism, sexism, and classism issues. He has served as Scholar-in-Residence at the U.S. Commission on Civil Rights and is the recipient of the American Sociological Association's W. E. B. Du Bois Career of Distinguished Scholarship Award. He was the 1999–2000 president of the American Sociological Association.

Kimberley Ducey, an Associate Professor at the University of Winnipeg and a recent graduate of Canada's esteemed Université McGill, does research on the historical and contemporary oppression of humans and other animals. Dr. Ducey is a Québec Forces AVENIR recipient – an award which aims to recognize, honor, and promote involvement in projects that contribute to the formation of conscious citizens.

A masterful deconstruction of the intersection of race, gender, and class inequality in the 21st century. A must-read book for anyone who cares about inequality.

Roy L. Brooks, *Warren Distinguished Professor of Law,*
University of San Diego School of Law

In *Elite White Men Ruling* Joe Feagin and Kimberley Ducey make an important, historically-grounded, contribution to our understanding of the intersectionality of class, racial, and gender domination in the United States that meticulously reveals the workings of the hugely consequential, but largely invisible, oligarchical rule of elite white men. Kudos to Professors Feagin and Ducey for both deepening our understanding of such oppression and for offering us a model of intersectional studies that not only casts a wide substantive net, but goes deep historically and conceptually in explaining both the specific workings of each oppressive system and their exponentially-increased power, as they feed off one another.

Noel A. Cazenave, *Professor of Sociology, University of Connecticut,*
and author of Conceptualizing Racism: Breaking the
Chains of Racially Accommodative Language

With eloquence and compelling scholarship, Feagin and Ducey offer a searing, profound analysis of the elite-white-male dominance system, an analysis that is both breathtaking in scope and persuasive in intellectual depth. The book will undoubtedly be viewed as a sociological *magnum opus* of this century.

Edna B. Chun, *Chief Learning Officer, HigherEd Talent, and co-author of*
The Department Chair as Transformative Diversity Leader

Feagin and Ducey pull back the curtain on abstract concepts of institutional power to show us the elite-white-male architects of inequality and oppression. In the Feagin tradition, the book does not hold back punches in examining – and often naming – the human sources of racism, sexism, and class exploitation.

Nestor Rodriguez, *Professor of Sociology,*
The University of Texas at Austin

Feagin and Ducey affirm the scholarship of a whole range of scholars from Du Bois and Cox to Patricia Hill Collins and Kimberlé Crenshaw. Their forthright and concise analysis provides a fresh and insightful analysis that demonstrates the historical roots and contemporary contexts through which elite white males create, maintain, and reconstruct their hegemonic control over most major institutions within western society. Feagin and Ducey posit that this hegemonic control represents a major challenge to effective democracy. Such a democracy requires embracing the efficacy of human rights as an instrument of social change and justice. This would require a revolution, of spirit if not of society.

Rodney D. Coates, *Professor of Global and Intercultural Studies,*
Director of Black World Studies, Miami University

Elite White Men Ruling

Who, What, When, Where, and How

Joe R. Feagin and Kimberley Ducey

Routledge
Taylor & Francis Group

NEW YORK AND LONDON

First published 2017
by Routledge
711 Third Avenue, New York, NY 10017

and by Routledge
2 Park Square, Milton Park, Abingdon, Oxon, OX14 4RN

Routledge is an imprint of the Taylor & Francis Group, an informa business

© 2017 Taylor & Francis

The right of Joe R. Feagin and Kimberley Ducey to be identified as authors of this work has been asserted by them in accordance with sections 77 and 78 of the Copyright, Designs and Patents Act 1988.

Library of Congress Cataloging-in-Publication Data
Names: Feagin, Joe R., author. | Ducey, Kimberley, author.
Title: Elite white men ruling : who, what, when, where, and how /
    Joe Feagin and Kimberley Ducey.
Description: New York, NY : Routledge, 2017. | Includes bibliographical
    references and index.
Identifiers: LCCN 2016052990 | ISBN 9781138191815 (hardcover : alk.
    paper) | ISBN 9781138191822 (pbk. : alk. paper) | ISBN 9781315640280
    (alk. paper)
Subjects: LCSH: Elite (Social sciences)—United States. | Men,
    White—United States. | Power (Social sciences)—United States. |
    Discrimination—United States. | United States—Politics and
    government.
Classification: LCC HN90.E4 F43 2017 | DDC 305.5/20973—dc23
LC record available at https://lccn.loc.gov/2016052990

ISBN: 978-1-138-19181-5 (hbk)
ISBN: 978-1-138-19182-2 (pbk)
ISBN: 978-1-315-64028-0 (ebk)

Typeset in Minion
by Apex CoVantage, LLC

In memory of Hernán Vera

Contents

Acknowledgments

We would like to thank Noël Cazenave, Edna Chun, Sean Elias, Melissa Ochoa Garza, Thaddeus Atzmon, Rachel Feinstein, Frank Ortega, Gabe Miller, Anthony Weems, Colin Goff, and Heidi Rimke for their comments and suggestions on various versions of this manuscript.

Introduction
Elite White Men:
The 21st Century Problem

The central problem of the 21st century is elite white men. They long ago created what we term the *elite-white-male dominance system*, a complex and oppressive system central to most western societies that now affects much of the planet. This small elite rules actively, undemocratically, and globally, yet remains largely invisible to the billions of people it routinely dominates. In the U.S. case, which we focus on here, few people outside the top rank of this powerful elite or its immediate subordinates can name more than a tiny number of the mostly white men at the pinnacle of major U.S. institutions.

While we include these immediate powerful subordinates in the term *elite*, we seek to accent the *top* rank of that elite—the mostly white men who occupy the loftiest apex of societal power and control. This small ruling class holds exceptional social rank and privileges, and they have much more power than non-elite members of society. Those in the top rank of the elite form a dominant oligarchy in which they, a very small minority of U.S. residents, rule over all others in society.[1]

The director of one media research project, Soraya Chemaly, has summed up the extensive white male dominance across major U.S. economic, political, educational, and media institutions:

> [Currently] white men make up more than 80% of Congress, 78% of state political executives, 75% of state legislators, 84% of mayors of the top 100 cities, 85% of corporate executive officers, 100% of CEOs of Wall Street firms, 95% of Fortune 500 CEOs, 73% of tenured professors, 64% of newsroom staffers, 97% of heads of venture capital firms, 90% of tech jobs in Silicon Valley, 97% of owners of television and radio licenses, 87% of police departments and 68% of U.S. Circuit Court Judges.[2]

A very unusual *New York Times* article recently presented photographs of top elite and other powerful decision-makers. Unsurprisingly, it showed a huge sea of white, and especially white male, faces of societal decision-making power.[3] As Chemaly adds to her analysis, if a novelist presented a fictional story in which the gender of these powerful decision-makers were *reversed*, the "reviewers would describe this world as a violent and emasculating feminist tyranny or a frightening male dystopia."[4]

One goal of this book is to move away from the typical passive tenses and vague nouns in discussing those who have ruled this country for centuries. In our experience, almost no social analysts have made regular and systematic use of a specific term and concept like "elite white men," for those who constitute the overwhelming majority of the most powerful decision-makers whose everyday choices and actions have regularly shaped both the United States and other societies across the globe.

One only has to skim a typical U.S. history textbook to see that almost all of the top economic and political *decisions* made by Americans since the 1600s have been made by *elite white men*. Some actions taken by these elite white individuals, or by elite subgroups, have been relatively progressive or potentially beneficial to ordinary people—for example, the elite's asserting equality and justice themes in the Declaration of Independence, creating 1930s New Deal social welfare programs, joining the European war against Nazism in World War II, helping to create a United Nations, and passing significant civil rights, health, and social welfare laws since the 1960s.

However, a great many other choices and decisions made by this elite have been oppressive for centuries, for very large numbers of people in North America and overseas. These have included, to name a few, creating North American colonies by killing off and stealing land from indigenous Americans, creating and maintaining African American slavery for more than half of U.S. history, fighting a bloody Civil War over slavery, maintaining Jim Crow segregation for many decades, establishing a sexist and heterosexist legal system, creating an auto-centered and petroleum-dependent transportation system, creating exploitative capitalistic corporations, militarily invading countries to build a U.S. empire, becoming the largest seller of weapons abroad, using the first nuclear weapons, and starting wars in countries such as Iraq and Afghanistan. Today's white male elite, and the organizations they head and are thus empowered by, still engage in many similar actions, including the large-scale parasitic exploitation of people of color globally. Note too that this elite has historically generated much of the racial, gender, and class framing rationalizing their actions.

For centuries, since Europeans began imperialistic and colonial expansion, a powerful white male capitalistic elite has emerged and thereby replaced earlier aristocratic elites by generating great wealth from extensive theft of the labor, land, and other resources of peoples across the globe. They have engaged in new nation-building and positioned themselves at the top of the overarching elite-white-male dominance system and, thus, of three of its major subsystems—systemic sexism (heterosexism), systemic classism (capitalism), and systemic racism—that we examine in this book.[5] These highly oppressive and globally determining subsystems usually appear together in societal operations and are regularly interlocking, codetermining, and coreproducing in a helix-like fashion. This is true for several reasons, but one primary one is that the same or similar elite white men have long ruled at the *top* of each subsystem, and thereby over the entire elite-white-male dominance system.

A typical definition of "modernity" emphasizes features of western countries, such as advanced industrialization, extensive urbanization, substantial secularism, and developed technologies. This modernity, which supposedly includes a superior rationality, has long been accented by western scholars and other analysts, from German sociologist Max Weber's time to the present. What is missing from such conventionally positive portrayals of modernity is what is central to this book—the elite-white-male dominance system and its many negative impacts for much of humanity. In many ways the elite-controlled, colonized world created by European expansion, imperialism, and colonization from the 16th to the 19th centuries gave birth to many oppressive structures and other oppressive aspects of western societies that persist to the present day.

Social Science Analyses of the Elite

Since early in the history of western social science, most mainstream social scientists have tiptoed around the major issues of elite power and coercion, especially in regard to systemic racial, gender, and/or class oppression. Unsurprisingly, these social sciences have long been molded by their national contexts, and thus relatively elite white men have generally shaped the dominant theoretical and methodological perspectives on stratification issues.[6] As sociologist William Carroll has argued, this powerful white group has greatest access to information about how major institutions operate, while those in subordinated positions have much less information. As a result, most people have to put some "trust in the managers, officials, and professionals who occupy the higher echelons of the system." Drawing on sociologist Howard Becker's earlier argument, Carroll explains that if social scientists do research and teaching from some version of the dominant racial, class, or gender framing, "there is no charge of bias. . . . It is when sociologists give credence to subordinate perspectives and experiences, thereby challenging the hierarchy of credibility, that they may be charged with bias."[7]

Nonetheless, a significant number of social scientists have examined, with varying degrees of critical insight, aspects of western political and economic elites. Numerous mainstream political and organizational theorists, such as the conservative James Burnham, have provided insightful analyses of the role of managers, professionals, and think-tanks in important societal decisions.[8] In this book we have drawn most often on the social science tradition of investigating the U.S. elite from a more critical class (e.g., neo-Marxist) perspective. For instance, in the 1950s the critical sociologist Floyd Hunter demonstrated the absence of real democracy in decision-making in a major U.S. city, while sociologist C. Wright Mills probed beneath everyday events to major societal power inequalities and the actors shaping them. Mills documented, at the helm of U.S. society, a small tripartite elite—those few people in big corporations, major government agencies, and large military institutions who typically make many of society's most important decisions.[9] A little later, in 1960, political scientist Elmer Schattschneider argued that the array of powerful pressure groups did not add up to the "democratic" U.S. political system claimed by many pluralist analysts.[10]

More recent class-critical social scientists, such as Philip Burch and Bill Domhoff, have shown in empirical detail that the U.S. is governed at the top by an upper-class elite that is empowered by the organizations they operate from and the networks they have emerged from. Their work has influenced our understanding of the role of corporations and other important organizations in the power and development of the country's elite. Domhoff, for example, has demonstrated well that major capitalists and their close subordinates rule in the United States, in part, by serving in top positions in government and in private policy-planning organizations.[11] This critical social science theorizing and empirical research has mostly accented aspects of the social *class* dimension of the dominant elite, and we will draw on research on class and capitalism in our analysis.

However, there is much more to the dominant elite's social dominance that must be fully delineated and assessed. Throughout this book, we demonstrate that *whiteness* and *maleness* are extraordinarily important social dimensions shaping this elite's personal and collective reality, including their dominant social framing and their decisions flowing from that framing. As we demonstrate, these elite white men have for centuries constituted the group at the top of three major social hierarchies—the capitalistic, sexist, and racial hierarchies. They have long created, maintained, and extended these inegalitarian hierarchies that are imbedded in and shaping all societal institutions. Generally speaking, contemporary social scientists and other social analysts have substantially bypassed an in-depth analysis of the reality and significance of the *white* and *male* aspects of this controlling elite's motivations to act and, thus, the important decisions that result.

The partial exceptions to this generalization are mainly a few research studies and theories of scholars of color and white women scholars. For instance, one social scientist who pioneered in bringing issues of racism into a neo-Marxist class analysis was Oliver Cox, an African American sociologist. Between the 1940s and the 1970s he did penetrating analyses of the intertwining of white racism and class-exploitative capitalism. Breaking with white social scientists in that era, he contributed significantly to our understanding of this intertwining of racial and class oppression, seen as a single phenomenon with white capitalists generally at the top. From his empirically honed perspective, that ruling elite had aggressively exploited black labor and thus succeeded in proletarianizing "a whole people—that is to say, the whole people is looked upon as a class—whereas white prole-tarianization involves only a section of the white people."[12] The concepts of capitalists and white people seem "to mean the *same* thing for, with respect to the colored peoples of the world, it is almost always through a white bourgeoisie that capitalism has been introduced. The early [white] capitalist settlers . . . were disposed to look upon the latter and their natural resources as factors of production to be manipulated impersonally with 'white capi-tal' in the interest of profits."[13] Early on, Cox had assessed how the western ruling elite not only is made up of controlling capitalists but also has histor-ically been almost entirely white and male.

Moreover, in the midst of the 1960s civil rights movement, black activ-ists and activist-scholars increasingly accented the problem of an oppres-sive U.S. power structure. In their influential book *Black Power*, Student Nonviolent Coordinating Committee leader Kwame Ture and historian Charles Hamilton analyzed the racial and class aspects of what they called out as the "*white* power structure," especially how that power elite had cre-ated racially oppressive institutions that did much more harm than did isolated white bigots. Although they did not accent the gendered aspect of this oppression or call out and assess elite white men more specifically, they took a major step in naming and critiquing the collective white power structure and demonstrating that its power flowed from institutional positioning.[14]

In recent years a few other scholars have done some research on another juncture of the racial and class hierarchies—ordinary white men in the working class. Sociologist Michael Kimmel has analyzed the views of angry white men in the working class who have faced declining deindustrializa-tion and loss of jobs in recent times; he briefly calls out elite actors for suc-cessfully hiding their role in this crisis: "This has been the cultural mission of the ruling elites—to deny their own existence . . . and pretend that they are on the side of the very people they are disenfranchising. . . . The anger of middle-class white Americans is . . . misdirected not toward those who are the cause of their misery but against those who are just below them on the economic ladder."[15] Still, Kimmel's discussion is brief and he does not probe more deeply into the who and what of these "ruling elites."

The *Triple Helix* of Class, Racial, and Gender Domination

The influential sociologist Patricia Hill Collins, whose pioneering work on intersectionality theory is discussed in the next chapter, has suggested that the racial-gender intersectionality she probes deeply is part of an overarching system of oppression she terms the "matrix of domination"—the interconnecting matrix of the gender, class, and racial oppressions. Drawing on the tradition of black feminist thought in assessing the oppressive situations of black women, Collins argues that an accent on a single matrix structure should replace older models that just add up oppressions: "Race, class, and gender represent the three systems of oppression that most heavily affect African-American women."[16] A few other scholars of color have briefly underscored this tripartite system of oppressions. For instance, bell hooks too has pioneered in assessing the intersectionality of women of color. She labeled the system at the root of white violence against women and men of color as the "white supremacist capitalist patriarchy."[17] These scholars of color have laid one major part of the conceptual basis on which we build in this book.

Here we add to existing intersectionality theory and critical elite theory by accenting additional theoretical dimensions and empirical realities. In particular, we provide a *specific and detailed focus* on those white men who are the key decision-makers at or near the apex of society's elite-white-male dominance system. We primarily assess their centrality in three of this larger system's complex subsystems of racial, class, and gender oppression.

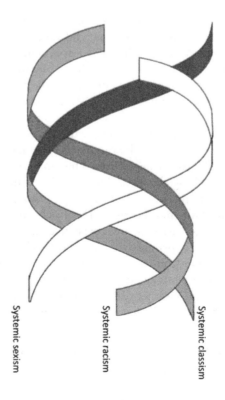

Systemic sexism   Systemic racism   Systemic classism

The Triple Helix

These oppression subsystems, which elite decision-makers play a central role in controlling and perpetuating, are much more than separate societal vectors that are "pointing in different directions and crossing at one point."[18] They do much more than intersect. Generally, they are intimately *intertwined* and *interlocking* at several levels, like a triple social helix, and they have *codetermined* and *coreproduced* each other at these levels for centuries. Thus, in their everyday actions elite white men constantly have a great impact on the shape and trajectory of society. Regularly, over short and long periods of time, they seek to protect and expand capitalistic profit and property, their position in the national and global racial hierarchy, and their hegemonic masculinity in the global gender order. As we will demonstrate, they are so powerful substantially because of the major networks and major organizations in which they are groomed, situated, and/or operative.

Among the specific questions we raise about these elite white men and their determinative actions are these: How has a rather small number of people, these very powerful white men, come to control most of the western world, and increasingly much of the globe? How does their racial and gender position and framing shape their actions in sync with their capitalistic position and class framing? What has motivated these elite men to create and perpetuate a geographical empire of centuries-long exploitation and dominance? Given that mostly elite white men still control this empire of hundreds of millions of people, where and how do they maintain that extensive national and global dominance? And how have they viewed and framed themselves, especially in comparison to those they have exploited and subordinated in class, racial, and/or gender terms?

So let us, indeed, position and assess these exceptionally powerful white men and their huge number of concrete societal-shaping actions as the *global problem of the 21st century* when it comes to many matters of human rights and human survival, to real "liberty and justice for all" of humanity.

Over the centuries since this early imperialistic colonization, the most powerful European and European American men, with aid from enabling acolytes, have regularly imposed or substantially shaped sexist, classist, and racist hierarchical structures in countries across the globe. Today, as in the past, this elite-white-male power is rooted in and buttressed by major societal organizations and institutions—and thus is systemic, firmly established, and undergirded by threats of force.

Intersectionality, Interactionality, and Coreproduction

Given this overarching elite-white-male dominance system, let us explore a bit more the relationships of its gender, class, and racial oppression subsystems. How are these component subsystems related and interrelated? Especially since the 1960s civil rights movements, numerous social science and humanities scholars have focused on certain aspects of the *intersectionality* of these important subsystems. These intersections seem to have been analyzed in detail for those most oppressed, especially the intersectionality that situates African American women and other women of color. Indeed, some groundwork for analyzing the intersectional situation of African American women appeared well before the 1960s movements in the work of activists and analysts from Sojourner Truth and Frances E. W. Harper in the mid-19th century to Anna Julia Cooper and Maria Stewart later in that century. For example, in her 19th century speeches and novels Harper provided penetrating assessments of the dominance of patriarchal norms as they negatively affected all women, and especially black women.[3]

Most recently, several African American scholars such as Kimberlé Crenshaw, Angela Davis, and Patricia Hill Collins have been in the forefront of those accenting a much more developed intersectionality theory and empirical analyses. Coining the term "intersectionality" for critical race studies, Crenshaw was a pioneer in critiquing mainstream feminist studies for not considering the intersectional position of black women, who jointly face both systemic sexism and systemic racism. In her work Davis has examined, among other intersectionality issues, how enslaved black women were long racialized and gendered—exploited for their labor and "breeders" of enslaved children. In her pioneering intersectionality research, Philomena Essed has examined what she terms the "gendered racism" faced by black women in the United States and Europe.[4] As suggested previously, Collins has provided a major and detailed social science analysis of intersectionality issues in regard to how racial oppression intersects with gender oppression, and how understanding these intersections forms a distinctive black feminist epistemological perspective.[5]

In addition, over the last century white Marxist-Feminist scholars have examined the intersectional relationship of gender oppression and class oppression, with a particular emphasis on the materialistic basis of this oppression. They have been critical of mainstream Marxists for paying little attention to the conditions of women and of the radical feminist tradition for being too psychological in analyses of such issues as marriage and women workers. Marxist-Feminist researcher Zillah Eisenstein has analyzed how the contemporary United States still has a well-developed patriarchal system in which women must struggle for their liberation and a positive sense of self.[6] A Marxist-Feminist perspective, as Heidi Hartmann argues, regularly defines "patriarchy as a set of social relations between men, which have a *material* base, and which, though hierarchical, establish or create interdependence and solidarity among men that enable them to dominate women."[7] Well-established societal institutions, such as monogamous heterosexual marriage, thus provide male control over women's access to essential productive resources (e.g., their relationship to the job economy) and control over women's family and sexual labor. In this way, the early European patriarchal system and its male exploitation of women's labor provided a major template for the later exploitation of colonized peoples overseas.[8]

In this book we add to social science analysis of these systems of oppression by examining in specific detail the most powerful group, the elite white men, at the intersectional top of the hierarchical gender, class, and racial subsystems. This society-creating and society-shaping group is rarely called out as such and has almost never been systematically analyzed by social scientists. This group of societal overlords makes many of the most important everyday decisions that create, shape, and sustain the sexist, classist, and racist subsystems. They interlink and interconnect these subsystems—physically, materially, and socially.

In addition, these subsystems do much more than accommodate each other, for they regularly *codetermine* and *coreproduce* one another. One subsystem rarely operates in isolation of the others. For example, within the modern capitalistic system important economic positions are often significantly determined and defined by the intersecting impacts of the sexist and racist subsystems. The hierarchical arrangement of jobs often has a major gendered component (e.g., women disproportionately in clerical positions, men disproportionately in senior management) or a racial component (e.g., blacks disproportionately in lower-paying jobs, whites disproportionately in better-paying jobs) that is not understandable just from an economic-class viewpoint. Theoretically, a profit-oriented capitalistic system does not require such gendered and racialized placements of workers. In turn, the long-term patterns of gendered and racialized job positions within the capitalistic economy help to reproduce other aspects of the larger sexist and racist subsystems of oppression. Additionally, the latter subsystems work to reinforce and coreproduce the class subsystem in numerous ways, including the gender and racial splitting up of the working class to the general benefit of the dominant capitalist class. For example, these subsystems create within capitalism a distinctive "reserve army of labor"—for instance, workers of color who are paid less by discriminating employers, and thereby also undermine the wages of many white workers. Unmistakably, over centuries critical aspects of these subsystems of subjugation have become interlocking and resistant to change, so that one subsystem significantly and regularly helps to coreproduce the others.[9]

Throughout this book we see how powerful this *coreproduction* process is in maintaining the elite-white-male dominance system. Some decades back, a group of critical social theorists briefly developed this useful concept, which they defined as a major "causal force at work in historical development. Spheres co-reproduce when the dynamics of one reproduce the defining relations of others."[10] We adopt here a holistic social science perspective that accents this reality of the major subsystems of sexist, classist, and racist oppression being coreproducing, interconnected, and intertwined. For the sake of a clearer explanation, we mainly consider in this book these three coreproducing subsystems of the elite-white-male dominance system, but we must keep in mind the interconnections of these particular systems of oppression with other systems of oppression in western societies like the United States. Thus, our approach will be to look beyond surface appearances and prevailing mythologies to critical societal realities that have long been regularly hidden and thoroughly disguised.

Unity and Divisions in the Ruling Elite

Many analysts who research or theorize systemic sexism, classism, and racism are periodically accused of "essentialism." This often involves the claim that there is such diverse experience within these categories that generalizing is unwarranted. However, other analysts counter that this "postmodern" attention to human differences has become so exacting that it leaves little room for the necessary unifying claims against major societal oppressions. That people in categories such as "women" or "African Americans" do not always experience subordination in the same manner does *not* mean that most do not share many similarly oppressive experiences as part of a socially oppressed group. As legal scholar Kimberlé Crenshaw has put it, a major project for all oppressed people is reflecting deeply on the "way in which power has clustered around certain categories and is exercised against others. This project attempts to unveil the processes of subordination and the various ways in which those processes are experienced by people who are subordinated and people who are privileged by them."[11]

As we will see throughout this book, much research demonstrates that substantial majorities of large subordinated groups such as women or

African Americans face broadly many similar gender and/or racial experiences with the dominant white male group. In that sense they do constitute oppressed *groups* because that oppressor group has routinely and powerfully made that so in material, legal, and other social terms.

Much empirical evidence demonstrates that the major institutions of U.S. society have long been shaped and operated by a small white and male elite, one that has taken on a more or less oligarchical form since the earliest century. Consider the foundational example of the 55 delegates at the 1787 U.S. Constitutional Convention. They were all white men, and almost all were members of a privileged elite within the colonial society. All agreed that the new U.S. government must be powerful enough to protect private property, and thus undergird and sustain current and future class and racial inequality. Well-off white Americans had to protect themselves against rebellious enslaved workers, indigenous Americans, and landless whites—a principal reason for the second amendment protecting armed state militias. James Madison, the influential shaper of the Constitution, wrote of the "class with" property and the "class without" property and thereby noted increasing national inequality, which he wished to be constitutionally protected. A leading northern delegate, Gouverneur Morris, likewise agreed that property is the "main object of Society."[12]

These Constitution-makers did protect propertied interests, again mainly those of white men with substantial property such as early capitalists. For instance, Article I of the Constitution prevents state governments from interfering with contract obligations, and the Constitution's Fifth and Fourteenth Amendments prohibit federal and state governments from taking private property without "due process of law" and "just compensation." Ever since, the mostly elite or elite-vetted federal and state judges have generally made certain that propertied wealth is well-protected.[13]

The U.S. Constitution, together with other early political documents, did not create a true democracy (literally, rule by "the people"). The "founders" actually created a nation-state with a federal government that has drawn higher-level officials typically from the white upper class or upper middle class. From the beginning, this increasingly bureaucratized government has provided a major power base for the dominant elite; its operation has generally been elitist in regard to most significant foreign and domestic policy-making. Moreover, the U.S. political system has sharply limited the degree of democratic input into its major political institutions by most adult citizens. Indeed, the new U.S. Constitution was *never* ratified by the mass of the country's adult citizens in a free election. The white male founders intentionally created an inegalitarian and undemocratic political system where most adults then—especially white women and women and men of color—had very little or no input into the shape and operation of the political institutions. The few who sought a much more democratic political system had lost out.[14] Thus, the U.S. Constitution and political actions taken after its ratification essentially established a "white man's republic" built to a substantial degree on African American slavery and the genocidal theft of indigenous peoples' lands.

Still, within this dominant oppressor group there were, and still are today, significant social divisions. There is indeed no one societal place called the White Male Dominance Headquarters, "with flags and limousines, where all the strategies are worked out."[15] There are conflicts within the top rank of the ruling elite that are revealed in major institutions, and especially in such realms as politics and corporate competitions. One important political or corporate faction periodically comes into conflict with another. For instance, when it came to some constitutional and other political issues, the founding elite had a conservative wing and a moderate wing, both rooted in empowering social networks and organizations. Those in the moderate wing of this elite were the most supportive of some greater class equality and of more political and legal rights for ordinary Americans (that is, ordinary white men). The more conservative wing included delegates who sought some form of monarchy, and many were anti-democratic and feared, as they said, "the masses." Indeed, the moderate wing was unable to get a specific list of individual civil rights into the initial Constitution, and these had to be added *later* in a more democratic Bill of Rights, substantially because of pressures from ordinary whites (i.e., white men with influence in various states).[16]

Since the founding period, the factions in the ruling elite have also been differentially represented in various U.S. regions, with the majority of the southern elite often being more conservative on certain issues than those in other regions. In some situations the factions within this powerful elite have found themselves in temporary or permanent political and economic conflicts. Even so, there is nearly unanimous commitment to maintaining the top status of elite white men in the country's gender, racial, and class hierarchies and thus in the overarching elite-white-male dominance system. Note too that over the last century or so the dominant U.S. elite has shifted from one that was in early centuries virtually all northern European in origins—mostly white Anglo-Saxon Protestants—to a more ethnically diverse group including growing numbers of Irish Catholics and southern and eastern Europeans (mostly Catholics and Jews). Today the power elite is characterized by a *multiethnic whiteness*. More recently and slowly, token or modest numbers of other men and women, including from groups that are not white, have been added to the margins of this still very disproportionately white and male elite.

Frequently, as we provide details on this elite, we will observe that just below its top social rank is a larger class of acolytes and assistants who provide everyday enforcers and coordinators of this integrated system of gender, class, and racial oppression. These powerful implementing decision-makers tend to be disproportionately white and male, but in recent decades modest numbers of white women and people of color have also moved up into these important societal positions.

Moreover, as we will document throughout this book, the tripartite sub-systems of the elite-white-male dominance system are operative within most U.S. major institutions and at various social levels within them, including groupings such as families, schools, workplaces, and civic organizations. Indeed, these latter social arenas are where much critical socialization into the dominant societal frames take place—the dominant frames that rationalize and legitimate the subsystems of gender, class, and racial oppression.

The Patriarchal-Sexist System and European Colonialism

In terms of historical time, patriarchal-sexist domination both predated and greatly shaped the historical emergence of the subsystems of capitalistic class dominance and white racial dominance in western countries, and in the global spheres they have since controlled.

We previously noted the ancient Greeks' great-chain-of-being framing of reality, which was later adopted and adapted by Europeans in the Christian era. Men were viewed as socially superior and women socially inferior, and thus necessarily subordinated. This patriarchal-sexist system has long had a strong misogynistic aspect; women are not only legally subordinated by superior men but often feared, disliked, or hated as dangerous. Researcher Jack Holland has traced the roots of this misogynistic perspective to the 8th century BCE, in both Greece and Judaea. There religious creation myths arose describing "the Fall of Man"—that is, myths about "how woman's weakness is responsible for all subsequent human suffering, misery and death." These "man's fall" myths (e.g., Eve tempting Adam) became central in western civilization through the Greek and Jewish traditions; they were used by powerful men to rationalize the oppression of women in patriarchal-sexist societies. Later on, male oppression and misogyny were intensified in the Christian tradition, which accepted the old Adam and Eve "Original Sin" myth. Woman is therein considered responsible for the "falling away of man from the perfect state of grace with God into the horror of the reality of being."[17] The male leaders of the western religions, together with other male leaders, were key figures in this misogynistic subordinating and dehumanizing of women. A central concern was full social control of women, their bodies, and their lives.

Conditions for women got even worse in many areas toward the end of the European Middle Ages, the era in which modern capitalism emerges in the context of a patriarchal-sexist and feudal system faced with increasing peasant protests. Public witch trials and burnings, usually of women, were part of the state violence that put down peasant rebellions against feudal elites. These trials also ensured, as Silvia Federici has demonstrated, that women had to submit to an amplified patriarchal system "where women's bodies, their labor, their sexual and reproductive powers were placed under the control of the state and transformed into economic resources."[18] From the 16th century onward, this extensive suppression of women was part of the great societal changes brought about by Europe's religious, political, and economic elites. The landed feudal elite oriented to agriculture was often struggling against the emerging urban capitalistic elite, yet both groups were almost always male and patriarchal-sexist in orientation. The capitalistic elite in various countries expanded its business enterprises by means of often violent "colonization and extermination of the populations of the New World, the English enclosures, [and] the beginning of the slave trade."[19] Organized state (especially military) violence has been *central* to capitalistic expansion and imperialism ever since.

Thus, the expansion of European countries overseas, the creation of empires, was simultaneously gendered, racialized, and classed. In this colonizing process, European male conquerors assumed male character to be virtuous and western Christian civilization to be a superior gift to a supposedly uncivilized world. This imperialistic expansion was often led by European men from the male-dominated occupations of entrepreneurs, state officials, ministers or priests, traders, and soldiers. Unsurprisingly, an individualistic and assertive masculinity developed in connection with the greedy and violent conquests of indigenous peoples on several continents. The European sense of masculinity was reinforced by ever stronger and imperialistic European states and large professional armies, whose operations in overseas colonies and European wars further institutionalized and universalized the patriarchal-sexist power and often violent orientation of European men.[20]

Unsurprisingly, when they imposed colonial rule on indigenous and African peoples in North America, European colonizers operated from a patriarchal-sexist framing. Virtuous European (soon "white") men were superior physically and morally, while women were weak and unvirtuous: "Marital, familial, and communal order all hinged on God's sanction of male superiority."[21] The English colonists, both the ruling male elite and ordinary people, adjusted the patriarchal-sexist patterns in the law, church, and community customs to "new social and demographic conditions, implementing a brand of patriarchalism that reflected not only Old World practices but also a commitment to . . . creating godly communities on the American coast."[22]

For instance, in his 1711 sermonizing pamphlet, *Manly Christianity*, the powerful Puritan minister and leader Cotton Mather made clear the necessary connection between white manliness and good Christian virtue. In this view male colonists' patriarchalism sustained a godly society; it was linked to "Christian manhood and the system by which men enjoyed primary authority in both family and society."[23] Their patriarchal-sexist model was authoritarian. To be a Christian patriarch, a man was supposed to be virtuous and a "strict father" figure. Early colonial laws "dealing with adultery, rebellious children, recalcitrant servants, single people, and the poor all served to reinforce the importance, power, and interests of independent married men and underscored the centrality of patriarchalism to colonial life."[24] Clearly, this European manhood framework not only set the normative patterns for men and women, but also shaped relationships between men of different social classes, ages, and family positions. Unsurprisingly, too, the elite European men extended patriarchal-family imagery to white male leadership in colonial communities, imagery that signaled their asserted control there and over the larger society.[25]

This European American patriarchal framework combined racial and masculinist views that shaped the approach these European American Christians took to Native American men. In the early colonization period major attempts were made to convert Native Americans to Christianity, including converting indigenous men to the English patriarchal ideal. Soon, however, this Christian missionary approach was pushed to the side as greedy colonists developed an even more substantial warfare approach to gain a firm hold on more land belonging to others. Early on, "manly" warmaking was central to the English Americans' view of Christian manhood. Their warmaking was contrasted in their minds with the supposedly unmanly and dishonorable warmaking conducted by Native American men who were, in fact, defending their invaded communities.[26]

Early male European leaders strongly shaped and maintained an inegalitarian, gendered society substantially through economic, legal, political, religious, and other institutional means. Ever since that era, in these institutional spheres, white men have generally averaged much more privileged and powerful positions and have received an array of better socioeconomic benefits and resources than women of all backgrounds. The European imperialistic and colonizing efforts were heavily gendered, masculinist, and patriarchal in what we term their *male sexist framing*. This aggressively male sexist framing is seen everywhere in the accounts of European explorers, entrepreneurs, and colonizers operating across the globe.[27]

Conceptualizing Systemic Sexism

Let us pause to underscore our systemic sexism perspective. Over the last century feminist scholars of diverse backgrounds have analyzed sexism (patriarchy) as deeply structured into U.S. society. Contemporary feminist scholars such as Patricia Hill Collins and Judith Lorber have strongly accented the reality of gendered institutions and the role of a gender ideology in perpetuating them. Some decades back in the 1970s, author Joe Feagin helped to accent the concept of *institutional* sexism, thereby taking analysis of gender discrimination beyond individualistic prejudice-centered theorizing.[28] Too often sexism, like racism, is viewed by the public and mainstream scholars as mainly a matter of relationships between individuals, between one or a few who are prejudiced perpetrators and one or a few who are the targets. In our view, however, sexism, like racism, cannot be adequately understood just in this individualistic framework.

Such asymmetrical interpersonal relationships are part of much larger systems within which more powerful people *repeatedly* and *profitably* impose their interests and goals on much less powerful people. At the heart of an analysis of this well-institutionalized sexism is this *material* reality of highly gendered exploitation and discrimination. It is centrally about who has the dominant power and who has much less or no power in recurring situations involving the societal groups concerned. We noted this materialistic accent above in the work of early African American feminists and of Marxist-Feminists. Gendered oppression has long been institutionalized and has thereby allocated, to quote the early feminist Gerda Lerner, "resources, property, and privileges to persons according to culturally defined gender roles." Furthermore, this has involved "male dominance over women and children in the family and the extension of male dominance over women in society in general."[29]

Generally speaking, we use *systemic sexism* to refer to well-institutionalized societal patterns of subordinate and dominant social positions and roles, respectively, for women and men in a male-dominated hierarchical society. To catalog key dimensions of systemic sexism specifically, we should underscore the following: (1) the many discriminatory practices of men directed against women; (2) the social privileges and power unjustly provided to men and enshrined in the dominant gender hierarchy; (3) the maintenance of these major gender inequalities by institutionalized social reproduction mechanisms; and (4) the many sexist prejudices, stereotypes, images, ideologies, emotions, interpretations, and narratives that constitute the dominant *male sexist frame* (male worldview) that rationalizes and implements the everyday oppression of women.

The dominant male sexist frame is a male-imposed worldview from which virtually all men routinely operate. As with all dominant frames, there are some significant variations associated with particular groups, such as certain racial and ethnic groups. (Yet, white masculinity dominates.) And numerous individuals in all groups may have some distinctive "bits" in their particular male sexist framing, but their individual bits are usually imbedded in, and elaborations of, collective group knowledge. As the sociologist Karl Mannheim argued, "Strictly speaking it is incorrect to say that the single individual thinks. Rather it is more correct to insist that he [or she] participates in thinking [to] further" what the relevant others have thought before.[30] Individuals always find themselves in societal settings where they learn and participate in inherited patterns of thought.

For centuries this male sexist frame has come to include both a deep-seated *pro-male subframe* (a positive placement of men and male superiority) and an *anti-female frame* (a negative placement of women and female inferiority). This male superiority subframe is the center of the dominant male sexist frame and aggressively accentuates male superiority, virtue, and associated elements. It thus emphasizes male supremacy (patriarchy) and hegemonic masculinity (superior manhood), the latter being typically viewed in U.S. society as white-racialized and heteronormative.[31] Significantly, the English word *virtue* is derived from the Latin word *vir*, which literally means *man*. Early in the development of North American colonies, white men were supposed to exhibit the *manly virtues* of courage, physical strength, and patriarchal dominance.

Consider a major contemporary example. This male sexist frame was obvious in the way the mainstream media recently covered the extramarital relationship between well-placed whites—Paula Broadwell, a counterterrorism expert and Army reservist, and David Petraeus, a former top U.S. general. In media discussions Broadwell was often negatively viewed out of the male sexist frame as very unvirtuous—with sexist language like "his mistress," "shameless," "self-promoter," and "femme fatale" who "got her claws" into Petraeus. He, in contrast, was portrayed from the virtuous-male center of that sexist frame as a "leading" and "honorable general," "gentleman," and "family man" who "let his guard down."[32] He had made a "grave error," but his career achievements were celebrated; she was "his mistress" without significant career achievements.

This negative framing of Broadwell lines up with centuries of negative framing of women who step outside the male-imposed normative expectations of women being married, child-bearing homemakers. As Lisa Wade notes, for many centuries and to the present day, many women living outside these strong domesticity norms have been conceptualized as in a "virgin" or "whore" category. In all these cases, however, women are viewed as subordinate to men, and their bodies are under male control.[33]

Women who conform to the virgin status or move into a conventional domestic setting are "good" according to the male-crafted norms of the patriarchal-sexist system. Even today, women are expected to be more sexually "pure" and religiously "pious" than men. Sexual activity by women outside the conventional norms often brings implicit or explicit criticism, in part because they are not supposed to have male-type sexual desires. In contrast, men are usually not judged so negatively for their sexual behavior, but are excused or expected to be sexually active outside of marriage ("men will be men"). Women who break strongly with these conventional male-crafted norms about domesticity and sexuality—such as those seeking careers outside the home, especially in male-dominated fields, or feminist activists—have long been considered to be "unfeminine," "immoral," or even "feminazis."

The "Founding Fathers": More Patriarchism and Intense Misogyny

In the early centuries of European colonization, the European American elite was substantially composed of large hereditary landowners and their business allies in the towns and small cities. By the 1660s the explicit term "patriarchism" was consciously developed for the sexist system by white men who headed up slave plantations, other large farms, and other important economic institutions. Slaveholders and other slavery-related elite men (e.g., merchants, bankers, lawyers) constituted the dominant wing of this country's white elite until the Civil War. And slaveholding communities, especially in southern and border states, were often organized around white male patriarchs who were extremely powerful and generally capitalistic in their business perspectives.[34] Note that their hierarchical *class* framing of society was constantly intertwined with their *racial* and *gender* framing of society. Thus, the white patriarchal worldview of this European American gentry *motivated* their aggressive control over women and children on their agricultural plantations and farms and over workforces in the fields and town enterprises, including over enslaved indigenous and black workers and low-status white workers who generated significant profits for them.

Still, these men viewed themselves as highly virtuous men of principle, as powerful and strict "fathers" controlling not only families but often communities and the larger society. For instance, in the 18th century the powerful Virginia slaveholder William Byrd II described himself: "Like one of the [biblical] patriarchs, I have *my flocks and my herds, my bond-men and bond-women*, and every soart of trade amongst my own servants, so I live in a kind of independence. . . . I must take care to *keep all my people to their duty*, to set all the springs in motion, and to make every one draw his equal share to carry the machine forward."[35] He makes clear in various writings that his wife and family are included in his broad patriarchal sphere. Now that they had driven or killed off most indigenous Americans in the area, Byrd and others at the top of the white gentry even "appropriated the newly invented reputation of Indian men for virility."[36]

One can use the term *patriarchy* to refer to this coercive, often violent dominance of these "fathers" over their lands and animals and over all aspects of the lives of their workers and family members. Moreover, for leading whites the immediate patriarchal family was a source of broad male-dominant metaphors used to interpret and conceptualize other important areas of socio-political life—including their patriarchal-like dominance over their communities and the larger society. Constantly, we see how intimately interwoven and coreproducing were (and still are) the sexist, classist, and white-racist hierarchies and their rationalizing frames.

We notice too how important the religious legitimation of the elite-white-male position in society was, as in their accent on being like *biblical* patriarchs. Influential religious leaders, especially but not exclusively in the South, such as minister James Henley Thornwell (1812–1862), defended slavery as a positive system under which white men had a moral and legal right to enslave others. In Thornwell's view this racialized and gendered system perpetuated the Bible's patriarchal admonitions—with a white father as ruling head of a household that included not only his wife and children but also men, women, and children he enslaved. Leading white slaveholders, ministers, and publishers of pro-slavery publications regularly cited Israel's patriarchs in the Bible as examples of their God-ordained legitimacy as patriarchal enslavers of African Americans.[37]

Unsurprisingly, too, the white slaveholders made clear their fear that enslaved African Americans, especially men, would revolt against their enslavement. They secured many laws, including the U.S. Constitution, that supported armed militias and other policing organizations to protect slavery from revolts. Black men were viewed as threatening their dominant white masculinity, to the point that many slaveholders made black men and boys wear dress-like shirts (female clothing) and barred or restricted their wearing *pants!*[38] Such actions again demonstrate the close connections between this country's systemic racism and sexism.

In addition, significant fear of white women was regularly expressed by members of the white male establishment. The powerful slaveholder William Byrd II and the leading slaveholding intellectual Thomas Jefferson kept diaries that presented themselves as virtuous patriarchs and provided very negative commentaries on white women (e.g., as "female *monsters*"). They sprinkled diaries with misogynistic commentaries on women's supposedly abhorrent and corruptible bodies. The young Jefferson even penned a misogynistic fantasy of a better world *without women*.[39]

Like other white men, they drew on these misogynistic images as metaphors for broad discussions of political or societal corruption, accenting that a good society must avoid these serious woman-like faults. Unsurprisingly, too, this white manhood perspective encompassed a heavy accent on heterosexism and hostility to gay and lesbian relationships. While gay relationships were occasionally tolerated if kept strictly private, leading founders such as Jefferson supported severe laws, including one that made castration punishment for gay men and facial mutilation for lesbian women. Numerous "sodomy" laws prescribed death for violations of heterosexist laws.[40] Being at the top of the societal hierarchies, these men played the central role in constructing who is the "normal" human being to judge others against—a male being bearing white heterosexist masculinity.

Archly patriarchal views extended well beyond the elite southern leaders. For example, the white "liberal" Benjamin Franklin insisted that "Every man that is *really a man* is master of his own family."[41] In his emphatically *masculine* view a real man must be dominant; he accented that his wife too was "obedient." Pervasive masculinist framing among leading white founders was shared by ordinary white men. It emphasized that girls and women were naturally unequal, suited for family life, should be dependent on men, were too emotional, and were unfit for full citizenship.[42] In the early centuries of this country's history, we observe key dimensions of what is still the dominant U.S. masculinity: male authority, dominance over women and children, toughness and aggressiveness, and heteronormativity.

The leading white men extended their patriarchal view to include their domination of the entire society. Like many others, Jefferson not only spoke of female relatives and those he enslaved as his subordinated family—in his words, he was "blessed as the most fortunate of patriarchs"—but also viewed the United States as a larger extension of the elite white families.[43] These men viewed themselves as deserving patriarchal rulers of their families, plantations, communities, and society. Indeed, they, and those who have celebrated them since, have regularly used clear patriarchal language for them—e.g., "forefathers," "founding fathers," "fathers of their country," and "fathers and guardians of their people." A myriad times since the founding era, George Washington has been labeled the "father of his country" or the leading "founding father." Such repeated *fatherly* language for and by the leading white founders further encouraged all white men, then and now, to obey elite male leaders "without feeling they had to sacrifice their own manly independence."[44]

Metaphorical and Other Language Control

Significantly, such patriarchal-sexist metaphors have been commonplace in much elite and ordinary white framing of political and racial matters since the days of slavery and the American revolution. As a result, white Americans have long spoken of their "forefathers" or "founding fathers," with an understanding that the white-dominated United States was the "family" of concern.

Reflect for a moment on the power of certain metaphors and of other language in shaping some ways that many people think about society. For centuries, powerful elite-generated metaphors have helped to legitimate this country's systems of oppression. Authoritative metaphors channel what ordinary people are encouraged to believe about our society's origin, development, and stratification systems. Cognitive linguists have underscored the importance of the creation and imposition of social, political, and moral metaphors that operate to protect existing structures of inequality. Much of how we know, and what we know of, the society is shaped by important concepts and metaphorical understandings that we are taught. In this way, key metaphorical themes and the frames that embody them function to serve the powerful elite and, more extensively, the country's dominant groups.[45] In subsequent analyses we will assess the importance of these elite-generated metaphors and linguistic expressions in a myriad of societal contexts.

We will see, for instance, how the dominant (white) manhood ideology has drawn for centuries on an array of metaphors and other linguistic expressions to spread the concept of "manly men." As linguist Eliane Luthi Poirier has emphasized,

> Sexist idioms and expressions, such as "be a real man," "take it like a man," "separate the men from the boys," and "boys don't cry" are all used to pressure boys and men into conforming to traditional ideals about masculinity and masculine behavior. It also serves to create deep fear in the hearts of boys of exhibiting any kind of *behavior that could be remotely considered feminine.*[46]

Members of the male elite, including presidents, and ordinary men have *regularly* used such harshly differentiating and gendered expressions to legitimate and buttress this society's oppressive patriarchal-sexist institutions.

Beyond this linguistic buttressing of the patriarchal-sexist system, throughout this book we will also show how much of the language of society's dominant racial and class framing is likewise developed and circulated by the ruling elite to undergird their societal control. New metaphors, expressions, and concepts arise in all corners of society. Once these appear, the mostly white male elite and its implementing subordinates have historically had great power to select and firmly institutionalize their preferred metaphors, expressions, and concepts.

When key metaphors and other language expressions become central to the dominant societal framing, they regularly influence what many people can or do think about, and especially what they do not think about. For example, in discussing the impact of the elite's historical framing of Native Americans as inferior and "uncivilized savages" on *recent* decisions of Supreme Court justices, the scholar Robert Williams captures the thought-shaping power of that negative framing on elite and ordinary Americans today: "It's that unthinking, unconscious, and unreflective state of mind and belief embedded in the American racial imagination . . . that determines and defines what most Americans care to think about Indians and Indian rights."[47]

National White Manhood Framing

Early national *manhood* framing, as historian Dana Nelson has shown, constantly accented its virtuous *whiteness*. The Declaration of Independence and the U.S. Constitution, crafted by powerful white men, implicitly or explicitly excluded white women and people of color from full U.S. citizenship. As it spread thereafter, this white manhood identity was very much a national identity spread by the ruling elite as an "ideal for guaranteeing national unity," especially among non-elite classes of white men.[48] Soon after the Constitution was implemented, the *Naturalization Act* (1790), passed by an all white-male Congress, made explicit these leaders' central concern for making only *white* immigrants into naturalized citizens of the new United States, as did later legislation at various government levels. (That act also used the pronoun "he" for these desirable immigrants.) Interestingly, too, during this era the image of "Uncle Sam" as a powerful and bearded *white man* came to personify the new United States.[49]

The privileged reality of national white manhood early articulated by influential propertied white men spread over the early 19th century to ordinary white men. Because of organized pressures by the latter men, important voting and other political rights were expanded across the class line to working class white men. However, they paid a heavy price for buying into an elite-generated, national white manhood. As Nelson notes, their identification with this white manhood blocked them "from being able efficiently to identify socioeconomic inequality," which greatly hurt them and their families, "as structural rather than individual failure." They were thus further socialized into the individualism of elite-run capitalistic markets and competition.[50]

By subscribing to this national white manhood the ordinary white men foregrounded the sexist and racist interests they shared with that white male elite, often instead of pursuing their class interests. They thus paid a personal price by collaborating in the oppression of other Americans (e.g., black Americans) and thereby helping to shut themselves and the country out of real democracy. As the social scientist W. E. B. Du Bois explained, these ordinary men got a "public and psychological wage of whiteness" in return for giving up important socioeconomic advancements, such as they would likely have had if they had organized in unions with workers of color to counter powerful capitalists' economic domination. We might add to Du Bois's concept that these ordinary men also got a public and psychological wage of *white maleness*. Ever since, this constantly proclaimed white brotherhood has regularly reinforced the exclusion of other Americans—white women, Native and African Americans, foreign immigrants—from voting and other citizenship rights.[51]

This national manhood framing included an emphasis on *toughness* and aggressive *manly* action to uphold white male interests, a militant perspective extended to white-controlled government action. For example, serving as the seventh U.S. president in the 1830s, Andrew Jackson was a former general with a strong white manhood identity, gained as a violent slaveholder and Indian-killing "pioneer" who helped expand the U.S. "frontier."

A patriarchal authoritarian in his general social framing, he endured and inflicted much pain—the enduring model of hegemonic white masculinity. He insisted that Native Americans relinquish ancestral lands to whites, in accordance with ideals of republican white manhood. In condescending communications with them, Jackson portrayed himself as "your father the President."[52] Jackson was a leading example of an elite figure who sought to spread the reality of privileged white manhood to white men of all classes. Indeed, the hyper-masculine Jackson's mythologized story has inspired subsequent politicians to use similar images of arrogant and heroic white masculinity in their political strategies. Since the early U.S. decades, this dominant manhood framing has constantly been linked, implicitly or explicitly, to assessments of who has the "*true* American" civic identity.[53]

Over the course of the 19th century after Jackson, according to an analysis of Google's huge book and article collection by the scholar Anthony Weems, the use of the concept of "manliness" increased dramatically in popular literature. These included numerous popular books by white Protestant authors like these: E. H. Chapin's *Christianity: The Perfection of True Manliness* (1856); T. Hughes's *True Manliness* (1880); and J. B. Figgis's *Manliness, Womanliness, Godliness* (1885).[54] They accented a hard-working, courageous, and Christian white male ideal, while stereotyping (white) women as necessarily docile and subordinate. The aggressive styles of these books and pamphlets can be seen in this passage from Figgis:

> Most young [white] men know that the Latin word for "man"—at least, for a *right manly man*—is the word from which our English word virtue comes. . . . And it has risen in the English word virtue, to the act and habit of duty. We may feel a modest national pride in this, and may gratefully conclude that in the thought of Englishmen *virtue* is the highest quality of a man; and so that manliness is most fully developed—the virtues, shall we say, of bravery, honesty, activity, and piety.[55]

The linkage of white men to high *virtue* is conspicuous in this literature. Notice the accent on *white Englishmen* as leading exponents of manly virtues of courage, duty, physical strength, and Christian piety. These important publications were designed to vigorously communicate this virtuous image to ordinary white men.

The great power of this manhood ideology over many decades, to the present, can be seen conspicuously in the history of major sports. In the late 19th and early 20th centuries, as amateur sports spread in the U.S. (and British) middle and upper classes, it became clear, as the scholar Tony Collins puts it, that "sporting ideals were underpinned by concerns about masculinity and its importance to capitalist society." The amateur sports sense of masculinity "was squarely based on Muscular Christian ideals. A gentleman amateur . . . was physically courageous, strong-willed, prepared to give and take orders, and, above all, *not feminine*. True sport could only be a masculine kingdom."[56] This dominant white masculinity was contrasted with an inferior and necessarily subordinate womanliness. In one 1912 *Ladies Home Journal* essay, "Are Athletics Making Girls Masculine?" a white male doctor highlighted his and others' concern with girls and women participating in "men's athletics" such as baseball, boxing, and basketball. Such participation makes them *too masculine*. In "man-splaining" to mostly women readers, he asserted that sports as played by boys and men are bad for girls and women; he suggested how to make them less vigorous for the latter.[57] Like many male authors who have written on such topics, he asserted a white male framing of superior (white) manliness over inferior (white) womanliness. This perspective persists in many sectors of society to the present day and remains important in the perpetuation of this country's systemic sexism.

Enshrining Male Dominance: The U.S. Legal System

From the beginning, most of this society's legal system, including the Constitution, has historically been crafted and controlled by white men. The powerful white men who crafted that Constitution assumed women's gendered subordination, then in place in numerous court decisions and state laws. This included the principle of "coverture"—that married women were not legal "persons," the term used in the Constitution, but are legally subordinate to husbands. Coverture laws and other laws imposing discriminatory restrictions on single women were instituted by (white) male-only state legislatures, and the Constitution-makers clearly did not wish to contradict those laws.

In 1848, a few decades after the ratification of the Constitution, a conference of 68 women and 32 men was held in Seneca Falls, New York, to press for full rights for women. The conference's Declaration of Sentiments forthrightly referenced the male-made Declaration of Independence:

> We hold these truths to be self-evident: that all men *and women* are created equal; that they are endowed by their Creator with certain inalienable rights. . . . The history of mankind is a history of repeated injuries and usurpations on the part of man toward woman, having in direct object the establishment of an absolute tyranny over her.

They then penned a long list of the ways in which women were oppressed by men, including these:

> He has compelled her to submit to laws, in the formation of which she had no voice. . . . He has monopolized nearly all the profitable

employments. . . . He closes against her all the avenues to wealth and distinction which he considers most honorable to himself. . . . He has created a false public sentiment by giving to the world a different code of morals for men and women, by which moral delinquencies which exclude women from society, are not only tolerated, but deemed of little account in man. . . . He has endeavored, in every way that he could, to destroy her confidence in her own powers, to lessen her self-respect, and to make her willing to lead a dependent and abject life.[58]

The document then concludes that "because women do feel themselves *aggrieved*, *oppressed*, and *fraudulently* deprived of their most sacred rights, we insist that they have immediate admission to all the rights and privileges which belong to them as citizens of the United States." As we will see throughout this book, women have not yet secured these full equal rights and privileges as U.S. citizens.

Systemic Classism and Systemic Racism: Theft of Land and Labor

Let us now consider the historical development of western capitalism in more detail. The Marxist theoretical tradition has provided a powerful theory of class oppression centered on key concepts like worker exploitation and class struggles. Marxist analyses typically identify the basic social forces undergirding capitalistic class oppression, show how human beings are alienated from each other by class relations and struggle, and point toward activist remedies for class oppression.

As we document throughout this book, there is much going on in this capitalistic system or, as we also term it, *systemic classism*. Briefly summarized, this systemic classism involves (1) well-institutionalized social patterns of subordinate and dominant class positions and roles, respectively, for ordinary working people and capitalists (owners and top executives) in a hierarchical capitalistic society; (2) the many exploitive practices of capitalists directed against workers of all backgrounds; (3) the social privileges and power unjustly provided to capitalists and enshrined in the class hierarchy; (4) the maintenance of major class inequalities by institutionalized social inheritance mechanisms; and (5) the many class prejudices, stereotypes, images, ideologies, interpretations, and narratives that constitute the capitalistic *class frame* that prizes the capitalist class and rationalizes the everyday exploitation of working people. We should note, too, that particularly important in most critical analyses of this systemic classism are those corporate capitalists who head up the larger enterprises with considerable employees, as distinguished from small business owners with relatively few employees.

There is a commonplace myth that these capitalists are no longer dominant in this society because about 47 percent of Americans are said to also be "owners" of corporations—that is, they directly, or in retirement accounts and the like, own some corporate stocks. What this notion elides is that the majority do *not* own stocks, and that those who do mostly own a modest number of shares. Moreover, because one major corporation's stock is usually held together with other stocks by institutional investors (e.g., mutual funds) that do not run companies, often one individual or small group needs only 5 percent or so of a corporation's stock to control it.[59]

Situated in important economic networks and organizations, today's corporate capitalists have decisive control over the economic means of production, distribution, and exchange; over land and buildings; and over the labor power of others, including many working class and middle class Americans in all racial and gender groups. Their power generally comes from their important networks and their location in powerful organizations such as the larger corporations. They and their acolytes often gain additional social power and critical coordination as they move into upper reaches of major government, civic agencies, and private policymaking organizations (e.g., the Business Roundtable)—and then often back again to capitalistic enterprises. This process is essential to the *coordination* and *integration* of the ruling elite.

Societal "power" is not some vague or magical reality, but comes from these specific organizational positions, operations, and resources. As sociologist Bill Domhoff has emphasized, these networked organizations are "power bases due to the information and material resources their leaders control, along with the ability leaders have to hire and fire underlings, form alliances with other organizational leaders, and many other prerogatives.... the specialists in managing, coordinating, and obtaining outside resources have the power advantage from the start."[60] For several centuries, clearly, executives at the top of large corporations and other major economic organizations have had a very disproportionate ability to substantially shape the economic and political development of societies like the United States.[61]

Historical Stages of Capitalism

Western capitalism and its developed class system have gone through historical stages in North America. Early on there was agricultural capitalism, essentially mercantile and slave-plantation capitalism, from about the 17th century to the mid-19th century. Wealth generated overseas from theft of indigenous lands and African American labor played a major role in creating urban-industrial societies in the colonizing countries in Europe. By the mid-19th century U.S. agricultural capitalism was accompanied by expanding urban-industrial capitalism. Over time smaller-scale industrial capitalism morphed into a modern form often termed "oligopolistic capitalism"—that is, a capitalistic economic system were major economic sectors are increasingly dominated by a few large national or multinational corporations.

Over the last century, this era of oligopoly capitalism has seen much corporate centralization and many mergers, emphasis on consumerism, and more government support for corporate profitmaking. Today in the United States, the capitalistic market remains central; direct or indirect control of major corporations and other economic institutions still lies in the hands of a small group of powerful capitalists (owners or top executives). Roosevelt Institute researchers emphasize that today U.S. capitalism is "more concentrated and less competitive than at any point since the Gilded Age"—the 1870s–1890s peak of early monopoly capitalism.[62] Additionally, to prosper, these dominant capitalists have long required a society in which both economic and noneconomic structures are substantially supportive of capitalistic norms, especially profitmaking. Throughout these eras the more powerful capitalists, usually white men, and the capitalistic system they crafted have made certain types of economic activity the central goal of numerous societies. They have operated according to the "mystique of gain." And "what they gained, others lost."[63]

A critical feature of contemporary oligopolistic capitalism is the dramatic increase in large U.S. multinational corporations operating around the globe. For many decades much of the globe has been available for U.S. capitalists' investments, and they have exported billions in capital and millions of jobs overseas in the process of creating profitmaking facilities that employ many workers, heavily workers of color, in less industrialized countries at significantly lower wages than U.S. workers. Disproportionately white and male, top corporate executives have become the major decision-making force in expanding the capitalist world economy and its international economic institutions and problem-creating social forces. Operating out of a strong capitalistic framing of society, these executives have regularly fought strong worker organizations globally, organizations that engage in a class struggle with capitalists to secure better wages and workplace conditions.[64] In later chapters, we will assess the impact of these multinational executives' operations globally.

Stealing Land and Labor: Original Capital Accumulation

Modern capitalism *began* with the great overseas expansion of European colonizers in the 16th and 17th centuries. The Spanish and Portuguese were the first to colonize the Americas for economic reasons, but were followed by colonizing English, Dutch, and French nation-states and private companies seeking economic wealth. In North America, English firms often made huge profits from agricultural farms and plantations, commonly using enslaved

indigenous and African labor on stolen indigenous peoples' lands. Stockholders in these exploitative firms included scientists, authors, bankers, and
members of the English legislature—most leading white men.[65] The North
American colonies began as state enterprises created under the auspices of
the king or as state-fostered companies developed by entrepreneurs and
plantation owners. Early capitalistic companies, such as the Southern Company, were formed by merchants under the auspices of James I of England.
This company's employees settled Jamestown, Virginia, the first colony to
enslave African laborers. Land worked by those enslaved was often taken by
genocidal force or crafted treachery from indigenous societies, and Europeans developed a brutal Atlantic slave trade to exploit these land resources.

The political-economist Karl Marx was perhaps the first to analyze
critically the reality of early modern capitalism being grounded in great
wealth stemming from European imperialism in the lands of non-western
indigenous peoples. In his book *Capital* he captured the significance of this
exploitative foundation:

> The discovery of gold and silver in America, the extirpation, enslavement
> and entombment in mines of the aboriginal population, the beginning
> of the conquest and looting of the East Indies, the turning of Africa
> into a warren for the commercial hunting of black-skins, signaled the
> rosy dawn of the era of capitalist production. These idyllic proceed-
> ings are the chief moments of primitive [original] accumulation. . . .
> [C]apital comes dripping from head to foot from every pore with
> blood and dirt.[66]

The early and dramatic growth of modern western capitalism was solidly
built on the wealth generated by this extensive, regularly violent seizing
by Europeans of the resources and labor of non-European peoples across
the globe. The leading oppressors in this original capital accumulation
and human destruction were aggressively masculinist European men—
especially capitalistic entrepreneurs, top religious leaders, and top military and other nation-state officials—who headed up extremely profitable,
world-changing societal developments. Over centuries, in this capitalistic
and imperialistic process, these men came to dominate a world social order.

Consider too the centrality of this so-called primitive accumulation
to capitalism, to the present day. Profit from exploiting urban workers in
the West is not enough. Scholars such as Silvia Federici have underscored
the point that extraordinary levels of exploitative accumulation beyond
western borders have always been essential. For centuries a universalizing
capitalism "has been able to reproduce itself . . . only because of the web
of inequalities that it has built into the body of the *world* proletariat, and
because of its capacity to *globalize* exploitation."[67]

Throughout this book we observe how central organized white male violence, including state violence, has been in the origin and continuing operation of capitalism. As the scholar Maria Mies has concluded from her research, "direct violence was the means by which women, colonies and nature were compelled to serve the 'white man.'"[68] In her view the supposedly enlightened modern world was created in this violent western process of subordinating most of humanity and of nature as well.

Genocidal Seizing of Native American Lands

The scholar Roxanne Dunbar-Ortiz has likewise described European and European American capitalism and colonialism as being "modern" from the beginning: "the expansion of European corporations, backed by government armies, into foreign areas, with subsequent expropriation of lands and resources."[69] Central to the expansionist oppression of Native Americans was the increasing power of private companies and government agencies, especially military organizations. Such bureaucratized organizations accented organizational discipline and written rules to facilitate their "efficient" operation. Large-scale attacks on Native Americans, and soon large-scale enslavement of African Americans, would not have been possible without them. Ever since, such extensive oppression has required these bureaucratized organizations and their empowered decision-makers.

To take a signally consequential example of United States expansion, in 1846 the slaveholding President James Polk invaded Mexico with a large U.S. army, thereby creating a trumped-up war that led to the United States seizing more than half of Mexico. This U.S. and European colonialism was modern in its use of well-organized government violence to overcome indigenous resistance to the new European-created societies in the Americas. Certainly, too, from the first century of European invasions, indigenous peoples living in strong communities had the cultural and other strength to fight back against oppression. They did so with "defensive and offensive techniques, including the modern forms of armed resistance. . . . In every instance they have fought for survival as peoples."[70] The intent of the European colonizers was not just to secure indigenous lands and other resources by treachery and violence, but often to destroy their very existence as peoples. European imperialism frequently involved intentional genocide in the name of an asserted European "right" to expand across indigenous peoples' lands.

One of the myths in the U.S.-origins narrative emphasizes that Europeans invaded North American lands that were unoccupied or underutilized. As Francis Jennings has underscored, the reality was the opposite:

Had it been pristine wilderness then, it would possibly be so still today, for neither the technology nor the social organization of Europe in the sixteenth and seventeenth centuries had the capacity to maintain, of its own resources, outpost colonies thousands of miles from home. Incapable of conquering true wilderness, the Europeans were highly competent in the skill of conquering other people, and that is what they did. They did not settle a virgin land. They invaded and displaced a resident population.[71]

Until they were well-established, European invaders depended heavily on the skills, food, and hunting technologies, and developed infrastructures of indigenous societies *already* present in the Americas.

Whites' often genocidal wars targeting indigenous peoples lasted for centuries, before and after the official creation of the United States in the late 18th century. This savage warfare was led by white men and was central to what white Americans saw as necessary land grabs for their own prosperity: "Owners of large, slave-worked plantations sought to expand their landholdings while small farm owners who were unable to compete with the planters and were pushed off their land now desperately sought cheap land to support their families."[72] Ever since these early conquests, many white analysts have assumed, implicitly or explicitly, that modern American "civilization" was created by early Europeans "in a struggle against the savagery or barbarism of the nonwhite races. . . . civilization was able to triumph because the people who bore it were unique from the beginning—a Chosen People or a super race."[73] Empirically speaking, however, the *most extensive savagery* was generated by white European invaders and their descendants.

Ever since the founding century, this much-heralded sense of U.S. exceptionalism—of being a "chosen people" with the God-given right to expand—has insisted that the U.S. government, its military, and private corporations bring "progress" and "civilization" to "uncivilized" peoples across the globe. As early as 1630, on a ship that brought Puritans to the Massachusetts colony, their leader John Winthrop gave a sermon setting forth the view that their colony was destined to be a world model: "The Lord will . . . make us a praise and glory that men shall say of succeeding plantations, 'the Lord make it like that of New England.' For we must consider that we shall be as a city upon a hill. The eyes of all people are upon us."[74] These colonists saw themselves as religiously and culturally distinctive from the "savages" they encountered, and as setting a spiritual example. Ever since, this exceptionalist perspective has played a key role as part of a distinctive nationalistic "American" identity.[75]

Seizing Labor and Land: The Material Basis of Systemic Racism

The massive amounts of land stolen from indigenous societies created the possibility and reality of much white wealth. Europeans, self-defined as white by the late-1600s, racialized the large-scale exploitation and enslavement they aggressively spread across the Americas and other parts of the globe. Long ago, the astute African American social scientist Oliver Cox was perhaps the first U.S. scholar to develop a systematic analysis of the role of white-seized labor in North America and elsewhere in creating the modern world, with its interlocking and codetermining systems of capitalism and racism:

> Seizing the labor of non-Europeans in North America and elsewhere is actually the beginning of modern racial relations. It was not an abstract, natural, immemorial feeling of mutual antipathy between groups, but rather a *practical exploitative relationship* with its socio-attitudinal facilitation. . . . As it developed, and took definite capitalist form, we could follow the white man around the world and see him repeat the process among practically every people of color.[76]

Without a doubt, systemic racism in the modern world began *not* with an ingrained white racial prejudice but with the extensive exploitation for profit of the world's peoples of color.

During centuries of subordination of Native Americans and associated land theft, together with centuries of enslavement of Africans and their descendants—and later oppression of other people of color such as Chinese and Mexican Americans—whites created and maintained not only modern capitalism but also the extensively *racialized* oppression that was also foundational and systemic. Generally speaking, we use the term *systemic racism* to refer to these well-institutionalized patterns of subordinate and dominant social positions and roles, respectively, for people of color and whites in a white-dominated hierarchical society. Specifically, this *systemic racism* has included: (1) the many exploitative and discriminatory practices of whites targeting various people of color; (2) the significant resources, privileges, and power unjustly gained by whites and enshrined in a dominant racial hierarchy; (3) the maintenance of major racial inequalities by long-standing social reproduction mechanisms; and (4) the many racial prejudices, stereotypes, images, ideologies, emotions, interpretations, and narratives that constitute the dominant *white racial frame* (white worldview) that rationalizes and implements everyday racial oppression.[77]

In addition, it is useful in thinking about what "systemic" means in the cases of systemic racism, sexism, and classism to consider the difference between *single-factor* and *systemic* causes.[78] For example, systemic racism has generated unjust enrichment for early and later generations of white Americans and unjust impoverishment for the early and later generations of black Americans through a web of different and interacting systemic causes. Immediate single-factor causality for a racist action is usually easier to see, such as in the beating by a white slaveholder of an enslaved black worker or a white employer discriminating against a black person today. However, the causal impact of such immediate individual subordination on racial inequality is only one part of the *systemic causation* that has shaped centuries of well-institutionalized racism. This systemic causation is harder to see if one operates mainly out of the standard U.S. framing that accents more individual and limited causality. That is, in the case of black Americans systemic causation has operated by means of multiple specific causes accumulating, interacting, and creating joint impacts to shape their lives across many generations. Indeed, once a group such as black Americans was thoroughly exploited and subordinated by whites in early generations, this over time created major feedback loops—that is, most blacks secured little or no socioeconomic resources to buttress their resisting oppression or to pass along to assist the social mobility of their descendants. Additionally, extensive white discrimination targeting those later generations created yet more systemic racial inequality.

Rationalizing Capitalistic Oppression: White Racial Framing

Over the centuries, the peoples invaded and exploited by early European and European American colonizers have been mostly non-European. From the very beginning of this European colonization an aggressive *ethnocentric* and *predatory* ethic was central to the thinking and motivation for the actions of the early male European entrepreneurs and other leaders of overseas imperialism. Their central value system was much more than the ascetic Protestant Ethic accented by theorists like Max Weber, for it entailed the view that people (men) of European descent had a God-ordained *right* to conquer new worlds, kill or "civilize" the "savage" (un-Christian) inhabitants, and seize lands and laborers in the interest and name of superior European religion and culture. Thus, not only economic greed but also extreme Eurocentrism and ethnocentrism (soon to be white racism) appear as major motivations behind the European land and labor expropriation and exploitation—actions often euphemized by many white analysts, then and now, as "overseas exploration" or "settlement of unoccupied lands."

This greedy and bloody theft of lands and labor was soon rationalized beyond ethnocentrism in an expanding white racial framing of the superiority of "whites" and the inferiority of the exploited others—early on, labeled "blacks" and "reds." For example, in 1836 a powerful U.S. senator from Virginia, Benjamin Leigh, boasted of supposed racial white superiority: "It is peculiar to the character of this Anglo-Saxon race of men to which we belong, that it has never been contented to live in the same country with any other distinct race, upon terms of equality; it has, invariably . . . proceeded to exterminate or enslave the other race in some form or other, or, failing that, to abandon the country."[79] Such dominant and predatory destructiveness by whites was in his mind a positive feature of the white "race" and of white manhood, a reality illustrating the constantly interlocking and coreproducing character of systemic classism, racism, and sexism.

Each of these "other races" faced a rationalizing white-racist framing from Europeans and European Americans. The European colonizers had brought earlier hierarchical notions privileging European peoples and cultures over other peoples and cultures. They extended the understandings from this hierarchical great-chain model to prescribe the racial hierarchy in which they were dominant over indigenous peoples and African Americans. In North America much white racial framing, of elite and ordinary whites, has for centuries been shaped by key framing elements that emerged in early imperialist wars against indigenous peoples and in the development of the extensive European enslavement system, the latter lasting for about 246 years. Thus, the conceptions of who is virtuous and "white," who is not virtuous, what the characteristics of whites and nonwhites are, and what "race" means, are all rooted in centuries of Native American and African American oppression. Those exploited, enslaved, and killed were viewed as biologically and culturally inferior. In contrast, the invading people of European ancestry were viewed as racially *virtuous* and *superior*—and regularly viewed as "white" by the late 1600s. As W. E. B. Du Bois noted, this "discovery of personal whiteness among the world's people is a very modern thing. . . . The ancient world would have laughed at such a distinction. . . . We have changed all that, and the [white] world in a sudden, emotional conversion has discovered that it is white and by that token, wonderful."[80]

Indeed, since the 17th century, elite self-defined "whites" and their acolytes have adopted and helped to institutionalize certain color labels (e.g., "white," "black," "red," "yellow," "brown") for the racial identities they have imposed on these human beings. Obviously, people are usually not these colors; "race" colors are not empirical observations but part of an imposed metaphorical system.[81] The historical metaphor themes attaching good and light/white versus bad and black/dark in European minds made it easier to associate "black" people with negative notions and "white" people with positive notions. Such metaphors intentionally direct the mind away from the empirical realities. As the scholar Andrew Goatly puts it, "Those who defend the existing classifications of society, for example race/colour, in which they are the most powerful group use the *language of nature* to justify this classification. This is an exceedingly important motive for the adoption of power-aggression theories of nature since the celebration of the winners in a competitive struggle is useful to those in power."[82]

The white male founders of the United States were very aware of the oppressiveness of the slavery system that their coterie controlled. Indeed, as they rebelled against the British, they insisted that they *as white men* would not give up their freedom and be, as they said, "enslaved" by the British. For instance, in 1774 George Washington, one of the largest slaveholders and chair of the later U.S. constitutional convention, described the crisis over white colonists' rights thus: "The crisis is arrived when we must assert our rights, or submit to every imposition, that can be heaped upon us, till custom and use shall make us tame and abject slaves, as the blacks we rule over with such arbitrary sway."[83] Another major constitutional convention delegate and Pennsylvania slaveholder, John Dickinson, argued too that: "*Those* who are *taxed* without their own consent . . . are *slaves. We are taxed* without our own consent, expressed by ourselves or our representatives. We are therefore—*slaves*."[84] Many white men made similar comments, including references to British authorities tying to strip them of "their manhood."

Additionally, a strong and distinctive white sense of individualism—one still significantly different from that in most European countries—has deep roots in the centuries of slavery during which whites could, or must, position themselves as individuals who were not enslaved and thus were distinctively "free." This long slavery era, as Greg Grandin has noted, included the emphasizing in the United States of a long-lasting "illusion of individual autonomy" among ordinary whites. The prosperity directly and indirectly generated by the huge slavery system "generalized these ideals of self-creation, allowing more and more [white] people, mostly men, to imagine themselves as autonomous and integral beings, with inherent rights and self-interests not subject to the jurisdiction of others." This individualistic process involved a white racial framing because of a white man's "emotional need to measure [his] absolute freedom in inverse relation to *another's absolute slavishness*."[85]

"Manifest Destiny": More Racist and Masculinity Framing

The racialized predatory ethic was given a boost in an enhanced white-rationalizing frame called "manifest destiny" in the late 19th and early 20th century, a framing that reasserted the white right to expand across others' lands to increase their prosperity. This capitalistic expansion again included the destruction or reduction of Native American societies and extensive theft of their lands in what became the western United States. It also included greatly increased overseas expansion of U.S. corporations.

Around the turn of the 20th century, the famous President Theodore Roosevelt operated from an aggressive manifest destiny view of the United States. The often violent subordination of indigenous Americans was, he bluntly argued, "as ultimately beneficial as it was inevitable. Such conquests are sure to come when a masterful people [whites] . . . finds itself face to face with the weaker and wholly alien race which holds a coveted prize in its feeble grasp."[86] Like most whites for centuries, he framed indigenous peoples as alien and racially inferior to superior and deservedly dominant whites. Soon, given the strong sense of territorial destiny and the needs of U.S. capitalism, this imperialism was globalized in the seizure of overseas territories of yet more people of color in such places as Puerto Rico, Cuba, and the Philippines—areas taken into the U.S. empire after the 1898 Spanish-American War. Ever since, the elite-dominated U.S. government (see Chapters 3 and 4) has engaged in much international imperialism, usually at least in part on behalf of U.S. capitalists' interests. These actions have also been regularly intertwined with this country's dominant white-racist framing of its manifest destiny to expand and dominate across the globe. As one historian has underscored, today the "sun never sets on American territory, properties owned by the U.S. government and its citizens, American armed forces abroad, or countries that conduct their affairs within limits largely defined by American power."[87]

Clearly, too, this global imperialistic enterprise was not only capitalistic and systemically racist, but heavily gendered. The accent on *virile* white manhood was again conspicuous. Hyper-masculine white men, principally from upper-income strata, were asserted to be necessary leaders in these imperialistic efforts. As scholar Mrinalini Sinha has underscored, those men opposed to this U.S. imperialism were described as *effeminate*. This sense of national white manhood was shaped by, and shaping of, members of the power elite. Theodore Roosevelt illustrated this process: "His reinvention of himself from a somewhat 'effete' and 'weakling' New Yorker into a symbol of US imperial masculinity was capped by his exploits as a 'Rough Rider' during the Spanish-American and Philippines-American wars."[88] Roosevelt's ideology of "strenuous life" hyper-masculinity was tightly linked to his view of superior Anglo-Saxon Protestant virtue, which had long been part of dominant racial framing. Indeed, Roosevelt was fond of the sport of U.S. football, at the time a very violent sport with no helmets or padding and numerous men being killed in play. Roosevelt called football leaders to the White House to help improve its rules and used football metaphors, without critical reflection, to accent the importance of assertive white masculinity: "In short, in life, as in a football game, the principle to follow is: Hit the line hard: don't foul and don't shirk, but hit the line hard."[89] The great expansion of college fans of this violent sport around the turn of the 20th century demonstrated and reinforced aggressive white masculinity, much of which has persisted in many areas to the present day.

Moreover, as with most other white men, Roosevelt's manhood framing accented a global militaristic stance, one lasting to the present day. As president, he was given to aggressive masculinist gestures such as sending the United States "Great White Fleet" to overseas ports to show U.S. prowess and international influence. He and other top elite men, viewing themselves as necessary global leaders, made great use of technically advanced and bureaucratically organized violence not only in colonial wars, but eventually in major European wars.[90]

Aggressive white masculinity has been connected to U.S. militarism and imperialistic wars for centuries. We saw it in connection with early military attacks on Native Americans by white leaders such as Andrew Jackson. To take another example, the white southern writer W. J. Cash underscored the hyper-masculinity of millions of ordinary white men who fought as Confederate soldiers during the Civil War. He describes the strong masculinist ethic they shared with leading slaveholders: "the individualism of the plantation world . . . like that of the backcountry before it, would be far too much concerned with bald, immediate, unsupported assertion of the ego . . . one, in brief, of which the essence was the [male] boast, voiced or not . . . that he would knock the hell out of whoever dared to cross him." A few pages later, he notes that the reason millions of ordinary white southerners would charge up hill after hill into heavy gunfire during the Civil War was their hyper-masculinist conviction "that nothing living could cross [them] and get away with it."[91]

Over the last two centuries, the heavy accent on a national white manhood has helped to generate among most ordinary white men strong support for white leaders' capitalistic expansionism at home and abroad. They could buttress their own sense of white manliness by reveling in the domination of people of color overseas in imperialistic government and corporate interventions, as well as over women in their social class at home. Additionally, economic and political trends *within* the United States in the first half of the 20th century buttressed this linkage of elite interests to the interests and perspectives of ordinary white men. Central to this was the country's continuing and advanced industrialization, which continued to link dominant manliness to dominant whiteness. Working-class and middle-class white men, as Thomas Winter has underscored, framed white women and men and women of color as mostly *not* having the essential and virtuous white masculine characteristics, including true rationality and intelligence, necessary for significant success in an advanced economy. Clearly, the capitalistic system has been constantly intertwined with both systemic sexism and systemic racism.[92]

Moreover, as we discuss later, these close connections between systemic classism, systemic sexism, and systemic racism have persisted over ensuing decades. For example, from the 1930s Depression era, through the World War II period, and in the postwar era up to the 1960s, top government officials developed many support (public welfare) programs, such as those creating jobs, providing business and housing loans, and setting up veterans' educational programs. Repeatedly, it was whites, especially white male "heads" of households, who were the principal, sometimes only, beneficiaries of these extensive and substantial government assistance programs.

These social welfare programs helped greatly to put a majority of white male "breadwinners" (and their families) into the middle class. Those citizens who were not white and male were often excluded or marginalized in terms of direct assistance from these extraordinarily important government programs.

Other Lasting Impacts of Racial Slavery

In many ways, the white-controlled, slavery-centered world of Europe and North America gave birth to, or shaped substantially, much of what most people think of as the "modern world." It is hard to exaggerate the deep, lasting, and long-term impacts of this extensive racialized slavery system, which lasted several centuries during and after the founding eras of European colonial societies in the Americas and Caribbean. Let us consider briefly a few more examples of the ways in which centuries of slavery-centered capitalism not only had an enduring U.S. impact but created a lasting *template* for later economic development, including much labor exploitation, by the capitalistic elite and its minions.

Consider, for instance, the early and central consumerism template. In North America, enslaved African workers generated many commodities, such as sugar and cotton, that became essential in the 18th and 19th centuries to Europe's and North America's growing economic prosperity, especially the expanding consumption of the newer middle and older upper classes. These mostly white consumers, notes Guy Mount, "were at once purchasing an abstract commodity removed from the brutal system that produced it" and thereby "enmeshing themselves in a transatlantic trade network that tied the daily nourishment that they put into their bodies directly to the institution of slavery and the slaves that suffered to produce it." That is, the slavery system "*consumed* slaves" to "produce *consumer* goods."[93]

In effect, without millions of those black workers and other workers of color, there probably would be no modern western world. In the massive slavery system not only white wealth, but also significant consumption opportunities and expanded leisure time, were systematically created—first for the white upper class and then, over time, for a growing and mostly white middle class. Indeed, contemporary western consumerism is still grounded in the very disproportionate exploitation of workers of color, this time in a globalized economy. One cannot understand consumer capitalism well without understanding these critical and systemic realities of U.S. and other western history.

A Distinctive Accent on Private Property

Another major example of the great long-term impact of slavery-centered capitalism is the U.S. legal system, with its very distinctive conception of *private* property. The systemic oppression of slavery, and its successor Jim Crow, included the creation and perpetuation of a dominant white perspective on who was legally a person and full citizen, on who or what could be considered personal and collective property, on who did what sort of labor, and on how the country should expand territorially. Thus, viewed by wealthy and better-off whites as their "property," enslaved workers were valuable as *embodied* capital. They were profit-generating on slave plantations and in other workplaces not only as enslaved workers and by producing more enslaved workers, but also as "commodities" in regional and national capital markets used as human "collateral" that a slaveowner could regularly borrow against.[94] This human labor and commodity system, developed by white male slaveholders, permanently shaped many aspects of the U.S. legal system, including its still distinctive property laws, to the present day. The Supreme Court's white supremacist *Dred Scott* decision (1857)—decreed by an all-white-male slaveholding majority—insisted that African Americans had "no rights which the white man is bound to respect." Additionally, in a less often discussed provision, that ruling decreed that no act of Congress depriving a white citizen of his enslaved human property "could hardly be dignified with the name of due process of law."[95] Quite clearly, these elite white men framed the world not only in class terms but also in white racist terms. In addition, this racialized ruling on enslaved human "property" (the black man Dred Scott) set in place, to the present day, a *highly privileged* legal status for private property that does not exist in many other countries. Over time, this extreme property-rights template has greatly affected workers of all racial backgrounds, by assisting in making capitalist property-holders and their corporations much more powerful, and workers and their organizations weaker, than in other western countries.[96]

To the present day, the extreme legal protection of corporate and other "private" property has blocked important changes in the U.S. system of racial oppression. For example, many whites have argued that desegregation and other redress for brutal Jim Crow segregation sought by black Americans in the 1960s and afterward has conflicted with the private "property rights" of white employers, landlords, and other discriminators. Given this accent on the *sacredness* of private property (often, no matter how gained), it is unsurprising that in our contemporary era the white conservative political-economic resurgence has brought much "renewed popular white support for private property rights over human rights."[97] This intensified accent on personal property rights is often just a diversion from the actual white concern over control of people of color in U.S. society.

Persisting Labor Management Techniques

In addition, U.S. slaveholders and other allied management experts greatly shaped what became capitalistic management practices for labor control after slavery's demise. Again systemic racism and capitalistic classism are closely intertwined. The scholar Karen Brodkin has underscored how the enslavement of African American workers became a centuries-long "template for an enduring organization of capitalism in which race was the basis for the organization of work."[98] The slavery-centered system of intensive worker exploitation over two-plus centuries was followed by nearly a century of the near-slavery of intensive Jim Crow labor exploitation, with much of that modeled on elements of the slavery system. In fact, in the early 20th century the white "father" of scientific management, Frederick Taylor, perceived well the business profitability of encouraging *racialized* competition between workers in the supposedly scientific management practices he suggested for top corporate executives and their managers. This management perspective was heavily influenced by the inherited racial framing of blacks, whites, and others as bad or good workers that was generated during the slavery and Jim Crow eras. White company managers and owners intentionally communicated this racist framing to millions of new European immigrant workers coming into the United States in the first half of the 20th century, so that these white immigrants would view black workers as racially inferior—again dividing workers racially for easier capitalistic control.[99]

The long era of extreme labor exploitation under slavery and Jim Crow generated a lasting management template from which contemporary white (and some other) employers and their managers have continued to interpret, manage, and exploit the labor of many workers of color, and thereby often to pit them against usually more privileged white workers. This is yet another example of the historical and contemporary interconnectedness of systemic racism and class-riven capitalism.

The Capitalistic Class Frame

These last sections on the extraordinary accent on private property and on aggressive worker management signal how strong the capitalistic *class* framing of U.S. society has been. Much of what has been written by analysts on the capitalists' frame of mind has discussed their view of the rational pursuit of profit and reinvestment, and other "Protestant Ethic" orientations.[100] In our view new social science analysis needs to focus on the broader class framing of the capitalist class. From the beginning, western capitalists have had a *hierarchical* view of society in line with the old great-chain-of-being framing. And some good historical research has examined key aspects of the capitalist class frame's negative view of workers. In the late 19th century leading capitalists developed a Social Darwinist perspective, one viewing most workers, especially those poor and nonwhite, as morally weak, lazy, and inferior. From this Social Darwinist perspective, there must not be union or government efforts—e.g., regulating work conditions or public education—to improve the lives of these socially inferior workers and their families. At that time, and often today, leading white male free-marketeers have "placed their faith in economic salvation." For them it is "as unnatural to fetter the rich as it was hopeless to uplift the poor."[101]

Clearly, since at least the late 19th century, this capitalistic class frame has encompassed a central pro-capitalist subframe (positive view of capitalists as virtuous and superior) and an anti-worker frame (critical view of workers as lower status and justifiably managed). Today, the capitalist superiority subframe is the center of the still-dominant class frame, which does vary somewhat across the society. Both subframes contain an array of class stereotypes, images, interpretations, and narratives. Unsurprisingly, too, workers of all backgrounds, and their families, are aggressively socialized to accept much of this class framing and their subordinate class position under contemporary capitalism, the latter being said to allow them the "freedom" to choose the work they do and to be consumers in a "free market" system superior to other economic systems. Note too that racial, gender, and occupational divisions within the U.S. workforce also help to reinforce the capitalist class system and its dominant framing by making workers' organized resistance less likely.

Conclusion

In this introductory chapter we have laid out, with important examples, much of our theoretical perspective on the centrality of *elite white men* in building and maintaining what is for a great many people a very oppressive contemporary world. During the early centuries of European imperialistic expansion and usually violent colonization these powerful social actors created an overarching system of elite-white-male dominance with its major interlocking and coreproducing subsystems of oppression—systemic sexism, systemic classism, and systemic racism.

Over subsequent centuries, to the present day, more generations of these elite men have further developed and mostly maintained their dominance in these and other subsystems of the overarching elite-white-male dominance system. We have examined here some of their actions and orientations, mostly prior to the 1970s in the United States. In the chapters to come we will examine many more examples of the power and impact of elite-white-male actions and orientations, as they have continued to maintain this elite-white-male dominance system in the United States and globally.

We have only touched briefly in this chapter on certain large-scale national and international impacts of this elite-white-male dominance system. We will enumerate these more fully in subsequent chapters. Earlier historical developments do greatly impact the present. For example, one central and lasting impact is that, over the black-enslavement centuries, thousands of small and large capitalistic enterprises—including slave plantations and associated merchant, banking, and law firms—generated much of this country's white economic prosperity and wealth. That particular oppression era was followed by a huge and unjust generation of more white prosperity and wealth over nearly a century of legal segregation. Over many generations, including the few since the end of Jim Crow in 1969, these socioeconomic resources have often been passed along in families, thereby generating unjust enrichment and prosperity for many tens of millions of white Americans, to the present. This massive exploitation over three and a half centuries of slavery and Jim Crow simultaneously created large-scale unjust impoverishment that has greatly impacted many generations of African Americans, as well as some other Americans of color. Though usually hidden from view, this white-generated process of unjust impoverishment for generations of Americans of color is *directly* linked to the unjust enrichment of generations of white Americans, now well into the 21st century.

One central aspect of the triple helix of interrelated and codetermining racial, class, and gender oppressions is that they operate routinely and often in the background. Reflecting on systemic sexism and its heterosexist masculinity, anthropologist R. W. Connell underscores how such *normalized* oppression works over time:

> Given that heterosexual men socially selected for hegemonic masculinity run the corporations and the state, the routine maintenance of these institutions will normally do the job. . . . What is brought to attention is national security, or corporate profit, or family values, or true religion, or individual freedom, or international competitiveness, or economic efficiency, or the advance of science. Through the everyday working of institutions defended in such terms, the dominance of a particular kind of masculinity is achieved.[102]

This normalized and often concealed operation is also characteristic of systemic racism and classism. An aggressively overt and direct defense of systemic racism, classism, and sexism is often not required because mostly elite white men and their immediate acolytes control the majority of major private and government institutions. As we see throughout this book, these societal realities of national security, corporate profit, family values, religion, individual freedom, competitiveness and efficiency, and advance of science affect all Americans, but they are still mostly elite-white-male generated, shaped, and/or controlled through the normal and routine operations of major U.S. institutions.

C. Calhoun. Calhoun was a defender of enslaving black people to generate white wealth and white "freedom." Today there is also a huge statue in Charleston, South Carolina, of this slaveholder, racist demagogue, and one-time U.S. senator, a man still regarded as more powerful than any president of his day. Revealingly, too, four of the twelve Yale colleges are (currently) named after white male slaveholders, and eleven are named for white men.[8] These and many similar examples indicate the *architecture* of systemic racism and sexism, of how such oppression gets actually built into *physical* structures that outlast many generations of human beings.

Clearly, when it comes to this form of elite-white-male domination, the past has affected and infected the racial present in a great many ways. For instance, in 2010 the elite-white-male Republican politician Trent Franks, who served for a decade in Congress, naively declared that present government policies on abortion were more devastating to African Americans than the "policies of slavery."[9] The arch-conservative Pat Buchanan—a white media commentator and advisor to presidents Richard Nixon, Gerald Ford, and Ronald Reagan, and who sought the Republican presidential nomination in the 1990s—has insistently declared that:

> America has been the best country on earth for black folks. It was here that 600,000 black people, brought from Africa in slave ships, grew into a community of 40 million, were introduced to Christian salvation, and reached the greatest levels of freedom and prosperity blacks have ever known. . . . no people anywhere has done more to lift up blacks than white Americans.[10]

Clearly, the arrogant Buchanan presumes to speak for generations of African Americans. And he does not mention the extreme human devastation created by this white-imposed slave trade for several centuries.

Today, many influential whites, including otherwise critical scholars, are sometimes implicated in constructing this whitewashed version of the centuries of North American slavery. That white male slaveholders were responsible for the great violence and other savagery, pervasive sexual abuse, and extreme immorality of slavery excludes the possibility that, as some white scholars and other whites like Buchanan argue, they were just *lifting up* Africans.

Moreover, the many rationalizing commentaries on slavery like these attempt, overtly or inadvertently, to legitimate centuries of whites' owning millions of human beings. In U.S. society, where an already existing faith in white *virtuousness* is propagated at the center of the all-pervasive white framing of society, such rationalizing comments are highly problematic. What's more, a thorough retelling of this bloody slavery has been largely absent from or whitewashed in most information-transmission institutions, including major educational institutions and mainstream media. Unmistakably, there is a distinctive absence in most such institutions of specific and sustained analyses of the overarching societal dominance and world-shaping oppressive actions of the founding era's most powerful white men, called out as such.

In the 17th century, European and European American elites began the often genocidal attacks on Native American societies, theft of Native American lands, and exploitation of the labor of Native Americans and African Americans. In every era since then, the white elite has persistently reinforced a white racial framing of society, as well as constructed or maintained economic, political, and other social organizations and institutions that mirror white or white male interests. Their actions—formerly as slaveholders, traders, and merchants and later as industrialists and other business leaders—have proved critical to the establishment and preservation of the elite-white-male dominance system. Pointedly, too, the demographic makeup of those drafting the 1787 U.S. Constitution (all influential white men) is *still* similar to the makeup of those Americans who are today mostly in control of numerous major institutions. We will return to numerous examples of contemporary racism in later chapters.

Systemic Sexism Today

Today, systemic sexism likewise remains central to U.S. society. A constitutional amendment to give women equal rights with men (the Equal Rights Amendment) was passed by both houses of Congress in 1972, with this wording: "The equality of rights under the law shall not be denied or abridged by the United States or by any State on account of sex." However, because only 35 of the 38 required state legislatures ratified it, there is today *no* such equal rights guarantee in the U.S. Constitution. Numerous legislatures that did not ratify it were, unsurprisingly, in white-conservative-run southern states. To a substantial degree, this lack of ratification was because of the strong opposition of mostly white state legislators and of organized (male and female) conservative groups that argued the amendment would erode women's traditional gender-role requirements and supposed "privileges."[11] An Equal Rights Amendment has been reintroduced, periodically, in Congress but still has not been ratified.

In this book we often show how this sexist system constantly intertwines with and coreproduces systems of racial and class oppression. Since the 1980s a renewed men's movement has developed, one that has accented the usually modest price that men sometimes pay, compared to most women, for the sexist system (see Chapter 8). Unsurprisingly, the defenders of this movement rarely examine in detail society's deeply imbedded sexist system.[12] Yet, a serious analyst can demonstrate from social science studies that for centuries (mostly white) men have had controlling economic, political, and other social power in myriad important societal areas, including in the (white) patriarchal family that has been a major site for reproduction of the dominant gender, racial, and class systems.[13]

Today, most men continue to benefit substantially from the age-old gender subordination of women in the home. Women are expected to do more housework, which is still conceptualized in the "domesticity" terms discussed in Chapter 1. Negative framing of women inside and outside of home and family reinforces this gendered family reality. Girls and women are commonly framed in restrictive male sexist terms, such as being "by nature" flaky, emotional, or less intelligent. Seen from society's dominant male sexist framing, they can be employed outside the home—for economic reasons they often have to be—but most are best suited for traditional female jobs, marriage, and a male-dominant family setting. While some gender and family changes have taken place, usually because of collective pressures from women, conventional male sexist norms are still pressed on women in many areas of U.S. society.

Men Controlling Women's Bodies

This sexist system includes a heavy focus on cissexuality and on heterosexuality, as is evident in societal pressures on women of all backgrounds for heterosexual marriages, heteronormative sexual relations, and conventional childbearing. Today, as in the past, one observes a great many examples of men—and at the top of the society, powerful white men—still controlling women's bodies and choices. Thus, in one recent year the anti-abortion bills in Congress were sponsored by mostly white male members. To be specific, these members of Congress had an average age of 60 years, were more than 80 percent male, and were about 80 percent white. This meant that disproportionately older and white men were legislating about all women's bodies and choices. They frequently took such actions assertively, even though studies showed that many did not understand basic facts about women's bodies.[14] Powerful white men have long played the central role in subjugating women's bodies, often out of fear of losing their hold on their sexist-patriarchal power.

Women of various backgrounds who break the conventional normative code of sexist subjugation are often hostilely framed as "bitches," "barren," or "unwed mothers," while the offspring of unmarried mothers are termed "illegitimate" or "bastards." Note again how elite and non-elite men in this way assume the right to define what women's virtue is and who is virtuous. Moreover, despite seemingly substantial gains in a few anti-sexist Supreme Court decisions, when a woman discards the traditional conventions of the dominant sexist system, there are strategies for reigning her in. For example, the male violence experienced by lesbians is extensive, including in the military and on college campuses. They face sexual harassment, stalking, and gang rapes. Certainly, too, a great many other women face this controlling male violence inside and outside home settings, with much of that perpetrated by their male attackers with societal impunity.[15]

Moreover, the indoctrination in gender stereotypes and other sexist framing that is propagated today by the majority of white families is usually linked to a racial framing that accents white girls being virtuous in certain particular ways. Full access to the realm of white social privilege is contingent on white girls and women having intimate relationships just with white men.[16] The sexist system has long ensured that most white men have intimate access to and control over women, often irrespective of their consent. For instance, the historical examples of enslaved black female bodies and of seemingly free white female bodies illustrate how white male patriarchy has long served the interests of white men, both elite and non-elite. For 60 percent of this country's history, subordinated black female bodies "were needed for the reproduction of a slave labour population," whereas the usually subordinated white female bodies were also "needed for the reproduction of European domination."[17]

For centuries now, the derogation and criminalization by powerful white men of interracial and nonheterosexual relationships have demonstrated well the overarching elite-white-male dominance system central to U.S. society. Anti-intermarriage laws and laws criminalizing same-sex relations have been common in white-dominated societies, including the United States. Not until 1967 did the white-male-controlled Supreme Court rule that laws prohibiting interracial marriage were unconstitutional. Recent studies on the experiences of white women who partner with men of color still reveal that they often suffer physical and verbal attacks by white male family members.[18] Moreover, for the dominant sexist-racist system to effectively function, men of color have for centuries needed to "know their place," one subordinate to all white men. Black men have historically been framed in the dominant white racial frame as sexually aggressive and dangerous, especially to white women, and this racist framing remains central to how much of white America still views them. Around 1900, the black sociologist Ida B. Wells-Barnett was the first social scientist to assess in some detail how "white womanhood" was regularly used to justify white lynchings of black men.[19]

Such white-racist justifications persist. Consider the recent case of the white man who murdered black churchgoers at a South Carolina church. As if it were his civic duty to act out a racist framing of African Americans, the shooter spouted racist mythology to his victims, "I have to do it. . . . You rape our women and you're taking over our country and you have to go."[20] Social commentator Chauncey DeVega has linked this violence to a growing sense of threatened white manhood—that is, the *learned* "fear of the world chang-ing to the disadvantage of white men."[21] Among the contradictions in the young killer's assertion is the fact that white men have long been the ones to control, often violently, the reproductive processes of *all* women. Ironic, too, is that far from African Americans "taking over our country," the overarch-ing dominance system that has long been in place still ensures that mostly white men control U.S. society at the top.

Note too the centrality of powerful guns and white male shooters in mass killings like this one. A substantial majority of the mass killings in recent decades have been done by angry white men. The aggressive celebrating of guns has long been associated with toxic white masculinity. The large white-owned gun corporations usually profit handsomely when an inci-dent like this happens, and many whites (disproportionately men) fear that gun controls will be imposed. As one investigative reporter noted about the owners and top executives of the leading gunmakers for the United States:

> They are *all white, all middle-aged, and all men.* A few live openly lavish lifestyles, but the majority fly under the radar. . . . these are America's top gunmakers—leaders of the nation's most controversial industry. They have kept their heads down and their fingerprints off regulations designed to protect their businesses—foremost a law that [uniquely] shields gun companies from liability for crimes committed with their products.[22]

These white owners and top executives often contribute to or maintain close ties to the National Rifle Association, from which they often get special awards. Note too that gun sales to *whites* were especially brisk during the years when an African American, Barack Obama, was U.S. president.

The Sexist System: Shaping Capitalistic Workplaces

As we suggested earlier, the sexist system is closely linked to the capitalis-tic system, and they are coreproductive. For centuries male employers and workers have created and maintained gender segregation and other discrim-ination in capitalistic workplaces, generally by using the traditional gen-dered framing and discriminatory techniques of an age-old sexist system. Today, the negative stereotypes and other negative framing of women noted previously are commonplace in a great many U.S. employment settings.

For instance, one recent study of Wall Street firms concluded that bla-tantly sexist framing is a central part of these firms' typically male corporate cultures. The highly disrespectful sexist "Bro" commentary and framing of (mostly white) male executives, traders, and other employees there "makes it very difficult for women to ascend the Wall Street ladder. When you create a culture where women are casually torn apart in conversation, how can you ever stomach promoting them, or working for them?"[23] Of course, a great many other U.S. workplaces have similar situations where male executives' and other employees' aggressively sexist framing of women—in all-male backstage settings and in frontstage settings where women are present—not only limits women's advancement but also makes their workday lives troubling and difficult in other ways.

In countless workplaces institutionalized sexism means that a great many women must accept occupational positions that are lower status and lower-paying compared to the occupational positions that men who are comparably (or less) qualified can secure. For many decades women have been concentrated in a smaller number of U.S. occupations than men—occupational settings such as domestic worker, fast-food worker, nurse, clerical worker, retail sales worker, and schoolteacher. In addition, women frequently have to endure various discriminatory barriers in regard to hiring and promotions, often in spite of the same or better educational attainments than men. Often too, they experience sexual harassment, and significant resistance to sexist discrimination can mean losing a much-needed job. The result of these discriminatory patterns is much socioeconomic and other loss for women, their families, and their communities. Especially great are losses to society of the abilities and creativity of millions of women who have faced entrenched gender discrimination over lifetimes, now for generations. In Chapter 8 we will provide further details on contemporary sexism in the U.S. workplace.

Shifts in Heterosexist Dominance

The societal dominance of heterosexism has been challenged by organized efforts in recent decades, but these have had much pushback. Heterosexism has long been central to the dominant male sexist frame. Indeed, the American Psychiatric Association listed "homosexuality" as a mental disorder until the 1970s. Not one state barred discrimination against gay and lesbian Americans until the 1980s. Yet, by the 1990s, the legal situation for gay and lesbian Americans was changing significantly. In 1993 they were allowed to serve covertly in the U.S. military, but that "Don't Ask, Don't Tell" policy was not officially changed until 2011. (Even today many LGBTQ people there remain silent, fearing retaliation.) Moreover, upset at pressures for change, in 1996 a majority of members in a male-dominated Congress passed, and President Bill Clinton signed, a discriminatory Defense of Marriage Act stipulating that federal recognition was granted only to heterosexual marriages. Nonetheless, that same year the Supreme Court knocked down a Colorado law allowing discrimination against gay and lesbian citizens, and in 2000 Vermont became the first of numerous states to allow a civil-union form of gay marriage. Soon, gay marriages were allowed or recognized in several states. In 2008 a California referendum banned gay marriage, even as the state Supreme Court permitted it. Between 2008 and 2015 gay marriage was gradually legalized in Iowa, Vermont, New Hampshire, New York, and D.C.—and then nationally by the Supreme Court in mid-2015.[24]

Still, as of 2017, there is no federal law banning LGBTQ discrimination, although one has been introduced in Congress since the 1990s and presidential executive orders have provided some protection for LGBTQ Americans. A majority of states do not yet have comprehensive laws that prohibit discrimination on the basis of sexual orientation and gender identity for all types of employment. Moreover, in 2016–2017 there were successful legislative attempts in numerous states to make discrimination against LGBTQ Americans *permissible*, including overturning existing anti-discrimination laws. Still, this mostly male-led, often arch-conservative, anti-LGBTQ action brought much public protest and substantial economic retaliation against the affected states. This uneven and oscillating legal situation for LGBTQ rights reveals that overt, subtle, and covert heterosexist and homophobic framing is still commonplace. A great many people openly conceptualize "real men" as not being gay and "real women" as not being lesbian, and both men and women as being defined only by the sex listed on their birth certificates.[25]

Elite Economic Dominance: Contemporary Capitalism

We have already discussed briefly the male-normed and male-framed character of many U.S. organizations, including workplaces. These institutions are also class-normed and class-framed, as well as racially normed and framed.

White Male Dominance among Contemporary CEOs

Today, most U.S. economic organizations remain white-normed and white-framed in their internal sociocultural structures, and white individuals are mostly in command at and near the top of these organizations that effectively empower them. Even after decades of official attempts to desegregate economic institutions, the overwhelming majority of those heading up most major powerful economic and associated political organizations are still white and male. They make up most higher-level executives across many business sectors. In a 2016 count whites made up 96 *percent* of CEOs of Fortune 500 companies. And 93 percent were white men. White men constituted 85 percent of corporate executive officers and nearly all CEOs at Wall Street and venture capital firms. (No major investment bank has yet had a woman head.) Yet, the U.S. workforce is currently about 64 percent white workers—and only about a third white male. This dominance is an old phenomenon, for over the last century almost all Fortune 500 corporate CEOs have been white men.[26] White men have *long* dominated among the top executives and owners of major U.S. companies, including multinational corporations. Recall, thus, the analyst who said that if these gender numbers were reversed, many people would consider U.S. society to be an "emasculating feminist tyranny."[27]

While data displaying this corporate dominance are striking, the stories behind the data are also arresting. Take, for example, two famous corporate executives, Thomas J. Watson, Sr., and Thomas J. Watson, Jr. This family lineage, father and son, was empowered by and controlled one of the world's most significant international corporations (IBM) for several decades (1914–1971). They provide an example of the nepotistic cloning of high economic officials. Note, too, that it was not until 2011 that an elite (white) woman was appointed as CEO of IBM—the first in its long history, and significantly just in time to preside over significant corporate decline there.[28]

Like many other elite U.S. families, the Watsons illustrate some ways in which elite white men take *specific* actions to maintain great power and wealth over generations. The legal and political system has long been arranged by men like them for this purpose. They can do this by passing along economic and other social inheritances across family generations and by creating and regularly utilizing elite white networks and other exclusive social organizations. Not only is their present dominant individual and family position greatly rooted in their family's past dominance, but it is also rooted in these high-level networking and organizational arrangements that lay the groundwork for future generations' power and wealth. Systemic racism, classism, and sexism all operate with this type of social reproduction process of racial, class, and gender group privilege from one generation to the next. These systems of well-institutionalized oppression constantly reinforce and codetermine each other.

In the contemporary era, major corporate CEOs, mostly white and male, are still among the highest paid societal decision-makers. Today, they are situated in an era of economic inequality unmatched since the 1920s. Consider just one year's (2014) bonuses for Wall Street executives; they totaled *twice* the annual incomes of *all* minimum wage workers in that year. Since 1990, CEO compensation has snowballed. CEOs in 1965 received approximately 24 times the annual amount of the average U.S. worker. Currently, these CEOs receive *325 times* that of the ordinary worker.[29]

Additionally, white men dominate among the wealthiest 400 Americans. A recent *Forbes* study found that almost all were white. Blacks and Latinos made up less than 2 percent; women were rare in the group as well (about 13 percent). Just the top 100 in this group had more wealth than all African Americans and Latinos combined. The study found yet again that most had *inherited* substantial financial capital and significant cultural capital, such as access to a very good education and important social networks that enabled them to move up economically. Most were not "self-made men."[30] Today the concentration of great wealth and luxury of this white male cadre has become extraordinary. Even more importantly, "More than any category of people before them, they collectively have the power—the accumulated resources, the physical and social techniques—to shape the [world's] future."[31]

Note too that this male dominance of wealth is a global reality. Another *Forbes* study found that more than 91 percent of the world's 1,226 billionaires were men, yet men make up only half the world's population. As in the United States, most of the few non-U.S. women among these super-wealthy people had gained their wealth through marriage, divorce, or inheritance.[32]

Modest Racial and Gender Desegregation: The Corporate Elite

Much research shows there is a concrete ceiling generally blocking Americans of color and white women from higher-level positions in many workplaces. Over many decades now, few men or women of color have ever served as heads of a Fortune 500 company. As of 2014, Asian, Latino, and African Americans taken together made up just 4 percent of Fortune 500 CEOs. Only in 1999 did Franklin Raines become head of the Federal National Mortgage Association, as the *first* black male CEO of a Fortune 500 company. More than a decade would pass before the first black woman was appointed CEO of a Fortune 500 company. Between 1999 and 2015, only ten other African Americans were appointed as CEOs. In 2015 the number of black CEOs was still only five, a mere 1 percent of the Fortune 500 corporate heads.[33] Corporate boards of directors reveal similar patterns of white male dominance. An Alliance for Board Diversity study reported that among Fortune 500 companies, black men and women totaled just 7.4 percent of corporate board members. (African Americans were about 13 percent of the population.) White men held about 73 percent of corporate board seats, with white women holding only 13 percent.[34]

Ronald Parker, head of a group representing top black executives, has explained a key reason for this continuing dominance of powerful white men as CEOs. In a type of socio-racial cloning process, the latter are greatly inclined to offer high-level employment opportunities to white men who act and "look like them."[35] Those hired usually benefit from extensive white male networking. Again, we observe just *how* this elite-white-male dominance system gets perpetuated by specific decisions. Such a glaring selection bias continues despite the fact that research reveals that persisting corporate homogeneity does not push a business's market development and generate business innovation as well as substantial employee diversity does.[36] In addition, these and other corporate workplace data indicate that commonplace claims that most corporations are committed to racial and gender inclusion are suspect.

Additionally, one review of CEO changes at Fortune 500 companies over a recent period found a propensity to thrust executives of color or white female executives into top leadership roles as a white-male-generated *last resort* in companies facing crises. Extending the metaphor of the glass ceiling, some have dubbed this process the "glass cliff." If the corporation's functioning declines during the tenure of the nontraditional executive, these men and women of color or white women tend to be quickly traded in for a conventional white male executive. In fact, the evidence suggests that even when women CEOs fix problems inherited from male predecessors, they are eventually removed from power to make room for a white male successor.[37] While we have not seen systematic data on the highest-level positions in major noneconomic institutions, we suspect that this process is often likely there as well.

General Motors CEO Mary Barra, the first female head of a major global automaker, is a case-in-point. Following decades of employment experience at the company, in 2014 she was appointed CEO directly before revelations over major car safety issues there emerged. Barra was well-qualified, but the timing of her promotion was suspect. In her first months she was grilled by Congress and faced a public relations nightmare. She had to make a public apology for the company's decision not to recall many GM vehicles despite internal long-term knowledge of a serious design flaw. Some analysts have insisted that Barra was a scapegoat for male executives' mistakes.[38]

Social scientists Allison Cook and Christy Glass have emphasized the motives often behind hiring an executive who is not a white male during challenging corporate times, including as a gesture to indicate diversity changes supposedly taking place.[39] Traditional gender and racial stereotypes also play a role. That is, female executives are typically seen as more capable of uniting people and being more believable in apologizing for company shortcomings. A company often publicizes such a historic-first appointment while setting up that person to fail. What's more, in order for nontraditional executives to rise to the top, they have to be relatively flawless in major decision-making and overcome never-ending gender or racial framing throughout their corporate careers. Unsurprisingly, the nontraditional CEOs who have not succeeded in turning around unproductive corporations are also less likely to be selected for future leadership positions.[40] Moreover, one scholarly study of 1,085 corporations found that "mergers, the closure of corporate subsidiaries that had numerous women and people of color on their management teams, and emergence from bankruptcy all led to reductions in corporate diversity."[41]

Researchers have demonstrated that top corporate CEOs who are not white men mostly share the same social class backgrounds as the latter, with the exception of African American CEOs. White women CEOs are generally comparable to the white men in terms of class backgrounds. Nonetheless, researchers Domhoff and Zweigenhaft have established that women who serve as corporate CEOs and board members of Fortune 500 companies do tend to be more highly educated than their white male colleagues. They are more likely to have attended top colleges and universities and to have graduate degrees. To get ahead in a corporate world that discriminates, women and others facing discrimination generally have to be better educated, as well as generally do better in major decision-making, than their conventional white male rivals.[42]

Framing an Oppressive Society: Top White Male Executives

Rarely do we get to see the actual thinking of powerful white male executives in regard to critical racial, class, and gender issues. One reason is that they often have public relations officials to protect them. However, on one rare occasion recently, the wealthy CEO of the huge financial and insurance company AIG, Robert Benmosche, commented from his posh estate on the European debt crises. Revealing his elite class framing, he suggested that these crises could be solved if the "normals" (that is, ordinary workers) there would work a lot more, including into their 80s.[43] The prominent CEO of the computer programming company AngelHack, Greg Gopman, demonstrated a similar class-biased perspective in an attack on San Francisco's poor on Facebook. He accused the "lower part of society" of ruining the downtown for people like him. There, he asserted, the "degenerates gather like hyenas, spit, urinate, taunt you, sell drugs, get rowdy, they act like they own the center of the city." He later apologized, but his outburst demonstrated a harsh classist (and probably racist) framing of modest-income urbanites.[44]

In another case the racist framing of elite men came to light because of a lawsuit. According to a 1990s *New York Times* report, top executives at one of the country's largest oil companies were taped discussing a discrimination lawsuit filed against them by black employees. There the white executives argued their employees were like "black jelly beans" who just "stuck to the bottom of the bag." Other lawsuit materials revealed that a white company executive at another office commented on an employee's formal discrimination complaint by saying he would "fire her black ass." When it was pointed out that company policy did not allow that, he replied, "I guess we treat niggers differently down here."[45]

On another such occasion recently, the prominent CEO of CBS, Les Moonves, was presented with an opportunity to reject racist and sexist commentary during his network's reality television series *Big Brother*. The season garnered attention because of many racist, sexist, homophobic, and other bigoted comments regularly made by white participants vying for a prize. At a Television Critics Association meeting, Moonves explained that he and his wife, *Big Brother* host Julie Chen (an Asian American), had discussed the international controversy over the program's extreme bigotry. He referred to it as "appalling, personally," but explained it was an unfortunate reflection of "how *certain* people feel in America." He defended as appropriate his and other executives' profitable decision to keep the offensive participants on the show.[46]

Some critics underscored the CBS elite's problematical standard in much other programming. While network executives did criticize *Big Brother* participants for offensive comments, their main characters in other highly rated CBS programs also frequently made racist jokes about racial and ethnic groups.[47] Unsurprisingly, more than 6 million viewers tuned in for *Big Brother* after the racist framing and other bigoted framing garnered news headlines. Of course, the large advertising revenues are a major reason for the continuation of *Big Brother* and similarly offensive shows. Indeed, the year that the *Big Brother* controversy arose, Moonves' salary was a *huge* $66.9 million.[48] These revealing examples signal why and how elite-white-male capitalists rarely show a moral backbone in regard to highly racist, sexist, and homophobic programming when that morality conflicts with corporate profitability. They routinely operate not only out of a capitalistic framing accenting their high-class superiority and interests, but often out of an insensitive racist and sexist framing of society.

In addition, many top white executives, especially white men, are convinced we now live in a post-racist, post-sexist country. One interviewing project involving corporate executives encountered frequent assertions like this from a top executive. Asked about his view of affirmative action, he made these generalizations:

> I'd like to believe that over the last 30 years of having those kinds of programs however, that attitudes have changed dramatically enough that maybe those programs aren't as necessary as they were before. So I'd like to see them either phased out, I'm actually very pleased to see the courts now starting to review some, some of these cases and viewing them as being reverse discriminatory.[49]

In this common view of elite and ordinary whites not only have things improved dramatically in white attitudes so that positive remedial programs are no longer necessary, but also there is now a supposed problem of "reverse discrimination," a term first popularized by elite whites in the 1970s backlash against civil rights progress.[50]

Occasionally, too, we get a glimpse of the views of top corporate executives on women and women's issues. For instance, Mike Jeffries, the

Abercrombie & Fitch CEO, admitted that for years his company did not sell plus-sized clothes for women because the corporation did not want to attract larger women customers as part of its clientele.[51] In another example of male sexist framing the former CEO of General Electric, Jack Welch, articulated a negative view of developing women's networks ("victims' units") and mentoring programs ("you should see everyone as your mentor") to help women improve their employment situations. His view was that "women should just work hard, over-perform and that will take them straight to the board." Welch is also famous for accenting in his writings "about what fun it was to go into the office on Saturday morning and hang out with the guys."[52] Also, the powerful JPMorgan Chase CEO, Jamie Dimon, recently commented condescendingly at a Chicago Executives Club gathering on U.S. Senator Elizabeth Warren, a published researcher of the financial system, for her accurate criticisms of Wall Street: "I don't know if she fully understands the global banking system."[53] Dimon is famous for his aggressive support of the U.S. banking system, in spite of its determinative role in the damaging Great Recession of the early 21st century.

When a hackers' group published documents from Sony corporate files, just how some white CEOs in media companies operate out of a male sexist frame came to light. Sony CEO Michael Lynton and the billionaire CEO of Marvel Entertainment Ike Perlmutter were seen to be discussing how female-centric "superhero" films are *bad* business; they cited the failure of three such films. As one commentator, Jessica Goldstein, wisely asked, "does it only take three poorly-executed and badly-received examples to prove a person of a certain gender can't star in a certain kind of movie?" Underscoring sexist framing inherent in the CEO exchanges, Goldstein listed numerous poor movies with white male superheroes, concluding that there never seems to be gendered talk about them being bad for business.[54]

Other powerful white men, including those who are not CEOs, have revealed their male sexist framing. For example, the *St. Louis Post-Dispatch* columnist George Will was replaced with another columnist in part because, as the newspaper editor explained, Will had "suggested that sexual assault victims on college campuses enjoy a privileged status. . . . The column was offensive and inaccurate." Will had argued U.S. colleges "make victimhood a coveted status that confers privileges, victims proliferate."[55]

While we stress that it is powerful white men who have played the most vital role, to the present day, in the construction and sustaining of the gender, racial, and class systems, the aforementioned Sony document release also offers a look into the backstage views of a few influential white women. In the documents, Scott Rudin, a top white male Hollywood producer, and Sony Pictures CEO Amy Pascal joke about President Barack Obama's film preferences as just being for black-populated films like *Django Unchained*, *12 Years a Slave*, or *The Butler*. In what the progressive group Color of

Change called a "more troubling exchange," Pascal also said that getting one's own television show is "the new Black baby" for celebrities, as if black children are a trendy craze. Pascal's remarks were seen as verification of the exploitative relationship that corporations such as Sony have with African Americans: "We must hold Amy Pascal accountable here; not just for her horrendous comments, but also for her role at the helm of a corporate agenda that views Black America as one big, lucrative joke."[56]

Unmistakably, we observe here and elsewhere throughout this book that the relatively few CEOs who are not white men are nonetheless socialized into white-male-generated corporate values and conventional elite racial and class framing, so that they generally behave in important decision-making much like their white male counterparts.[57]

New Technology Sectors: White Men Rule

Executives of the U.S. high-technology sector—computer companies, and social media, communications, and other Internet-oriented companies— like to boast that they are the cutting edge in society's innovation and concern for reflecting a global and future-oriented perspective. If so, they frequently do not demonstrate this commitment in actual reality, and certainly not in their substantially segregated employment patterns. They undoubtedly drive much profitmaking in contemporary oligarchic capitalism across the globe, but their top executives, while often a bit younger on average, do otherwise look much like older white male executives who have run most major companies for generations.

When Dominic Rushe, business editor for the *Guardian* newspaper, asked about the growing high-technology sector, "What's white, male, straight, and occasionally hangs out with Asian guys?," he was not kidding about who runs Silicon Valley. Lack of significant diversity is a serious industry-wide reality, and California's famous Silicon Valley technology companies are no exception. Recent data indicate that about half of information technology businesses have no women on their boards, compared to 36 percent of the largest U.S. public companies. Top executives of major globalizing firms like Facebook, Twitter, and Google are all part of a rather homogenous corporate coterie of overwhelmingly elite white men.[58] Indeed, Silicon Valley has been called "a place where it's possible to have all white male meetings all day every day," certainly a far-cry from the frequently proclaimed imagery of corporate *meritocracy*.[59]

One reason for this male dominance is the power of the male sexist frame's stereotypes of women as particularly "emotional" and "irrational," while the central pro-male subframe of that dominant frame insists that men are especially "rational." As anthropologist R. W. Connell notes, this stereotyped male rationality is now linked to better-paying occupations involving new technical knowledge and expertise, such as those in Silicon Valley. That is, the assertion and perpetuation of male dominance in the economy is done not only by direct domination, but also by the segregated hoarding of technical knowledge and control in specific occupational settings.[60] This pattern also is evident in regard to the way the white male technological elite frames potential and actual employees of color. Again, we observe the role of *specific* decisions and decision-makers in routinely perpetuating the elite-white-male dominance system.

Unsurprisingly, thus, the high-profile tech executives have been relatively slow in *revealing* data on employee diversity in their corporations. When CNN researched U.S. technology companies in 2011, they could only secure public diversity data on a few. Additionally, the data made available as of this writing have usually been incomplete—for example, they rarely include information on promotion and retention rates for employees of color. When queried, numerous high-tech companies have claimed that public disclosures would result in "competitive harm."[61]

Some change has come more recently. For example, after years of trying to keep employee diversity data secret, Facebook's executives made their figures public in 2014. Facebook executives then professed they were "serious about building a workplace that reflects a broad range of experience, thought, geography, age, background, gender, sexual orientation, language, culture and many other characteristics."[62] Notably, however, racial and ethnic diversity was not explicitly named. What's more, employment data tell a different story. Globally, 85 percent of Facebook's tech employees are men. In the United States, 63 percent of Facebook's employees are white, and 24 percent are Asian American. Only 8 percent are Hispanic and African American.[63]

The diversity organization Color of Change pressured Twitter, the social media company, to release its employment data. Reflecting on these often difficult efforts, the organization's executive director has described a culture of denial in Silicon Valley—people "who like to think of themselves as liberal, progressive or at least open minded." Aware that it is part of an Internet industry with dramatic imbalances in corporate diversity, in 2014 Twitter did declare its commitment to inclusiveness, as "a cornerstone of our culture."[64] However, company data then showed that 70 percent of employees were male, a percent that increased to 79 percent for the company's leadership and to 90 percent of tech employees. Some 59 percent of Twitter employees identified as white, 29 percent as Asian, and just 5 percent as Hispanic or African American. These employee statistics are in dramatic contrast to Twitter's user base, where a disproportionate share (22 percent) of their online users is African American and another significant percentage of users is Latino.[65]

Of the major Internet companies detailed, Google has so far been the most candid in admitting uneasiness in publishing statistics. The company's executives, with little attention to systemic racism and sexism issues, finally offered poor excuses as to why tech companies like Google "struggle to recruit and retain women and minorities." These included citation of lower rates of computer science degrees among women and of lower college graduation rates for students of color. Claiming the company is not where it wants to be on diversity, their 2015 data revealed that 70 percent of employees were men. In terms of racial groups, 60 percent were white, 31 percent were Asian, and just 5 percent were black or Latino. Moreover, blacks occupied just 1 percent of tech jobs, with Latinos at just 2 percent.[66]

About the same time, the Apple corporation revealed that 70 percent of its worldwide employees were men, a figure that increased to 72 percent for those in leadership roles and 80 percent for technical positions. Asian Americans comprised 15 percent of its personnel, Latinos 11 percent, and blacks 7 percent—the best percentages for employees of color at major high-tech firms. Apple CEO Tim Cook has steadfastly said that diversity and inclusion are "top priorities."[67]

About this time Cook joined a few of the world's wealthiest individuals and families and vowed to dedicate the majority of his wealth to serious philanthropy. This wealthy group has argued that philanthropy can accomplish "public goods," goals that the government and most of the private sector in capitalistic countries like the United States are no longer willing to pursue.[68] Declarations of major commitments to diversity represent a relatively recent change for most top corporate executives. Actions are yet to follow, and most corporate executives still seem tone deaf. For example, the influential white CEO of Twitter, Dick Costolo, took offense to the critical comments of Asian American entrepreneur Vivek Wadhwa concerning Twitter's lack of gender equity. Its governing board was then all white men.[69] Costolo side-stepped the issue, instead mocking Wadhwa as the "Carrot Top [a stand-up comedian] of academic sources." In additional exchanges via Twitter, Costolo continued to avoid a candid discussion of systemic racism and sexism issues. In contrast, Wadhwa pointed out that Twitter's CEO was typical of white men in this high technology sector, describing them as "a boys' club—a fraternity of the worst kind. It stacks the deck against women. It leaves out blacks and Hispanics. And it provides unfair advantage to an elite few who happen to be connected."[70] That is, this problem involved *systemic* racism and sexism. In recent years, many lawsuits have made public a volley of backstage sexist and racist comments and decisions by executives in high technology companies; they provide another reason to remain skeptical about their nods to diversity.[71]

For critics of the white men's club that is Silicon Valley, their public companies have an obligation to reflect the diversity of customers who make top executives and their investors wealthy. Interestingly, companies with the greatest percentage of women directors on their boards on average have a significantly higher return rate on invested capital.[72]

An even more troubling issue with the lack of diversity in these high tech and Internet firms, and thus in their everyday decision-making, is that they are on the leading edge of a technological revolution that is reshaping millions of lives, young and old, and helping to create more unequal societies globally. A recent book by Robert McChesney and John Nichols suggests that this *automation revolution* is soon to hit most countries even harder:

> Unemployment will spike as new technologies replace labor in the manufacturing, service, and professional sectors of an economy that is already struggling. The end of work as we know it will hit at the worst moment imaginable: as capitalism fosters permanent stagnation, when the labor market is in decrepit shape, with declining wages, expanding poverty, and scorching inequality.[73]

Some analysts seem to think the greatest danger here is to manufacturing jobs, but numerous technological developments in the robotics, artificial intelligence, and computing power areas already suggest that a substantial array of white-collar jobs are in danger, including many clerical, consumer service, and professional jobs that involve routinized tasks.[74] However, also missing in discussions of the impact of new technologies is *who controls them*. Under oligopolistic capitalism the decision-makers are still mostly elite white men. In our final chapter we will return briefly to the related issue raised by analysts of the possible worker-liberation effects of this new technology revolution.

Elite Political Dominance

As we discussed earlier, the white "founding fathers" of the United States broke with their British overlords using a democratic origins narrative that was substantially mythological. In this story, seen clearly in accounts of the Declaration of Independence, these mostly anti-democratic white men were proclaimed as heroes championing ideals of freedom, equality, and democracy. Contrary to this sacred mythology, the U.S. Constitution these powerful white men prepared, one that is still the U.S. political and legal foundation, did *not* come close to creating a real people's democracy where most adult Americans had the right to participate substantially and freely in major, democratically structured political institutions.

The New Deal and After

Not until the middle of the 19th century did ordinary white men, those with modest amounts of property, gain the right to vote in most areas, thereby having the opportunity to engage in some important political activities.

Even then, white men mostly of affluent backgrounds were the only members of the Congress until the Reconstruction era (late 1860s–1870s). The United States became more democratic with slavery's abolition and the temporary enfranchisement of black men after that war, but Reconstruction reforms were soon reduced or eliminated with the rise of legal racial segregation. Even later reforms moving in a democratic direction, especially in the 1930s New Deal era, did not move the United States to a full-fledged democracy. Sociologist Bill Domhoff has challenged pervasive notions concerning the supposedly "weak" corporate power and "liberal" government expansion from the New Deal to the 1960s. Actually, President Franklin Delano Roosevelt's (1933–1945) New Deal government was in trouble by 1937 and was under even greater corporate control by 1939. Since that time, top corporate business executives have very often prevailed on key economic matters involving government action—such as in undermining labor rights, including the 1935 National Labor Relations Act.[75]

The New Deal interventions in a depressed U.S. economy often triggered a militantly conservative response. Much of this came from intensely racist and powerful white men, many from the South, in Congress. Their racist and gendered-racist framing shaped many New Deal decisions. They passed legislation guaranteeing these government programs would be implemented with aggressive discrimination against black Americans. Local officials, usually white men, systematically favored whites over blacks in unemployment and other Depression-era programs. Repeatedly, too, this *systemic* racism heavily influenced the free-market actions and goals of capitalistic employers. These white businesspeople, heading firms small and large, routinely operated out of their own white racial framing and thus hired white workers first, no matter how unqualified they were and how costly that was for the employers. Ever since, this systemic racial discrimination has continued to regularly trump free-market goals in the implementation of many employers' decisions.[76]

Additionally, in the 1930s some powerful white capitalists created an attack organization, the Liberty League, to fight New Deal programs seen as limiting their capitalistic operations. Funded by manufacturing, banking, and other corporate capitalists, this League began politicized attacks on the Roosevelt administration as a "dictatorial" threat. The National Association of Manufacturers also became a major player in political assaults on New Deal reforms. Expanding unions and enhanced worker rights were major targets. Some company executives stockpiled weapons to fight a feared uprising of workers. Some in a reactionary wing of the elite actually plotted to violently *overthrow* the Roosevelt administration. The era's very conservative political-economic organizations, all led by white men, laid the groundwork for later expansion of conservative political movements, to the present day.[77]

After significant expansion in government programs for ordinary Americans from the Franklin Roosevelt era of the 1930s–1940s to the Lyndon Johnson era of the 1960s, over the subsequent 1970s and 1980s the federal government and the major political parties became generally more conservative and tilted toward corporate interests and away from support of expanding social support programs. Many have termed this the corporate-shaped *right turn* in U.S. politics. Not only was there less support for government programs for ordinary Americans, but moderately liberal Democratic officials such as President Jimmy Carter (1977–1981) got less congressional support for new domestic programs. Conservative pressures resulted in yet more support for military expenditures and related intervention overseas, usually to the benefit of profit-seeking corporate executives and often exemplifying an aggressive display of age-old *white "tough-guy" manhood* internationally.[78]

For decades, military-related federal expenditures and arms production have been significant areas of government *economic* intervention. Numerous scholars and a few political leaders, including President Dwight Eisenhower as early as the 1950s, have warned of the negative impact of this still-huge military-industrial complex.[79] Given close ties to conservative corporate elites, since the 1960s the Republican Party has taken up the political platform of increased military expenditures, cutbacks in domestic social spending, and corporate tax cuts. In contrast, the Democratic Party has become a party of oscillating political-economic goals, sometimes supporting multinational capitalists' interests, but at other times working for significant employment and other social programs for ordinary Americans.[80]

From the beginning, major U.S. institutions have been shaped and governed at the top by a white ruling elite and its immediate implementing acolytes. This has been true for the capitalistic economy and major political institutions—in spite of the "freedom, liberty, and justice" rhetoric that tries to cover up great economic and other social inequalities. Since the 17th century, successive oligarchical regimes have created, maintained, and/or extended very inegalitarian economic, political, and educational institutions.[81]

Undemocratic Governance for Centuries

Because this country's leading white founders wished it to be so, the U.S. Senate is an undemocratic political institution set up to protect their gender, racial, and class interests. Said to be the "brains" behind the U.S. Constitution, a fearful James Madison noted that this Senate would protect ordinary Americans "against the transient impressions into which they themselves might be led."[82] The Constitution specifies two senators per state, an anti-democratic provision that created a Senate in which people in a sparsely populated state (e.g., Wyoming) get the *same* numerical representation as those in a far more populous state (e.g., California). Noting this reality, scholars Winters and Page have pointed out that Senate elections in small states are frequently swamped with cash from outside organizations and "often result in victories by multi-millionaire candidates (or candidates backed by multi-millionaires), who are likely—consciously or not—to have special sympathy for the views of the wealthiest Americans."[83] Additionally, the Constitution provides these powerful senators with six-year terms, much longer than for representatives in the more democratically structured U.S. House of Representatives.

Additionally, the influential white men who made the U.S. Constitution gave senators extraordinary decision-making power on key government matters, including the sole power to ratify treaties and approve major court appointments. For centuries the undemocratic Senate has played a central role in protecting the economic, political, and other social interests of powerful white men. For instance, for the 80 percent of U.S. history that was slavery and Jim Crow segregation, just two dozen or so southern senators manipulated anti-democratic Senate rules to kill almost all anti-slavery legislation in the 19th century and, later on, almost all significant civil rights legislation until the 1960s. Thus, the "Constitution's fundamental arrangements of federalism and separation of powers provide multiple veto points at which any serious threat to an oligarchy-friendly status quo can be blocked."[84] Moreover, until 1868 all members of Congress were white men, and until 1916 all were men. A substantial majority of U.S. adults had little or no real representation in Congress for much of U.S. history. Clearly, the congressional structure has not been one of truly representative democracy.

Undemocratic Governance Today

A key part of elite control of the political system is that a majority of elected politicians to major state and federal offices come from the most affluent and powerful 10 percent of Americans. Most members of Congress have significant business or professional backgrounds; most head affluent-to-rich families. Most are members of the top elite or are in the associated strata just below. From the beginning, affluent white men have constituted almost all of the top political leadership positions, including in the White House and Congress. Most recently, rare exceptions have included the examples of President Barack Obama (2009–2017) and House Speaker Nancy Pelosi (2003–2007). Yet, even Obama had to have strong backing from segments of the country's mostly white and male elite. Without that backing, he could not have become president.[85] Today, powerful whites still overwhelmingly dominate major political institutions. A consideration of the 114th U.S. Congress (2015–2017) brings vibrancy to the point of white male dominance. It was mostly white and 80 percent male. In fact, while white men make up a statistical minority (about 31 percent) of the population, they currently hold 65 percent of elected offices in the United States. They are about 84 percent of mayors in the largest 100 cities, about three quarters of state legislators and governors, nearly 70 percent of U.S. circuit court judges, and 87 percent of major police officials. In addition, in the United States most law cases are tried at the state level, where about 10,000 judges try 90 percent of cases. Whites make up 80 percent of these judges, and white men alone are a significant majority. Clearly, the latter possess far more political and legal power than Americans of color and white women, taken together.[86]

Consider the great implications of the lack of representation for just women in cities. Nowadays only a fifth of cities with populations over 30,000 are governed by female mayors. Just 30 percent of council members in major metropolises are women. They are also inadequately represented in most public planning agencies and most private architectural and real estate development agencies, particularly at upper levels of decision-making. The local white male political-economic establishments mostly ignore many of local women's everyday needs, even exposing them to preventable risks of urban violence and other discrimination in public spaces. Decisions regarding urban accessibility issues and zoning for housing and transportation design often fail to take into account certain requirements of women or people of color. As a result, for example, many women feel very unsafe in venturing into the streets after dusk. Indeed, cities at night are frequently "cities of men." Day and night, urban socio-spatial design generally communicates the influence and control that powerful white men have over the gendered and racialized others in terms of city governance and planning, and thus over daily urban life patterns. Cities are often used differently by white women and people of color than by most white men. For example, men and women of color are more likely to live in poverty than white men, and they have different needs; they frequently have different transportation requirements resulting from the combined requirements of low-paid work and domestic duties. This means that the cities *of* and *for* white men function poorly for a great many women and men of color, as well as often for white women.

Consider too that, since the beginning, the incomes and wealth of members of Congress have been far above average. Those elected to Congress have mostly shared the conditions of the upper 5 percent or so of U.S. individuals and families in terms of economic security, wealth, and investments. In 2014 the median net worth for lawmakers in the House and Senate was more than $1 million. More than half of the members of the House and Senate, who determine laws regarding how affluent and wealthy Americans are taxed, were millionaires in terms of assets.[87] When their total financial assets were pooled for just one year (2013), they were collectively worth about $4.3 billion, a 10 percent increase from the year before. This was the equivalent to the wealth of about 76,000 average U.S. households.[88] Unsurprisingly, most members of Congress also have intimate links to the capitalistic economy. In a recent year their most prevalent investment was real estate holdings—with an estimated value between $357 million and $1.2 billion. The securities and banking sectors drew the greatest congressional investments after real estate.[89]

Even the election of historically atypical political officials, such as a few white women and people of color, does not necessarily weaken the hold of elite white men as a group on government. Consider the administration of President Barack Obama (2009–2017). With some major exceptions, he appointed members of the established white elite to the majority of very top administration positions. Most had served in previous presidential administrations and/or corporate positions. A substantial majority in traditional cabinet positions were white; most were from very affluent or wealthy backgrounds.[90] Unsurprisingly, thus, on most important economic issues, Obama opted for numerous centrist policies. Princeton professor Cornel West, a leading black intellectual, argued harshly that Obama had become little more than a "puppet of corporate plutocrats."[91] In addition, sociologist Michael Dyson has documented how Obama mostly catered to white opinion in speeches on racial matters. He was more likely to accent individual black responsibilities for socioeconomic difficulties than the systemic white racism that routinely creates or exacerbates those life challenges.[92] In the elite-white-male dominance system it is difficult for a particular political (or corporate) official, especially one not white and male, to stray far from a societal framing acceptable to the ruling white elite, or at least one major faction within it. Operating in well-established organizational settings they must, almost always, conform to the *white male normative structure* there.

Unsurprisingly, prominent white men effectively control numerous other sociopolitical institutions. In recent years an estimated 11,000 or more political lobbyists, the majority white, have been registered to lobby Congress and government agencies. Most powerful lobbyists are white men. The growth in lobbyists has been dramatic. Only five registered lobbyists worked for large-scale corporations for every one of the 535 members of Congress in 1970. Currently, there are about 22 such lobbyists for every congressperson.[93] Over a recent decade, lobbying firms and agencies have spent an estimated $1.6–$3.5 billion annually to persuade members of Congress and the heads of important government agencies to act in the interest of corporations and other economic organizations they represent. These are the officially recorded dollars, yet much more is spent in unrecorded ways. Those groups and companies that spent the most on this government lobbying between 1998 and 2010 were, with one exception, linked to major corporations and corporate associations.[94] There is also the infamous "revolving door," the process in which members of Congress and other important federal government employees—again, mostly white men—are employed by lobbying firms and groups, and other large corporations or business think tanks, after their employment in government (see Chapter 5).[95]

Moreover, since the late 1970s those who directly advise elected and other government officials have grown in number and shifted significantly in a more conservative direction. Until that time, a majority of outside experts frequently consulted by government and media officials came from centrist or moderately conservative think tanks. Yet, in recent decades they have increasingly been countered or displaced as very wealthy business conservatives began to substantially fund an array of right-wing think tanks. These very conservative organizations have been able, usually with the collaboration of friendly media executives, to place numerous right-wing experts into media and other public discussions. These organizations have thereby significantly shaped the information, and much misinformation, available to the public on major societal issues.[96]

Still, as of 2016–2017, there were signs in a few states of coming political change. In the most racially diverse state (California), where whites are a demographic minority, a 2016 candidate with African American and Asian-Indian American ancestry, Kamala Harris, won a U.S. Senate seat. Additionally, Obama's 2009–2017 presidency is assumed by many to foreshadow a time when racially diverse voters will be reflected in the more representative faces of Democratic politicians. However, in spite of Obama, the Democratic Party's top elected officials in early 2017 were still noticeably white and primarily men.[97]

Political Gatekeepers: Economic Dominance

Most major elections are substantially controlled, directly or indirectly, by powerful corporate executives and other wealthy Americans. These election contests are nowhere close to the ideal of real political democracy. In the case of both major U.S. political parties, disproportionately white top officials often operate as allies of elite wealthy backers. As noted previously, many leading politicians are from major business sectors. As we have also noted, the important state and national candidates who are elected from the major parties, as well as those appointed to top government positions, generally come from the elite or near-elite sectors of the population. As a group, they are certainly not representative of the general population.[98]

As a result, for many decades the major political parties have adopted economic and related policies that are mostly in line with the economic interests of the elite white men who have had the greatest influence over the economy. Given the capitalistic context, the Democratic Party and the Republican Party have generally operated as variations of one dominant "property party." Their top leaders are not just interested in their ordinary voters turning out, but are often very concerned with building up party power by getting major funding and other resource support from major "political investors," especially those connected to large capitalistic firms.

When major business blocs *differ* on important government policies because of differing economic and other social interests, the political parties commonly associated with those blocs also often differ in their approach to those policies. Economic blocs contribute substantially to party campaigns and hire effective lobbyists—and thereby seek to shape major party policies and, ultimately, the decisions of their elected officials. Frequent linkage of party policies to major capitalistic blocs has been highlighted in an *investment theory* of politics developed by political scientists Thomas Ferguson and Joel Rogers. Over long centuries, the U.S. economy has periodically changed in terms of which business blocs have had the greatest economic and political influence. The white owners and executives who mostly have led the companies in these major blocs have sometimes shifted political allegiances from one party to the other depending on their particular business needs and related concerns.[99] Additionally, on some government policy issues, especially on those not central to business profitmaking, the power elite does sometimes split into a conservative faction and a moderate faction. Those in this moderate faction—together with a small liberal faction—have periodically been more supportive of some reduction in class inequalities and increases in certain social and political rights (e.g., expanding LGBTQ rights) of ordinary Americans.

Most members of Congress, most top staff members, and most influential lobbyists are members of either the white elite or the affluent enabling class just below the elite. Most seek to foster the political-economic interests of well-off Americans. For instance, although national surveys reveal a substantial majority of Americans favor tax increases for the rich in order to deal with problems like government budget deficits, such liberal views often have little impact on congressional actions in regard to these tax and budget matters. The reason is simple: the congressional decision-makers usually pay much more attention to the views of the country's elite.[100] Unsurprisingly, the upper 1 to 5 percent of Americans in political-economic power and wealth very disproportionately influence congressional decision-making on issues of major concern to them. One research examination of voting records of U.S. senators found that they were far more responsive to views of very "affluent constituents than to the opinions of middle-class constituents" and, most strikingly, that the views of "constituents in the bottom third of the income distribution have *no* apparent statistical effect on their senators' roll call votes."[101] If well-off voters, especially white voters, favor or oppose an important government policy, their views are far more likely to prevail.

Another group of researchers set out to examine the political actions of wealthy Chicagoans, who averaged annual incomes of more than 1 million dollars and whose median wealth was 7.5 million dollars. More than two-thirds had contributed substantial money to political campaigns, as compared with just 14 percent of the general population. Over half reported having specific and recent personal contacts with senators, representatives, and other important political officials about government policy issues. Unsurprisingly, they were usually much more conservative than the general public on issues of business regulation, taxes, and social programs. They reported seeking their own socioeconomic interests in being active politically. The researchers concluded that their "distinctive policy preferences may help account for why certain public policies in the United States appear to deviate from what the majority of US citizens wants the government to do," and that this certainly "raises serious issues for democratic theory," both serious *understatements* about the significance of their disturbing findings.[102]

Moreover, even though privileged whites, especially white men, have been contributing to political campaigns for many decades in attempts to make their presence felt in politics, more recent Supreme Court decisions have unlocked fresh paths for unrestricted political giving. Consider the Court's 2010 decision *Citizens United v. Federal Election Commission*. This ruling in favor of a conservative nonprofit organization freed such groups to use huge amounts of corporate and other elite funds to organize political campaigns. As a direct consequence, of all the traceable money donated to candidates during the 2012 presidential election, 28 percent came from just 31,385 individuals in the U.S. population. For instance, Sheldon and Miriam Adelson, a very wealthy and conservative husband-and-wife team, who are foes of labor unions and the Democratic Party generally, contributed $97 million themselves.[103]

Then, soon after the Supreme Court's contentious 2014 *McCutcheon vs. Federal Election Commission* decision, talk again turned to the exclusive group of campaign donors who unleashed a flood of money into a political structure already overflowing with large donations from moneyed interests. The very wealthy have thus come to further dominate among the mega-donors to important political campaigns.[104] The political influence of the predominantly white and male elite has spread, as signified by a vastly unbalanced increase in their political donations. Nonpartisan organizations regularly document how a group of ultra-wealthy donors now dominates much of U.S. politics. Most are male. Almost half reside in the richest 1 percent of urban neighborhoods; fewer than 1 in 50 live in areas with a majority of African American or Latino residents. In most areas we observe these wealthy donors dominating political campaigns and institutions.[105]

Another indication of elite political influence is the fact that funds from the most generous backers have contributed greatly to the election of almost all successful congressional candidates. Indeed, "84 percent of those elected in 2012 took more money from these 1% of the 1% donors than they did from *all* of their small donors (individuals who gave $200 or less) combined."[106] The idiom "money talks" has never been more fitting for the U.S. political scene. However, it is still rare for most of these white, male, and ultra-wealthy people to be explicitly named and seriously analyzed in mainstream media accounts—doubtless, because they also have significant input into, or influence over, much of the mainstream media.

These huge money contribution numbers are very significant in shaping the everyday operations of the U.S. government. Recall that elite and ordinary Americans are often poles apart when it comes to certain political priorities, especially regarding government social support programs. When they differ on such policy issues, most elected officials have been found to side with the dominating elite much of the time. For generations now, this has generally been the case throughout all U.S. presidential administrations.[107]

Wealthy White Political Funders Today

To truly understand the impact of mega-donors on the political landscape, one can follow the money trail. In regard to candidate-specific political advertisements alone, the billionaire brothers Charles and David Koch, among the richest men on the planet, raised and distributed $400 million during the 2012 elections and another $53.5 million for the 2014 elections. Most went into political issue ads. The expressed aim is to convey a message about a public issue without directly encouraging voters to take explicit action. Despite such rationales, conservative groups spending huge dollars on these ads aggressively endeavor to sway voters to actively work and vote for conservative causes and candidates. At one benefactor's conference, a Koch official explained that advocacy ads reduce the popularity among voters of political candidates the Koch group opposes.[108]

The billionaire Sheldon Adelson spent nearly $100 million in an attempt to ensure that the White House would not be returned to President Obama in 2012. Adelson's disappointment with his political investment did not stop prospective Republican presidential candidates in later elections from trying to win him over, and Adelson periodically announced his desire to bankroll more of them.[109] Harold Simmons is another white political "investor" who spent much money to secure influence in Washington. During just one recent presidential election he contributed in excess of $25 million to Republican super PACs, the latter a kind of political action committee created after the elite-favorable outcome of a federal court case.[110]

By the conclusion of the 2012 presidential electoral cycle, this *dark money*—so called because it is not included in federal disclosure rules—skyrocketed, reaching at least $400 million, a huge increase from the 2010 election. These funds were mostly earmarked for electoral and issue advertising. Dark money dominated again during the 2014 and 2016 electoral cycles.[111] A *New York Times* editorial observed that the U.S. Senate was elected, as of 2014, in the "greatest wave of secret, special-interest money ever raised in a congressional election." Calling much defense of these unrestricted clandestine campaign expenditures "phony free speech," the editorial described the dark money that dirtied that electoral cycle, including the many super PACs established for political candidates to side-step federal restrictions and permit wealthy donors to back individual candidates with huge contributions.[112] Striking also is the fact that this subterranean money has gone *very disproportionately* to Republican Party candidates. Still, non-profit groups associated with the Democratic Party did contribute much more modest sums (about $27 million) during the 2014 electoral cycle. This massive and usually hidden political funding, often defended as a type of "free speech," actually results in a *silencing* of much necessary political speech, especially of the views of those who cannot compete money-wise with the powerful white elite for mainstream media airtime.

Throughout the data for these and later elections we observe the enormous U.S. political influence that comes with giving hundreds of millions to disproportionately conservative political candidates. Occasionally, wealthy donors receive ambassadorships and other plum political appointments in return for their "generosity." Far more common, however, is the bounty that comes with having an elected official more or less in one's pocket. An official of the Campaign Legal Center, which works on campaign finance, has explained the major problem:

[We] would like to see an American democracy that is truly democratic that reflects the vast diversity of our country. . . . When you look at who's contributing to bankroll the system, we are seeing an overwhelmingly white and male and wealthy donor base that doesn't look [like] the America I live in.[113]

An Undemocratic Supreme Court

Consider another undemocratic institution created by the powerful white founders—the U.S. Supreme Court. This high court was set up, intentionally, to be an unelected political body with little democratic overview. In an early Court decision (*Marbury v. Madison*), the *unelected* white male justices by themselves decided the Court had the power to decide whether congressional legislation is constitutional.[114] Unlike other western countries, the Court can in effect *legislate* without the consent of the legislative branch, yet the latter's actions can be overturned by a judicial veto involving only five members of this unelected judicial elite. The Court has vetoed congressional legislation two dozen times as unconstitutional, and in many other cases interpreted (often, distorted) the laws in the interest of a segment of the ruling elite.[115] Consider, too, that from the 1790s to the 1950s, most of this country's history, an *all-white-male* Court protected the slavery and Jim Crow systems of racial oppression. More recently, especially since the Richard Nixon era (1969–1974), a conservative Court majority has weakened federally protected civil rights that were enshrined in the 1960s civil rights laws and knocked down moderate affirmative action programs that seek to eliminate the effects of past and persisting racial and gender discrimination.[116]

As of this writing, just 112 Americans, 108 men and 4 women, have ever served on this high court. About *97 percent* have been white, and those mostly white men. Given this extremely skewed demographic composition, the historical and current dominance of sexist framing and white racial framing in many Court decisions, and thus in much law, is unsurprising. Significantly, after President Barack Obama's appointments of Supreme Court Justices Sonia Sotomayor and Elena Kagan, many white media pundits and other analysts boasted that the Supreme Court was the most diverse ever—with three of nine justices being women and one a black man (Clarence Thomas). However, Justice Thomas was intentionally appointed by a Republican president (George H. W. Bush) because he was a rare black conservative and would *not* represent black majority views on most discrimination issues before the Court. Thomas has delivered on that expectation, such as by voting against racial desegregation efforts of great concern to most African Americans. Indeed, a significant social science literature exists on the ways in which some people of color aggressively adopt elements of the dominant white racist framing, often to the harm of communities of color.[117] Justice Thomas appears to be a major example of how the dominant white elite has worked, directly or indirectly, to control much of the thinking of Americans, including many people of color, on racial, gender, and class issues—especially on issues where they seek to maintain the societal status quo in their favor.

Judge Antonin Scalia: The Power of One White Man

Long gone are the powerful white male slaveholders, ministers, and publishers of pro-slavery publications who cited biblical patriarchs as examples of their God-ordained patriarchal, racial, and class legitimacy. Nevertheless, members of today's white male elite still regularly raise themselves to almost godlike stature in societies like the United States. These white men are indeed part of a powerful societal *system*, for their substantial power comes both from their elite family and other social networks and from powerful institutional positions they hold.

The elite's societal power often appears transcendent, for in death they can still greatly shape a society, still affecting those they considered below them in status. Consider the major example of the late Supreme Court justice Antonin Scalia (serving 1986–2016), an arch-conservative white man. With his demise in 2016, progressive causes seemed to benefit. If he had lived a little longer, a major ruling against public workers' union dues by the then-conservative-controlled Supreme Court would have likely devastated the public union movement. Instead, the court's 4–4 tie meant that an earlier pro-union ruling by a lower court was decisive.[118] Other rulings that would have been decided by 5–4 conservative margins also ended up as ties, and more progressive decisions by lower courts stood. Scalia's death favorably impacted cases about legislative redistricting, making it more difficult for conservative state legislators "to redraw districts to favor white, rural, Republican voters."[119] Another tied Court ruling was likewise a triumph for women's health. Scalia symbolizes how the elite firmly positions itself at the political helm of the overarching elite-white-male dominance system and its major subsystems.

Additionally, conservative members of the white elite, mainly in the Republican Party, tried to determine Scalia's judicial successor, aggressively arguing against President Barack Obama making a Supreme Court nomination. Interestingly, even the deceased Scalia was part of this effort. In an interview before his death, he named another white conservative as his preferred heir apparent.[120] Like the powerful white men who uncompromisingly perpetuated the gendered-racist hierarchy long ago, Scalia dedicated his life (and death) to ensuring that the same social order, with moneyed white heterosexual men highest on the ladder of human beings, would long endure.

Scalia and his conservative male judicial brethren put into place considered plans to protect their vision of U.S. society in the aforementioned Supreme Court decisions, most especially the 2010 *Citizens United* decision. That ruling mostly eliminated federal and state legislative efforts to regulate the huge election expenditures of corporations and other powerful groups for political advertising.[121] This far-reaching decision followed the election of an African American president and came at a time when voters of color were becoming more influential. As sociologist Glenn Bracey has noted, the "combination of black and brown leadership, increased black and brown voting activity, decreased white voting potential, and sufficient noncorporate funding pools for campaigns was a new threat to which whites were compelled to respond immediately."[122] Most whites appear to believe they will lose political and racial dominance as they become a statistical minority (see Chapter 8). Indeed, since the Richard Nixon administration, the intentional packing of the Supreme Court by Republican presidents with conservative judges has provided important votes for anti-democratic Court decisions. A key justice in this effort, Scalia recognized what a more liberal court meant. As one social scientist summarized, "A more liberal court could overturn *Citizens United*, restore voting rights and workers' rights, protect women's right to abortion, allow the president to address climate change, keep affirmative action in jobs and education, and deliver many other important rulings."[123]

The Supreme Court Echo Chamber: Male Dominance

Since the Obama judicial appointments noted above, the Supreme Court has been more inclusive than the powerful lawyers who argue directly before it. Little known to the public, an exclusive cadre of mostly white male lawyers is considered elite because their Supreme Court appeals are far more likely to be accepted than all others filed. One study noted that for the period 2004–2012 just 66 such lawyers accounted for less than 1 percent of lawyers who filed appeals, yet were engaged in 43 percent of cases heard. Some 63 of the 66 elite lawyers were *white*, and 58 were *men*. Many had elite network connections, such as formerly clerking for a Supreme Court justice or holding prominent posts in the Office of the Solicitor General. Moreover, most primarily represented corporate interests.[124]

White male lawyers often enjoy great societal privileges. In 2013, for instance, mostly white male lawyers appeared before the Court. Among the few lawyers of color who appeared before the Court in that 2004–2012 period was Neal Katyal. Born to Asian Indian immigrants, Katyal was just one of three top 66 lawyers who was not white. Still, he is male and was supported by powerful white male mentors and worked under several federal justices and as deputy solicitor general. Finally, like the majority of these top lawyers, he is in the business of protecting corporations and their interests.[125]

Some legal authorities insist that such dependence on a few legal specialists, who mostly advocate for corporations, has transformed the Court into an echo chamber where an exclusive corporate-oriented group of jurists are intimately linked to a select group of top business lawyers. The two groups collectively reinforce narrow notions of how laws should be interpreted. In exclusive interviews with Reuters news agency, a majority of the eight justices interviewed did indicate that racial or gender diversity among legal counsels is *not* a priority and that such "efficient" legal representation best serves the interests of the U.S. legal system.[126] Nonetheless, the evidence suggests that this echo chamber is real and, conspicuously, antidemocratic. Lawyers who become sufficiently elite-networked to present cases before the high Court enjoy numerous litigative and access advantages that most lawyers and their clients do not enjoy.

Unsurprisingly, thus, leanings toward corporate interests have been obvious under the Supreme Court headed by Chief Justice John Roberts. Consumer, environmental, and union groups have had great difficulty getting legal appeals before the Court. The aforementioned elite lawyers have been three times more likely to petition the Court on behalf of businesses than for these groups. In one nine-year period (2005–2014), the Roberts Court ruled for business parties 60 percent of the time, a significantly greater percentage than for the previous Court headed by William Rehnquist.[127]

Some justices have argued that the corporate bias resides not in them, but in the nature of modern-day litigation. More business patent and property cases, as well as government regulatory issues, are coming before the Court. Additionally, some justices have argued that there are capable legal advocates who do defend individuals against corporations. However, in making this latter argument they tend to mention only two major attorneys, one of whom has pointed out that they are *not* a realistic alternative to powerful corporate law firms.[128] Thus, numerous critics see these common attempts to defend the corporate-centered Court as mainly justifications concealing white-run corporations' great and persisting legal power.

We have already underscored the distinctive U.S. emphasis on protecting property, especially that of wealthy property holders, since the making of the Constitution. By 1819, the U.S. Supreme Court had created a legal status for U.S. corporations. Over the subsequent decades the all-white-male Court took historic steps to advance the legal status of the corporation above what had existed in previous Anglo American law. In so doing, the Court sowed the seeds for a reduction in government sovereignty over these corporations, thereby helping businesses become more impervious to government regulation. Over the course of a century, corporations—and thus the executives at their helms—acquired numerous new constitutional "rights" as a consequence of Supreme Court decisions, including actually being considered legal "persons."[129]

By the end of the Civil War it was clear that corporations were often powerful organizations with legitimate hierarchical structures; major decisions were made by top, usually white male, executives, with lesser decision-making as one moved down the corporate hierarchy. In 1864, even President Abraham Lincoln, earlier a railroad company lawyer, wrote of his fear of the growing power of corporate executives and the corporations they led:

> As a result of the war, corporations have been enthroned and an era of corruption in high places will follow, and the money power of the country will endeavor to prolong its reign by working upon the prejudices of the people *until all wealth is aggregated in a few hands* and the Republic is destroyed.[130]

Since that time, presidents, other top administration officials, and members of Congress have been intensively involved with the problems of corporations, in the United States and across the globe. On a recurring basis, the executive and congressional branches of the U.S. government have assisted particular firms and also bailed out the white-run corporate economy when in economic predicaments. Such undemocratic intervention is sought and won by elite business interests, even though it limits government actions that can be taken for non-elite Americans.[131]

Other Powerful Legal Officials: Mostly White Men

We should note the racial and gender bias in other parts of the legal system. Few judges at most levels are people of color. Many white judges appear to have little understanding of the lives of those Americans, especially working class people of color, that they frequently face in courtrooms. Additionally, one study found the overwhelming majority (95 percent) of elected U.S. prosecutors are white, and 79 percent are white men. (White men are less than a third of the population.) Indeed, across the country only 4 percent of elected prosecutors are men of color, and a mere 1 percent are women of color. A substantial majority of the states that elect prosecutors have *no* African Americans in such positions. These figures underscore the dearth of racial and gender diversity among those entrusted to bring criminal charges and help confer prison sentences. These important justice system officials substantially control who gets tried, how trials proceed, and often what the punishment will be. Brenda Carter, who led this study, summed up the issue: "We have a system where incredible power and discretion is concentrated in the hands of one demographic group."[132]

Yet again, the vague "one demographic group" phrasing refers to mostly powerful white men. In contrast, the majority of those arrestees processed by them in the justice system typically do not come from their racial or socioeconomic backgrounds. Indeed, research has shown that arrestees of color are frequently described in court proceedings and other settings by these mostly white criminal justice system officials—prosecutors, judges, and others—in quite inhumane and overtly racist terms taken directly from the white racial frame.[133]

A Too-Powerful Chief Executive

As we have seen numerous times already, the elite founders created a strong central government that would not be too influenced in major decision-making by most of the voting public. Since the founding era, the operation of federal and state governments as mostly elite-male-controlled in top positions and in making important domestic and foreign policy decisions is what the principal founders sought to create. As of 2017, all U.S. presidents but one (Barack Obama) have been white men. None has been elected directly by the people, as the *undemocratic* constitutional insti- tution called the electoral college actually selects a president. In several U.S. presidential elections, including the 2000 election of George W. Bush and the 2016 election of Donald Trump, the candidate receiving the most votes nationally did *not* become U.S. president because of the imposition of that undemocratic electoral college.[134]

Most countries with a president allow that official only modest power, but in the U.S. case the president has become an extraordinarily powerful elected official. As in the corporate world, members of the U.S. political elite have decision-making power only because this society has long been struc- tured to provide the essential levers of that power. The U.S. president's veto of congressional legislation can be overridden only with an unlikely two- thirds vote of the House and Senate, another feature of the Constitution designed to keep government decision-making in the hands of a small elite. Over time, too, the executive powers of the president have substantially expanded. Together, this strong executive power and an undemocratic Sen- ate have often provided relatively unrestricted opportunities for that elite to aggressively pursue some of its political-economic interests nationally and globally. For example, the oligarchical structure of elite president plus elite Senate has long provided much support for imperialistic U.S. expansion globally.[135] In addition, since the country's founding, U.S. presidents, other top executive officials, and members of Congress have had to get substan- tially involved in numerous national and international crises faced overseas by U.S. corporations. Critical economic decisions made by top government officials in regard to "taxation, central bank operations, debt management, banking, trade and tariffs, and financial rescues or bailouts" have regularly increased or protected economic wealth, especially that of wealthy whites.[136] Every so often, too, the federal executive and congressional branches have had to bail out the U.S. economy and numerous corporations in the recurring economic crises the latter often create, such as in the destructive 2007–2009 Great Recession.

Elite Educational Dominance

College Presidents and Faculty: Much Cloning of White Men

Historically, the U.S. educational system has been run by powerful white men. In the 1980s the typical college president was a middle-aged white man, Protestant, and married. Twenty-five years later that demographic profile remained mostly intact. In one recent period the racial diversity in top educational positions *declined*—from 14 percent in 2006 to 13 percent people of color in 2011.[137] When educational institutions predominantly serving students of color are omitted, the percentage of college presidents who were people of color was just 9 percent in both years. Today, white men, usually from higher social status backgrounds, continue to dominate the top jobs, despite the growing diversity of students on many campuses. Women of all backgrounds (but disproportionately white) make up just 30 percent of chief executives, although women students are currently about 60 percent of college undergraduates. Among other major college administrators, most are also white and disproportionately male.[138]

This persistence of powerful white men at the top of most university hierarchies has great educational significance. They and their immediate assistants have long controlled much of how colleges and universities are structured and operated over time—including staffing, curricula, graduate requirements, and other regulations—and with numerous broad consequences. According to a recent report, of the 1.5 million full-time instructional faculty in degree-granting postsecondary institutions, about 44 percent are white men, 35 percent are white women, 6 percent are black, 4 percent are Latino, 9 percent are Asian or Pacific Islander, and less than 1 percent are American Indian, Alaska Native, or multiracial. Among *full-time professors*, moreover, the majority are white men and just one-quarter are white women; these are the more secure and influential faculty members.[139]

Recent research on Brown University (in the Ivy League) offers insights into the dominance of white faculty, especially on campus climates. White students there outnumbered students of color, and there were ten times as many white faculty as faculty of color. Brown's students of color felt they were at a disadvantage as they toiled to find supportive mentors who understood their difficult experiences in a mainly white learning environment. They reported problems in lecture sessions, including white faculty members' avoidance of important racial issues and unawareness of their own white racial framing. In contrast, the significantly underrepresented faculty of color were described as essential enablers of students of color.[140] This dearth of faculty of color is also a great loss to white students, who miss out on their societal perspectives. As an African American colleague recently told us, the lack of racial diversity in students and faculty results in higher-level administrators more easily sweeping their institution's "racist legacies, as well as recent and recurring racist incidents, under the proverbial rug."[141]

These commonplace data on the lack of diversity at historically white institutions may shed light on why Saida Grundy, an African American professor at Boston University, was met with intense white hostility there. In 2015, after racist chants of fraternity brothers at that university's Sigma Alpha Epsilon (SAE) came to light, Grundy went to social media to explicitly call out "white college age males" as a "problem population."

Unsurprisingly, an aggressive white backlash ensued.[142] A petition appeared calling for her dismissal because her "radical idealism" produced a "counterproductive learning environment." Yet another petition in defense of her "right to express her views as an individual" also materialized.[143] That petition opposed assertions that her comments were "racist," explaining that she "as a sociologist, recognizes that racism is a system of oppression in which people of color are denied political, economic, and social power. . . . Calling Professor Grundy's tweets racist minimizes the very real effects of racism for people of color in the U.S."[144] Indeed, for some years now, social science research has shown that many college students tend to consider white male heterosexual professors more "objective" than faculty of color, women faculty, or LGBTQ faculty.[145]

Grooming Young White Men: Dominant Racial Framers

Beyond lecture halls an unsettling pattern of grooming affluent young white men as racial framers and discriminators is apparent on most college campuses. For example, in 2015 the University of Oklahoma's own Sigma Alpha Epsilon (SAE) fraternity made disturbing headlines. White fraternity brothers chanted that they would never include a black male student and referred to lynching a black person. When the incident made national headlines, SAE's national president claimed the organization was "not only shocked and disappointed but disgusted by the outright display of racism. . . . SAE is a diverse organization, and we have zero tolerance for racism or any bad behavior."[146] However, a university investigation found that the young men had actually learned the racist chant on a leadership cruise *sponsored* by that national SAE organization.

Back in 1856, the founding members of SAE then limited the fraternity to the South. One charter member explained that "the constant agitation of the slavery question was a barrier to northern chapters, as it would preclude the possibility of harmony."[147] The bonds of this white brotherhood seem enduring to the present day. In recent years the University of Memphis SAE chapter was also investigated after a new member protested racist remarks made by fellow members about his black girlfriend. Washington University suspended its SAE chapter while probing allegations that pledges participated in racially offensive behavior, and Clemson University suspended the fraternity after white members dressed in shirts displaying racist images at a gang-themed "Crip-mas party."[148]

The exclusive social networking provided by these fraternities and similar white-run organizations is critical to the social integration and routine perpetuation of elite male dominance. To take another example of this, a study of historically exclusive country clubs showed that most continue as places where overwhelmingly white, male, and well-off members customarily socialize among themselves. In such private fraternity-like settings they exchange important business information, make key contacts, and craft significant decisions for their corporations and other important organizations. This helps to integrate and sustain the country's power elite. Note too that in most such settings there are now token numbers of white women and men and women of color—most of whom have been voted into exclusive country clubs relatively recently. Yet, by no means does the presence of a token number of people who are not high-status white men significantly affect how exclusive these social clubs remain, nor does it signal a real change in the way they routinely operate and buttress this country's elite-white-male dominance system.[149]

Higher Education Research: Bias in Private Funding

One reason there is too little critical research on key social issues coming out of many colleges and universities has to do in part with how they are funded, including by conservative white legislators and private donors. For example, the aforementioned white billionaire Koch brothers, among the top contributors to conservative causes, give many millions to higher education. In one recent year they donated nearly $13 million to 163 colleges and universities, with implied or explicit conservative goals. For example, when Charles Koch donated $1.5 million to hiring faculty for the economics department at Florida State University, his representatives *screened* hires for a program supporting conservative "political economy and free enterprise."[150] The Koch foundation reserved the right to revoke funding if new hires did not meet conservative objectives. Consider too Virginia's George Mason University. This public university has received more than $30 million from one Koch foundation to finance their Mercatus program, said to be the "world's premier university source for market-oriented ideas." Thus, when President George W. Bush named 23 government regulations he wanted to jettison, 14 had been originally suggested by Mercatus researchers.[151] Other wealthy white donors—many conservative and a few liberal—run their charitable foundations with the purpose of greatly shaping teaching and research in higher education.

Media Dominance: The Propaganda of Oppression

Ordinary Americans have learned most of what they know about society from sources they consider authoritative—parents, other relatives, friends, teachers, ministers, and selected media sources. Thereby they learn well the established social views—including the dominant gender, racial, and class frames that rationalize societal hierarchies. As a result, most think from these dominant conceptual frames. They rarely think critically about these frames, but accept what they have inherited from family and other social networks or from society's authority figures. As philosopher Jason Stanley has put it, "Even to begin the process of indirect voluntary control over belief is clearly an arduous, often life-changing task, one that often involves separation from family and community."[152]

The mainstream media, especially movies and television and radio networks, are important authoritative sources of information for most people. Once again, those in control at the top of major media organizations are still *overwhelmingly white and male.* In one recent year Hollywood movie studio heads were 94 percent white, and all were male. Their immediate senior managers were 92 percent white, and 83 percent male. Similarly, television network and studio heads were 96 percent white, and 71 percent male. In addition, white men made up almost all the owners of radio and television licenses and were the substantial majority of newsroom staffs.[153]

Today, the media outlets for elite information control include not only older radio, film, television, and print media, but also music videos, satellite transmissions, Internet websites, and social media. In recent decades the mostly white male controllers of societal information have used these increasingly powerful means in their quest for the production and diffusion of racist, sexist, and classist ideas, images, and narratives from the dominant racial, gender, and class frames. This dominant group controls much essential information, and provides much misinformation, through major educational and media conduits. These powerful decision-makers do not need to directly control all of society, for they have historically established media, educational, and other socialization institutions to help them with indirect control. That is, the dominant elite's leg-men and leg-women in these major institutions routinely perpetuate and operate out of the dominant racial, class, and sexist frames.

Using local and national media, the white male establishment normally has the ability to shape a mass consensus on numerous elite-generated opinions or societal goals. As a result, an apparent majority consensus often conveys a false impression of the United States as genuinely democratic. Through these influential media, powerful white men and their acolytes foster much misinformation and shared ignorance in the non-elite population. They do this in part by methodically denying the latter access to accurate information and analyses that are critical of the society's major institutions. Thus, because of a widespread lack of *critical* awareness of the country's actual racial, class, and gender realities among ordinary Americans, especially whites, they can be more easily manipulated in their socio-political thinking, framing, and actions.

Today, just a few hundred top executives and heads of corporate boards of the largest western media corporations constitute a *global* media elite. Media analyst Noam Chomsky has examined how these powerful executives select and disseminate much information to a global public—information routinely screened to be in their corporate or political interest. Very disproportionately white and male, they use their opinion-shaping programming and advertising to increase their already great corporate influence globally. An important part of media executives' indoctrination efforts involves deflection and diversion of public attention from certain underlying societal realities. Analyzing the public's obsession with sports, for example, Chomsky has argued: "That keeps them . . . from worrying about things that matter to their lives that they might have some idea of doing something about. . . . And in fact it's striking to see the intelligence that's used by ordinary people in [discussions of] sports."[154] Sports media coverage and similar media diversions are, in effect, a soporific drug for the general population, to take their minds off what they should be paying attention to—including corporate-generated societal problems and corporate subversion of efforts at expanding economic and political democracy.

Unfortunately, the white-controlled mainstream media often manipulate Americans into supporting destructive political or corporate decisions made by leading members of the elite. For example, Stanley has summarized the build-up and consequences of the Iraq war (see Chapter 4) begun by the George W. Bush administration in 2003:

> [The white] elites exploited a free press to convince a large majority of American citizens of beliefs that lacked so much real world evidential support that those very elites later repudiated being associated with them. . . . the multi-trillion dollar cost of the Iraq War, not to mention the lives lost on both sides, was *not* in the interest of the nearly 70 percent of Americans convinced by the flawed ideology of patriotism and demonization used to motivate it.[155]

Additionally, social science research confirms that those who most often consume material presented by conservative media outlets, such as the predominantly white viewers of Fox News and listeners to right-wing talk radio, are significantly less informed about many current societal issues than other media consumers. Moreover, the more conservative men among top media executives and producers have demonstrated significant and *overt* racial, class, and gender biases in media programming in recent years, such as in openly biased reporting on the Barack Obama presidential administration. Some conservative television programs actually cut to commercials when Obama was giving important speeches, conservative media commentators bashed his exceptional educational credentials, and some arch-conservative commentators viciously caricatured him, including negative references to his supposed lack of U.S. citizenship.[156] In response to numerous racist media attacks on Obama and his family, a great many white Americans engaged in cheering or stayed silent.

The White Racial Frame: Mainstream Media and Beyond

Actually, all mainstream media regularly disseminate certain stereotypes and images of Americans of color straight out of the prevailing *white racial frame*. As we noted previously, centuries of western imperialism and the consequent systemic racism are widely legitimated by this dominant racial framing. This is a white-imposed worldview from which virtually all whites, and many others, operate to varying degrees. Recall that it includes not only racial prejudices and stereotypes, but also racialized images, ideologies, emotions, and narratives that rationalize and implement racial discrimination and other racial oppression. For centuries this frame has come to include both a deep-seated *pro-white* subframe (a positive placement of whites and white *virtue*) and *anti-others* frames (a negative placement of people of color, viewed as unvirtuous). This pro-white subframe is the center of the dominant racial frame and aggressively accentuates white superiority, virtue, and moral goodness. One example of this heavy accent on virtuous white exceptionalism is seen in early European American colonizers reframing their bloody oppression of Native Americans in positive terms as bringing the latter a superior (Christian) religion and "civilization."

From the distant past to the present, much of the effort to create and maintain this dominant white racial frame has come from powerful white men. This is not surprising, for they are central to the frame—especially its accent on *virtue*. As we discussed earlier, the word virtue is derived from the Latin *vir*, which means *man* or *hero*. Early on, in the development of the North American colonies, white men were supposed to exhibit the so-called manly virtues of courage, strength, and piety. Most white men, then as now, have implicitly or explicitly accented certain masculine virtues. They have often exuded an arrogance about what is human virtue and what is not, about who is virtuous and who is not, and about where and when there is virtue. Not surprisingly, the dominant white frame has been replete with anti-black and other anti-others subframes—that is, subframes targeting "those people" as generally *unvirtuous*.[157]

Cognitive scientists have studied how relatively unconscious frames in people's heads influence socio-political proclivities and activities. Frequently the dominant white racial frame is implemented in half-conscious or unconscious ways. Additionally, much scientific research on social movements accents how people often use a conscious subframe of some larger societal frame in guiding their actions, and significant media research also emphasizes the conscious media micro-framing of news stories in which narrow facets of a topic are chosen to advance a particular reading of it.[158]

Frequently, too, the dominant white frame operates in relatively conscious ways to shape much racialized behavior that perpetuates systemic racism.

Over centuries European and European American elites have developed this white racial frame to defend their exploitation, enslavement, and other oppression of many peoples of color. As they enslaved increasing numbers of Africans and African Americans over the 18th century, white slaveholders, government leaders, and intellectuals explicitly portrayed "negroes" they subordinated as a biologically distinctive "race" quite different from "white" European Americans. The major U.S. theorist of liberty and equality, Thomas Jefferson, in his book *Notes on the State of Virginia* (1785), was thorough in his very negative framing of black Americans, whom he viewed as racially inferior to supposedly virtuous and civilized whites. Jefferson was certainly not unique, for virtually all the white founders and most other white Americans then operated out of a negative racial framing of African Americans.[159]

Racist, Classist, Sexist Framing: The Contemporary Scene

The scholar Edward Hall has emphasized how deeply learned that conventional framing, such as the dominant white racial frame, usually becomes: "Once learned, these behavior patterns, these habitual responses . . . sink below the surface of the mind and . . . control from the depths."[160] Developed by and habitually imposed on the minds of all whites, the white racial frame is their learned "frame of mind" and "frame of reference" in regard to racial matters. Additionally, most Americans who are not white often incorporate certain elements of the white racial frame in their minds because it is so commonplace in U.S. society.

The white framing of Americans of color, especially as reinforced in families and in the mainstream media, helps to explain why many whites fail to comprehend racial realities routinely faced by Americans of color. One large national survey found that 61 percent of whites viewed, inaccurately, the average black person as having health care access at least equal to that of the average white person. Half also felt that black Americans had a level of education similar to or better than whites, and half felt that whites and blacks were equally as well off in the jobs they hold. In contrast, much social science research demonstrates that none of these white views is accurate. A substantial majority of whites hold factually erroneous beliefs about white-black inequalities. Today, most whites are ignorant or misinformed when it comes to understanding the difficult and racialized life conditions that African Americans and other Americans of color face.[161] In another survey nearly two-thirds of whites indicated they believed that the quality of life for black Americans had gotten significantly better over recent years. In contrast, 61 percent of black respondents disagreed, reporting that the quality of life had stayed the same or gotten worse.[162] These erroneous white beliefs are likely to have resulted from, or been reinforced by, watching and listening for years to white-framed programming in the mainstream media that suggests in images and white-framed discussions that black Americans as a group are doing at least as well as whites.

Note too that this mainstream media programming sustains and propagates dominant sexist and classist frames. As a result, in the lives of specific individuals all three important societal frames frequently come into play in particular situations. For example, commenting on the actions of one white man who killed an unthreatening black teenager, the scholar bell hooks has described the murderer's framing:

> White supremacy has taught him that all people of color are threats irrespective of their behavior. Capitalism has taught him that, at all costs, his property can and must be protected. Patriarchy has taught him that his masculinity has to be proved by the willingness to conquer fear through aggression; that it would be unmanly to ask questions before taking action.[163]

The overarching elite-white-male dominance system and three of its major subsystems, including the media-reinforced racial, class, and gender framing that sustains them, are evident in such recurring events across this society.

Rarely do mainstream media commentators analyze in any detail the central dominance of elite white men and their principal acolytes, including those who regularly control mainstream media operations. Numerous reports reveal the absence of women and people of color. For example, one recent analysis by journalist Sarah Seltzer discovered only 38 women columnists are among the 143 columnists working for major newspapers and syndicators. Men were also quoted much more often than women in front-page stories, including 3.4 times more in front-page stories in the *New York Times* for a recent period. Indeed, in many news stories about issues affecting women, the experts quoted are overwhelmingly men, especially white men.[164]

Additionally, the overwhelming majority of reporters working in newsrooms are white, often middle-aged, men. Unsurprisingly, thus, much news that Americans view is reported through a white-framed, male-framed, and/or class-framed perspective of a white male reporter. As media critic Terrell Starr notes, whether it is a trade magazine like *Variety* running a headline exclaiming that "Rock 'n' Roll" originated with Elvis Presley, or a *New York Times* article that claims that black women are not characteristically attractive, mostly white men control much "information" that gets communicated to the public.[165] White media executives also frequently make racialized decisions about employees. There is the major example of the white television anchor Jennifer Livingston and the black television anchor Rhonda Lee. When a male viewer criticized Livingston's weight, she went on the air to blast him. The station management backed her, and her story garnered favorable headlines. In contrast, Lee, whose natural hair was attacked by a Facebook user on her station's webpage, was fired by her manager after she openly and respectfully defended herself.[166]

In major cable news programming, we encounter very disproportionate numbers of conservative white male experts and their often limited white-male-framed worldviews. Between 2004 and 2012, for instance, Sunday morning talk shows were dominated by white male Republicans. Between June 2011 and February 2012, one-on-one interviewees on leading political talk shows—NBC's *Meet the Press*, ABC's *This Week*, CBS's *Face the Nation*, and *Fox News Sunday*—were skewed greatly in favor of Republicans (70 percent), white guests (92 percent), and men (86 percent).[167] Moreover, in the aftermath of President Barack Obama's regulation mandating that health insurance plans offer free birth control, Fox, Fox Business, MSNBC, and CNN all asked *men* to comment by a nearly 2–1 margin over women. Twice as many men were asked to comment on an issue that so directly impacts *women*.[168] The operation of systemic sexism is illustrated clearly in these media settings where mostly or only men are drawn on for much important social commentary.

Similarly, the dominant presence of (white) men in cable news discussions and debates has been well-documented. Of guests interviewed on six prime-time programs or taking part in discussion segments over a five-week period in just one year (2014) on CNN, Fox News, and MSNBC, 84 percent were white, and 72 percent were male. Latinos were especially underrepresented, accounting for 3 percent even though they constituted 16 percent of the population. Women of color made up *only 5 percent* of sources across programs, even though they comprised 18 percent of the population.[169]

One major reason for the disproportionate role of conservative whites in the mainstream media is because of the ability of elite conservatives and their powerful organizations to place them there. Since the 1970s, the right-wing of the white establishment has developed conservative and arch-conservative think tanks such as the American Enterprise Institute and the Heritage Foundation. These well-funded think tanks have been successful in getting very conservative, mostly white male experts and their often reactionary ideas into the mainstream media. These experts have helped to further indoctrinate non-elite Americans into the dominant racial, class, and gender frames.[170]

Reflecting on North American media, the prominent South American journalist Eduardo Galeano once put the matter this way:

More and more have the right to hear and see, but fewer and fewer have the privilege of informing, giving their opinion and creating. The dictatorship of the single word and the single image, much more devastating than that of the single party, is imposing a life whose exemplary citizen is a docile consumer and passive spectator built on the assembly line following the North American model of commercial television.[171]

As we show throughout this book, there is a certain "dictatorship" of the white racial framing, the sexist framing, and the capitalistic framing of society. These dominant frames regularly create highly conforming media consumers out of much of the general public—and thereby often stifle critical thought about societal oppression and inequalities.

Conclusion

Actually diversifying most U.S. institutions is very difficult when most top officials refuse, resist, or slow down such change. For instance, the country's largest city, New York City, has a population that is two-thirds people of color. Recently, the white male commissioner of its Department of Cultural Affairs launched a major study to assess the diversity of the boards, staffs, and audiences of the city's cultural organizations, including orchestras, museums, and dance troupes. The study was announced as being about just celebrating "best practices." To a significant degree, the results were known in advance, for few large New York cultural organizations had ever had boards that were not overwhelmingly white. The timid study announcement made clear that there was *no* intention to deal with the racial roots of the problem. There was *no* intention to enforce concrete goals for diversity changes if these were found to be needed, such as by enhanced city funding for groups with an improved diversity record.[172]

As we have shown, such elite sentiments about "diversity" are at best vague, and at worst another way for whites to delay change and ensure continuing white domination of key public and private organizations. If the commissioner of New York's Department of Cultural Affairs and other private and public leaders are legitimately concerned about untapped talent among citizens of color, they should be willing to admit that the lack of diversity is very much about systemic racism and purposeful exclusion of people of color for centuries, and to the present day. From much social science research, we suggest that the acknowledgement and drive to change things in the direction of social justice is not just a desirable humanistic and democratic goal, it is a smart thing to do for such organizations, and the larger society generally, to expand their knowledge base and, thus, longterm effectiveness, a point we consider further in Chapter 8.

In a world where whites are increasingly a statistical minority, their powerful, constant, and distorted white racial, class, and gender framing already creates major disadvantages for a society like the United States, both nationally and internationally. Those disadvantages will grow larger in the future. White ignorance of, and isolation from, people of color is, or will soon be, a major handicap for U.S. (and European) corporate and government executives and other officials engaged in international cooperation, trade, and diplomacy in a world where international leadership is becoming more diverse and where non-European countries are becoming more powerful. Excluding and marginalizing Americans of color in economic, political, and cultural settings—which can be termed *epistemic* oppression—means excluding and marginalizing much *knowledge, creativity*, and *understanding* that is necessary for U.S. society to persist and prosper, especially if it is to become truly democratic. No society can successfully ignore the great stores of human knowledge and ability that its array of knowledgeable but oppressed members possess. Indeed, one observes clear evidence of how this epistemic ignorance becomes problematical when white policymakers, sometimes assisted by white acolytes, have frequently made poor decisions on many domestic and foreign policy issues, such as in catastrophic U.S. interventions overseas in recent decades (see Chapter 4).

Before we return to these contemporary political-economic realities, we will first detail some major historical developments that reveal the great determining power and concrete actions of elite white men as they have created and maintained racial, class, and gender oppressions that are foundational and central to the "modern world."

The overseas expansion of U.S. and Europea.   ..ıul
white men in the decades just before and after t.   . .as dramatic
and world-changing. As we discussed previously,   ɔ.ɔbal expansion by a
small number of white men involved a predatory approach to stealing land,
mineral resources, and labor from people of color globally. In their view, the
white male conquerors had a right to seize new worlds in the name of white
Christianity and "superior" European culture. Their imperialistic enterprise
was capitalistic, systemically racist, and heavily gendered.

Recall how sociologist W. E. B. Du Bois underscored the racial aspects
of this exceptional imperialistic expansion: "The discovery of personal
whiteness among the world's peoples is a very modern thing." He added
that "Whiteness is the *ownership* of the earth, forever and ever, Amen."[1] He
aptly described the obsessiveness of white (male) predation and control
that was part of the motivation for the efforts by powerful white Americans
and Europeans to exploit and oppress people of color globally.

Since the earliest era of U.S. imperialism, the military and political interventions implemented by formidable white men have characteristically
evoked a white racial framing of overseas societies in ways similar to the
centuries-old white framing of African Americans. The focal point of this
framing centers on the assertion of powerful whites, mostly white men, that
they have a *right* to intervene in the affairs of other peoples whenever their
economic and political interests are at stake. Non-European peoples—e.g.,
Africans, Latin Americans, the Japanese, the Koreans, the Vietnamese, and
Middle Easterners—have long been common targets in a vast array of U.S.
imperialistic, and usually military, interventions.[2]

Regularly, the powerful men who have led these interventions overtly
demonstrate their sense of a superior whiteness that is also deeply gendered
and hyper-masculinist. Historically, their public rhetoric has included the
defense of (subordinated) white womanhood, but their top priority has
been to protect or enhance the dominant framing of a *virile white manhood*.
Hyper-masculine men have usually been the leaders in major imperialistic
efforts. Recall that Theodore Roosevelt was once considered an "effete" New

become a very masculinist leader in efforts to secure
...ifest destiny" in the country's imperialistic actions across

...prisingly, the elite decision-makers implementing imperialism
...regularly made use of assertively masculinized and bureaucratized
...e.g., military) violence in their colonizing invasions and wars. In concert
with them, ordinary white men have buttressed their sense of white masculinity by reveling in domination of other peoples in U.S. imperialistic efforts.
Warmaking in the name of white "civilization" has been central to the rule
of powerful white men in the West, to the present day. As the scholar Maria
Mies has noted from global research, "violence is therefore still the secret of
modern capitalist–patriarchal civilization."[3]

World War I: A Clash of Growing Empires

World War I (1914–1918) involved the military coalition called the Central
Powers (Germany, Austria-Hungary, Ottoman Empire, Bulgaria), which
was fighting the Allies coalition (United Kingdom, France, Russia, United
States, and Japan). Although at war's end many in the Allies' countries
blamed Germany for the war, this was incorrect. More accurately, that war
was generated by mostly white nations competing for resource-filled colonies. According to the critical view of W. E. B. Du Bois, the white elites
surveyed the world and saw places where "darker peoples"

> are cheap and the earth is rich. . . . white masters may settle to be
> served as kings, wield the lash of slave-drivers, rape girls and wives,
> grow as rich as Croesus and send homeward a golden stream. They
> belt the earth, these places, but they cluster in the tropics, with its
> darkened peoples.[4]

World War I was not the noble fight for liberty and justice that the ruling
elites in Europe and the United States claimed. War was waged substantially
in pursuit of white power and control, of colonialism and imperialism.
Soon there would be a more imperialistic "despising and robbing of darker
peoples" on several continents. Du Bois also foresaw the resistance that was
coming; the war was a "prelude to the armed and indignant protest of these
despised and raped peoples."[5]

Like many analysts of color, Du Bois rejected the lore of superior white
virtuousness and its artificial zeal for rhetorical "liberty and justice for all."
Nearly as many soldiers as had died during World War I had *already* per-
ished under the white Belgian King Leopold II in the colonized African
Congo. What Belgium suffers as a result of World War I "is not half, not
even a tenth, of what she has done to black Congo."[6] Du Bois highlighted

the West's civilized savagery, its brutal destructiveness amidst claims to superior civilization. In the aftermath of war, with white male conceits in tow, victorious European leaders determined which colonized territories belonging to defeated Central Powers would now belong to them. Observe how western wars have often involved the simultaneous coreproduction of global imperialism, capitalistic exploitation, and systemic racism. European disarmament after World War I, with its supposed international policing, was set up amid expanding imperialist ambitions. Insincerely discussing peace, the European and U.S. elites championed global imperialist ambitions via more international aggression.[7]

The fate of seized overseas colonies and their racialized populations was decided by the elite founders of the new League of Nations, including U.S. President Woodrow Wilson (1913–1921). These white men created three racialized categories of mandates for the "administration" (i.e., domination) of newly colonized territories. White nations' leaders acted as Mandatories of the League of Nations, and as such would oversee the territories' governments and economies. Class A mandates comprised territories that white leaders deemed equipped to handle eventual independence. All were in the Middle East and were administered by Britain or France. Class B and C mandates encompassed territories for whom these white leaders deemed independence a remote possibility or to have no prospect of independence.[8]

Today, western students commonly learn that the provisions of this mandate system inferred a recognition that colonial territories could be "given" independence if they were viewed by western leaders to have attained a "sophisticated" level of development.[9] Such terms were code for mostly negative white attitudes toward peoples of color, which also assumed superior white virtuousness. This elite recognition mostly came from white men (to a lesser degree by the elite of Japan, the one non-western country among the Allies). These powerful white men would grant independence only when "backward people of color" attained a level of development determined to be sufficient.

In summer 1919, acting as an official peacemaker, President Wilson brought the Treaty of Versailles and the Covenant of the League of Nations before the U.S. Senate for ratification. Du Bois noted the irony involved in this: "*No nation is less fitted for this role.* For two or more centuries America has marched proudly in the van of human hatred—making bonfires of human flesh and laughing at them hideously, and making the insulting of millions more than a matter of dislike—rather a great religion, a world war-cry."[10] Wilson failed; the Senate refused to ratify. Many in the white political-economic establishment feared that the treaty and League would diminish the ability of the U.S. government and corporations in increasing their imperialistic reach.[11]

From the late 1890s to the 1930s, leading U.S. government officials, drawn from or assisted by top corporate executives, were increasingly interventionist and imperialistic in dealing with countries populated mostly by people of color. These included Haiti, Mexico, Cuba, Hawai'i, Puerto Rico, Guam, and the Philippines. When it came to Asia, U.S. leaders had long worked to force an isolationist Japan to trade with western countries, using threats of military violence. They unilaterally declared an Open Door Policy in China as a means of assuring U.S. corporations would have opportunities equal to those of Europeans in exploiting China. They and European leaders sent troops to China to assert white corporate and political supremacy there. In Latin America, this white male elite aggressively engineered a local revolution against Colombia and split off what became the U.S.-controlled country of Panama to build the profitable Panama Canal. Over the early 20th century the U.S. government intervened militarily in Nicaragua, the Dominican Republic, Haiti, Cuba, Panama, Guatemala, and Honduras, often numerous times. By the 1920s the finances of many Latin American countries were to some extent controlled by U.S. government and corporate officials.[12]

As Robert Gilpin has underscored, mature capitalistic economies go through regular periods when profit rates necessarily fall, so their top executives often must "seize colonies and create dependencies to serve as markets, investment outlets, and sources of food and raw materials. In competition with one another, they divide up the colonial world in accordance with their relative strengths."[13] Unsurprisingly, the expanding U.S. empire came into conflict with other capitalistic empires, thereby helping to generate World War II.

Repeatedly, one sees in these historical details how the foundation of the modern world was substantially laid by the studied decisions of the well-established white rulers of western countries. The perspectives and actions of these powerful men routinely demonstrated the triple helix of systemic classism (capitalism), systemic racism, and systemic sexism. Five centuries of European and U.S. imperialism across the globe have not only spread capitalism but created at the same time a global racial order and global gender order. These imperialist ventures thereby created numerous colonies globally. After later colonial rebellions, most of these became western-influenced or western-controlled countries. Unsurprisingly, many elements of the elite's white racial frame and (white) male sexist frame have penetrated the worldviews of non-western leaders and others in former colonies on several continents, especially in regard to their economies, educational systems, and political institutions.

World War II: Another War of Empires, and a People's War

World War II was a somewhat different kind of war. As historian Donny Gluckstein has shown, two interlocking wars were going on from the late

1930s until 1945. At one level, there was again a battle among several empires seeking and maintaining territories for political control and economic exploitation. The Allied powers included the old European imperialistic powers Britain and France (controlling about 35 percent of the globe) and the somewhat newer imperialistic powers, the United States and the Soviet Union. All but the Soviet Union were capitalistic, and the Soviet elite created what some term state-directed capitalism. The competing Axis powers included nation-states seeking to expand their imperial reach—Germany, Italy, and Japan.[14] The most powerful blocs in all these states, except for the Soviet Union, involved major capitalistic executives and their companies.

At the same time, a second type of war was going on, one constantly contending or integrated with the war between the Allied and Axis empires. This war involved the efforts of ordinary people's movements who fought against the imperialistic goals and undemocratic leaders in countries *within* both the Allied and Axis coalitions. (We discuss a U.S. example in a later section.) These people's movements were usually anti-fascist and sought major democratic and social justice goals. Gluckstein has described the people's uprisings that punctuated World War II and some elite reactions to them: "In many European countries sections of the upper class eagerly *collaborated* with the Nazis (the classic example being Vichy France), because they feared the radicalism of their own working class *more than* German occupation."[15]

Gluckstein provides examples of elite-white-male leaders of the Allied powers who openly viewed the western wartime actions as necessarily aimed at extending capitalistic empires. One was the imperialistic Winston Churchill: "Churchill was always very clear that his mission in the war was to defend the British empire, not promote the interests of ordinary citizens. He was *not ideologically committed to destroy fascism*."[16] U.S. and French leaders largely shared such imperialist and capitalistic goals, often seeking to expand their own economic and political empires.

During the 1930s, before direct U.S. participation in military conflicts in Europe, elite U.S. officials worked with leading corporate executives to extend their sphere of political and economic influence. For example, when Italian dictator Benito Mussolini attacked Ethiopia, these officials allowed U.S. businesses to export oil to that fascist regime and its military. Capitalistic profits again took precedence. Then, when civil war broke out in Spain (1936–1939) between those loyal to the democratic Spanish Republic and a fascist group led by Francisco Franco, the U.S. elite backed a supposed "neutrality" act that permitted Germany's Adolf Hitler and Mussolini to provide aid to Franco. This led to Franco's fascist dictatorship. Despite the thousands who suffered violence during Franco's brutal dictatorship, U.S. officials continued to support his fascist regime *long* after World War II.[17]

In the 1930s and 1940s numerous influential white Americans, especially capitalist owners and CEOs, profited greatly from certain pro-fascist, including pro-German (see below), policies of U.S. government officials. However, once imperialistic Germany dramatically interfered with U.S. global imperialistic ambitions, an anti-Nazi position became central. Certainly, over time German chancellor Adolf Hitler's obsession with the threat of this expanding U.S. international influence blended in his thinking with the mythical threat of a "world Jewish conspiracy," as Adam Tooze notes:

> In Hitler's mind, the threat posed to the Third Reich by the United States was not just that of conventional superpower rivalry. The threat was existential and bound up with Hitler's abiding fear of the world Jewish conspiracy. . . . Germany could not simply settle down to become an affluent satellite of the United States . . . because this would result in enslavement to the world Jewish conspiracy, and ultimately race death.[18]

Expansion into Asia: More Clash of Empires

In the early decades of the 20th century, much of the U.S. elite's imperialistic efforts in the Asia-Pacific region involved attempts to expand the reach of the government and multinational corporations. These white men tried to gain white supremacy over a growing Japanese empire in the Pacific. The 1941 Japanese bombing of Pearl Harbor has usually been framed by U.S. officials and conventional analysts, then and now, as an abrupt and infamous attack that was unanticipated. However numerous critical scholars have assessed the Japanese attack on Pearl Harbor as the logical result of a long succession of jointly aggressive imperialistic acts in the Pacific realm by the U.S. and Japanese governments.[19]

It was *not* the earlier violent attacks on Ethiopians, Czechs, Poles, and other victims of the (white) German Nazi officials and their European allies that became the main trigger for the initial U.S. entry into World War II. The U.S. elite entered the war *only* when Japanese leaders, seeking to protect their own imperial expansion, attacked Hawai'i's military bases in a failed attempt to hem in the U.S. Pacific empire. As long as Japanese leaders were *obedient* to U.S. interests—e.g., willing to share economic exploitation of China—Washington's white elite did not view Japan as a serious enough foe for war. Only when Japanese leaders threatened prospective U.S. markets in Asia—particularly southeast Asia's rubber, oil, and tin—did influential white men turn to aggressive action, including a U.S. embargo on scrap iron and oil to Japan in summer 1941. This put Japan's very economic survival at stake, triggered the Japanese attack, and put two imperialistic countries on the road to a major war.[20]

The real war story has never been properly explained to the U.S. population. Significantly, after the war, the Asian-Indian jurist Radhabinod Pal was the sole judge—out of eleven Allied judges—who handed down a "not guilty" judgment on Japan's wartime leaders at the Tokyo war-crimes trials (1946–1948). He accurately argued that U.S. economic embargoes before the war obviously posed a colossal obstacle to Japan's survival and, thus, U.S. officials *intentionally* incited the conflict. Prior to the attack on Pearl Harbor, the Washington elite had indeed *openly* talked of war with Japan and had even deliberated about how to sell an imperialistic war to the citizenry.[21] Judge Pal recognized Japan's significant war atrocities, but rebuffed the Allied charges of Japanese crimes against humanity as *ex post facto* law—in his dissent what he termed a "sham employment of legal process for the satisfaction of a thirst for revenge."[22] In his studied view, the U.S. atomic bombings of Hiroshima and Nagasaki were equivalent to Nazi war crimes because of huge civilian casualties (mostly civilians of color, too).

Even today, the central motives of the U.S. government's imperialistic expansion and associated elite capitalistic profitmaking in fighting World War II remain hidden in the rhetoric of many apologists who assert that the United States only fought virtuously to end fascist dictatorships and promote global democracy. Yet again, the principal U.S. decision-makers in this era were almost all elite white men.

Corporate Brotherhood: U.S. and Nazi Dealings in World War II

Many people know that during Hitler's rule numerous German corporate executives and their firms willingly partnered with the Nazi party and government. However, much less known is the substantial collusion between U.S. corporate executives and the Nazi government or German companies in the 1930s and 1940s. These firms included Chase Bank (now J.P. Morgan Chase), General Electric (GE), Kodak, Coca-Cola, Standard Oil, and International Business Machines (IBM), to name only a few. Many western capitalistic firms, again headed by powerful white men, aggressively sought profitable corporate contracts in Nazi Germany. This business dealing reluctantly ended only when the United States finally entered the European military conflict. Despite some corporate apologies, these U.S.-Nazi partnerships have never received much public attention. Elite executives who eagerly did business with the Nazis and made substantial corporate profits remain mostly unrecognized. They included the most powerful white men of the era. Prior to World War II, J. D. Rockefeller, a key shareholder in Chase Bank, openly financed the Nazi eugenics movement. Influential white executives at Kodak's subsidiaries, in so-called neutral European nations, manufactured cameras, film, and military hardware for Nazi Germany. High-ranking GE executives made significant pre-war purchases of shares in the German company Siemens, implicating them in the manufacture of gas chambers.[23]

The previously mentioned Thomas Watson, Sr., founding CEO of IBM, provides another example of troubling business choices that elite capitalists who run multinationals have made in constant pursuit of private profit. IBM played a *significant* business role in connection with Nazi Germany's various campaigns. The IBM founder approved the 1939 release of alphabetizing machines that helped organize the German occupation of Poland. Thereby, leading U.S. executives allowed their punch-card technology to be used in organizing Germany's anti-Jewish programs. This work was overseen in New York's IBM headquarters, and later via German subsidiaries in various European nations.[24] In 1937 Hitler bestowed on Watson *a medal* for his services. (In 1940, in reaction to public indignation, Watson returned it.) Edwin Black, author of *IBM and the Holocaust*, describes a U.S. Justice Department memo produced during a later investigation of IBM and its German subsidiary. He quotes the memo: "What Hitler has done to us through his economic warfare, one of our own American corporations has also done."[25] However, in this regard IBM executives were not unique, for numerous other U.S. executives guided their companies in doing profitable business with the Nazi regime.

U.S. Anti-Semitic Framing and Action in the World War II Era

Elite and Popular Anti-Semitism

Although unknown to most Americans, in the 1930s top U.S. government officials intentionally made major *conciliatory* efforts towards the Nazi government of Germany, even as the Nazis repeatedly demonstrated violent anti-Semitic framing and actions. Whatever their private concerns for victims of Nazi persecution might have been, President Franklin Delano Roosevelt (1933–1945) and many other powerful white men in the public and private sectors were reluctant for much of the war to openly condemn Germany's anti-Semitic policies. Indeed, many members of the powerful white elite, predominantly Protestant men, were anti-Semitic in their own racial framing and actions.

While Roosevelt did take numerous actions during World War II that benefited Jews in the United States and Europe—such as bringing numerous Jewish professionals into the U.S. government workforce, including as advisors—he articulated numerous anti-Semitic views before and during the war, thereby revealing his own racial framing. In the 1920s he supported a quota limiting Jewish students at Harvard, and in the late 1930s he argued that Polish Jews had been responsible for stimulating violent anti-Semitism by their economic successes. During the war he also argued there should be a discriminatory quota for Jews in professions in North Africa. He privately confided to acquaintances that Jewish American leaders' calls to help refugees from Nazism were "Jewish wailing" and made numerous other anti-Semitic comments. He described some Jewish professionals' tax actions as "a dirty Jewish trick" and spoke of Jews as having too much influence in the United States. Roosevelt himself operated to a significant degree out of a traditional anti-Semitic framing.[26]

Assertive anti-Semitism was commonplace in this country's white elite from the 17th century onward; it was especially strong in the decades leading to World War II. For instance, the very famous auto entrepreneur Henry Ford controlled a Detroit newspaper that published anti-Semitic articles, including Nazi-like attacks on a "world Jewish conspiracy" and on Jews, mainly Jewish men, for supposedly weakening business standards and corrupting "morals." Elite and affluent whites were involved in much anti-Semitic discrimination. From the 1920s to the 1950s, numerous U.S. college and university officials, almost all white and male (gentiles), engaged in anti-Jewish discrimination, including using overt admissions quotas to keep out Jewish students. Unsurprisingly, white male (gentile) university students also engaged in anti-Semitic actions, such as those who hung a sign reading "Scurvy kikes are not wanted at New York University. If they knew their place they would not be here. Make New York University a White Man's College."[27] One notices too in much of the anti-Semitic writing and cartoons of this era the interconnection between the systemic racism directed against Jews, who are racialized as *not* white or not truly white, and the white masculinity at the center of systemic sexism. Much anti-Semitism in this era, in the United States and Europe, portrayed *Jewish men*, not women, as the threat to white gentile men, their hegemonic masculinity, and thus their families.

From the early 1900s to well beyond the 1940s extensive anti-Semitic thought and action was also demonstrated by many ordinary Americans, much fueled by racist demagogues on the radio.[28] More than a hundred organizations, including the Ku Klux Klan, circulated much anti-Semitic propaganda. Opinion polls demonstrated that a majority or near majority of Americans held firmly to numerous blatantly anti-Jewish stereotypes, such as Jews being too powerful or "greedy."[29]

U.S. Government Collusion with Nazi Anti-Semitism

A good example of U.S. government unwillingness to offend anti-Semitic German leaders is seen in what happened in the movie industry. In the 1930s Hollywood executives faced intense pressure from top government officials to *appease* Hitler's government. These leading white officials' diplomatic and economic concerns led them to warn these movie executives against provoking the Nazi government. In 1939, the powerful former U.S. Ambassador to Britain Joseph Kennedy (father of President John Kennedy) spoke unequivocally to Hollywood executives on behalf of the Roosevelt administration: Do *not* make anti-Nazi films. Kennedy explained that Nazi leaders enjoyed U.S. films and wanted the studios to keep making them, but studio executives must remove references to Jews. Thus, half the people who worked on the Warner Brothers' 1939 film *Confessions of a Nazi* specifically removed their (Jewish) names from the credits, and anti-Semitism was *never* mentioned in the film. Studio head Jack Warner, who was Jewish and responsible for the film, nonetheless received *reprimands* from Washington's white gentile elite. Indeed, the powerful U.S. House Leader Martin Dies, Jr. openly claimed the film actually vilified a "friendly country."[30]

Additionally, the Nazi government banned U.S. films considered anti-German. A few independent anti-Nazi films were made, but because of German pressure on theater chains these films were often *not* released. The financial reliance of Hollywood on the German market, U.S. isolationist sentiment, and the movie industry's self-censorship help explain these extensive U.S. movie-censoring actions.[31]

Like many male congressional leaders, Martin Dies was obsessed with fighting "Communism." In 1938 he co-founded a U.S. House Committee investigating "un-American activities," one eventually named the House Un-American Activities Committee (HUAC). Fixated on the supposed Communist threat, Dies focused on spies of the Soviet Union (a U.S. wartime ally) and not on the spies of Nazi Germany—even in the midst of World War II. And German American involvement in U.S. Nazi and Ku Klux Klan activities did *not* interest his investigating committee. As a HUAC spokesperson said, the Klan is an *old* U.S. institution. Indeed, the Klan has long carried, to the present day, the banner of the country's most visible anti-Semitic and anti-black organization.[32]

Roosevelt and Congress: Anti-Semitism and Collusion in the Holocaust

Even when they ceased pro-Nazi appeasement after the United States officially entered the Allied military conflict, elite U.S. officials, virtually all white gentile men, did not rush to counter the horrific Nazi actions against European Jews. Controversy continues over whether President Roosevelt was helpful to enough Jewish refugees from the Nazi Holocaust. Historian David Oshinsky has argued that Roosevelt had to make national concerns (e.g., unemployment, bank failures), and not European Jews' oppression, his governing priorities in the 1930s.[33] In this exculpatory view, even if Roosevelt had been willing to substantially assist oppressed Jews, such as by lobbying to bring many refugees to the United States it would have proved difficult because of powerful members of Congress who were anti-Semitic.

These white men did not see Jews as desirable immigrants, or even as "white." Reflecting national anti-Semitic sentiment, even a modest 1939 congressional bill to admit some Jewish children was met with much white male hostility in and out of Congress.[34]

For most of his long presidency, Roosevelt did relatively little to help European Jews. We have noted his anti-Semitic views. He privately feared being dubbed pro-Jewish in his actions, and this mostly outweighed his concern for Jews. Nevertheless, he did occasionally act to rescue some. His administration agreed to ease visa regulations after prominent Jewish Americans put pressure on him, yet he still met with U.S. Jewish leaders only once. He did instigate an international conference to tackle the refugee problem in 1938. Representatives of 32 countries met, but amidst declarations of sympathies for the Jewish plight, all were opposed to allowing large numbers of refugees into their countries. In reaction, Nazi government officials said it was "astonishing" that the officials who criticized Germany did not want Jews either.[35]

White Subjugation: African Americans and Japanese Americans

By the time Franklin Roosevelt and Winston Churchill met in Casablanca in 1943 for a crucial wartime meeting looking forward to an Allied victory, the Axis powers had dramatically endangered U.S. and U.K. economic interests, including those of their global capitalist enterprises. The Allied powers called for an *unconditional* surrender. In one tragic irony, at this meeting Roosevelt hypocritically explained that this unconditional surrender was necessary for "the destruction of the philosophies in those countries which are based on conquest and the subjugation of other people."[36]

Jim Crow Oppression: African Americans

The great irony was obvious: There was *much* negative white racist framing and "subjugation of other people" across the United States. From the 19th century to the 1960s segregation (Jim Crow) was legalized in southern and border states—and informally enforced in other states. For generations, where black Americans could get a job, where their families could live, where they could go to school, and how they could travel were substantially determined by elite and ordinary whites. Many faced daily threats, brutal beatings, or worse, especially if they resisted. Most were at an extreme economic, political, and social disadvantage compared to whites. Their lives were significantly shortened, and their inherited socioeconomic resources were mostly nonexistent.

Well aware of this racist system, Roosevelt was leader of a party powerfully represented in Congress by white male Democrats, especially southerners, who defended this U.S. racial totalitarianism. His hands were said to be tied when it came to moving the country legislatively toward more equality. Still, he took small steps. He appointed African Americans as a federal judge and Army general. He called lynching "a vile form of collective murder," the first president to do so. The number of African Americans working for the federal government increased. At the 1936 Democratic Convention, he pressed the Democratic Party to incorporate the first explicit civil rights plank in its platform.[37]

Still, Roosevelt, like most presidents before and after him, failed to substantially advance racial justice and equality. He did *not* work to eliminate significant discrimination in housing, employment, wages, and working conditions. Roosevelt's New Deal, as experienced by black Americans, was very different from that experienced by white Americans. Even a contemporary organization now promoting Roosevelt's legacy has admitted that his New Deal did little to remedy the horrific injustices that African Americans had to endure daily, and even routinely buttressed legal segregation.[38]

As further evidence of Roosevelt's lack of commitment to genuine racial equality, his administration did not effectively challenge occupational segregation during World War II, even when black labor was essential for the war effort. At one important aviation plant on the West Coast, for example, African Americans were only hired as janitorial staff, even if they were trained aircraft workers.[39] Segregation was still a common reality. Again, we observe how systemic racism—specifically, the white-racist framing in the heads of powerful whites—interfered in *major* ways with the capitalistic production in this era—and thus with prosecution of the war effort. Particularly striking, too, was preferential treatment by white male military officials given to white German prisoners of war (POWs) held in the United States during the war. Incredibly, black military police had to sit in the back of buses traveling south while their German prisoners remained in coveted front seats.[40]

Jim Crow America and German Anti-Semitism

Adolf Hitler and other Nazi officials were inspired by the well-developed systemic racism of the United States. Prior to and during the war, they cited U.S. Jim Crow segregation, when they were criticized by outsiders, in defense of their highly discriminatory treatment of European Jews. As historian Ira Katznelson has described, Nazi news media "frequently printed anti-Black cartoons, reminded its readers that southern public accommodations were segregated, and delighted in reporting how blacks . . . could not sleep in Pullman cars and could not exercise the right to vote."[41] German segregation laws were influenced by U.S. racial segregation laws, the latter declared constitutional by an all-white-male Supreme Court long before the German Nazi racist laws. Leading Nazis defended their racist world with references to U.S. literature, movies, and speeches with an overt white supremacy tilt, including those of President Woodrow Wilson. Moreover, before World War II, numerous U.S. scientists and other leaders praised Germany's "rational" implementation of eugenics laws, while Nazi scientists drew on the research of U.S. colleagues who sought eugenics control over Americans of color.[42]

Repeatedly, we observe the operation of the all-encompassing, elite-white-male dominance system and the constant integration of its major subsystems of systemic sexism, classism, and racism. These operated in somewhat *similar* ways before and during World War II in both the United States and Nazi Germany. As social scientist Judith Goldstein dramatically underscores, elite and ordinary white men

> idealized and enforced male dominance, military prowess and violence against their enemies: in the Third Reich, Aryan warriors as pagan gods and, in the South, white males as Confederate heroes as part of the "honor" culture. Both racist systems depended upon the critical docility, acquiescence and political impotence of women. . . . Germany and the South extolled the sexual purity of white—and in the German sphere—white Aryan women. Both targeted and exaggerated the threat of predatory men—blacks in the South and Jews in Germany—to justify intimidation and violence against the racial enemies.[43]

Sadly, this critical U.S. history of systemic racism and systemic sexism is today little known to most Americans, and major vestiges of these views persist in the United States today.

Black Resistance to Imperialism and Racism: The "Other War"

The historical circumstances of centuries of extensive racial oppression—slavery and Jim Crow—have caused African Americans to advance national and foreign policy analyses and action in opposition to the imperialistic actions of the white elite. This has especially been true since the early 20th century. Early on, African American scholars and activists, including Rayford Logan, Alain Locke, Du Bois, and Ralph Bunch, laid the groundwork for the development of what only later became a white-dominated discipline of "international relations" studies.[44] These and other black scholars openly questioned U.S. imperialism, and the white-racist framing that went along with that, long before most white scholars ventured into such critical analyses. Ever since, black civil rights leaders, elected politicians, and appointed officials have often raised significant critical queries concerning the U.S. government's military and other international interventions. They also have led the war within the larger wars, the internal war against U.S. racial oppression.[45]

Recall that World War II involved not only a war between the imperialist Allied and Axis coalitions, but a less remembered war involving organized efforts of ordinary people fighting against undemocratic institutions in both Allied and Axis countries. For example, African Americans fought against Nazi oppression and fascism in Europe and Asia even as they had to fight internally to make the United States more just and democratic. Soon after the United States entered World War II combat, James Thompson, a courageous black cafeteria worker, coined the "Double Victory" slogan, which laid bare this white-racist reality:

> The "V for victory" sign is being displayed prominently in so-called democratic countries which are fighting for victory over aggression, slavery and tyranny. If this V sign means that to those now engaged in this great conflict, then let we colored Americans adopt the double VV for a double victory. . . . The first V for victory over our enemies from without, the second V for victory over our enemies from within. For surely those who perpetrate these ugly prejudices here are seeking to destroy our democratic form of government just as surely as the Axis forces.[46]

Without a doubt, most African Americans were not fooled by white leaders' rhetoric about "fighting for democracy."

The internal black war for democratic representation was accelerated in 1941, when black rights activists and organizations led by A. Philip Randolph, the head of a black union, pressed the Roosevelt administration hard to desegregate wartime industries. They announced a major march in Washington, D.C., to protest job discrimination. Working from centuries-old, experience-based, anti-racist counter-framing, these brave activists brought "power and pressure to bear upon the agencies and representatives of the Federal Government to exact their rights in National Defense employment and the armed forces of the United States."[47] Reluctantly, Roosevelt signed an executive order establishing a Fair Employment Practices Committee (FEPC) to oversee desegregation of wartime defense-industry jobs. However, while the FEPC did officially require companies with government contracts not to discriminate, their antidiscrimination regulations were mostly unenforced. Still, this threatened protest and its result in executive action helped to set a precedent that would bear fruit decades later with the 1960s civil rights laws.[48]

Note, too, that centuries of African American experience with systemic white racism has led many to be skeptical or pacifistic in regard to U.S.

imperialistic wars and colonial interventions. In the World War II era, several black civil rights activists were pacifists. The brilliant activist Bayard Rustin was jailed for refusing to serve in World War II, but later played a major role in the 1960s civil rights movement and in international movements against nuclear weapons.

Many African Americans were ambivalent with regard to U.S. involvement in World War II because in their view, in a world where the Japanese proved victorious over imperialistic white Allied powers, people of color across the globe might be better off. In this critical assessment, the shackles of white supremacy might be smashed.[49] Earlier, to counter the white elite's Pacific imperialism and anti-Japanese framing, Japanese officials had sought a trans-Pacific alliance with African Americans. Some African American leaders and political leaders in Japan looked to one another for support in their mutual desire to challenge the racist international policies of elite white men. African American civil rights leaders and scholars were influenced by contacts with Japanese leaders, including in efforts to rid themselves of the white-racist framing of Asian "racial inferiority." In the assessment of Japanese leaders, moreover, African Americans were often viewed as "colored yet modern and westernized" and a model for Japan "in its endeavors to reach a 'higher' level of civilization and become a member of the western world."[50]

Of course, these communications stopped as war began, and African American communities provided many who served in U.S. armed forces. Yet, African American leaders had gained significant knowledge of global realities of white-imposed racism. As a result, they explained to U.S. officials that whites' racist framing of the Japanese was partly to blame for their initial gross underestimation of Japanese military forces.[51] Over many decades now, African American leaders, both intellectuals and activists, have worked abroad with anticolonial and other human rights groups to counter white imperialism in its many manifestations, thereby honing their own ability to understand and better resist the elite-white-male dominance system.

Postwar Black Resistance: More Internal War

After World War II returning black veterans still faced blatant racism, including beatings and lynchings. A letter written to President Harry Truman (1945–1953) about an attack on a returning black veteran by white police officers illustrated violent white supremacy: "To 'gouge out the eyesight' of a man who had used his eyes to safeguard the freedom of his country," the author wrote, "is surely a disgrace unheard of in any other country of the world."[52]

At war's end, the NAACP executive secretary Walter White visited the European, Pacific, and Mediterranean theaters to chronicle the experiences of black military personnel. Inspired by what he saw in 1945, with the war concluding, he and W. E. B. Du Bois appeared before a United Nations conference to endorse the eradication of the U.S. and European colonial systems. This was followed in 1947 when African American leaders presented to the UN "An Appeal to the World," a well-documented petition outlining links between slavery, Jim Crow segregation, and colonial imperialism. With much social science data, it insisted that "a great nation, which today ought to be in the forefront of the march toward peace and democracy, finds itself continuously making common cause with race hate, prejudiced exploitation and oppression of the common man. . . . Peoples of the World, we American Negroes appeal to you."[53] However, the mostly white officials in the Roosevelt administration blocked the delivery to the UN General Assembly, doubtless fearing it would hurt the desired U.S. image globally. Later, in 1951, African American leaders delivered an even stronger indictment of U.S. racism to the General Assembly. This petition, titled "We Charge Genocide: The Crime of Government Against the Negro People," detailed the federal government's role in Jim Crow discrimination, which was empirically documented as *genocidal* according to the new UN Genocide Convention. Again, the white elite in control of U.S. representation at the United Nations saw to it that this accurate petition was rejected.

Still, in the war's aftermath, the home front war for racial justice was occasionally successful. In a 1948 letter to President Harry Truman, African American civil right activists threatened a boycott of the highly segregated armed forces. Soon, Truman did issue an important executive order, starting the process of ending racial segregation in U.S. military forces. He also issued an executive order establishing a President's Committee on Civil Rights, whose report *To Secure These Rights* asserted all Americans had civil rights to be protected and calling for federal action for those rights.[54] One reason for these more assertive presidential actions was that millions of black southerners had moved in previous decades to northern cities, where they could organize and vote. Their substantial voting power had positive political impacts on some white Democratic politicians in northern cities. These occasional progressive white political reactions signal the great importance of people's organized resistance to white (male) political dominance.

African American criticism of, and action against, imperialist wars persisted over ensuing decades, indeed to the present. One famous example of an African American who aggressively resisted was world champion boxer Muhammad Ali. Proud of his African American heritage and religious commitments (Nation of Islam), in 1967 he refused the military draft, citing religious doctrine and his disapproval of the imperialistic U.S. war in Vietnam. In spite of vicious white-racist attacks on him for draft refusal, he stood firm, which cost him his world heavyweight title. One of his perceptive comments about this matter resonates to the present: "I am not going ten thousand miles from here to help murder and kill and burn another poor people simply to help continue the domination of white America."[55] This comment garnered him much respect and praise from African Americans and many people outside the United States.

More White Racist Action: Japanese Americans

Another wartime example of elite decision-making from the white racial frame involved imprisonment of most Japanese Americans in U.S. concentration camps in World War II. This highly racist action was taken by white officials with *no evidence* of Japanese Americans being a security threat. Such actions actually interfered with the war effort. The principal reason for this economically irrational decision involved decades of negative white-racist framing and actions targeting Japanese Americans and other Americans of Asian descent. Just before and after 1900, influential white politicians in the United States and other western countries worked aggressively to *prevent* Asian immigration. Racial heterogeneity was undesirable for them, and they viewed the exclusion of many people of color as a reinforcement of a "white republic." In fact, whiteness was an official criterion for U.S. citizenship from 1790 until the 1870s, when African-descended people could officially become citizens. Moreover, not until the 1950s were all immigrants of color allowed to become naturalized citizens.[56]

In the early 20th century, significant numbers of Japanese workers had been imported by some white employers to fill agricultural jobs in Hawai'i and on the West Coast. That is, these employers' capitalistic framing of profitability motivated their hiring actions. Nonetheless, other whites aggressively opposed these immigrant workers on blatantly racist grounds. Asian immigrants endured white-supremacist attacks that characterized them as unintelligent or unassimilable. Leading members of the white male elite, such as the prominent U.S. senator from California, James Phelan, insisted Japanese Americans threatened the "future of the white race, American institutions, and western civilization."[57] This widely accepted racist framing was a chief factor leading to passage of very restrictive immigrant legislation. The all-white, heavily Protestant members of Congress overwhelmingly passed the 1924 Immigration Act establishing racist immigrant quotas giving preference to northern Europeans and completely excluding Japanese immigrants. The white male chair of the House immigration committee insisted such exclusion was needed to stop a "stream of alien blood," language similar to continuing common white nativistic views of immigrants to the present day.[58] Highly racist immigration laws restricted Japanese and other Asian immigration into the United States *until the mid-1960s.*

From the early 1900s to the 1940s, many members of the white male elite increased their assertion of an array of anti-Japanese views. Such racist framing was shared by Franklin Roosevelt well before he became president. In articles for the Macon, Georgia, *Daily Telegraph* and for some magazines in the 1920s, he had warned against granting citizenship to "non-assimilable immigrants" and opposed Japanese immigration because "mingling Asiatic blood with European or American blood produces, in nine cases out of ten, the most unfortunate results."[59] Similarly, the writings of Ernie Pyle, the most famous U.S. journalist who reported from military theaters in World War II, reveal blatantly white-racist framing of the Japanese: "In Europe we felt that our enemies, horrible and deadly as they were, were still people. But out here I soon gathered that the Japanese were looked upon as something subhuman and repulsive; the way some people feel about cockroaches or mice. . . . I wanted a mental bath after looking at them."[60] Such openly racist and anti-immigrant imagery of numerous immigrant groups has been seen in numerous public statements of white commentators and politicians ever since.

Racialized Internment: Japanese Americans

Unsurprisingly, given such highly racist framing, the white national origin groups from enemy countries in Europe and Asia were treated in radically different ways by elite and ordinary whites during World War II. For example, the Italian language was prohibited on some radio stations, a small percentage of Italian Americans thought to be a security threat were imprisoned at one Montana camp, and many had to carry identity cards. German Americans faced similarly mild discriminatory treatment, with only a tiny percentage interned. Elite federal officials' wartime actions against white Italian and German Americans were mostly unjust, but far less severe than those against Japanese Americans. The wartime experience actually contributed to Italian and German American socioeconomic mobility, even as it devastated the lives of Japanese Americans. The solidarity with other whites, including in whites-only military units, helped German and Italian Americans to further prosper during and after the war in the country's white-dominated institutions.[61]

The treatment of Japanese Americans was dramatically different. The U.S. West Coast military commander—instructed by Roosevelt's officials and with racist discriminatory actions declared *constitutional* by an all-white-male Supreme Court—established western California, Washington, Oregon, and southern Arizona as areas where no Japanese, Italian, or German "aliens" could live. Yet, mostly Americans of Japanese ancestry were detained in barbed-wire concentration camps guarded by soldiers. Camps for them were erected in western states, holding about 115,000 people, mostly U.S.-born citizens.[62]

Even in wartime, there was constant evidence of an aggressively racist framing among the powerful white men and their acolytes who ran the war effort. White framing was evidenced by the huge wave of political, media, and public support for the internment of Japanese Americans. A white *Los Angeles Times* reporter wrote with an assertively racist voice: "A viper is nonetheless a viper wherever the egg is hatched," suggesting that a Japanese American born on U.S. soil "grows up to be a Japanese, not an American." Note too that these elite and ordinary white commentators were almost always white men who targeted Japanese and Japanese American *men*. Exhibiting aggressive white masculinity, they often portrayed, in their writings and stereotyped cartoons in magazines and newspapers, Japanese men as very racially threatening to white women and children. Yet again, we observe the intertwining and coreproduction of the white racial frame and the male sexist frame, in both elite and ordinary white minds.[63]

Leading white commentators and officials advocated or went along with the internment, which openly violated U.S. constitutional protections. Earlier, after Pearl Harbor, the rabidly racist and powerful Representative John Rankin of Mississippi declared the need for an internal war: "I'm for catching every Japanese in America, Alaska and Hawaii now and putting them in concentration camps and shipping them back to Asia as soon as possible. . . . This is a race war, as far as the Pacific side of the conflict is concerned."[64] Numerous white male politicians and millions of ordinary whites also believed that the country was actually in such a "race war," including Roosevelt and other top administration officials.

Nonetheless, some in the moderate wing of the white establishment voiced objections. Curtis Munson, a State Department official, concluded that Japanese Americans were no more disloyal than other groups. Even FBI director J. Edgar Hoover stated the internment had no security evidence to back it. Nonetheless, such contrarian views had no effect on federal government officials' actions to put most Japanese American citizens into barbed-wire concentration camps. Moreover, also forgotten is that there were many acts of Japanese American resistance in asserting their U.S. civil rights in this era, including within these military-controlled concentration camps and in federal courts.[65]

After the war, a commentary in *Harper's* by leading scholar Eugene Rostow dubbed the internment "our worst wartime mistake."[66] The internment of Japanese Americans, with *no* evidence of a security threat, contradicted the liberty-and-justice frame that governing white male officials had long endorsed. Elite and ordinary whites' hostility towards Japanese Americans was not new. For instance, the white executive heading the powerful California Grower-Shipper Vegetable Association told a *Saturday Evening Post* reporter that white farmers could easily replace "Japs," insisting that

"Japs" would not be welcomed back after the war. In part because of this long-term white opposition, the property loss to Japanese Americans from these extraordinarily racist government actions, which were often similar to early German Nazi actions against Jewish property holders, was a huge $1.3 billion.[67]

Collectively, Italian and German Americans did *not* suffer such extreme wartime oppression by the government, or such massive economic losses. This differential policy paralleled the white-racist framing evident in U.S. wartime propaganda. Anti-German war propaganda was mostly directed at Nazi *officials*, whereas anti-Japanese propaganda was highly racist and targeted *all Japanese*. While German or Italian civilians were white and at worst viewed by other white Americans as unwise dupes of their authoritarian leaders, the Japanese people were regularly dehumanized and portrayed out of the white racial frame as a very "inferior race" and commonly called "yellow vermin."[68] This highly racist framing was spread aggressively and successfully via the mainstream media and other war propaganda outlets by numerous powerful white men.

Still Justifying the Internment: Racialized Thinking Today

A mythological view of World War II still shapes the thinking of many elite and rank-and-file whites. Relatively recently, Howard Coble, an influential white congressional representative, declared the discriminatory wartime actions against Japanese American citizens to have been appropriate. "We were at war. We were under attack by a sovereign nation," he said. Without evidence, he arrogantly insisted that "Some [Japanese Americans] probably were intent on doing harm to us, just as some of these Arab Americans are probably intent on doing harm to us [today]."[69] When Coble first came to Congress in the 1980s, he even headed Republican opposition to a bill to compensate Japanese Americans for their racially discriminatory and unconstitutional detention.[70]

Recently, some influential white men or their acolytes, the latter including a few people of color, have endorsed this type of racialized detention of people of color as a possible way to deal with *contemporary* domestic security threats. In their current arguments, they have justified the World War II internment of many thousands of innocent Japanese Americans. Today, such white-generated racial framing by U.S. analysts of color is certainly less common than such framing by whites, but is still seen in some recent ill-informed analyses. Recently, for example, Michelle Malkin, a conservative pundit and herself Asian-Pacific American, authored a best-selling book justifying the internment of Japanese American citizens. She also defended more government use of such discriminatory racial and nationality profiling of nonwhite people today.[71] Significantly, the Historians' Committee for Fairness, an organization of major historical researchers, has described her work as "a blatant violation of professional standards of objectivity and fairness."[72]

Postwar Capitalism and Imperialism: The United States as Superpower (1940s–1950s)

The Atlantic Charter, a 1941 agreement between top U.S. and British political leaders, outlined their public vision of the postwar world. The words of these elite white men confirmed that global power and profit were driving forces behind the U.S. entry into World War II. Signed before the Pearl Harbor attack, when the United States was not directly part of the war, the Charter contained claims that U.S. and British governments would pursue "no aggrandizement, territorial or other" and that both respected "the right of all peoples to choose the form of government under which they will live."[73] Reality proved *quite* different. Only weeks before it was signed, the U.S. Under Secretary of State, Sumner Welles (1937–1943), had assured the French government that it could preserve its overseas French empire at war's end. In 1945 President Truman offered similar guarantees.[74] The white male elite was fully in charge of what was now the world's dominant superpower, the United States, with major gatekeeping power even in regard to the old European colonial empires.

U.S. National Self-Interest: Oil, Money, and Banking

The imperial ambitions of this Washington elite directly contradicted their claim of wanting to prevent the "territorial aggrandizement" of all nations in the Atlantic Charter. During World War II, white male diplomats and corporate executives worked tirelessly to ensure that when hostilities concluded U.S. economic and military power would sustain unrivalled world superpower status. In pursuit of this, U.S. corporate and government leaders infiltrated new geographical and political areas long dominated by the British.[75]

Control of Middle Eastern oil is an illustration of this elite push. By war's end, Britain was no longer the leading influence in oil-rich Saudi Arabia. Middle Eastern dominance had shifted to the top U.S. government and corporate leaders, substantially owing to efforts of those in the Roosevelt administration. The U.S. president met with the dictator of Saudi Arabia, who controlled Middle Eastern oil reserves, to work out U.S. dominance there. The U.S. elite's preoccupation with oil even led the poet Archibald MacLeish, then Assistant Secretary of State (1944–1945), to write: "the peace we seem to be making, will be a peace of oil, a peace of gold, a peace of shipping, a peace, in brief . . . *without moral purpose*."[76] As we document throughout this book, powerful oligopolistic capitalists regularly seek new types of overseas imperialism—in this case, more western profitmaking by the dispossession of others' oil resources. They and the government officials they influence have long used U.S. military might to back this highly exploitative process of resource dispossession. Moreover, as here, much U.S. postwar imperialism involved non-western peoples, whose domination was often racialized in terms of bringing them elements of white western "civilization."

Additionally, in 1944 with war still raging in the Pacific and Europe, the International Monetary Fund (IMF) was established. Again the U.S. elite guaranteed that they would dominate the IMF organization through voting power directly related to the amount of capital contributed by member nations. Unsurprisingly, major IMF decisions about international financial matters were typically made without serious dialogue with less powerful nations. The IMF came to be controlled by the Group of 7—the principal government donors. Consisting of the finance ministers and central bank governors of the United States, Canada, France, Britain, Germany, Italy, and Japan, plus those of the European Union (EU), this mostly white male club has possessed great global economic dominance now for several decades.[77]

Moreover, the creation of the United Nations in 1945 was presented in noble terms—supposedly, to sow seeds of international cooperation and prevent wars. However, the mostly white principal founders of the organization ensured that they—from the imperialist United States, Britain, France, and the Soviet Union—would remain in substantial control of this supposedly democratic body. The UN Charter essentially gave U.S. government leaders a veto of UN actions.[78] As we demonstrate in Chapter 4, the control that the United States later exerted over UN actions has periodically had disastrous consequences for people of color on several continents.

Corporate Power and the Rise of the Military-Industrial Complex

Recall that several researchers have shown that U.S. electoral candidates tend to support views popular with wealthy interests, because most rely substantially on prosperous backers to get elected. This money often shapes who wins major elections. These heavily white and male capitalistic blocs "invest" in candidates and have thus long had great political influence. Periodically, from their elected representatives, a majority of ordinary voters would doubtless like to see things such as more substantial government support for programs like Social Security, Medicare, and unemployment insurance that they rely upon. However, since they do not have real control over the funding and selection of their representatives, they often do not have the required muscle to substantially influence numerous government policies they prefer.[79]

Despite the fact that under Franklin Roosevelt's leadership the Democratic Party became more politically liberal—including in support of social welfare programs, unions, civil rights, and business regulation—the party leaders were no exception to this investment theory of politics. An influential coalition of corporate leaders were important in backing the administration. Especially important were executives of high-tech companies, international energy corporations, international media corporations, and investment banks—i.e., mostly capital-intensive firms with a multinational orientation. In contrast, numerous older and nationally focused large companies mostly stayed with the more conservative Republican Party. In part because of this multinational corporate umbrella, a strong international "free trade" position and significant involvement in international monetary matters were adopted as major strategies by the Roosevelt administration, indeed by many Democratic Party officials to the present day.[80]

Accordingly, a major aim in the World War II era was expansion and revitalization of white-run oligopoly capitalism. Ongoing integration and cooperation between the capitalistic elite and the Washington political elite ensured that the greatest economic beneficiaries of the war were mostly powerful white male corporate executives and their large corporations. Contrary to interpretations of Roosevelt's New Deal as "too liberal," this period saw a major increase in corporate dominance in government affairs. Industrial mobilization, essential to the World War II efforts, resulted in wealth converging on a relatively small number of corporations and associated executives. A Senate report titled "Economic Concentration and World War II" confirmed that while 2,000 corporations had competed for government wartime contracts, 40 percent of money awarded went to just *ten* big white-run corporations. Corporate executives mostly retained full control of company decision-making during the war, even though millions of U.S. workers were organized in unions. From 1938 onwards, most important economic laws passed by Congress reflected elite corporate interests.[81]

Nonetheless, organized workers did try to fight back. Fixed wages and great corporate profits led to a record number of strikes during the war, involving millions of workers. Exploited workers in mines, textile factories, and other industries took to the picket lines. In 1944, the final full year of the war, more strikes took place than in any previous year. Resistance to capitalistic classism was commonplace in these years.[82]

One major enduring result of World War II was the creation of an extraordinarily powerful military-industrial complex. As we noted previously, in the 1950s President Eisenhower, the former general heading the Allied military, warned about the dangers of this complex. Since that war, it has come to dominate much of the U.S. and global economy and politics. The military-industrial complex greatly expanded during World War II, continuing to mushroom in subsequent decades. Consider too the Selective Service Draft. Established in the 1940s and ending in 1973, this imposed draft gave the top white male decision-makers a relatively unrestricted right to send millions of mostly younger men of all backgrounds into military training and combat. After 1973 the aggressive military recruiting continued, this time in a supposedly all-volunteer military force. During this long era, old and new forms of mainstream media helped to spread military propaganda to mass audiences in effective ways. A recent analysis of the subtexts of this government propaganda during most of the military draft era has revealed insights into how the military elite framed the military institution. Drawing greatly on and reinforcing hegemonic masculinity, in photos and other materials the military personnel were routinely represented as mainly white, male, heterosexual, and physically powerful. This created an unambiguous image of the U.S. armed forces that not only succeeded in aggressively foregrounding a type of white hyper-masculinity (and increasing recruitment), but also bolstered the larger elite-white-male dominance system and its chief subsystems in the larger society.[83]

For decades this military-industrial complex has been composed of a massive interlocking array of government agencies and corporations profiting from massive government military expenditures. Thousands of companies, large and small, are still linked to the U.S. Department of Defense by large, often extremely wasteful military contracts, exchanges of personnel, advisory committees, and lobbyists. This setup has been called the "Iron Triangle" because thousands of people are interlinked, and many move from job to job in it. They often rotate around its three main job sectors—military services jobs, Defense Department jobs, and jobs in military-related industries. Such incestuous government-corporate networking is commonplace and, most importantly, essential to the contemporary operation and integration of corporate dominance in this society.[84]

The mostly white male capitalists in the military-industrial complex generate more or less guaranteed profits for their corporations and stockholders. This military-industrial complex has consumed trillions of dollars of public tax money, yet such spending is difficult to reduce because of congressional and public support, an orientation rooted in part in a sense of global (white) dominance. This corporate welfare system is sustained by the fact that military-related companies employ people in many congressional districts, and by the reality that the companies spend millions lobbying Congress and contributing to congressional campaigns. Even though the "Cold War" with the former Soviet Union ended by the 1990s, which destroyed much of the official rationale for the huge U.S. military-industrial complex, this complex has aggressively persisted. Moreover, the impact of actual or possible cutbacks in U.S. military expenditures is offset by massive U.S. arms sales overseas, where major U.S. firms do at least half of the international weapons business. This situation creates what sociologist C. Wright Mills long ago called a "permanent war economy," a situation that not only bolsters contemporary capitalism but also white western global dominance.[85]

White Men Carving Up the World: More Imperialism

Most geopolitical crises threatening the world today have their roots in the shifting decisions of the past that have been made by those at the top of the now global elite-white-male dominance system. For instance, Russian relations with the West reveal how war and aggression occurs in a distinctive loop through which hegemonic white supremacy and masculinity are recurringly maintained and legitimated globally, while national rivalries are also periodically produced and sustained.[86] This has disturbing ramifications for the prospect of authentic peace, security, and justice across the globe now and in the future.

Even today, ongoing tensions between Russia and the West have their origins in elite men's grab for national and personal power at the end of World War II. Recall that British Prime Minister Winston Churchill viewed western wartime actions as inescapably tied to extending their capitalistic empires. Post-war agreements between him, U.S. President Franklin Roosevelt, and the General Secretary of the Soviet Union Joseph Stalin (1922–1952) at the famous 1945 Yalta Conference help to explain enduring hostilities between Russia and the West since World War II. At Yalta these powerful white men bestowed many areas to the western powers, and granted eastern Europe to the Soviet Union, the latter decision resulting in Russians immigrating there. These elite decisions, substantially rooted in white predatory framing of the colonized societies, continue to generate contemporary geopolitical conflicts.[87]

Conclusion

Certainly, World War II did pit the U.S. and other Allied powers against Axis adversaries who proved capable of great genocidal crimes, including the massive German Holocaust. Operating from their version of the white racial frame, these self-styled white male "Aryans" saw themselves as a "superior race" fated to rule much of the world. Nazi Germany was indeed an immoral foe. Given such evil adversaries, one can be grateful for those who sacrificed to end their rise to global power and to publicly question central tenets of their infamous white framing of supposedly superior and inferior racial groups.

Nonetheless, as African American leaders such as W. E. B. Du Bois explained at the time, there is much more to the long history of white western atrocities. He put it bluntly: "There was no Nazi atrocity—concentration camps, wholesale maiming and murder, defilement of women and ghastly blasphemy of childhood—which the Christian civilization of Europe *had not long been practicing against colored folk* in all parts of the world in the name of and for the defense of a Superior Race born to rule the world."[88] This idea that Adolf Hitler was rivaled in his global and genocidal ambitions by other European and U.S. imperialism is likely a disconcerting idea for many white westerners. But the evidence is clear. Just to take one example, remember that during the late 19th century reign of King Leopold II, white male officials were responsible for the forced labor and mass killing of an estimated *10 million Africans* in the Belgian-colonized Congo Free State. One social critic has asked why the genocidal Leopold has not taken his place alongside the genocidal Hitler in U.S. and European school curricula.[89]

Moreover, some have raised the question of whether in the postwar era the U.S. government elite has, in its domestic and foreign policies, embodied the liberty-and-justice principles for which World War II was ostensibly fought.[90] As we show throughout, the answer to this is a definitive "no." This is true not just for the post–World War II era, but for U.S. history generally. From their national and overseas depredations over current and previous centuries, and backed by the institutions they head, powerful white (male) capitalists have regularly gained vast profits, which have translated for them into great institutional power as well as reinforced the individual and societal realities of white masculinity and superiority. As a result of this hegemonic white power, there are still numerous oppressed groups within and beyond U.S. borders that suffer extensive economic exploitation and political domination. In recent decades, frequently under the rubrics of neoliberal austerity or privatization directed at capitalistic restructuring of societies, a succession of racial-class assaults have been carried out against people of color globally.

Neither protecting destitute citizens in faraway lands (such as European Jews), nor the preservation of the celebrated ideal of "nonintervention in the affairs of other nations," were the most important impetuses among the U.S. leadership for entering and winning World War II. In their long imperialistic histories, Allied governments had not often typified the "freedom" and "democracy" values for which they supposedly fought that war. As for the U.S. white male elite specifically, framing the United States as a virtuous democratic guardian of oppressed citizens in Nazi-occupied Europe was highly inaccurate and hypocritical. The racist and sexist framing and discriminatory treatment that they and ordinary white men have directed at people of color, Jews, white women, and others has been constant throughout U.S. history. Indeed, the ultimate triumph of the Allied powers over the Axis powers was never intended by those in control to be the major blow to white racism, imperialism, and militarism that many wartime advocates of the "war for democracy" would have us believe.

Here we challenge with much evidence the commonplace framing of U.S. wartime leaders as highly virtuous white men, as being centrally concerned with authentic freedom and justice values. Instead, we observe that they were frequently unresponsive to the extreme suffering of millions of fellow human beings. U.S. foreign policy as dictated by these white men has usually been racialized and masculinized in character and consistent with U.S. imperial and capitalistic interests before, during, and after World War II.

4
White Imperialism, Racism, and Masculinity
Globalization Since the 1950s

In the contemporary era, no national government or other interventionist group has even come close to matching the U.S. record on political and economic intervention in the affairs of other societies. In the last chapter we cited earlier examples of this global intervention by powerful white men in the federal government and heading up major corporations. Understanding well the harsh realities of U.S. foreign policy, especially in regard to countries predominantly composed of people of color, requires that one adopt an analytical perspective emphasizing and assessing key elements of systemic white racism, which is still essential and foundational to white global dominance. Additionally, this global imperialistic enterprise not only has been systemically racist but, as we have frequently seen in previous chapters, is usually oligopolistically *capitalistic* and heavily *masculinist*. Repeatedly, in case after case of U.S. imperialism, past and present, an accent on virile white manhood has been conspicuous in the actions of white political and economic leaders and their principal acolytes.

To recoup perceived injuries to the white manhood of the U.S. elite, and to keep people of color globally in their "place," these powerful men have long worked assiduously to fortify their often masculinized foreign and domestic policies. Unsurprisingly, most overseas interventions have involved manly and military *violence* to achieve U.S. national goals. Our goal in this chapter is to now examine major examples from a more recent era of imperialistic U.S. intervention overseas. There are many to choose, but we have space to detail only a few. We begin with major military coups that the highest federal officials, virtually all white men, were heavily involved in—the 1953 Iranian coup, the 1954 Guatemalan coup, and the 1973 Chilean coup. These U.S.-facilitated coups have had *lasting* impacts that greatly shape global politics to the present day.

U.S. Imperialism: Iranian and Guatemalan Military Coups

Consider the 1953 Iranian military coup against democratically elected Iranian Prime Minister Mohammad Mosaddegh (1952–1953). Initially,

President Harry Truman (1945–1953) declined an official British offer to jointly solve the "problem" of this elected prime minister who would not acquiesce in British and U.S. goals for exploiting Iran's oil. However, the next president, Republican Dwight Eisenhower (1953–1961), was more imperialistic and agreed to get U.S. government agencies secretly involved in the expansion of U.S. oil-related capitalism.

This imperialistic involvement in Asia was also substantially shaped by the dominant racialized and white-masculinized framing of U.S. goals. For example, during the years 1949–1950 China and South Korea fell to Communist control, and the Democratic Party, in power at the time, paid an election price for this result. In the 1952 presidential election former General Dwight Eisenhower, a Republican, won. One reason was that many voters, especially the then-dominant bloc of white male voters, viewed the Chinese and Koreans out of a racial framing as "backward" and "weak," for only weak men would allow Communism to prosper. U.S. diplomacy and military policy under Eisenhower was permeated with noticeably hyper-masculine values and terms. *Brinkmanship* was the idea that the world's capitalistic and Communist countries were perpetually on the threshold of nuclear war. *Massive retaliation* was the phrase for reacting to an enemy country's military action "with an all-out attack." *Rollback* was the term for pushing back the Soviet Union's sphere of European influence. All implied a certain white masculine assertiveness and virtuousness. Indeed, the manly President Eisenhower, the former top military general, was seen by many Americans as an iron-fisted defender against the challenges of international Communism.[1]

In this atmosphere local political uprisings, many of them popular and relatively democratic, were seen by Washington's white male leaders as a threat to their global power—and implicitly to their white manhood perspective. Stephen Kinzer, a researcher of U.S. interventions, has outlined the parallels between two big U.S.-engineered political coups of the 1950s—the 1953 Iranian and 1954 Guatemalan coups. Both countries had democratically elected leaders who were *not* U.S.-controlled. (They were also not controlled by the Soviet Union—the myth often constructed by the U.S. elite to defend interventions.) The so-called transgressions of these democratic leaders were in deciding to put their people's interests ahead of those of U.S. and European government and corporate elites. Specifically, they often dared to insist their countries' natural resources belonged to their own citizens and not to white American and European corporations.[2]

In the case of Iran's elected prime minister Mosaddegh, the U.S. Central Intelligence Agency (CIA) later acknowledged that the 1953 Iranian coup was carried out "as an act of U.S. foreign policy, conceived and approved at the highest levels of government."[3] Under Eisenhower's control, the CIA was in charge of the antidemocratic coup's implementation, which included bribing high-ranking Iranian officials, as well as launching a biased propaganda campaign against the democratically elected Iranian government.[4] In the buildup to the western imperialistic coup, conflict had emerged over the Anglo-Iranian Oil Company (AIOC), a British corporation that had exclusive control of Iranian petroleum reserves, a result of past British imperialism. Widespread Iranian dissatisfaction with the AIOC was rooted in that corporation's exploitative policies. Initially, Iranian Prime Minister Mosaddegh sought only to reduce the corporation's exclusive control over Iran's reserves. The company's refusal even to accommodate the Iranian government's modest requests resulted in Iran nationalizing its oil industry and expelling nonnational corporate representatives.[5]

Following the 1953 U.S.-British-generated coup, an autocratic military government replaced Mosaddegh, leading the way for the rule of the "Shah" of Iran. An obsequious U.S. ally, he depended on U.S. military support to retain his dictatorship.[6] The coup generated great anti-U.S. opinion throughout the Middle East. The Iranian people eventually rebelled; their 1979 overthrow of the brutal Shah marked the emergence of the country's often anti-western theocratic rulers. Many analysts have noted that the September 11, 2001 attacks on the United States can be traced in part to the impact in the Middle East of the 1953 Iranian coup engineered by the CIA, since the Shah's reign and eventual demise encouraged anti-U.S. radicals in the region. If democracy had been allowed to flourish much earlier, Iran might have become an example to other countries there. The 1953 anti-democratic military coup is a clear example of how organized U.S. imperialistic intrusions have had devastating long-term effects.[7]

In the case of Guatemala, the U.S. power elite once again backed the toppling of another democratically elected leader, President Jacobo Árbenz (1951–1954). The country's economy had long been substantially controlled by white male executives heading up just *one* U.S. corporation, the United Fruit Company, which had powerful connections to the Washington elite. Influential white men in the Eisenhower administration sat on its corporate board or were otherwise intimately linked to it. U.S. Secretary of State John Foster Dulles (1953–1959) was once an attorney for the corporation.[8] U.S. capitalists' interests were threatened when President Árbenz pushed progressive land reform. The resulting law required United Fruit Company to sell much of the country's best uncultivated land to the Guatemalan government. The company's executives convinced Eisenhower administration officials that the democratically elected government was "antagonistic" to U.S. corporate interests (profits) and falsely portrayed Árbenz as an "instrument" of the Soviet Union. This was the Cold War era, and these powerful white men were mostly anti-Communists for whom fabricating political lies about a country's situation was unimportant.[9]

Those Guatemalan military leaders doing the killing often had support from U.S. intelligence officials. Taking their directives directly from Washington's elite leadership, the CIA and the U.S. ambassador there backed the autocratic Guatemalan military leaders in the coup. During the "Cold War" with the Soviet Union, these elite men favored the government doing whatever it took to impede real or mythical Soviet influence.[10]

The U.S. Intervention in Vietnam and Chile

The presidents immediately after Eisenhower continued as "Cold Warriors." The only non-Protestant president, the Catholic John Kennedy (1961–1963), was regularly represented in assertively masculine terms—including in his own representations. Under Kennedy, white men would "boldly go" where they had not gone before, as could be seen in his administration's talk of space travel that would signify white male courage. In opposition to Cuban leader Fidel Castro, Kennedy's foreign policy emphasized the old Theodore Roosevelt virtues of white male supremacy over peoples of color who had the gall to assert their freedom from U.S. political-economic control. This strong accent on white manhood was illustrated in the 1961 Cuban Missile Crisis, where Kennedy "stood tall" against Cuban and Soviet leaders. Similarly, the aggressive white-male-savior postures of presidents Kennedy and Lyndon Johnson (1963–1969) helped to get the country involved in a disastrous new war in Vietnam.[11]

Johnson and other white men high in his administration decided to engage heavily in the Vietnam War for what were, yet again, substantially hyper-masculine reasons. In 1965 John McNaughton, a high official in Johnson's administration, crafted a report explaining the reasons for intervention: "70% to avoid a *humiliating* blow to our reputation; 20% to keep the area from China; and 10% to bring the people of South Vietnam a better, freer way of life."[12] Johnson viewed the Vietnam war in a very masculine way:

> He saw the war as a test of his own manliness. In LBJ's world there were weak and strong men; the weak men were the skeptics, who sat around contemplating, talking, criticizing; the strong men were the doers, the activists, the ones who were tough and always refused to back down.[13]

Opponents of the war were often described, as with previous wars, as anemic, effeminate, or homosexual.

President Richard Nixon (1969–1974) continued this tradition of hyper-masculine Cold Warriors in regard to the Vietnam War. Thus, in the 1970s the lesson he, like other top white male leaders, took from the U.S. defeat in this war was that "America had fallen victim to a debilitating 'syndrome' of passivity and weakness."[14] That is, there was a failure in (white) *manliness*. Additionally, Nixon and imperialistic advisors like Henry Kissinger pursued efforts against democratically elected governments that were committed to controlling their natural resources by reducing U.S. control over them. Thus, Chile's Salvador Allende (1970–1973), a democratically elected president, also fell prey to an anti-democratic intervention of the U.S. elite, in this case white male officials in the Nixon administration. Coveted Chilean natural resources were controlled by highly exploitative U.S. and European corporations. With a goal of improving his people's living conditions, the democratically elected President Allende began to nationalize the Chilean land holdings of these companies. Prominent members of the conservative Chilean elite were outraged and met with U.S. Secretary of State Kissinger (1973–1977). Shortly afterwards, Nixon determined that Allende's tenure as an elected president had to be ended, if necessary by U.S. intervention.[15] In addition to concerns that U.S. corporate interests would be harmed by Allende's democratic policies, top Nixon administration officials feared that he would embolden other Latin American leaders to "bring about socialism by democratic means" and thereby reduce U.S. economic and political imperialism in Latin America.[16]

In the aptly titled article "The Other 9/11," a former CIA agent who was dispatched to Chile to facilitate the autocratic military coup there has discussed his agency's role. He described major U.S. support for General Augusto Pinochet, the leader of the military junta that overthrew Allende and who then ruled over Chile with great brutality from 1974 to 1990. He further explained that the CIA directives came from the White House, including for economic and political sabotage. With strong (white) masculinist language, Nixon vigorously instructed his administration to make the Chilean economy "scream," so that a military coup would ensure the removal of the elected president. Washington's white male elite inaugurated an economic blockade and thwarted Allende's attempts to secure loans from international organizations also controlled by powerful white men. Later on, investigators concluded that thousands were assaulted and killed by Pinochet's brutal minions.[17]

Arrogant White Interventionists: Richard Nixon and Henry Kissinger

Arrogant hyper-masculinity is often obvious in powerful white men, for they brook no criticism and many have had great power for long periods. Consider National Security Advisor (1969–1975) and Secretary of State (1973–1977) Henry Kissinger. In these positions under presidents Nixon and Gerald Ford, and as an advisor of other presidents, Kissinger controlled much U.S. foreign policy at the height of the Cold War. His "tough-minded" white masculinity often translated into policy action of a white imperialist variety. In spite of his Nobel Peace Prize, several critics have portrayed him as in some ways an international war criminal because of certain shadowy or questionable Cold War dealings, including the clandestine bombing of Cambodia during the Vietnam war.[18]

Given that the white men at the top do not generally tolerate censure, and because they generally see their actions as valid and involving civic duty, the full consequences of Kissinger's tactical and ethical failures have largely been hidden from the public. A reflective Kissinger, for example, might want to reconsider his defense of the saturation bombing of Cambodia given the estimated 150,000 noncombatants killed by U.S. bombs.[19] Even late in his life, the pivotal role he played in Chile, Cambodia, and other such imperialistic bloodshed was still substantially whitewashed. He long remained a "distinguished" Harvard professor, foreign policy advisor, and media expert.[20] In numerous books he defended *realpolitik* in U.S. foreign policy. *Realpolitik* is a German word for a very masculinist form of international power politics centered mainly on considerations of global U.S. supremacy rather than democratic ideology and ethical principles. Unsurprisingly, Kissinger's "tough-minded" brand of U.S. *realpolitik* resulted in contentious U.S. political decisions. Moreover, prizing an increase in national power, Kissinger once remarked that "power is the ultimate aphrodisiac."[21]

In many ways Kissinger has become a major symbol of arrogant white male western imperialism, as seen in his support, alongside President Nixon, for West Pakistan's military dictatorship in East Pakistan. The scholar Gary Bass has detailed the U.S. role in the 1971 massacre of Hindu Bengalis in East Pakistan by the Pakistani leader there. Nixon and Kissinger were steadfast supporters of this brutal leader, even though U.S. diplomats warned them of an impending genocide being orchestrated by him. International geopolitics, reflecting the arrogant masculinity style, played a decisive role in U.S. support for this Pakistani architect of genocide and a hatred for the female leader of Bangladesh's struggle for independence, Indira Gandhi. Behind closed doors, Nixon referred to Gandhi as a "bitch" and a "witch." Acting as a man's man, Nixon preferred the whisky-drinking Pakistani general. On advice from Kissinger, Nixon sent military planes and weapons to Pakistan, even though he knew this violated U.S. law.[22] The resulting genocidal massacre of Hindu Bengalis in East Pakistan is sadly reminiscent of the story of the United States' mostly elite-white-male leadership in regard to the 1990s Rwandan genocide (see below).

Kissinger and Nixon might also have been responsible for far more spilled blood had the Soviet Union's leadership retaliated to certain U.S. anti-Soviet interventions with their nuclear bombs, which was a possibility at the time. But in a world where elite white men rule, such reckless and masculinist political gambling is often lionized or hidden from the public.[23]

More Hyper-Masculinity: The Reagan and Bush Eras

With the elections of Ronald Reagan (1981–1989) and George H. W. Bush (1989–1993), the Cold War received a new dose of aggressive white masculine policymaking and action targeting the Soviet Union. Space-based anti-missile systems (i.e., Reagan's Strategic Defense Initiative) were no longer science fiction. Supporters of Reagan—a former gunfighter in movies—and George H. W. Bush have credited their Cold Warrior masculinity poses with ending the Cold War with the Soviet Union in 1985–1991. However, this crediting seriously neglects the important role of the General Secretary of the Communist Party of the Soviet Union, Mikhail Gorbachev (1985–1991), and his policies of *glasnost* and *perestroika* (Soviet restructuring for more social and economic freedom).[24]

In this era of warrior masculinity in government action, numerous movies and other media efforts attempted to reassure a concerned public that its white male patriarchs and heroes still knew best. In the 1980s Reagan-era entertainment industry, the virtuous white male prevailed over effeminate or degenerate foes. Movie protagonists played by movie icons like Harrison Ford, Arnold Schwarzenegger, and Sylvester Stallone were recurring symbols of white male prowess. The scholar Randy Laist put it thus:

> The father figure these Reaganite fantasies elevates to godlike priority symbolizes not only the integrity of the United States itself as a world power or Reagan himself as a benevolent patriarch, but also an entire metaphysical condition of stability and coherence. . . . If an emerging climate of globalism, multiculturalism, and feminism had threatened the white male's cultural supremacy, the Cold War provides a metanarrative that consolidates power in the hands of the *father* while simultaneously anchoring reality itself to a stable set of familiar coordinates.[25]

The Soviet Union was replaced in 1991 by a smaller Russian-dominated confederation that has continued in great political tension with the United States; white male leaders in both countries still periodically engage in assertive masculinity posturing.

Later on, the U.S. victory in the 1991 Gulf War (over control of Middle Eastern oil resources) under the direction of President George H. W. Bush, reinforced customary views of male toughness and wartime gallantry, served to quash antiwar discourse, and to some degree made up for previous assaults on white male superiority that came from the U.S. defeat in Vietnam by Asian men believed, then and often now, to be racially inferior and effeminate. In these events, repeatedly, we observe the close intertwining in male decision-makers' minds of strong masculinist framing, white racial framing, and an elite classist framing that emphasizes the constant need for U.S. capitalistic expansion globally.[26]

The Imperialistic Wars of George W. Bush

A decade later, another President Bush engaged in two more wars that signaled more U.S. imperialism in the Middle East. George W. Bush assumed the presidency in 2001, and the removal of Iraq's dictator, Saddam Hussein, was made a priority in his national security meetings.[27] In defense of an imperialistic invasion, Bush and his mostly white male colleagues intentionally tried to deceive the Congress and public into believing that Hussein and the 9/11 terrorist leader Osama Bin Laden were allies, even though they were *enemies*.[28]

Two days before the Iraq invasion, a *Washington Post* headline read, "Bush Clings to Dubious Allegations about Iraq." The authors of the article noted that the administration was prepared to attack even though its allegations against Hussein had been challenged by U.S. intelligence reports, the UN, and European governments. However, so powerful is the Washington white elite that this significant article was buried deep in the newspaper. Yet, there was no evidence that Hussein had anything to do with the 9/11 attacks or possessed weapons of mass destruction. State Department officials and intelligence officials in the Department of Energy, which deals with nuclear issues, were among those dissenting from the administration's official line. They were silenced.[29]

Ever since, influential white voices have tried to recast the Bush administration's deliberate lies and misrepresentations as innocent errors. Laurence Silberman, a judge who co-chaired the 2004 Weapons of Mass Destruction Commission, is among these. In one article he claimed, inaccurately, that no one in Washington presented contrary evidence to the intelligence community before the invasion. Charles Duelfer, who led a post-invasion fact-finding mission, was also among the voices.[30] In these cases we witness powerful white men defining what political virtue is, who is virtuous, and where and when there is virtue. According to the narrative they weaved, Bush was innocently mistaken. For centuries white male decision-makers have portrayed themselves as tough-minded, heroic, and righteous, even as they often generate destruction and misery throughout the world. Note too that in this process most white men show little awareness of the problematical racial, class, or gender framing of their actions.

Many influential white men, especially conservatives, were far less generous when it came to President Barack Obama's (2009–2017) impact on Iraq. One scholar summed this up: "The rhetoric against the Obama Administration is quite robust in its harshness."[31] Some Republicans publicly suggested that, had Obama not withdrawn U.S. forces from Iraq, then the Prime Minister Nouri al-Maliki (2006–2014) would not have been able to brutally repress the Sunni Islamic minority there, and hence radicalize them further. The truth is less convenient. Bush had strongly supported al-Maliki since 2006 and aggressively worked to get his predecessor ousted from office. The influential white men who have been so critical of Obama's actions seem to have forgotten that *President Bush* was actually responsible for the agreement that paved the way for the U.S. withdrawal in 2011.[32] Moreover, a bitter legacy of the Bush presidency was that the 2003 Iraq invasion and change of control from Sunni leader Saddam Hussein to a Shiite-controlled state eventually served as a means for al-Qaeda to enter Iraq and restart a Sunni-led resistance movement, commonly known in the West as the Islamic State in Iraq and Syria (ISIS), and in the Arab world by its Arabic language acronym Daesh. Indeed, prior to the invasion the U.S. National Intelligence Council had told Bush that an Iraq war could lead to an anti-U.S. uprising and strengthen support for Middle Eastern terrorism.[33] Yet Bush and Vice President Dick Cheney (2001–2009) pressed ahead aggressively, with much hyper-masculine posturing in regard to bringing "freedom" to Iraq. Examining speeches by both presidents Bush, one sociologist has concluded that father and son relied substantially on the important gestures and language of vigorous white masculinity to effectively peddle their unnecessary Middle Eastern wars.[34]

The 2003 invasion of Iraq serves as one of many examples of white hyper-masculinity in the United States, past and present. This example brings us to a paradox: Unrelenting white domination of people of color disguised as the pursuit of democracy. For instance, when publicly speaking of his desire to remove dictator Saddam Hussein from power and eradicate Iraq's ability to develop weapons of mass destruction, President Bush enthusiastically spoke of a "world democratic movement," the "global democratic revolution," and the "forward strategy of freedom," all of which depended on nondemocratic U.S. military power.[35] Observe in Bush's words the durable view among white male conquerors that they have a natural right to invade or seize new worlds in the name of "superior" western culture. The global imperialistic enterprises here were, yet again, simultaneously capitalistic, systemically racist, and heavily gendered.[36] For centuries a U.S. or European grab for control of strategic materials and resources has resulted in a constant succession of wars and other unrelenting attacks on peoples of color throughout the world.

Additionally, throughout this book we have underscored the importance of the non-white-male Americans who have been allowed by white men into the lower reaches of the power elite. Since the 1970s token numbers of men and women of color and modest numbers of white women have played an increasingly significant role in sustaining and perpetuating the societal institutions, with their often oppressive norms and other structures, put into place historically by dominant white men. Unsurprisingly, thus, much white-male historical mythology and societal framing have been drilled into the heads of Americans of color and white women by the mainstream media, in schooling, and in other socialization institutions. Many elements of the dominant racial, class, and gender frames are learned, even sometimes aggressively embraced, by most people who are socialized into this elite-white-male dominated society.

Consider briefly two African Americans who served in the George W. Bush administration—Colin Powell as Secretary of State (2001–2005) and Condoleezza Rice (2001–2005) as National Security Advisor and then Secretary of State. Both operated to a significant degree from a mainstream white framing of national and international matters, and both helped, knowingly or unwittingly, to frame the fraudulent reasons for the 2003 U.S.-led invasion of Iraq.[37] Colin Powell was heavily involved in, and strongly defended, Bush administration decision-making about entry into the imperialistic Iraq War. Condoleezza Rice was Powell's successor as Secretary of State. She personally approved a CIA petition to use torture on suspected terrorists. Her role was reportedly far more substantial than she admitted in testimony to the Senate Armed Services Committee.[38] Arguably like other female acolytes of the white male elite, to rise in their ranks and culture, Rice appears to have adopted some hegemonically masculine attributes, including a "tough-minded" supporting of unchecked violence against a possible enemy. In the examples of Rice and Powell we observe that in the lower tier of the U.S. elite, or just below that elite, are often important enforcers and coordinators of the racial, class, and gender subsystems of the elite-white-male dominance system.

Moreover, arrogance on the part of the political members of the mostly white elite, or of their major political assistants, seems to regularly arise from their unreflective sense of holding superior white-western values and framing of international issues. Without this conventional and highly biased elite-white-male framing, leading U.S. policymakers might have listened to those who opposed the U.S.-led invasion of Iraq—and thereby saved a great many American and Middle Eastern lives.

Western Intervention in the Middle East

A major example of *recent* geopolitical crises being linked to white men's much earlier grab for global resources can be seen in the 1916 Sykes-Picot Agreement affecting the Middle East. This clandestine arrangement divided the Arab provinces of the defeated Ottoman Empire into British and French spheres of imperialistic influence. The British elite was interested in the region's petroleum; the French elite sought entrance to Mediterranean harbors.[39] Again we observe the aggressive predatory ethic of western capitalism in operation. Essential to this example of "free enterprise" was a destructive, gluttonous, and narcissistic orientation that asserted the rights of the mostly white, male, and Christian elite over other lands and peoples of quite different backgrounds—in this case, the mostly Arab and/or Muslim peoples of the Middle East.

In 1916 the elite European diplomats Mark Sykes and François Georges-Picot crafted this Sykes-Picot Agreement; they mostly ignored existing regional ethnic identities, tribal cultures, and theological divisions in carving up the region for European profit. Without consideration of local histories, their agreement resulted in splitting up significant ethnic groups among different countries (e.g., Kurds), while also forcing different unfriendly religious sects to live side-by-side. These elite white diplomats are long gone, but the western dominance they created or buttressed continues to greatly affect the Middle East. Indeed, for many Muslims the Sykes-Picot Agreement marked what they perceive to be a modern *western Christian crusade* against them.[40]

From this discriminatory 1916 agreement to the much later 2003 U.S.-led invasion of Iraq and beyond, Middle Eastern Muslim leaders have denounced the West for many alleged wrongs. The recurring grab for control of strategic petroleum and other resources has resulted in a constant succession of Middle Eastern wars. How arrogant was Vice President Dick Cheney, when prior to the Iraqi invasion that deposed Saddam Hussein he boasted, "We will . . . be greeted as *liberators.*"[41] White neoconservatives, including Cheney and Donald Rumsfeld, wanted Hussein removed from his position long before the invasion. Petroleum resources were central. In the 1990s, Cheney—then CEO of Halliburton, a large oil service company—remarked that "The good Lord didn't see fit to put oil and gas only where there are democratically elected regimes friendly to the United States."[42] Later, as vice president, he led a task force involving clandestine meetings with major oil company executives. Such private meetings clearly signal how the economic and political actors in the dominant white oligarchy routinely collaborate behind the scenes.

The U.S.-led invasion of Iraq was dubbed "Operation Iraqi Freedom" by Washington's political elite. When publicly speaking of his desire to remove Hussein from power and eradicate Iraq's ability to develop alleged weapons of mass destruction, President George W. Bush enthusiastically spoke of a "global democratic revolution" and the "forward strategy of freedom," but these efforts actually depended on a *nondemocratic* decision by mostly white U.S. officials to invade a country considered by many to be racially or culturally inferior. Echoing the opinions of the mostly white male neoconservative intellectuals and government leaders, Bush misrepresented the invasion as part of supposed U.S. "missions of rescue and liberation on nearly every continent."[43] Notice again here the power elite's control over language used to describe what is in fact something else—for example, the deflecting language of "freedom" and "democratic" for U.S. imperialistic invasions. The enduring view among these white male conquerors is that they have a natural right to seize new worlds in the name of "superior" white western culture, with its mythological commitment to democracy. Repeatedly, these white men thought they had the right to define globally what political-economic virtue is. Their global imperialistic enterprises were, then as now, not only capitalistic but often white-racist and heavily gendered. Both elite and non-elite whites in the West have long profited from the exploitation of the material resources of peoples of color across the globe.

Unsurprisingly, such western imperialism has been regularly challenged, including by militant groups such as the aforementioned ISIS (now self-styled IS). Indeed, their goal is the obliteration of the Sykes-Picot Agreement of 1916 that defined state borders in the greater part of the contemporary Middle East. The Sunni group's later name change to simply Islamic State is significant in that they have removed the reference to Iraq and Syria as separate countries. This assertive naming is directly related to the 1916 agreement forced by western powers on this mostly Muslim region. IS has celebrated their tearing down of the barricade forming part of the European-imposed boundary between Iraq and Syria.[44] Cruel, violent, and hyper-masculine themselves, the IS leaders have understood the western countries' leaders' historical competition for the exploitation of Middle Eastern resources.

Moreover, since the September 2001 attacks on the United States and other terroristic attacks on the U.K. and France since, ordinary citizens of these countries, among other non-elites in white-dominated nations, have been asked to back war and aggression for obscure reasons, reduce dissent, and surrender rights and liberties in the interest of "national security." Notwithstanding rhetoric to the contrary, seemingly nonracialized security initiatives by western elites are replete with religious, cultural, ethnic, and racial discourses and policies, as is evidenced in the contemporary profiling and criminalization of Arabs, Muslims, and others by influential white politicians in numerous western countries.

The Rwandan Genocide: Racialized Elite Responses

The 1990s saw the election of a Democratic president, Bill Clinton, whose presidency continued to encourage government and corporate leaders to be involved in pursuit of elite U.S. interests overseas. Consider the very important example of the large-scale genocide—one of the largest in human history—that took place in the African country of Rwanda, a western-colonized country that only became independent of Belgium in 1962. This is a major example of how elite-white-male dominance operates globally, especially toward people of color.

In 1994 extremists from one Rwandan ethnic group, the Hutu, murdered at least 800,000 Rwandans who were predominately from another ethnic group, the Tutsi. The origins of this genocidal slaughter are to be found substantially in that country's long colonial history. Pre-colonial ethnic antagonisms between the Hutu and Tutsi were strengthened during the Belgian colonial domination there after World War I. Using a divide-and-conquer strategy, the white Belgian invaders bestowed on the Tutsi minority a social status superior to the Hutu majority. However, contrary to remarks of influential U.S. policymakers during the 1990s genocide, made to justify U.S. abandoning of Rwandans, major intergroup violence between the Tutsi and Hutu groups was actually *unusual* in pre-colonial times.[45]

Before the end of their colonial rule, as retribution for the Tutsi leading Rwanda's independence drive, Belgian officials reassigned their preferential treatment to the Hutu majority. Juvénal Habyarimana, a Hutu, became the country's president. Later, in the 1980s, organized Tutsi exiles invaded Rwanda. In 1993 President Habyarimana did accept a peace treaty under whose terms the Tutsi political organization and the Hutu-led Rwandan government would share political power. However, in April 1994 a jet carrying the Rwandan president was shot down, and he was killed. The following day Hutu extremists unleashed mass violence against the Tutsi and more moderate Hutus who embraced peaceful reconciliation, thereby beginning a massive genocide.[46]

Much of the white world's elite initially paid little attention. The courageous Canadian General Roméo Dallaire, then commander of the United Nations Assistance Mission for Rwanda (UNAMIR), brought attention to the international white media's lack of interest in the fate of these thousands of black Africans. Comparing genocidal actions in Africa to the European war crimes happening about the same time in the Balkans war in the former Yugoslavia and getting great western attention and intervention, Dallaire astutely wrote: "There were more people killed, injured, internally displaced and turned into refugees in 100 days in Rwanda than during the six years of the Yugoslav campaign. It was as if those people *didn't count*."[47] One major example of such indifference involved 2,000 people who took refuge at a Catholic school. Guarding these Rwandans were Belgian soldiers, but they were dispatched away to assist in the exodus of their white "expats" there. The Rwanda survivors described the genocidal slaughter at the school that followed, and the white western notion that Africans are less valuable than Europeans became brutally apparent.[48]

Considering those officials who crafted the U.S. response to this Rwandan genocide, we observe at the top of the power pyramid very powerful white men. These included President Bill Clinton (1993–2001), White House National Security Council (NSC) official Richard Clarke (1992–2003), and Secretary of State Warren Christopher (1993–1997), all of whom shaped the feeble U.S. response to this large-scale genocide.

With declassification of documents, we now know a fuller story of what happened with the U.S. response, including the role of principal assistants to these elite men. These latter implementing officials included Ambassador to the UN Madeleine Albright (1993–1997); Susan Rice, Clarke's NSC deputy during the genocide; Christine Shelley, a state department spokesperson; Presidential Press Secretary Mike McCurry (1994–1998); and Donald Steinberg, a key presidential adviser. These important assistants to the top political elite helped to frame a fraudulent story of the U.S. response to the genocide that fit U.S. national interests and the enduring myth of superior white western virtuousness. There is a general phenomenon here to be noted, too. The immediate subordinates of top elite decision-makers usually seek to foster the latter group's political and economic interests. Indeed, the elite constantly depends on them to help enforce and coordinate the complex and extensive elite-white-male dominance system that, as is clear here, has a great global reach. While the elite's immediate subordinates tend to be disproportionately white and male, over the last few decades modest numbers of people of color and white women have moved into some important elite-support positions, as we see here.

In the Rwanda case, money was a clear measure of how little importance the elites and their subordinate officials placed on the genocide. For example, at the outset, the UN requested that the Clinton administration provide trucks for an evacuation of vulnerable Rwandans, but White House officials vacillated over who would foot the modest bill. In stark contrast, for an assortment of U.S. political and economic reasons, the aforementioned cases of Iran and Guatemala in the 1950s and Chile in the 1970s were of far greater importance to, and got much more attention from, Washington policymakers and U.S. corporations.

Elite Racial Framing: "Some . . . More Human Than Others"

The United Nations Assistance Mission for Rwanda (UNAMIR) was established by the UN Security Council in 1993. UN peacekeepers under General Dallaire were mandated to observe the Rwandan ceasefire and help fulfill a peace agreement between the Hutu-controlled government and the Tutsi rebel group, the Rwandan Patriotic Front (RPF). However, from the beginning, UNAMIR did not have the western and other political, logistical, and monetary backing it needed. Months before genocidal violence

began, Dallaire and his UN superior had incessantly, and often unsuccess-
fully, petitioned UN headquarters for necessary equipment.[49] In a later
book, Dallaire summed up lessons from the Rwandan events:

> We need to re-emphasize the principle of justice for all, so that no
> one for even a moment will make the ethical and moral mistake of
> ranking some humans as more human than others, a mistake that the
> international community endorsed by its indifference in 1994.[50]

Ever since, Dallaire has been critical of top U.S., European, and UN officials
for their racialized and unethical indifference to black Rwandans.

In important ways the negative white racial framing of Africa and Africans served as one basis for western powers' complicity in this genocide. The
readiness of white political leaders and other white officials to define the lives
of black Rwandans as *less valuable* than white Europeans and Americans
signaled a racist framing in ways similar to the dominant white framing of
black Americans over centuries. For example, in 1964 the white-controlled
U.S. media were unusually riveted on Philadelphia, Mississippi, where white
men in the Ku Klux Klan and at least one white police officer conspired to
murder civil rights workers, one black and two white. Civil rights leader Ella
Baker was asked to comment on these brutal murders: "The unfortunate
thing is that it took this [the murder of two whites] . . . to make the rest
of the country turn its eyes on the fact that there were other [black] bodies lying in the swamps of Mississippi."[51] Unfortunately, Baker's words are
applicable to the dramatically different official U.S. responses to the Rwandan genocide in Africa and the Bosnian war crimes in southern Europe that
occurred about the same time. The former genocide involved many black
deaths; the latter genocide involved many white deaths.

The focal point of much U.S. white elite framing of foreign affairs has been
the view that white officials have a *right* to intervene, or to not intervene,
in the affairs of other countries whenever they deem their vital political-
economic interests to be at stake. Sitting in government and UN offices in
Washington, New York, London, or Paris, mostly white elite officials and
their immediate subordinates assumed the right to determine if murders of
hundreds of thousands of black Rwandans were to be considered genocide
requiring a serious U.S. and international response.

Bill Clinton and U.S. Interests

The foreign policy scholar and diplomat Samantha Power has explained
why the mostly white Washington elite, including President Bill Clinton,
chose U.S. national interests over the obvious humanitarian concerns in
Rwanda. In her view these high-level officials were confident that "they

were doing all they *should*" given "competing American interests." Further, accepting their viewpoint, Power has suggested that these top policymakers "understandably" presumed that it would damage their credibility if they even referred to the Rwandan violence as "genocide" while doing nothing to stop it. Major U.S. news agencies, mostly controlled by powerful white executives, also concluded that the United States had "no recognizable national interest in taking a role, certainly not a leading role."[52]

In the decades since, Bill Clinton and other white officials have been unfavorably labeled *bystanders* by some analysts. However, they did do many things that allowed or facilitated the genocide. For instance, they refused to send U.S. Marines already in a neighboring country to Rwanda as a deterrent to early mass killings, but kept them nearby in case evacuation of U.S. nationals went wrong. U.S. officials also worked to get most UN peacekeepers withdrawn and refused to block a Rwandan hate-radio station organizing the genocide.[53]

Additionally, Clinton and his cabinet officials intentionally played down and whitewashed the genocide, including actually suppressing the word *genocide*. In 1998, before Clinton's claims of ignorance were exposed as deceitful by declassified documents, he offered a fake apology to the Rwandans:

> It may seem strange to you here, especially the many of you who lost members of your family. But all over the world there were people like me sitting in offices . . . who did not fully appreciate the depth and speed with which you were being engulfed by this unimaginable terror.[54]

Actually, Clinton knew of the "*final solution* to eliminate all Tutsis" as early as April 1994, the first month of the genocide. Numerous CIA briefings concerning the genocide had been circulated to Clinton and senior officials. Yet, most Clinton administration officials did not even recall one cabinet-level meeting to discuss the murderous events in Rwanda.[55]

The Black Congressional Caucus pressed Clinton to act, and human rights activist Monique Mujawamariya personally pled with him to do something to help halt the violence. She later recounted a conversation with a U.S. official responsible for Africa, who offered an explanation for her inability to convince Clinton: the U.S. "has no friends," only "interests," and "there is no interest in Rwanda. . . . we are not interested in sending young American Marines to bring them back in coffins. We have no incentive."[56] This official mirrored Clinton's words in a 1994 speech at the U.S. Naval Academy. Clinton asserted that whether "we get involved in any of the world's ethnic conflicts . . . must depend on the cumulative weight of the American interests at stake. . . . our interests are not sufficiently at stake in so many of them to justify a commitment." Most centrally, he meant the political-economic interests of the mostly white male U.S. elite.[57] In our view, a negative white framing of Africans seems to have been one root cause for Clinton's unwillingness to intervene. Ignoring African concerns when it suited him politically was not new; like most U.S. officials for decades he generally displayed very little interest in the conditions and politics of African countries.

While the Tutsi military organization did eventually defeat the Hutu authorities responsible for the horrific genocide, there were long weeks of killing, raping, and torture, weeks during which the Clinton administration *could* have acted to save many thousands. Once the classified files were public, Clinton did acknowledge that, had his administration intervened at the start, at least 300,000 Rwandans might have survived.[58]

High Administration Officials: Rationalizing and Resisting Action

In describing Donald Steinberg, the National Security Council Director for African Affairs during the genocide, commentator Iain Dale wrote critically that Steinberg advised Clinton

> to keep well out of [Rwanda]—possibly one of the worst pieces of advice given to an American President in . . . 20 years. . . . he is representative of a class of so-called public servants who . . . feel quite at home in the United Nations and thrive in making excuses for that organization's terrible failures.[59]

Another key white official, Bob Dole, the Republican Senate minority leader (1987–1995), also accented U.S. interest: "I don't think we have any national interest there. . . . The Americans are out, and as far as I'm concerned, in Rwanda, that ought to be the end of it."[60] Clearly, these top white officials made lethal decisions regarding the lives of hundreds of thousands of people openly deemed *irrelevant* to U.S. socio-political interests.

In October 1993, Tony Lake (UN National Security Adviser to President Clinton), Richard Clarke, and his Deputy Susan Rice submitted a draft letter to an adviser of the French president. The communication accompanying the draft clarified that, even though the United Nations Assistance Mission for Rwanda might have a chance of success, the Clinton White House was unenthusiastic. Clarke or Rice underlined text that read "*US troops will not participate.*"[61] As important Clinton emissaries, they were determined to set high ceilings for U.S. involvement in any peacekeeping operations.

In addition, for most of the 100 days in which genocidal violence unfolded, top officials publicly framed the violence there as only a "civil war." For a time Secretary of State Warren Christopher ordered spokespersons to *not* use the word *genocide*, even after reading a briefing describing

Hutu declarations of a "final solution to eliminate all Tutsis." This would have been imprudent because U.S.-supported intervention was never on the table. When he later permitted officials to sort of use the term, he weakened its impact by authorizing "acts of genocide" as the terminology.[62] This language suppression is an example of George Orwell's famous "newspeak," his term for elite thought control in his novel *1984*.[63] Once again, Christopher, a powerful white official, got to decide even what was genocide or what was not. Belatedly on June 14, Christopher conceded that the "operative term, from a legal standpoint" was genocide. The Tutsi, at the mercy of Hutu killers for 70 days, would certainly have considered the use of "genocide" appropriate long before. Additionally, the potential for the bloody news reports to upset the image of the mostly white-run U.S. government's *virtuousness* in its overseas efforts was great, so a belated attempt was made to publicly construct U.S. foreign policy as humanitarian. In contrast, however, in 2014 international experts gathered at a history conference to discuss the Rwandan genocide and agreed that the UN withdrawal, pushed by top U.S. officials, was a "green light" for that genocide.[64]

A Few White Dissenters to Whitewashing Genocide

A few powerful white men, mostly *outside* the United States, did dissent from the Clinton administration's whitewashed language and failure to act. They included Canadian General Dallaire; Canadian Major Brent Beardsley, who served as Dallaire's staff officer; New Zealand's Colin Keating, Ambassador to the UN; David Hannay, Britain's UN Ambassador; and Mark Doyle, a British journalist who reported from Rwanda. The lone American in this major group was the missionary Carl Wilkens.

Once the genocidal violence was unleashed, and under western pressure, the UN Peacekeeping Operations agency sent General Dallaire, in charge of peacekeeping in Rwanda, a cable. Reminiscent of the indifference that earlier 20th century European imperial powers exhibited toward colonial subjects of color, it read: "You should make every effort not to compromise your impartiality or to act beyond your mandate. . . . but [you] may exercise your discretion to do [so] should this be essential for the evacuation of foreign nationals."[65] U.S., French, Belgian, and Italian troops arrived to begin the mass evacuation of their citizens, but no others.

Comparing the genocidal actions in the European Balkans war to those in Rwanda, Dallaire shed light on the white racial framing of Africa among white North American and European elites:

> In Yugoslavia, the problems were portrayed as long-standing divisions that educated people had debated. It was religious and ethnic conflict, something studied and analyzed. As such, we brought in new terms,

like "ethnic cleansing" to describe Yugoslavia. In Rwanda, it was just a bunch of tribes going at each other, like they always do. Rwanda was black. Yugoslavia was white European.[66]

All western troops and UN peacekeepers were under orders from government officials not to evacuate Rwandans. Later, in 2004, the white Canadian officer Brent Beardsley explained what this meant:

[A]nybody that was white-skinned got to get on an airplane and fly to safety, and anybody that was black-skinned got to stay in Rwanda and get killed. . . . It still to this day leaves a very, very bad taste in my mouth that the United States of America could have 350 Marines sitting at Bujumbura Airport, that the French were able to get in 500 or so paratroopers.[67]

Beardsley angrily recalled that top-ranking U.S. and UN officials later claimed it was impossible to get troops to save the Rwandans. But these were face-saving deceits, for troops were actively deployed to "save white people. And that's what it came down to. . . . The [white] world just didn't care."[68]

On April 8, 1994 President Clinton chose to evacuate *U.S. nationals* from Rwanda, and the only American to remain was Carl Wilkens, a white missionary. He explained: "I've got this blue American passport. . . . But all of these people don't have a passport. They can't go."[69] Wilkens' courageous actions in Rwanda likely saved more lives during the genocide than the entire U.S. government operation.

Some Critical American Voices

Significantly, at a 2014 meeting of former Rwandan officials and international policymakers who managed the response to the genocide, Prudence Bushnell, a U.S. Deputy Assistant Secretary of State for African Affairs during the genocide period, supported the assessment that Clinton administration policymakers showed little interest in Rwanda. "I was way down the totem pole and I had responsibility for the Rwanda portfolio. That shows you how important it was in the U.S. government."[70] Her words captured the power differential between elite men at the top and their lower-level acolytes. Still, she clung to convenient myths which rested on a white racial framing, including that the White House did not know "it" was genocide. She has described the administration view: "What I was told was . . . 'these people do this from time to time.' We thought we'd be right back."[71] Here we observe stereotyped rationalizations about "these people" at the heart of much white racial framing of black Africans—what sociologist Ben

Carrington has called the old "white colonial frame."[72] Note that Bushnell was the major state department official in charge of African Affairs.

There is deep significance in white officials' constant racial framing of the people of Africa. Historically, as much of this book demonstrates, white westerners have *not* been less prone to horrific violence than Africans. White Americans have long been guilty of large-scale violence against people of color, including the centuries of genocidal targeting of indigenous Americans and of violent enslavement and segregation of African Americans.

Recall, for example, that in 1951 African American leaders presented a major petition to the United Nations that was entitled, "We Charge Genocide: The Crime of Government Against the Negro People." Drawing on a black antiracist counter-framing of U.S. society, the well-documented petition pushed back against the dominant white racial frame and comprehensively described how in the United States white officials had propagated for many decades Jim Crow's discriminatory, often violent actions against African Americans. These leaders rightfully judged these as genocidal according to provisions of the new UN Genocide Convention.[73] Moreover, echoing this petition decades later, Dr. Jeremiah Wright, then President Barack Obama's minister, famously proclaimed a critical black counter-frame that criticized the U.S. government's recurring racial oppression, exposing as false the superior white virtuousness central to the white frame. White officials had long engaged in the actions like those described in the 1951 petition:

> [W]hen it came to treating her citizens of Indian descent fairly, she failed. She put them on reservations. When it came to treating her citizens of Japanese descent fairly, she failed. She put them in internment prison camps. When it came to treating citizens of African descent fairly. . . . The government put them on slave quarters, put them on auction blocks, put them in cotton fields, put them in inferior schools, put them in substandard housing, put them in scientific experiments, put them in the lowest paying jobs.[74]

During the Rwandan genocide, numerous brave black voices called out U.S. and European elites' true motives. For instance, Paul Kagame, the black commander of the Tutsi military organization and later Rwandan president, has wondered whether such killings of many thousands of Americans would have been ignored. Years later, he discussed conversations he had with Secretary Bushnell during the genocide: "I hate remembering the conversations. Hundreds of thousands of people are being killed . . . [and she] was talking about something else that had nothing to do with saving the lives of these people."[75] Soon after the genocide ended, as the new Rwandan president, he had also told Bushnell, "You, Madame, are partially responsible for the genocide, because we told you what was going to happen and you did nothing."[76]

Failures in the U.S. and International Media

Unquestionably, the Rwandan genocide demonstrates that western media coverage of international humanitarian crises is very uneven and usually white-framed. During the genocide far greater attention was riveted on white European victims of the Balkans war. Indeed, the U.S. mainstream media even gave far more coverage to trendy topics like the rivalry between major U.S. figure skaters. During the genocide period only *one* significant editorial on Rwanda was ever published in the *New York Times* or the *Washington Post*, the country's major newspapers of record.[77]

Interestingly, David Bleich has argued that much academic analysis in his field of linguistics has been done from a heavily male viewpoint. His findings seem accurate for scholarship in many fields, as well as for mainstream media coverage of national and international issues. Actually, much scholarly and media analysis is presented from an *elite-white* or *elite-white-male* viewpoint. That elite-white-male perspective helps to explain, among other issues, why just the statistical *number* of people killed in the Rwandan genocide has become the common media and official gauge of that human catastrophe.[78] Other important aspects have gotten far less attention. Thus, thanks to mainstream media presentations shaped by disproportionately male producers, even the modest coverage of the Rwandan genocide rarely referenced the huge number of rapes of Tutsi and moderate Hutu women carried out by male Hutu extremists. This white male media perspective regularly sanitizes or limits media and other public discussions concerning the negative social and cultural climates, the systemic sexism, that women everywhere face.[79]

Conclusion

The implications of our analysis for understanding white-male-run, often imperialistic capitalism and other societal dominance go well beyond understanding that elite's discriminatory response to the Rwandan genocide or their interventionist role against democratization in Iran, Guatemala, and Chile. These are just a few cases out of many demonstrating the constant intertwining of centuries-old U.S. and other western capitalism, systemic racism, and systemic sexism. We observe their elite implementers' constant focus on their collective, usually elite-white-male, interests. This powerful group interest is usually constructed, rationalized, and legitimated in the shaping context of the dominant white racial frame and associated capitalistic and male sexist frames.

The U.S. Federal Bureau of Investigation (FBI) defines *terrorism* as

the unlawful use of force or violence committed by a group or individual, who has some connection to a foreign power or whose activities transcend national boundaries, against persons or property to
intimidate or coerce a government, the civilian population or any segment thereof, in furtherance of political or social objectives.

Philosopher Robert Elias notes that this definition fits many U.S. government interventions overseas.[80] Anti-democratic interventions in Iran,
Guatemala, Chile, and numerous other countries over the last century have
reflected not only the class (capitalistic) framing but also the white racial
framing of elite white, mostly male government and private decision-makers
that "western civilization" is under serious *threat* from groups of people
who are *not* white or European-descended. That is, they are "not like us" and
are cited as "those people." This sometimes subtle, often blatant racial framing frequently represents an emotional and defensive response to societal
changes, including a great and increasing fear of losing white (male) power
at home and abroad. Additionally, the white male elite's implicit and explicit
accents on national white manhood in their aggressive orientations and
actions also regularly helps to generate among ordinary white men greater
support for elite interests, as well as to buttress the latter's sense of their
own "tough-minded" manliness as they revel in the domination of people
of color overseas.

The case of Rwanda, one where top U.S. officials did not assertively intervene against the genocide, reflected cold calculations about white U.S. and
other western interests. General Roméo Dallaire underscored this: "It was
just an absolute perverse exercise of developed nations using excuses of
sovereignty and nationalism and involvement and self-interest, to argue
the way around one of the most fundamental premises: *Are these people
human?*"[81] These so-called developed nations are of course controlled by
powerful white men, and mainly in their own group's or country's interests. Their enduring legacy suggests that in their white racial framing they
consider themselves more *human*, virtuous, and deserving of personal and
group socioeconomic development, liberty, and justice than many other
human groups.

In some ways, little had changed since earlier western colonialism. In
the Rwandan case, most western policymakers still communicated a lack
of genuine concern with, and a racially framed understanding of, African
societies—which contain a large percentage of humanity. Arrogance among
elite whites and their major acolytes seems to regularly arise from their
unreflective sense of superior white values and common white western
framing of international issues. Without that racially framed orientation,

major U.S. policymakers would likely have listened to local African opinion on the coming genocide—and thereby saved many lives.[82]

Nor has U.S. imperialism ceased. Juan Cole, a prominent Middle Eastern scholar, has noted that the world's most populous country, China, has not "invaded anybody recently, whereas the US has thrashed about invading numerous countries, and droning the ones it didn't invade."[83] The asserted "civilizing" mission of classical U.S. and other western imperialism is ongoing, forcing many outside observers to perceptively ask today's white elite if *they* are civilized themselves.

5

More Oligopolistic Capitalism
The Current Neoliberal Era

It is Beijing, China. The future year is 2030. A Chinese professor lectures students on U.S. economic and political decline:

> Why do great nations fail? The Ancient Greeks, the Roman Empire, the British Empire, and the United States of America. They all make the same mistakes, turning their back on the principles that made them great. America tried to spend and tax itself out of a Great Recession. Enormous so-called "stimulus" spending, massive changes in health care, government takeovers of private industries and crushing debts. Of course, we [Chinese] owned most of their debt. So now they work for us.[1]

This 2010 advertisement revealed much about a major conservative shift in contemporary U.S. politics. Larry McCarthy, the white conservative behind other controversial political attack ads, produced this ad titled "Chinese Professor." Broadcast during the 2010 congressional elections, a conservative think tank paid for it.[2]

Observe the political attack on then-President Barack Obama's Affordable Care Act, which extended health care coverage to millions, and on his administration's stimulus package to jump-start the troubled economy inherited from Obama's Republican predecessor. The phrase "government takeovers" is a highly exaggerated attack on weak Obama administration commitments to reclaiming a little power that multinational corporations had stripped away from the U.S. government. The "Chinese Professor" ad endorses a version of capitalistic market fundamentalism known currently as "neoliberalism."

Neoliberalism: Privatization and Financialization

Contemporary U.S. capitalism in its neoliberal form is unlike classical economic liberalism of the 19th century because it views people as primarily market actors. Classical economic liberalism did assume human beings behave as market actors, but they are viewed as something else when it comes to their religious, familial, and political realms.[3] Because of the confusion caused by the term "liberalism" here, we will also use the more accurate phrase *oligopoly capitalism* for this reality. This contemporary capitalism, as noted throughout this book, is aggressively oligopolistic—that is, dominated in most of its major economic sectors by relatively few large firms. As we have already seen, it is also mostly white-male-controlled at the top, a reality that has routinely made a significant difference in how its capitalistic operations are also racialized and masculinized.

The geographer David Harvey has defined neoliberalism as a capitalistic system that involves an *accelerated* "accumulation by dispossession." This dispossession of others' lands and resources has always been central to western capitalism, but contemporary neoliberal capitalists often take their predatory ethic to a new level. As Harvey sees it, contemporary oligopolistic capitalism has these main pillars: accelerated privatization of public goods and services; aggressive financialization, in which many market goods are turned into instruments of economic speculation; increased economic crisis manipulations for capitalistic profit; and yet more government-assisted wealth redistribution upward to the top classes.[4] Neoliberals are market fundamentalists and insist that capitalistic market operations need little government regulation, that many government services should be privatized, and that much government social spending should be slashed. Actually much in this capitalistic approach, especially accenting privatization and austerity for most Americans, is not really new.[5]

In the United States and the United Kingdom, this particular reinvigoration of white oligopoly capitalism is commonly dated to begin in the era of the right-wing President Ronald Reagan (1981–1989) and right-wing British Prime Minister Margaret Thatcher (1979–1990), the powerful white politicians who helped to lead the charge to further exploit the labor and resources of people (mostly people of color) across the globe. At the core of this oligopoly capitalism is not only the old predatory ethic in a new disguise of "promoting democracy" across the globe, but also the celebrated mythology of "meritocracy" in regard to the United States and the United Kingdom. These countries are mythologically framed in mainstream media and elsewhere in classist terms as countries of great socioeconomic opportunity and mobility for all; as countries where racial, gender, and class hierarchies are now unimportant; and as countries where unrestricted competition does regularly compensate individual hard work and innovation.[6]

The "Chinese Professor" ad advocates the neoliberal ideas of government deregulation of commerce and labor, reduced government, and privatization of public programs. It implies an ominous "Yellow Peril" Asian stereotype, with ruthless Chinese looming over a complacent United States. The ad is meant to instill fear, especially among whites, that they will no longer dominate global commerce and politics. There is the implication that the United States is truly democratic and not itself sinister in global actions. Implied is that the entire world will be worse off if the white-controlled United States is no longer in charge of the global economy. Actually, however, several Latin American countries recorded a strong drop in poverty once the Washington elite shifted most neoliberal pressures and actions away from them to the Middle East and Asia. If the power of the mostly white male U.S. corporate and government decision-makers to shape the economies of other countries declined, such a shift would likely be good for most of the world's population.[7]

The neoliberal ideology accents a supposedly free and deregulated market with lots of competing businesses, yet neoliberal practice fuels the *oligopolistic* power of a modest number of large global corporations in ever-expanding neocolonial and economic-concentration efforts. Large multinational firms usually benefit much more than smaller businesses from most financial and business deregulation, removal of tariff barriers, and reduction of government support programs to reduce business taxes. The white male corporate executives often heading up the larger multinational corporations are also substantially responsible for the deindustrialization, automation, and export of jobs overseas that have in recent decades cost many U.S. blue-collar workers of all racial backgrounds their good-paying jobs.

These negative effects of neoliberalism—including, as Maria Mies underscores, "rising unemployment, a new wave of poverty, more exploitation of workers, more ecological destruction"—have obviously been noted by most working people. This has resulted in much political opposition to free-trade policies, but as Mies also notes, over time "this opposition became weaker, because the international corporations were able to throw more and cheaper commodities from 'low-wage countries' onto the global market."[8] That is, workers in rich countries are bought off by consumer goods, which heads off much protest there. Eventually, however, many workers "in the erstwhile rich countries lose their jobs and face poverty."[9]

Moreover, once firmly enshrined in political arenas, neoliberal "free market" values and associated political efforts have led to significant privatization of important public services and increased the profits of the corporations thus involved.[10]

Global Impacts: Contemporary U.S. Capitalism

The global economic reality is actually scarier than the "Chinese Professor" ad would have U.S. voters believe, and for a hidden reason. In the United States and Europe contemporary oligopoly capitalism has made international "emperors" out of privileged white men, while their corporate policies have frequently had negative impacts on workers and consumers the world over, including for people of color, who are most of the world's population.

Oligopolistic capitalism requires new types of overseas imperialism to keep it going. Central to this process is, yet again, accumulation by violent dispossession. Today, U.S. and other western corporate capitalists and the governments they control often use their police and militaries to back up these exploitative processes of resource and labor dispossession across the globe. In addition to the continuing theft of lands, mineral resources, and labor of peoples of color overseas, new capitalistic ways to dispossess people have been created. This includes aggressive corporate patenting and licensing of "genetic materials, seed plasmas, and all manner of other products," often thereby limiting necessary access to them by small farmers and other small producers.[11]

Moreover, the coalition of large Wall Street and other U.S. multinational corporations, the U.S. Treasury Department, and international financial organizations like the International Monetary Fund (IMF) dominates global monetary and financial transactions involving the world's many economies. Mostly dominated at the top by white men, this international network usually operates effectively because most of the world's major economic actors are well "networked and successfully hooked into . . . a structured framework of interlocking financial and governmental (including supra-national) institutions."[12] One additional aspect of such organizations is that they help to coordinate and integrate the various segments of the U.S. power elite.

A report by the UN Conference on Trade and Development on the dramatic *failures* of globalized neoliberalism should have served as the epitaph for the "free market" economic model developed by conservative economists. Given the report's sobering findings, the IMF, World Bank, Organization for Economic Co-operation and Development (OECD), countless business schools, and nearly every government should have done as some Latin American countries did and rid themselves of neoliberal market-fundamentalist thinking. However, the powerful whites who benefit greatly from this market fundamentalism, and who mostly control the world's major financial institutions and major western governments, do not want to see an end to the market fundamentalism associated with oligopolistic capitalism. It does not matter, as this UN report documents, that market fundamentalism has often produced devastating economic results contrary to those projected. The resulting greater economic inequality, less stable economies, and lower economic growth rates in part of the globe are of little concern to white elites made richer by neoliberalism. Nor does it matter to them that since the 1980s, with the onset of privatizing effects, deregulating labor, slashing taxes on the rich, and gouging social support programs, that economic growth rates have often plummeted and unemployment has often grown.[13] The ultra-rich white male establishment continues to endorse neoliberal economic theory and apply it, irrespective of its devastating human results.

The International Monetary Fund (IMF): Enforcing Neoliberal Capitalism

Over several decades, from Argentina to Greece to Zambia and many other countries, powerful IMF officials' "structural adjustment" programs have forced theoretically independent governments to adopt policies resulting in destruction of ordinary people's jobs, health, and other living conditions. The U.S. elite wields a disproportionate quota of the IMF votes. The market-fundamentalist goals have often been enforced irrespective of national contexts, as the IMF officials mostly have done the bidding of white male elites in the most powerful nations, and they often have forced subordinated national governments to discard their progressive social policies. Every country the IMF has colonized monetarily has been required to make inflation control its economic priority, lessen government expenditures, accommodate its banking system to outsiders, jettison obstacles to the flow of international oligopoly-capital, eliminate trade barriers, and privatize assets that can be hawked to outside investors.[14]

The IMF is a component in the time-honored ritual of advancing the imperialistic and pecuniary interests of western countries' white elites, while subordinating the human welfare of most others—and especially the world's majority, people of color. Indeed, the heartless IMF austerity levied on some southern Europeans in the 2010s was relatively modest as judged against previous varieties of austerity oppression imposed for centuries by elite western officials.[15]

The recent European example of Greece provides an example of what can happen when there are populist revolts against powerful white officials. The latter officials may be forced into temporary compromises. One economist referred to the Greek populace's protests against neoliberalism as a "heroic rebellion by a very beleaguered people against a doctrine which has been destroying their lives—the austerity doctrine and the whole neoliberal project."[16] Put simply, European banks headed by mostly white men agreed to accept 50 cents for every dollar owed to the banks by the Greek government. However, in exchange the embattled Greek government had to adopt severe austerity measures, including decreasing pay for public workers and sweeping cuts to social services.[17]

Neoliberal Attacks on President Barack Obama's Policies

The same year this critical UN report was released on neoliberalism, the "Chinese Professor" ad was re-aired during the U.S. 2012 presidential election. Despite the failures of neoliberal capitalism, casting then-President Obama and his more progressive social reforms as anti-corporatist was seen by Republican conservatives as a way to attack the incumbent president and elevate his rival Mitt Romney, a former corporate CEO. Obama's policies on healthcare, undocumented immigrants, solar energy, and civil rights enforcement were often at odds with the classist and racist goals of many in the large conservative wing of the corporate elite. While Obama adopted a moderate neoliberal approach to economic issues, Romney was a conservative oligopoly capitalist himself. The United States has often been distinguished by *aggressive* neoliberal control exercised by influential white men associated with large corporations—for example, the Romney team (i.e., Governors George and Mitt Romney) and the Bush team (i.e., Wall Street executive banker and Senator Prescott Bush, presidents George H. W. Bush and George W. Bush, and Governor Jeb Bush).

According to conservative rhetoric like that in the "Chinese Professor" ad, President Obama was too lenient in dealing with the Chinese government. Yet, as numerous research analysts have noted, an aggressive arms race is unnecessary because the Chinese government does not appear interested in empire-building outside its immediate geographical area. Instead, it seems intent on national and global economic growth. Currently, the United States has *hundreds* of military bases around the world, but China has *none* outside its borders.[18]

Those heading up the Washington foreign policy establishment, again mostly white men, have long been acclimatized to being dominant power players globally and have shown little willingness to share significant international power with emerging countries' officials. As is evidenced in the eastward expansion of the North Atlantic Treaty Organization (NATO) into former Soviet countries since the 1990s, the mostly white men who rule Washington seem intent on maintaining a globally expansive and imperialist U.S. foreign policy, even if this is not what a majority of Americans want.[19]

Oligopoly Capitalism: White Racial Framing and Non-Elite Whites

One of our terms for the realities of contemporary capitalism in the West, *oligopoly capitalism*, calls out the reality of relatively few people, in this case powerful white (male) corporate executives and government officials, who are mostly behind the recent resurgence of market fundamentalism. We adopt Noël Cazenave's call to reject the common practice of docile *linguistic accommodation* in assessing U.S. society. This unwillingness to name societal realities for what they really are has clearly slowed the development of our conceptual and empirical understandings of systemic sexism, classism, and racism. Linguistic *confrontation* is necessary for a candid analysis of these major systems of oppression.[20]

Market fundamentalism is intended to safeguard elite economic privileges globally through necessary neoliberal government actions. It is thus centrally about protecting white male power. But the public presentation of these neoliberal strategies by the capitalistic establishment generally obscures this truth. That the main actors behind market fundamentalism have mostly been powerful *white men* continues to be obscured in almost all media. Even progressive analysts celebrated for critiquing neoliberalism usually fail to address systemic racism's and sexism's central role in this neoliberalism.[21] Throughout this book our terminology brings important attention to the racial and gender dimensions of contemporary neoliberal capitalistic decision-making. Unmistakably, powerful white men play leading roles in oligopoly capitalism as most of its principal architects, implementers, and overseers.

They are often Orwellian in trying to make critical modes of thought difficult, such as when they effectively erase terms and concepts like *systemic racism* and *systemic sexism* from the public and academic lexicons. Powerful whites regularly circulate and act out of their racist and sexist framing even while arrogantly promoting the mythology of the United States being a post-racist and post-sexist society.[22] Thus, recent survey data indicate their continuing success in promoting such mythologies. For example, one U.S. survey found that 56 percent of men (higher for young men) believed that gender discrimination that "made it harder for women than men to get ahead" was *largely gone*, even though only 34 percent of women agreed.[23]

Still Trying to Buy Off Ordinary Whites: Images of Whiteness

As we have frequently seen, there are many close ties between contemporary capitalism, systemic racism, and systemic sexism. Today's mostly white male leading capitalists and their implementing assistants regularly downplay societal inequalities by means of racial and class framing, including meritocratic "bootstrap" narratives. Thus, according to this mythical storyline, whites sit atop the racial hierarchy because they possess the necessary mental and moral "superior stuff" to pull themselves up the societal ladder. In contrast, subordinate racial groups occupy lower rungs because they purportedly possess a proclivity for less intelligence, criminal behavior, laziness, and other individual and collective defects. Again, we observe key subframes of the dominant white frame usually in tandem: the deep-seated pro-white subframe (positive placement of supposedly *virtuous* whites) and then the anti-others frames (negative placement of supposedly *unvirtuous* people of color). The pro-white subframe articulated routinely by the ruling elite is central to white-run oligopoly capitalism, as it directly and indirectly legitimates the "superior" work values, intellectual acumen, and moral goodness of most whites.[24]

White-run oligopoly capitalism involves a racial framing favored not only by economically privileged whites, but also by non-elite whites. In understanding this phenomenon, recall the astute analysis of W. E. B. Du

Bois. Observing the impact of white racism on southern white workers in the mid-20th century, he described the wage of whiteness they accepted: "They were given public deference and titles of courtesy because they were white. They were admitted freely with all classes of white people to public functions, public parks, and the best schools."[25] For many decades the racial framing accenting white supremacy that was drilled into heads of ordinary whites by elite whites, and then perpetuated in their families, prohibited the possibility that they and black workers could unite against the exploitation of white male capitalists.

Just as white workers in earlier centuries accepted white privileges and status in the racial hierarchy, today the majority of non-elite whites accept a racially framed society with elite-generated language and action favoring government cutbacks and privatization as good for all people, and especially whites. Sociologist Randolph Hohle has explained how the reinvigorated, often somewhat coded, racial framing of powerful whites since the 1960s has been associated with an aggressive reinvigoration of capitalistic privatization and other market fundamentalism. The 1960s civil rights movement inadvertently helped the white corporate elite to push nationwide for corporate expansion and market fundamentalism, but especially in formerly segregated southern and border state areas.

Expanding their economic interests in these areas, the white economic elite successfully networked with formerly segregationist white government officials to reduce government regulations they deemed objectionable. This enabled the mostly white regional and national corporate capitalists—such as bankers, insurance executives, and manufacturers—to secure the implementation of market fundamentalism's goals of major reductions in taxes and government regulations and of the aggressive privatization of certain government services. Since the 1960s, the implicit or explicit racialized language and framing of *white = private = superior* has often characterized neoliberal corporate goals and associated government privatization policies, from which small and large white-owned businesses usually profit. In contrast, the implicit or explicit racialized language and framing of *black/brown = public = inferior* has frequently characterized white officials' views and policies on existing public school systems, existing public social services, and much proposed new public spending. Since this racialized neoliberal thinking came to the forefront in the 1960s and 1970s, to speak of "public schools" or "public spending" has often had very racialized, yet coded meanings for a great many whites.[26] Here again we see the deep-seated pro-white subframe (i.e., the positive evaluation of white actions and privatization goals) and the anti-others subframes (i.e., the negative evaluation of oppressed people of color and their needed public facilities) in a sustained and everyday political-economic example.

Today, neoliberal rhetoric has, yet again, depoliticized much class conflict by persuading ordinary whites to continue to view their dominant social status first in racial terms (i.e., "superior" white) and only secondarily in class terms (i.e., working or middle-class). A majority of ordinary whites, who have long adopted the dominant racial framing created by elite white men, fear or suspect that numerous government policies are much too oriented to African Americans and other Americans of color. Despite the detrimental economic and other impacts of this elitist market fundamentalism on *ordinary whites*, it persists because of the aforementioned psychological wage of whiteness strongly accepted by a majority of whites. Despite overwhelming proof that major tax cuts mainly or disproportionately benefit economic elites and other economically advantaged groups, and often do not generate the predicted job growth for ordinary workers or increases in government revenues, the white working and middle classes have continued to support oligopoly capitalism. Since the 1960s, as George Lipsitz underscores, numerous racially segregated white middle class neighborhoods and networks have provided major "sources of mobilization for tax limitation, defunding the public sector, and denying social services to minorities and immigrants."[27]

Clearly, too, contemporary neoliberalism has involved an elite male response to some attempts at women's liberation from systemic sexism in economic and government decision-making. While a rather small group of (mainly white) women have been celebrated for their advancements in corporate management, a great many women workers, especially those in the working and lower middle classes, have been disproportionately hurt by large neoliberal cutbacks in local, state, and federal government jobs and in certain government social programs (e.g., "welfare reform"). In contrast, well-off, mostly white men have benefitted much more than non-elite women of all backgrounds from the numerous neoliberal tax decreases and corporate privatization opportunities.[28]

The Great Recession and Bailouts: Oligopoly Capitalism in Action

We will now examine a few examples of important pro-business, antiregulation "ole boys" networks that link white Washington officials, Wall Street firms, and other significant economic organizations of contemporary oligopoly capitalism. Many people in these very powerful networks cling to market fundamentalism despite its demonstrated failures. Consider the inner workings of this government-linked oligopoly capitalism. It is still a restricted world of largely white and male privilege, one where in the first decade of the 21st century helicopters took corporate CEOs from the roofs of office buildings to golf weekends despite an impending financial meltdown. It is a world in which there is nothing odd about elites traveling by corporate jet to seek billions in bailout funds from government officials. It is a realm in which mostly white lobbyists think it is acceptable to pay homeless people of color a pittance to wait in line for them on Capitol Hill in order to get good seats for congressional hearings.[29] Indeed, such actions as these signal that these elite men are extraordinarily hypocritical when they frame poor Americans as "lazy" and "entitled."

Recession and the Troubled Asset Relief Program

Significantly, from the outset of his presidency, George W. Bush and his neoliberal advisers adopted a philosophy of significant government deregulation, a perspective that seeped into leadership in many federal agencies—thus freeing bankers and mortgage brokers from much government oversight. This approach was nearly catastrophic. Beginning in the Bush years, the "Great Recession" (2007–2009) brought major national and global fiscal crises. Washington and Wall Street powerholders knowingly left millions homeless and in dire financial situations.

The U.S. Treasury Department's $700 billion Troubled Asset Relief Program (TARP) is central to this dramatic tale. Treasury Secretary Henry Paulson (2006–2009) described this massive program as providing funds to "strengthen" banks in rough economic times. Observe the erasure of the term "bailout" from the political lexicon, as well as the role of powerful white men in this extreme financial crisis, which their economic class had created. The "Troubled Asset Relief Program" was not a *relief* program, but a large-scale corporate *bailout* to offset the huge contemporary damage done by white male corporate capitalists.

Difficult economic times did not appear out of nowhere; the predatory ethic and corruption of this white financial elite made it so. Paulson, former CEO of the investment firm Goldman Sachs, and President Bush, former oil baron, pushed TARP through Congress to rescue fellow members of the white elite. Treasury officials launched programs under the massively funded TARP that were supposed to help struggling families avoid mortgage foreclosures, stabilize the financial system, and revive economic growth. In actuality, operating out of the old profitmaking ethic, the mostly white male executives at various financial corporations hoarded much of the money they got, increased and tightened lending as they saw fit, bolstered their firms' capital, and made acquisitions of other troubled companies.[30] This TARP bailout became yet more government "socialism for rich whites." Accounting for the TARP and other federal bailouts, roughly $600 billion was invested, loaned, or paid out from taxpayer funds to mostly white and male top corporate executives.[31]

Business moguls responsible for the economic meltdown mostly escaped serious public censure or criminal prosecution, and were bailed out.

Nonetheless, in the time-honored tradition of poor-bashing, it was financially underprivileged Americans who continued to be cast publicly as lazy and entitled by elite whites and their acolytes. During the Great Recession economic losses, especially from defaulting on home loans, fell more heavily on blacks and Latinos than on whites. The main reason was that they had been disproportionately pressured to take high-interest home loans (see below). Nonetheless, Mitt Romney, the 2012 Republican nominee for president, accused President Obama's supporters of being overly reliant on government handouts and of feeling "entitled."[32] Romney seemed to be labeling people of color as such, but did not similarly condemn Wall Street executives who were reliant on large government subsidy handouts. The latter were mostly white, male, prosperous, and feeling entitled.

Additionally, the white CEO of Whitney National Bank, John C. Hope III, told Wall Street analysts that his institution did not plan to help struggling homeowners, despite the $300 million in federal bailout money it had been given *to do just that*. Most people might be afraid to publicly label a mogul like Hope as entitled, for his bank had branches from Texas to Florida.[33] Other powerful men demonstrated the same sense of white elite entitlement. The president of Boston Private Wealth Management deemed his bailout funds as a way to "ride out the recession," and PlainsCapital's top executive referred to TARP money as "opportunity capital." The chief executive of Flushing Financial in New York blithely described TARP as a way to up the "ante for acquisitions" of other firms.[34] These leading white male bankers highlighted the gap between the public's anticipation for how the $700 billion in TARP funds should be spent and the actual choices made by white financiers. The Treasury Department's main priority coincided with bankers' interests. By giving banks full autonomy to use TARP funds as they deemed fit, the Treasury indicated that the priority was just to stabilize markets, not to enhance the economic security of ordinary taxpayers.[35]

Yet, as leading white bankers raked in salaries in millions, another story of ordinary families unfolded. As of 2017, most white households had begun to recover from the most damaging consequences of the Great Recession, whereas a great many black households continued to experience economic troubles and declines. The opposing recoveries are significant since they added to the racial wealth gap. The long-term impact of the discriminatory lending practices is crucial. The Great Recession disproportionately affected, and its legacy continues to disproportionately affect, families of color.[36]

The White Oligarchy's Revolving Doors

The "revolving door" concept captures the tendency among elite Washington government officials and top corporate executives to shuttle back and forth between important government agencies and leading corporations.

For example, while working in Washington agencies the mostly white male finance capitalists often safeguard the privileges of Wall Street via favorable laws and regulations, thereby reducing government fortifications against corporate plundering. Back at Wall Street, many amass millions because of laws and regulations they instigated or eliminated when in government. Similar patterns develop for other corporate executives. Then, usually when their party's presidential candidate returns to the White House, they may return to federal agencies. Once more, they use the government power to guarantee that this oligarchical back-and-forth compensates them and other corporate executives generously.[37]

Describing this privileged system, Neil Barofsky, the Inspector General who oversaw the TARP program, has noted that, regardless of the escalating destruction of the financial crisis, top Washington officials seemed reluctant to question the honesty and virtuousness of their past employers and others in the financial elite.[38] Given the revolving door, the view among leading Washington decision-makers that those in the Wall Street elite were entitled to huge sums of money, even as regular Americans suffered greatly because of their actions, is substantially about their self-validation. Consider Henry Paulson, former top Goldman Sachs executive and Bush's Treasury Secretary. Several sources name Paulson as a major contributor to the financial collapse because he and Federal Reserve executive Timothy Geithner (later, Barack Obama's Treasury Secretary) had expedited bankruptcy claims of the global financial services firm Lehman Brothers. As a result, the commercial paper market collapsed. (Commercial paper is issued by large corporations to acquire funds to meet short-term debt obligations.)[39]

Once in Washington, Paulson was overly amenable to Wall Street demands. His potential conflicts of interest have been well-documented. Goldman Sachs received a TARP bailout estimated at $12.9 billion, the *largest* beneficiary of public funds from the insurance giant American International Group (AIG). To be sure, prior to appointment as Treasury Secretary, Paulson sold his stake in Goldman Sachs. Nonetheless, Paulson was a Wall Street insider whose relationships with the bailout beneficiaries, some analysts suggested, might have placed him in significant ethical quandaries.[40]

In Wall Street's private sector, former high government officials, mostly white males, receive much greater remuneration than in the public sector, as the corporate world sees the value in tapping their experience. Cerberus Capital Management LP, a private-equity firm, employed a former Treasury Secretary and a former Vice President. New York-based private-equity firm KKR & Co. employed the past CIA Director and Army General David Petraeus. New York-based private equity firm Blackstone Group LP appointed U.S. Army General Wesley Clark, former NATO commander in Europe, as an energy investments adviser. Even former President George H. W. Bush (1989–1993) is among the powerful white men who served as advisers to a Washington-based private equity firm.[41]

Neil Barofsky: Insightful White "Ole Boy"

Barofsky's description of the process by which he was made head of the TARP program demonstrates that he was in the white "ole boys" network. He was a senior prosecutor at the U.S. Attorney's office in New York when the massive economic crisis hit. A Democrat, he was nonetheless offered the TARP job by the departing Bush administration. In his book *Bailout*, Barofsky comments on the frequency and importance of these bipartisan alliances.[42] Top government financial officials under Republican and Democratic administrations have historically been pulled from an exclusive group of mostly white men on Wall Street. In Barofsky's case, the Republican Treasury Secretary Henry Paulson needed support to get the bailout passed through Congress, whose Democratic majorities might prove an obstacle.[43] Here again, another type of revolving door was in motion.

Barofsky recognizes this bipartisan network at work. However, like almost all participants and outside commentators, he does *not* acknowledge that it is largely white and male, as well as highly privileged. Commenting on the well-connected group of attorneys he worked with at the U.S. Attorney's office, he concluded that "largely because of my own membership in that club, they were welcoming me to Washington with open arms and conspiring with each other to get me through the confirmation process."[44] He makes a cursory observation that the office was mostly staffed with Ivy League graduates and second- or third-generation lawyers, but does not analyze the significance of these details. If he had, he might have noted the systemic inegalitarianism and white "ole boys network" there.[45] Such networking is essential to the integration of the factions within, and thus the maintenance of, the elite-white-male dominance system. Indeed, upper-class whites often insulate their children with the most prestigious educations and from real meritocratic competition. In countries like the United States, where white-run oligopoly capitalism has been aggressively maintained and expanded, social mobility for many ordinary people has declined considerably in recent decades. Note, too, that most whites among the latter do not understand the cause and are instead encouraged to blame immigrants and other people of color.

Barofsky offers a scathing review of the corruption defining the financial crisis and federal response, yet fails to assess the fact that the lawbreaking executives were mostly powerful *white men*. Their often arrogant white masculinist framing and their associated racial framing seem central to their decisions. In Barofsky's estimation the fraud-riddled "subprime" loans that were a crisis feature of the Great Recession were handed out to any applicant. But he is wrong, for these loans were *not* randomly given out. Subprime loans were very disproportionately targeted by lenders to African Americans and Latinos, who were thus much more likely than white homebuyers to take out these high-cost mortgages.[46] These subprime loans are customarily accompanied by higher interest rates, fees, and penalties—and are usually quite profitable for lenders.

In fact, the majority of black and Latino families had credit records good enough for loans with more favorable interest rates. These homebuyers were victims of discrimination by lenders, and thus much more likely than comparable white homebuyers to be offered high-interest loans. In Boston, for example, researchers found that black and Latino homebuyers were more than *four times* as likely as whites to have taken out a high-cost subprime mortgage.[47] In one New York case, a white loan officer at a leading white-owned bank admitted the bank's top officials viewed black families as targets for exploitative subprime mortgages. Numerous other white loan officers, some of whom referred to blacks as "mud people" and to subprime lending as "ghetto loans," methodically sought out blacks and Latinos for profitable subprime mortgages.[48]

The financial corruption that enraged Barofsky is only part of the private-public system of mistreatment and injustice where white officials operate out of a white racist framing of society. Despicable "pillagers" is how he describes the elite financiers responsible for the financial meltdown. That they were mainly white and male is *never* part of the otherwise critical account he offers.[49] That a knowledgeable analyst writes about the massive loan scandal without mentioning that fact and also that African Americans and Latinos were overwhelmingly its exploited victims is indicative of the white-male-dominated and white-framed world that powerful men like Barofsky occupy.

Some other white analysts went even further in demonstrating that they were operating explicitly out of a white racial frame of people of color. They portrayed the latter as substantially responsible for the subprime mortgage crisis. They used concepts like *cultural immorality* (e.g., "people of color are lazy") taken from the white frame. Yet, it was white executives and officials who held the reins of power and actually created these housing crises. As one anti-poverty activist has explained, "poor people have as much control over government . . . or think-tank theorizing about their future as lab rats have in a cancer experiment."[50] Repeatedly, the white male elite's choices in these and other critical decision-making settings are revealed to be greatly shaped by their racial, class, and gender framing of society.

Robert Rubin, Larry Summers, Timothy Geithner: More White "Ole Boys"

Prior to the massive 2008 financial crisis, the large corporations Citigroup and Goldman Sachs had made billions on unregulated contracts that former Clinton Treasury Secretaries Robert Rubin (1995–1999) and Larry Summers (1999–2001) supported while in public office. Rubin was linked to Citigroup and Goldman Sachs and was an economic chief advisor to

President Bill Clinton. Later on, under President Barack Obama, Rubin's protégés moved into many administration posts at Treasury, the Office of Management and Budget, and the White House.[51]

After his work as Treasury Secretary, Larry Summers served as Harvard president (2001–2006), but resigned after a no-confidence faculty vote. He then returned to Wall Street and gave highly paid lectures at financial institutions. In 2009 Summers came back to Washington to lead President Obama's National Economic Council, thus becoming a major decision-maker in regard to the large-scale bailout of U.S. banks that soon followed. After leaving the administration in 2010, Summers again walked through the revolving door and worked in the private financial sector.[52] Recently, Summers has given us insight into the thinking of the white elite about some of their decision-making issues, including within the capitalistic system. He has been critical of what he regards as too many top grades given at major universities, yet his commentary seems to reverse the likely influence process: "How can a society that inflates the grades of its students and assigns the top standard to average performance be surprised when its corporate leaders inflate their earnings, its generals inflate their body counts, or its political leaders inflate their achievements?"[53] To us it seems more likely that the everyday actions of these corporate leaders shape this problematical U.S. ethical culture far more than the grading patterns of college teachers.

Timothy Geithner is another prime example of the bipartisan "ole boys" network that has long ruled both Washington and Wall Street. His grandfather was Vice President of Ford Motor Company and adviser to President Dwight Eisenhower. Geithner followed in this legacy, working under three presidential administrations. He was president of the Federal Reserve Bank of New York at the onset of the 2008 financial crisis. He served as Secretary of the Treasury in the Barack Obama administration from 2009 to 2013. After this government service, he was hired by a Wall Street firm—going through the revolving door like other elite white men.[54]

As Obama's Secretary of the Treasury, Geithner essentially acted with unconditional authority. He had the power to determine what to do with the second half of TARP's massive $700 billion. He proposed, among other things, to develop a new $1 trillion lending program. The Treasury Department would infuse capital into troubled banks, which the bankers could use for lending, supposedly on condition that they cut executive salaries and curb corporate acquisitions. Unsurprisingly, this bank-coddling scheme was heavily panned.[55] Over time, nonetheless, taxpayer dollars were used by bankers for basically everything (e.g., buying securities, buying other banks), except major home lending to ordinary citizens. So powerful were the banks that their mostly white male executives publicly sneered at the notion they would use TARP money for public needs and purposes other than what they deemed appropriate.[56]

When the financial crisis struck, the huge insurance and financial company AIG could not pay off the billions it contractually owed to the troubled financial companies its insurance was supposed to protect. Preferential treatment for AIG was thus also glaring. The interests of its mostly white male top executives were placed far above that of ordinary taxpayers. In 2009, Secretary Geithner sanctioned more than $160 million in bonuses for AIG executives who had made bad decisions. Making such monetary windfalls available to executives after the company had already received hundreds of billions of taxpayers' monies in the bailout scheme was viewed by many as perverse. Yet, the notion that these top white executives were entitled to outrageous salaries was deep-rooted in the societal *class* framing of Treasury Department officials, even as ordinary people lost their homes.[57] Indeed, this assumed class and racial prerogative seems to be deeply rooted in the societal framing of most powerful white men at the helm of major North American corporations and government agencies.

Why would powerful government officials worship at the Wall Street altar? The white ole boys network, and its old revolving door, are the keys to understanding. Many people were initially optimistic that an Obama-led Treasury Department would be dedicated to holding financial institutions accountable for hundreds of billions they received from TARP and would give precedence to corporate fraud prevention. However, Obama Treasury officials were generally as willing to toe the Wall Street line as the Bush Treasury Department. Mostly the white "ole boys" in both Treasury Departments had close Wall Street connections and were primarily impelled by their individual and group self-interests, and not so much the national interest.[58]

Punishing White Collar Criminality: Minor or No Raps on White Knuckles

Obama's Attorney General, Eric Holder (2009–2015), did not prioritize sending executives in banking and other financial firms to prison for their often problematical role in the subprime mortgage and other aspects of the Great Recession crisis. His remarks about Wall Street might suggest why: "I am concerned that the size of some of these institutions becomes so large that it does become difficult for us to prosecute them. . . . it will have a negative impact on the national economy, perhaps even the world economy."[59]

The men who brought this economic crisis on much of the globe were overwhelmingly white and well-educated, often from prestigious universities, yet many seemed to have had little sense of their ethical obligation to the public good. Many clearly engaged in unethical or criminal activity, and much of the U.S. and international financial system was operationally corrupt at its core. Yet, as Holder implies, calling out the unethical and criminal actors and punishing them was very unlikely because of the high level of their political-economic positions and great societal power. Indeed, few analyses inside or outside of government agencies even specifically named them and analyzed them as unethical or criminal. Their actions were often seen as perhaps mistaken but not really criminal, even as normal, in part because they or men like them write or enforce the laws about what is serious white-collar crime. They generally decide what or who is to be punished, and how severely. Millions of Americans lost their homes, jobs, incomes, and pensions, yet rarely were the culpable white men targeted or treated as criminals.

Repeatedly, federal officials have allowed some leading bankers to escape the net of justice by insisting such inaction is in the best interests of the U.S. and global economy. In the interim, some of these financiers' highly exploited victims received modest compensation that amounted to two months' rent; others received nothing.[60] And taxpayers had paid out hundreds of billions in bailout dollars. Alan Greenspan, a white banker who greatly contributed as head of the Federal Reserve (1987–2006) to the financial meltdown, eventually admitted that he had erred in presuming financial institutions could safely self-regulate.[61] Additionally, we should note that powerful white men have controlled most U.S. media corporations—and thus controlled how whites and corporate corruption get portrayed for the larger society. Mainstream media commentators frequently portrayed the Great Recession and its financial causes as an economic reality for which "we are all responsible." Yet, the *major* culprits are the very powerful white male decision-makers who did in fact create most of this horrific political-economic reality, one from which much of the economic world will be recovering for some time to come.

Some "Difficult Women": Disrupting White Male Dominance

Anthropologist Janine Wedel has written about some women in powerful financial institution positions who are deemed "difficult" by male associates. These women are often organizational "disrupters" who, because they are refused full access to elite male privileges and spaces, are less likely than powerful men to submit to organizational "groupthink." Furthermore, they can "ruffle feathers not because they have a superior moral compass, but because, at least for now, they are dogged outsiders who've fought their whole lives to be with the big boys."[62] Despite commendable attention to gender discrimination, this analysis fails to consider the intertwined realities of systemic sexism and racism—i.e., systemic gendered racism. The *white* men who make things difficult for these elite women, who are also typically white, are not as such part of Wedel's assessment, nor are the women and men of color who are also often their economic victims.

Still, it is significant that women have been disproportionately represented among those most critical of the financial malfeasance of the powerful white male decision-makers during and after the Great Recession. One important disrupter is Senator Elizabeth Warren (2013–present), a consumer advocate and law professor who ran Congress's TARP oversight panel in 2008–2010. She has described how Washington insiders carried out a financial bailout protecting friends at Wall Street firms, while largely ignoring the depressive fate of ordinary people. She regularly documents the relentless strain between her, an outsider and a woman, and mostly male Washington insiders. Alas, even the usually astute Warren frequently hides behind vague nouns and passive tenses when dealing with this white male elite. She problematizes her experiences as a woman in a man's world, but misses an opportunity to show how interlocking major systems of gender, racial, and class oppression really are in the societal areas she knows well. She might have called out the key decision-makers specifically—mostly elite *white* men—and their frequent self-important racist and arrogant masculinist perspectives.[63] Evaluating the government response to the Great Recession, she criticized Secretary Geithner and his misplaced priority in supporting banks. She has written about small business owners, homeowners, and women and men whose jobs disappeared because of this elite's assertive greed. To her credit, Warren is celebrated for advocating for taxpayers and for proposing a law that obliged the federal government to divulge deals reached with suspected corporate criminals. Yet, the fact that major targets of subprime loans were Americans of color was little discussed even in her analyses of the malfeasance of government and corporate officials.[64]

The women disrupters in this era also included Sheila Bair, chairperson from 2006–2011 of a principal bank regulator, the Federal Deposit Insurance Corporation. Prior to 2007, she had challenged the financial elite's opposition to home loan modification programs. Later, she boldly declared that the financial executives' unwillingness to offer mortgage adjustments stemmed in part from their contempt for ordinary borrowers. She blasted President Obama's economic team for their eagerness to bail out banks no matter the broader economic costs, while being unwilling to risk censure for assisting troubled homeowners.[65] Despite such commendable attempts to highlight the unscrupulous actions of the Wall Street and Washington elites, Bair's public perspective was also devoid of attention to the centrality of the white and male aspects of this often arrogant and racialized decision-making. In her interviews and writings she too bypasses the opportunity to effectively accent how interlocking the systems of gender, racial, and class oppression were in her extensive experience with contemporary oligopoly capitalism.

From 1996–1999, Brooksley Born, another woman disrupter, was chairperson of the Commodity Futures Trading Commission (CFTC). She tried but failed to push the mostly white male Washington officials to regulate the burgeoning multi-trillion-dollar derivatives market whose crash greatly facilitated the financial meltdown. For her efforts, Born was labeled "irascible, difficult, stubborn, unreasonable" by male counterparts and superiors. Her efforts proved futile when then head of the Federal Reserve Bank of New York, Alan Greenspan, and Treasury Secretary Robert Rubin persuaded other financial leaders that Born's efforts to regulate the precarious derivatives market (which soon brought down firms like AIG) would likely cause economic chaos.[66] In 2009 Born, along with Sheila Bair, was honored with the Kennedy Profiles in Courage Award in acknowledgment of her political daring in challenging other top officials on financial deregulation.[67] Given her high position, however, it is disappointing that Born too failed to call out the major financial villains with regard to systemic racism and sexism issues, including their gendered and racialized framing of society.

The women disrupters also included Carmen Segarra, bank examiner for New York's Federal Reserve Bank. She recorded secretive exchanges with colleagues and shined a light on inappropriate relationships between Federal Reserve officials and the executives at large private banks they officially supervised.[68] Indeed, Segarra was an outsider to the elite financial scene in which she worked, twice over—first as a woman and second as a rare Latina in that world. Note that all these women operated, on occasion, as what Patricia Hill Collins has called the "outsider within." Collins has examined the impact of gender and racial characteristics in the "outsider" situations of black women who operate within historically white institutions. This concept can be extended to all women in major historically male institutions, as they do not have the gender privileges held by powerful men, especially white men, with whom they must deal on a recurring basis in their important jobs.[69]

Neoliberal Capitalism and the Bootstrap Narrative

In spite of contrary evidence, especially that of the Great Recession, the powerful and privileged white men examined here typically display great confidence in, and often masculinist arrogance about, the emancipatory power of white-run oligopoly capitalism. They and their managerial assistants have convinced most ordinary whites to believe the same. This is unsurprising, as most have learned and articulated the capitalistic class frame and associated racist and sexist frames since their youth. They thus become the leading class propagandists engaging in efforts to excuse the devastating societal damage that contemporary capitalism regularly creates as socially necessary.

In the process, the white racial frame's central *fictions* regarding whites' racial and moral superiority and the sexist frame's central *fiction* of male superiority are repeatedly enhanced. Nowhere is this outlook better illustrated than in the individual bootstrap narrative central to the American Dream of upward socioeconomic mobility within U.S. capitalism (see Chapter 7). According to this perspective anyone who will work hard can achieve the American Dream (a decent job, house, family security, funded retirement). However, while dreamed of by most Americans, the mythical American Dream has for the most part been *fully* achievable only by whites. Moreover, as the scholar Susan Strong has underscored, this white American Dream has been available to a great many whites (but not all) because people of color have historically been exploited to generate much white prosperity over the generations.[70]

Members of the Elite Rationalize Oligopoly Capitalism

At the 2012 Democratic National Convention, former President Bill Clinton acknowledged, albeit without reference to underlying systemic issues, the hollow conventional metaphor of individual bootstrapping. He spoke of a conservative narrative that falsely casts Democrats as distinctive architects of an "entitlement" society, thereby supposedly encouraging ordinary Americans to become too reliant on government support programs. That well-worn political narrative, explained Clinton, suggests that all virtuous politicians are totally self-made. He put a spotlight on distorted claims of individual bootstrapping. Even so, he made no explicit mention of the millions of men and women color, or of white women, who are disproportionately cut off from equal opportunity and economic empowerment by the everyday impacts of systemic racism and sexism.[71]

This bootstrap narrative is central to biographies of most influential white Americans. To take one example, Daniel Mitchell, a fellow at the Cato Institute, is representative of influential conservative whites who propagate this narrative. For elite men like him, market fundamentalism is the liberator of deserving Americans and the avenue to the American Dream. If the federal government could be kept more in check, this individualistic American Dream would supposedly thrive well into the future.[72]

The few white women who have managed to move up into top ranks of the corporate sphere, which is still largely controlled by imposing white men, usually must conform to the white male normative structure there. For instance, the former computer company executive Carly Fiorina's official narrative reveals her commitment to this bootstrap mythology. In 2015 she announced her campaign for the U.S. presidency. She has long touted the myth of the accessible-to-all American Dream. In her autobiography she writes about her supposedly modest beginnings in middle-class America. That story is *not* true, for her childhood offered great privileges. At four years old, she was studying French and frequenting operas. Her father was a federal judge and taught at major law schools.[73] Fiorina greatly exaggerated her background to seem an ordinary American. Additionally, she has publicly denied the systemic sex discrimination that all women face. As CEO of Hewlett-Packard (1999–2005), she was the first woman *ever* to head a top 20 U.S. corporation. Yet, even as she related personal examples of gender discrimination she faced in the corporate world, she also articulated the myth that the U.S. is a great "land of opportunity, not sexist oppression."[74] For this essentially *white* dream of great socioeconomic mobility she emphasizes to persevere, it would have to be real to begin with.

Unsurprisingly, young white Americans often aggressively assert this white framing of U.S. society. To take just one example, Tal Fortgang was a Princeton University student from an affluent family whose recent opinion piece on white privilege in his Ivy League student newspaper went viral. He censured those who asked him "to check his privilege," which, contrary to Fortgang's understanding, means being aware and critical of the subtle and covert negative operations of white male privilege and power. "It's not a matter of white or black, male or female or any other division which we seek," he argued, "but a matter of the values we pass along, the legacy we leave, that perpetuates 'privilege.'"[75] He drew on his difficult ancestral family history to argue, in an uninformed way, that anyone with the proper values and work ethic could overcome major societal barriers.[76]

For white-run oligopoly capitalism to prosper, ordinary whites, not just the elite, must believe in the fictional bootstrap narrative. Fortgang's unconditional faith in this mythical narrative doubtless stems in part from the white-controlled media and educational establishments that constantly press the all-pervasive white racial frame and male sexist frame on young minds. Fortgang was apparently shielded from a genuine telling of U.S. racial history, including the unrelenting struggles of Americans of color who survived whites' genocidal, enslaving, Jim Crow actions and now face contemporary discrimination. In our view the majority of whites need to pay much more attention to how Americans of color have experienced the harsh realities of white oppression in both the past and the present (see Chapter 7).

Negatively Framing Those Who Do Not Succeed

The bootstrap narrative shapes the life stories of some prominent people of color who serve as props to substantiate fictitious claims of a post-racial U.S. society. Such assertions sound something like, "If Oprah and Obama can make it, then every black person can." Accordingly, barriers of systemic racism and sexism are rejected. Misrepresented accounts of declarations of individual bootstrapping, and even genuine stories of people who did somehow move up the societal ladder, are frequently used by white politicians, media commentators, and corporate executives to cultivate a narrative in which working hard ("merit") supposedly leads to economic success. The implication is that if you are poor or otherwise struggling, blame yourself for not trying hard enough. Such racist or classist framing, and deflective rationalizing, overlooks the reality of millions of Americans working at least as hard as those in the corporate and political elites; indeed, many of the latter do not work as hard as ordinary Americans.[77]

Evidence of how central the white racial frame is to contemporary oligopolistic capitalism is found in the negative subframes commonly directed at Americans of color. Indeed, one major illustration of how systemic racial, gender, and class issues intersect is that of the fictional black "welfare queen." According to no less than President Ronald Reagan (1981–1989), such a person lived in Chicago and had many aliases and Social Security cards to gain welfare funds. However, neither Reagan nor any investigation by journalists provided *evidence* for this fictional villain. The racist image of the allegedly welfare-cheating and lazy black mother has been central to a dominant white framing of moderate-income black women for many decades.[78] Indeed, this racialization of black women is not unique, for other moderate-income women of color have faced similarly hostile white framing.

Sociologists Kenneth Neubeck and Noël Cazenave use the concept of *gendered racism* to explain white hostility to the clichéd welfare queen. They assess the ways in which negative racial, gender, and class descriptions of those who must rely on public aid are often accented even by the mostly white architects of government welfare support policies. Since a great many white women also depend on this public welfare, Neubeck and Cazenave question why whites only emphasize African American women and employ this coded racist language in policy discourse. As the counterpart of the bootstrap mythology, this coded racist imagery serves the purposes of the ruling elite.[79] This elite-generated discourse has proven alarmingly effective, to the present day, because most ordinary whites are willing to embrace such aggressively gendered racist mythology. "The Welfare Queen driving a pink Cadillac to cash her welfare checks at the liquor store fits a narrative that many white, working-class [and middle and upper class] Americans had about inner-city blacks," explains historian John Hinshaw. "It doesn't matter if the story was fabricated, it fit the narrative, and so it felt true, and it didn't need to be verified."[80] To understand why the "welfare queen" endures as white mythology is to understand more about the operation of systemic racism. Many whites accept the fictitious welfare queen narrative because they rely on such racist framing of alleged black criminality to help safeguard their institutionalized racial privileges and unjust enrichments— which they view as mostly a result of their virtues, including a virtuous work ethic. In this manner they refuse to recognize and understand the empirical realities of centuries of white racial oppression. But more is at work here. The "welfare queen" myth is an excellent example of the decidedly oppressive and globally determining racial, class, and gender subsystems that typically appear together in societal operations. Recall that these subsystems are interlocking, codetermining, and coreproducing in a helix-like fashion—in part because the same or similar elite white men have long ruled at the *top* of each subsystem, and thereby over the entire elite-white-male dominance system.

Indeed, more recently and regularly, candidates for the Republican nomination for president—such as Newt Gingrich, Rick Santorum, and Mitt Romney—have viewed themselves as "white knights" out to slay another version of the welfare chiselers stereotype. In 2012, for example, each of these powerful white politicians dubbed the African American President Barack Obama a "food stamp president" or proclaimed him the architect of a troubled "entitlement" society. Such racialized political claims are to be expected because any serious discussion of systemic classism (e.g., poverty) and systemic racism issues runs antithetical to white capitalistic fictions about individual work ethics and socioeconomic bootstrapping always leading to substantial economic and other societal success.[81]

Conclusion

In the early 2000s the United States and other western countries faced a devastating Great Recession, yet the framing and actions of very powerful white men have still not been fully assessed. One usually cannot do so in the elite-controlled mainstream media. It is impossible to call out and fully problematize the ruling white-male group, or even their immediate acolytes, in a sustained way as they have too much societal power and control. This means no real systemic financial reforms are possible.

In a recent book Rana Foroohar, a more critical financial analyst, points out that the U.S. financial system has as yet not been significantly reformed and that the extensive "financialization of America"—that is, the dominance of large financial institutions—constantly means there is a probability of at least another Great Recession. Only 15 percent of the money in the U.S. system runs through the real economy; *most* is looping around the financial sector. The tax system encourages major capitalists, owners and top corporate executives, to store money overseas or buy back their stock instead of reinvesting in U.S. jobs and to seek short-term profits rather than longer-term investments and innovations. Additionally, many financial regulations that were suggested as necessary right after the Great Recession have not yet been implemented.[82]

Significantly, a recent report from the research division of the International Monetary Fund (IMF) actually admitted that some of their and other leading financial institutions' neoliberal policies had been *a failure*.

Removing restrictions on the movement of capital across country borders and the fiscal approach called "austerity programs" (forcing governments to reduce deficits and debt levels) had not created in most countries the economic growth that the IMF had asserted would be the case and had actually increased socioeconomic inequality. These heavy costs of neoliberalism for countries, they note timidly, "epitomize the trade-off between the growth and equity effects of some aspects of the neoliberal agenda. Increased inequality in turn hurts the level and sustainability of growth." They further admitted that the IMF's top officials have been correct in moving recently to permit some governments to use their funds to support greater economic expansion rather than just austerity. They also noted that the IMF's views on country controls on private capital had changed "to greater acceptance of controls to deal with the volatility of capital flows."[83]

In addition, another major economic report makes clear the failure of the (overwhelmingly white) western economics profession to forecast the Great Recession accurately. Western economists have relied too heavily "on models that disregard key factors—including heterogeneity of decision rules, revisions of forecasting strategies, and changes in the social context—that drive outcomes in asset and other markets." That is, they often leave out research on the well-institutionalized actions of the white, mostly male powerholders.[84]

While the heralded rhetoric of contemporary oligopoly capitalism emphasizes individual choice and open meritocracy, an exclusive group of white male decision-makers mostly hold the corporate and government reins of great economic power. As a result, making good individual and family economic choices is still difficult for countless millions of Americans. Even with periodic people's protests, getting top decision-makers to accept major responsibility for persisting systemic class, racial, and gender discrimination is currently impossible.

One global survey of more than 1,000 major CEOs, the majority likely being white men, found important information on how they currently think about societal issues that might affect them and their corporations. The survey found that top among their priorities was government over-regulation, likely connected to concern for corporate profits. Strikingly, in their list of corporate and contextual concerns there is *no mention* of global warming, racial and gender discrimination, or growing economic inequalities.[85] One reason for this lack of concern with discrimination and inequality is the threat that progressive societal change in these areas would bring attention to their generally undeserved and unjust material standing in society. Indeed, despite the market causes of the financial meltdown of 2007–2010, most ruling-class whites continue to place their faith in market fundamentalism. Their celebration of oligopoly capitalism provides continuing legitimation for large-scale socioeconomic inequality and their quest for material aggrandizement.[86]

Well into the era of recovery from the Great Recession, three rich white men who were central to the Great Recession and the problematical recovery strategies had a good laugh about societal inequality issues. At a conference panel in plush Beverly Hills, the former Treasury Secretaries Robert Rubin, Henry Paulson, and Timothy Geithner were interviewed on the country's increasing inequality by media executive Sheryl Sandberg. When asked about this, Paulson said "he'd been working on income inequality since his days at Goldman Sachs, Geithner quipped, 'In which direction?' 'You were increasing it!' cracked Rubin, as everyone on stage roared with laughter."[87]

Imagine if the standards that most rich white men apply to poor Americans were applied to them. Most have received huge government subsidies, tax concessions, or bailouts of various kinds. They could be accurately labeled "corporate welfare bums" and "unworthy entitlement seekers." Wealthy Americans and their allies would protest legislation reducing their large-scale subsidies as unfairly targeting the "virtuous" well-to-do.[88]

Indeed, the large-scale corporate bailouts and other corporate welfare programs described in this chapter are at the heart of recurring fiscal crises at all government levels. The recurring capitalistic bailouts raise the major question of how much of the economic and other social costs of white-elite-run capitalism the government and its taxpayers should pay. There is a dramatic societal contradiction between the massive size of government expenditures for corporate subsidies and the social costs created by their operations and the large-scale government expenditures necessary to meet essential social needs of ordinary people, such as for Social Security and unemployment insurance programs. One repeatedly observes across U.S. history that the federal government *cannot* support corporate subsidies and then still adequately meet the substantial needs of working people without creating government and societal fiscal crises. In the future this basic contradiction has the potential to collapse the current U.S. political-economic system.

To hide underlying social class contradictions, top corporate and government officials have long promoted aggressive propaganda against the economically oppressed, especially Americans of color. Public social services, they often claim, are a waste of (implied as *white*) taxpayers' money. Racialized poor-bashing and other classist and racist framing work together to conceal the country's extensive corporate welfare and the everyday decisions of a powerful elite that make many people poor by means of exploitation in numerous workplaces and other economic areas. In addition, influential businesspeople and their government allies regularly come together to defend contemporary oligopoly capitalism against periodic attacks from unionized and other organized citizens. In these various ways, again and again, the dominant racial, class, and sexist/masculinist frames support and coreproduce each other across the society.

Meanwhile, the society's economic dissenters, a few even in the elite, must fight an uphill battle on behalf of the relatively powerless majority of Americans. They must try to articulate an effective social justice counter-framing, but this is exceptionally hard to sustain in face of well-established, long-existing systems of oppression.

6

The Politics of Systemic Racism
Domestic Change and Reaction

In the previous chapter we examined important decisions made by the mostly white male members of the elite in regard to the U.S. economic and class system. Now we turn to numerous significant decisions made by members of that elite in top government positions as they changed or perpetuated the country's foundational and systemic racism.

Recall from previous discussions that the operation of this country's government has long been elitist in racial, class, and gender terms. Indeed, since the election of the first president in 1789, the president has been an important member of the ruling elite. In most countries the person in the president's role holds modest power, but the U.S. president has come to be what many view as the "most powerful elected official in the world."[1] Until 2009, the 43 presidents were all elite white men. Elected on November 2008, Barack Obama was the first and only president of color, and even he relied heavily on experienced white male advisors and assistants. In turn, he was followed in 2017 by an elite white man. As we noted previously, *not one* president has been elected directly by the voters—because of the undemocratic electoral college that actually selects the president. This political framework is a white-elite-created reality with intentionally limited democratic input—including the ordinary citizen's "right" to vote for congressional and presidential candidates who are very disproportionately white men or others vetted or funded by elite white men.

In this chapter we examine the extraordinary power that a few white male presidents and their implementing acolytes have had in creating, maintaining, and changing aspects of the systemic racism that has remained central to the elite-white-male dominance system over the last several decades. Then we will examine the distinctive situation of President Barack Obama as he inherited and dealt with this system of racial oppression, including the large-scale racist attacks he experienced during his elections and presidential terms.

White Racial Framing and the Political Elite

As with decisions of top corporate officials, the decisions of most leading political officials, including presidents, have routinely reflected the dominant white racial framing of society. Recall from previous chapters that for centuries that omnipresent frame has provided an overarching worldview extending across class, gender, age, and other divisions among the dominant white racial group. Imposed on all white minds, this racial frame is still a prevailing "frame of mind" for most whites in regard to important racial matters. Remember, too, that it is often associated with the male sexist frame—thereby creating a widespread societal reality of dominant white masculinity.

The elite white, mostly male establishment is not monolithic on major political and other social issues. Today, as in the past, this elite has a rather large conservative faction and a significant moderate faction—and a relatively small liberal faction. Historical and contemporary data indicate that a large segment of influential whites in this conservative faction have regularly expressed an overtly racist perspective and framed such protests against oppression by Americans of color in racially negative terms. Moreover, among a majority of elite and ordinary whites, and especially conservatives, the pro-white-virtue narrative assumes that contemporary whites are now mostly *colorblind* (i.e., personal racism is dead) and that "reverse racism" (i.e., supposed discrimination against whites) is serious. An example of these white-framed notions has come from a famous member of the elite, Donald Trump, who became U.S. president in 2017. Trump once insisted that "A well-educated black has a tremendous advantage over a well-educated white in terms of the job market," adding that "I've said on one occasion, even about myself, if I were starting off today, I would love to be a well-educated black, because I believe they have an *actual advantage*."[2]

Over the decades since the 1970s, the right-wing of the elite establishment has grown in power substantially because well-off white conservatives have funded influential right-wing think tanks, such as the American Enterprise Institute and the Heritage Foundation. Their mostly white "experts" have been successful in getting the contemporary right-wing's very conservative ideas into mainstream media, and especially in media like the Fox cable channel and right-wing radio shows. Assisted by other conservatives, the commentators from right-wing think tanks have helped to indoctrinate ordinary whites and some people of color in an often aggressive and overt white framing of racial issues.[3]

Members of the white ruling class, including presidents and presidential candidates, have regularly operated politically out of versions of the dominant white racial frame. In quests to secure votes of fellow whites, they have drawn on its racial stereotypes, interpretive concepts, images, emotions, and narratives. Many emphasize aspects of white virtue, moral goodness, or superiority. On the flip side, they may depend on racial narratives accentuating what they and other whites frame as the mediocrity or inferiority of people of color and their vices, immorality, or deviant propensities.[4]

Lyndon Johnson: The 1960s Civil Rights Era

Let us consider some of this variation in racial framing and action across several contemporary presidencies. The white elite's more moderate and liberal members, though historically often the smaller group in the elite, have periodically been more positive in their framing of Americans of color and people's movements protesting discrimination. Under pressure from the latter, these moderates and liberals have been largely responsible for white contributions to liberalizing U.S. society on racial, class, gender, and other social hierarchy issues. This included their active support in getting rid of slavery in the 1860s Civil War era and eliminating legal segregation during the 1960s civil rights era. In that 1960s era, President Lyndon Johnson and a majority of members of Congress—most of them white men—did belatedly enact important civil rights laws—the 1964 Civil Rights Act, the 1965 Voting Rights Act, and the 1968 Fair Housing Act.

Legal scholar Derrick Bell has suggested that this type of political change in racial patterns usually entails significant "interest convergence" between some part of the elite and certain dissenting groups of ordinary Americans.[5] Ending totalitarian Jim Crow segregation involved convergence between interests of the white elite's moderate/liberal faction and the interests of black civil rights leaders and civil rights organizations.[6] The main goal of elite moderates was, then as now, the preservation of societal order by ending overt racial conflicts. The 1950s–1960s civil rights movements generated a *legitimation crisis* for this elite in the United States and abroad. They were concerned with how the Soviet Union seemed to be winning the "Cold War" with the United States by circulating media information (e.g., photos of black children attacked by police) to countries across the globe. This mostly white, mostly male elite has acted to end some racial discrimination *only* when it as a group profits in significant ways—in this case, from positive international press coverage about the end of Jim Crow segregation, and thus from the resulting greater U.S. influence in its international struggle with the Soviet Union.

The belated federal enactment of the 1960s civil rights laws, as well as the support of them by key Democratic Party leaders, has had significant effects on U.S. politics. Democratic Party commitments to civil rights laws have brought a major increase in the number of voters of color, and a positive orientation among them to the Democratic Party in numerous elections. Additionally, party reforms since the civil rights era have helped voters and officials of color to gain greater power within the more liberal wing of the Democratic Party. Still, these important civil rights laws and government attempts at enforcing them have persistently stirred up the racial fears of many whites and led them to move their allegiance from the Democratic Party to the Republican Party since the 1960s.[7]

Richard Nixon: Rolling Back Civil Rights Progress

Once the necessity of interest convergence over civil rights was reduced by the decline of the Cold War, and by the decrease in organized civil rights protests, most in the white male elite clearly felt much less pressure to end the reality of widespread and continuing racial discrimination against Americans of color. More conservative thinking came to dominate in regard to racial matters. Thus, conservative presidential administrations since the election of Republican President Richard Nixon (1969–1974) have intentionally weakened enforcement of civil rights laws and blocked numerous expansions of these laws.

In the 1968 and 1972 presidential campaigns, Nixon and his top advisers, all white men, developed the so-called southern strategy, which successfully targeted southern white voters. (Since many southerners are not white, it is more accurately termed the "white southern strategy.") Additionally, during and after these political campaigns Nixon made frequent use of racist code words ("states' rights," "law and order," "crime in the streets") to attract more whites to the Republican Party. He succeeded in relating to the widespread white discontent with the civil rights movement and desegregation efforts in the North and South.[8] White advisors working with Nixon, such as Kevin Phillips, helped to craft the white southern (and northern) strategy. Philips argued that the emerging "Republican majority" among voters meant the party did not need "urban Negroes" and other "vested interests" to win major political offices. They could successfully focus on the majority of white voters upset with racial change.[9]

In his first term Nixon made clear his white-racist framing and related discriminatory commitments. He welcomed former arch-segregationist and white supremacist Democratic Senator Strom Thurmond to the Republican Party, nominated southern racial conservatives to the Supreme Court, and reduced government efforts to desegregate schools.[10] He brought in conservative officials to weaken enforcement of school and other racial desegregation and covertly pressed the FBI to harass civil rights groups. In addition, Nixon appointed a former segregationist, William Rehnquist, to the Supreme Court. Rehnquist later became Chief Justice and shepherded the high court in a more racially conservative direction, including helping to roll back racial desegregation efforts.

Nixon's private actions regularly signaled his operation out of a blatant version of the old white racist frame. According to advisers, he frequently used racist words like "nigger," "jigaboo," and "jigs" for black people in private discussions and asserted that certain government programs could not benefit black Americans because they were "genetically inferior."[11] His chief white aide kept diaries of interactions with Nixon, one entry from which noted that the

President emphasized that you have to face that the whole [welfare] problem is really the blacks. The key is to devise a system that recognizes this, while not appearing to. Problem with overall welfare plan is that it forces poor whites into the same position as blacks. . . . Pointed out that there has never in history been an adequate black nation, and they are the only race of which this is true.[12]

Additionally, in 1970 Nixon and Vice President Spiro Agnew performed a piano duet at a Washington celebrity dinner. There Nixon sarcastically asked Agnew, "What about this 'southern strategy' we hear so often?" To great white audience laughter, Agnew answered in a mock black dialect, "Yes Suh, Mr. President, ah agree with you completely on yoah southern strategy."[13] Nixon and his high-ranking white associates regularly fostered a racist climate throughout the Nixon administration's halls of power.[14] Note too that one likely reason for Nixon's actions reflecting white conservative views of racial matters was the increase in (white) corporate lobbying in Washington, D.C., in this era. Indeed, ever since the Nixon administration, considerable business lobbying has been aimed at ending or reshaping government antidiscrimination policies that might affect corporate profitmaking—yet another intertwining of contemporary capitalism and systemic racism.

Jimmy Carter: More Variation in White Framing

In numerous ways the Nixon era civil rights rollbacks remained in place during the Democratic presidencies of Jimmy Carter (1977–1981) and Bill Clinton (1993–2001). In Carter's case, this might have been expected. Early in his political career, Carter had a strong positive orientation to white superiority and virtue and a strong negative orientation to African Americans. As a Georgia state senator (1963–1967), he was silent about the many beatings and incarcerations of black civil rights protesters for fear of alienating white voters.[15] During his 1970 bid for Georgia governor, he simultaneously pursued black voters and white segregationist voters.

In his successful 1976 bid for the U.S. presidency, his campaign statements were replete with sentiments supporting white in-group superiority and black out-group inferiority.[16] He pledged not to use the presidency for integration purposes: "I am not going to use the Federal Government's authority deliberately to circumvent the natural inclination of people to live in ethnically homogeneous neighborhoods. . . . it is good to maintain the homogeneity of neighborhoods if they've been established that way."[17] Later, he said this did not mean the federal government should oppose residential integration, but that it should not enact such changes. Clearly, he was trying to win over white voters.[18]

Unsurprisingly, Carter's presidential administration (1977–1981) had modest antidiscrimination policies and enforcement. The significantly increasing conservative political movement of this era meant that he faced an overwhelmingly white Congress where there was less support for expanding federal funding for important social welfare and antidiscrimination programs. Still, Carter did work to improve the socioeconomic and educational conditions faced by black Americans. He ordered federal agencies to undertake a Black College Initiative, which included more assistance for historically black colleges. His top officials worked on increasing opportunities to create minority-owned businesses and to enable them to be competitive for federal contracts. Carter and his administrators also committed themselves, under persisting pressures from civil rights organizations, to expand job programs to deal with youth unemployment.[19]

Later in life, after his presidency, Carter became *much* more openly and aggressively committed to change in the country's racist patterns and to international human rights expansion. When asked in 2014 by a reporter to explain why most white male southerners were Republicans, Carter offered the most critical anti-racist framing ever articulated by a white president: "It's race. . . . Ever since Nixon ran—and ever since [Lyndon] Johnson didn't campaign in the deep South, the Republicans have solidified their hold there."[20] In his astute analysis then the political positions of the right-moving Republican Party were designed to attract whites angry with racial changes. "Those kind of things just exalt the higher class, which is the whites," he said, "and they draw a subtle, but very effective racial line throughout the South."[21] In recent decades Carter's analysis of racial issues has been devoid of his earlier language evasion; he now speaks of changing systemic white racism in a very active voice.

Ronald Reagan: Again Moving Backwards on Civil Rights

The major conservative turn in U.S. politics that marked the Ronald Reagan administration (1981–1989) resulted in significant rollbacks of civil rights progress. Reagan had long operated out of an open racist framing. When he campaigned in 1976 against President Gerald Ford for the Republican presidential nomination, he specifically sought former segregationist George Wallace's voters, called for a constitutional amendment to ban bus transport for school desegregation, and advocated ending other government actions to desegregate. He thereby further developed the white conservative strategy of catering to white racial fears and desires to return to many of the overtly racist patterns of the past.[22]

Unsurprisingly, in his 1980s elections Reagan won a majority of white voters in southern states with appeals to white opposition to significant change in patterns of racial discrimination. After his elections, his governing strategy continued this pattern. One key Republican political activist and advisor, Lee Atwater, was blunt in explaining this white-framed conservative strategy:

> You start out in 1954 by saying, "Nigger, nigger, nigger." By 1968, you can't say "nigger"—that hurts you. Backfires. So you say stuff like forced busing, states' rights, and all that stuff. You're getting so abstract

now you're talking about cutting taxes, and all these things you're talking about are totally economic things, and a byproduct of them is blacks get hurt worse than whites.[23]

Atwater was, in effect, laying out how a racialized anti-government, anti-tax, privatization agenda has been presented in politically coded language, language that has been central to numerous Republican political efforts ever since.

Top Reagan administration officials signaled by their everyday comments that there was an openly racist climate in many areas of the administration. Michael Deaver, a major Reagan adviser, had a "penchant for telling racist jokes about blacks" and these "jolted associates and members of the White House press corps." Yet other Reagan aides engaged in racist joking, including references to Dr. Martin Luther King Jr. as "Martin Lucifer Coon." One high administration official, Terrel Bell, later wrote about his distress over the significant racist commentary among his fellow Reagan officials.[24]

One central feature of the Reagan administration was a heavy emphasis on a renewed and racialized "war on drugs," a strong metaphorical description intending to orient the public away from viewing drug addiction as a curable disease. This was then, and still is now, an obvious example of how the ruling elite creates and spreads *metaphorical language* in order to lure the unreflective majority of the public into accepting its often oppressive and destructive actions. That is, leading white political officials committed much federal funding and many federal employees to this supposed new "war."

A central goal was clearly racist—that is, to aggressively target drug use in communities of color while largely ignoring similar use in white communities. With media fanfare and local white support for this "war," expanded government funding assisted in greatly expanded, semi-militarized policing programs in most cities. Significantly, there was little conservative opposition to "big government" in this case. Greatly expanding police funding and the prison-industrial complex was viewed as necessary to sharply increase the number of incarcerated black and Latino Americans—and, not coincidentally, increase low-wage prison labor for corporations and at the same time reduce voters of color. This increase was substantially the result of the discriminatory enforcement of old and new drug laws. Only in the early 21st century did many conservatives start to question the high economic costs of this discrimination, and even then with much less concern for the human costs.[25]

George H. W. Bush: The Specter of "Willie" Horton

Since the 1960s, Republican candidates for the presidency and other high offices have generally been more explicit and open in their white-virtue sentiments and/or negative views of people of color than Democratic candidates.

One influential racist campaign involved the 1988 "Willie" Horton advertisement run by the George H. W. Bush presidential campaign. In that infamous ad the Democratic presidential hopeful Governor Michael Dukakis is attacked by Republicans for his allegedly soft-on-crime policies. It featured an ominous mug shot of a black prisoner, "Willie" Horton, who had raped a white woman and knifed her fiancé while out on a Massachusetts prisoner-furlough program, one put into place before Dukakis was governor there. It falsely suggested that Dukakis was responsible for dangerous black felons on the streets. According to its creator, white conservative Larry McCarthy, the ad's mug shot intentionally made Horton look disheveled and supposedly like "every suburban [white] mother's greatest fear."[26] It helped to cement George H. W. Bush's (1989–1993) victory in that presidential campaign.

The Bush campaign officially insulated itself from accusations of racism by maintaining the ad had been produced by an "independent" political action committee. However, Bush cited "Willie" Horton (William Horton was his actual name) frequently on the campaign trail, and campaign officials distributed thousands of copies of a magazine story about Horton entitled "Getting Away with Murder."[27]

Over the years since, Republican officials have frequently used an array of such strategies to tie Democratic candidates to negative images of Americans of color, and thereby attract more white voters. Larry McCarthy has continued to rely heavily on the negative placement of people of color in political ads. In a 2010 political ad for the American Future Fund, backed by white billionaires, McCarthy redirected public animosity for Muslims toward another Democratic candidate. Propagating the false notion that a proposed Mosque and Islamic Center for Manhattan were intended as monuments reveling in the 9/11 attacks, the intentionally distorted ad urged Iowa voters to vote against the Democratic candidate for his alleged support of that construction.[28]

In the George H. W. Bush period, another openly racist political ad was created for a leading Republican politician, former arch-segregationist Senator Jesse Helms (R-North Carolina). In his reelection campaign he was trailing his Democratic rival Harvey Gantt, an African American, in opinion polls. His minions created a racist television attack ad, in which the camera zoomed in on white hands holding a letter while a narrator remarked, "You needed that job, but they had to give it to a minority." Gantt's support of modest programs to remedy long years of anti-black discrimination had been identified in surveys as unpopular among white voters. This "white hands" ad, one for which there was no evidence, likely helped to secure the overtly racist Helms' reelection. Again, the ad's obvious intent was to make political use of many whites' resentments about racial change—which since the 1960s have been central to their racial framing of society.[29]

As continuously happens with the negative placement of people of color and the elevation of whites in the commonplace white framing, the ad effectively erased the personal biographies of both candidates. In fact, Gantt had a longstanding interest in civil rights. From an early age he had studied nonviolent protest techniques so that at sit-ins he would be prepared for the resistance of many whites. Blatantly racist views and actions had defined Helms' life, yet this fact was often side-stepped or softened in the mainstream media.[30] Later on, after Helms announced his retirement from the Senate, a *Washington Post* columnist captured the hidden workings of the pro-white subframe of the dominant racial frame thus:

> the *New York Times* described [Helms] as "a conservative stalwart for nearly 30 years," the *Boston Globe* as "an unyielding icon of conservatives and an archenemy of liberals." The *Washington Post* identified Helms as "one of the most powerful conservatives on Capitol Hill for three decades." Those were accurate descriptions. But they skirted the point. . . . the squeamishness of much of the press in characterizing Helms for what he is suggests an unwillingness to confront the reality of race [i.e., *white racism*] in our national life.[31]

A few years later, a leading Republican activist, Ralph Reed, described the contemporary orientation of the party thus: "You're going to see a new Republican party that is still primarily white and that is fiscally and morally conservative, but that also is attempting to project an image of racial tolerance and moderation."[32] Unmistakably, Reed was revealing that many mainstream white Republicans envisioned a Party that is primarily white but looks good publicly with its nicely veneered "image of racial tolerance."

Bill Clinton: Appealing to White Working-Class Northerners

To varying degrees, leading Democratic Party politicians have also operated out of overt versions of the white frame. For instance, revitalizing his lagging campaign for the presidency in 1992, Bill Clinton attempted to appeal to white working-class northerners by criticizing the African American recording artist Sister Souljah. Following the early 1990s black "riots" in Los Angeles, Souljah had offered an explanation as to why blacks had protested in the streets, as might be seen from the perspective a young gang member: "If the social and economic system has neglected your development and you have become a casual killer who will kill even your own brother, in your mindset, why not kill a white person?" She was *not* personally advocating violence, but sought to make whites understand that violence directed by blacks against nonblacks during the uprising was set within harsh white-controlled socioeconomic realities that unsurprisingly generated local urban violence.[33]

Seeking white votes, Clinton ignored her obvious reasoning and remarked that if one reversed the words "white" and "black," one might think a Klan member was speaking. The timing of his criticism, during an address to a civil rights group, was calculated. He attempted to distance himself from the Democratic Party's more liberal leaders. Later on, in his autobiography, Clinton did admit his racialized criticism was triggered by his faltering political campaign.[34]

Clinton's attack on Souljah only worked because ordinary whites mostly viewed black Americans as menacing, an assumption dependent on the old anti-black subframe of the dominant white frame. Interviewed after Clinton's remarks, Souljah noted that white

America needs Sister Souljah to be the black monster, to scare all of the white people to the polls because they were disinterested in a very boring, very sloppy political campaign that's been put forth by not only Clinton, but George Bush himself.[35]

In another interview she expanded her critique:

Bill Clinton is like a lot of white politicians. They eat soul food, they party with black women, they play the saxophone, but when it comes to domestic and foreign policy, they make the same decisions that are destructive to African people in this country and throughout the world.[36]

Significantly, too, no major white politicians or media commentators tried to seriously understand the black counter-framing of white racism eloquently presented by Sister Souljah.

Over his campaigns and presidency, Clinton and his close associates regularly played into the dominant white frame. These mostly white men periodically did this by distancing themselves from civil rights leaders and the aggressive civil rights enforcement Americans of color sought. On one occasion Clinton golfed at a racially segregated club with a television crew in tow. While he had played at the club for years in spite of its all-white exclusionary membership, the presence of the television crew suggested he was performing for white voters—with a message that "I am aware of your racial concerns and of the same mind as you."[37] Without a doubt, Clinton's campaign tactics contained an assortment of racial stereotypes and images that signaled allegiance to fellow whites. Researchers concluded that white voters took a greater shine to Clinton after he distanced himself from African American leaders and after his conventional white-framed statements about street crime and welfare reform, which suggested he did not believe white racism was responsible for the predicaments in which African Americans often found themselves.[38]

In numerous ways, the civil rights rollbacks of previous Republican presidents remained in place during Clinton's presidency. Over his two presidential terms, the Congress, often controlled by white conservatives, placed pressures on him for cutbacks in social programs assisting Americans of color. Then as now, elite Republicans like Newt Gingrich, a leader of House Republicans in the Clinton era, have taken a hard line against support programs for the poor. In 2011 Gingrich commented bluntly that "Really poor children in really poor neighborhoods have no habits of working and have nobody around them who works," even though most poor adults *do engage* in paid labor.[39] Clinton administration officials and other Democrats gave in to congressional and other political pressure by cutting back on social programs, as well as on racially conscious remedial policies for discrimination. In the interim, the Supreme Court was pushed toward an exceedingly conservative course by reactionary justices appointed by former Republican presidents. For a long period since this era, the Supreme Court has had a majority that is very conservative, and thus has played a pivotal role in reducing or reversing numerous civil rights and inequality gains of prior decades.[40]

To his credit, Clinton did appoint more African Americans to important government positions, including judgeships, than former Republican presidents. Some of these have worked hard to enforce and extend existing civil rights laws. Still, Clinton's positions on civil rights issues were often weak by the standards of more liberal Democrats. For instance, Clinton's weak commitment was evident in his poor treatment of the distinguished civil rights lawyer (later, Harvard professor) Lani Guinier. Clinton appointed Guinier as an assistant attorney general. After the white right-wing attacked her with white-framed language such as "Quota Queen" (similar to racist "welfare queen" language), a politically fearful Clinton backed off and did not defend her stellar qualifications and reasonable civil rights views, instead withdrawing her nomination.[41]

George W. Bush: More White Framing

As with the Reagan White House, there were numerous Republican reports of a negative racist climate created at the top during the George W. Bush presidential administration (2001–2009). Ron Christie, a black adviser there, reported that a white senior staff member once asserted that Christie's office area was "starting to look like a ghetto." Later on, Christie's reflections indicated his pain: "The ghetto? I was crushed."[42] In addition, throughout the Bush administration there were reports of the periodic criminalization and other racial stereotyping of black Americans by key white conservative administrators. For example, in discussions of a 2005 New Orleans hurricane disaster these administrators, as well as some mainstream media commentators, often described the city's hard-hit working class residents, many of them black and suffering greatly, as "thugs" and "hoodlums." In this old white framing, ordinary black Americans were again racially stereotyped as criminals.[43]

Numerous white government administrators over the course of Bush's eight years worked to weaken or end civil rights progress. A Commission on Civil Rights report described the administration's civil rights efforts as mainly designed just "to carry out official duties, not to promote initiatives or plans for improving opportunity." Their conservative policies were retreating "from long-established civil rights promises in each of these areas."[44] This strategy was unsurprising given that, since Nixon, numerous Republican administrators have tried to roll back or end efforts at racially desegregating major institutions. Bush's Attorney General, John Ashcroft (2001–2005), showed little interest in enforcing civil rights laws. He was even interviewed and praised by the white supremacist magazine *Southern Partisan*.[45] In addition, over the next decade Bush's Supreme Court appointments tipped the court in a more conservative white-framed direction in rejecting efforts at expanding voluntary desegregation and other civil rights programs.

Voter restriction efforts, almost all by Republicans, expanded during the Bush years. Ballot security programs frequently entailed the use of "intimidating Republican poll watchers or challengers who may slow down voting lines and embarrass potential voters by asking them humiliating questions," "people in official-looking uniforms with badges and side arms who question voters about their citizenship," and advertisements "targeted to minority listeners containing dire threats of prison terms for people who are not properly registered—messages that seem designed to put minority voters on the defensive." Bush's Justice Department did little to discourage these voter restriction efforts.[46]

During the Bush years, there was an acceleration of negative, often quasi-racialized framing of Middle Eastern Americans (typically assumed to be Muslim), especially by white conservative activists and commentators. In 2004 Bush reelection advertising, Americans of Middle Eastern descent were explicitly linked to terrorism. In an ad entitled "Wolves," a pack of the animals (animalized Middle Eastern terrorists) invade a forest (the United States). George Bush, as a white Christian man, is portrayed in hyper-masculinist terms as skilled enough to vanquish these Middle Eastern "wolves." According to the narrator, Bush's Democratic challenger John Kerry in that 2004 campaign would be unable to defeat these terroristic "animals." Appealing to similar xenophobic fears, another ad showed Bush hugging a girl whose mom died in the 9/11 attacks. The girl declares that Bush is "the most powerful man in the world and all he wants to do is make sure I'm safe."[47] Broadcast 30,000 times, the masculinist ad was accompanied by a barrage of such images on the Internet and in millions of political brochures.[48] So effective was the appeal to irrational xenophobic fears that Senator Kerry, a man awarded major medals for outstanding military service, was apparently viewed by many voters as not manly enough to lead the country on national security matters.

The Barack Obama Era: Extensive Racist Attacks

The election of the first African American president, Barack Obama, generated many elite and ordinary white actions signaling that the United States was anything but post-racial. During the 2008 election many racist attacks, verbal and otherwise, were made on Obama by conservative activists and commentators. Supporters of his Republican opponent, John McCain, used racist epithets for Obama at rallies; some held signs with "Vote Right, Vote White" or with racist (e.g., ape-like) figures of Obama. Influential conservatives frequently led, joined, or ignored these very racist activities. A Republican Party official in Washington state had to apologize for his group's selling "$3 bills" with Obama in Arab dress and mocking "black speech."[49] Significantly, too, such extreme racist commentary did not end after Obama became president.

During his presidency subtle and overt racial insults and other attacks continued from ordinary and elite whites. A strategist for Obama's campaigns, David Axelrod, noted that

> no other president in US history had had a member of Congress shout at him in the middle of a major address—as Joe Wilson of South Carolina did in 2009 with his "You lie!" rebuke—or faced persistent questions about his American citizenship, as Obama did from the so-called "birther" movement.[50]

Axelrod concluded that many whites seemed unnerved by shifting racial demographics that meant they would be a minority in the near future. "To those people," he suggested, "Obama is a living symbol of something they fear, they don't like, and some of that has spilled into our politics."[51] In his view racial fears contaminated the political realm and were partially responsible for Republicans' unyielding opposition toward Obama's legislative agenda.

This extensive white hating on Obama has usually been from versions of the dominant white racial frame—a framing of black people as inferior and white people as superior. In an early defense of Obama, former President

Jimmy Carter suggested that many whites believe that a black American cannot effectively lead the country. He was troubled by the emotional racist framing among whites: "I think people who are guilty of that kind of personal attack against Obama have been influenced to a major degree by a belief that he should not be president because he happens to be African American. . . . It's a racist attitude."[52] Carter's analysis made clear that whites in various social classes are responsible for this racist framing and explicitly positions them as active agents of racism.

Additionally, President Obama endured often racialized anti-Muslim sentiments. Despite the fact that he is not Muslim, persistent rumors, especially among whites, insisted that he was. At a time when national security concerns were on many minds, efforts to link Obama with various extremists usually reflected some overt or subtle racial framing. For example, prominent Representative Steven King (R-Iowa) drew on anti-Muslim sentiment in challenging Obama's leadership. While claiming he did not ridicule people on the basis of "their race, their ethnicity, their name," King nonetheless said,

> When you think about the *optics* of a Barack Obama potentially getting elected . . . what does this look like to the rest of the world? . . . if he is elected president . . . the radical Islamists and their supporters, will be dancing in the streets in greater numbers than they did on September 11.[53]

By linking Obama with radical terrorism, King tried to portray him as not a true American. King was well-known for persistent white-framed assertions about a supposed national targeting of white men: "There's been legislation . . . that sets aside benefits for women and minorities. The only people that it excludes are white men. . . . Pretty soon, white men are going to notice they are the ones being excluded."[54] Today as then, the white-framed notion of virtuous white men under threat of exclusion seems to be widely shared. This is not new in white pushback against racial change, for such racially framed views have endured among elite and non-elite whites for centuries. For example, in the 19th century fearful whites argued that the abolition of black enslavement would result in enslavement of whites. Later on, in the post-slavery and post-Jim-Crow eras, the racially framed concept of "white subjugation" was asserted by whites who feared the democratic expansion of voting and other civil rights for African Americans and other Americans of color. Today, claims of a metaphorical "war" on whites purposefully fuel white racist fears, and thereby generate more discriminatory actions. They also help to conceal regressive government policies backing off on expanding civil rights. Central to this contemporary white racial framing is, as we show further in the next chapters, the white fear of losing racialized power and privilege as Americans of color grow in number and political power.[55]

Certainly, Republicans are not the only ones who have operated out of a white framing of Obama. In 2008, then New York Attorney General Andrew Cuomo (2007–2010), a Democrat who had thrown his support behind Obama's primary opponent, commented on one Obama press gathering in this way: "You can't shuck and jive at a press conference."[56] Roland Martin, a black media commentator, explained the offensiveness of this: "When African Americans hear former President Bill Clinton call Obama a kid, that is seen as an insult. . . . It is remindful of grown black men being called 'boy' during the Jim Crow era. . . . The same goes for shuck and jive."[57]

Racist Framing during and after the 2012 Election

In the 2012 presidential election, Obama's Republican challenger was former corporate executive Mitt Romney. He too engaged in subtle and overt racialized attacks. At one fundraiser he chastised Obama supporters for being too reliant on government aid and for a sense of entitlement to "health care, to food, to housing."[58] He repeatedly claimed that Obama wanted to transform the country into an entitlement culture, with the implied beneficiaries being heavily Americans of color. Numerous other influential white Republicans claimed Romney was correct.[59]

In similar fashion, Newt Gingrich and Rick Santorum, also candidates for the Republican nomination, referred to Obama as the "food stamp president" and proclaimed the United States was becoming an "entitlement society."[60] Campaigning in Iowa, Santorum exclaimed, "I don't want to make *black* people's lives better by giving them somebody else's money."[61] The only coded message in this case was that the "somebody else" meant *whites*. Such racialized comments caused one critical columnist to ask, "Has the time finally come for social scientists who blame the so-called culture of poverty for the lowly status of the black underclass to start focusing on the equally pathological culture of the wealthy, powerful—and, not coincidently, virtually all-white elite?"[62] This comment implicitly referenced such negative societal events as the 2007–2009 Great Recession which was triggered by the corrupt actions of a mostly white and male corporate and political elite.

Yet other powerful whites engaged in an array of racist commentaries about Obama around the time of this election. One prominent federal judge emailed acquaintances a fanciful animalizing yarn wherein Obama's white mother jokes to then-young Obama that his mixed racial ancestry might be linked to her having wild party sex, joking that alluded to potential sex with a dog. For centuries now, elite and ordinary whites have mongrelized black Americans out of the dominant white racial frame. Aggressive animalizing of President Obama and his family was widespread throughout the Obama elections and presidency—and continues to the present. For instance, in 2011 one important Republican official sent acquaintances a photo of President Obama's face on a chimpanzee. Moreover, as with many other whites, these leading Republican officials insisted, when they were called out, that they were just joking and "not racist."[63]

During and after the 2012 election numerous white political commentators made their racial framing clear in other ways. After Obama's reelection one elite commentator proclaimed that "Voters with forty years of politically correct [read: anti-racist] education are ecstatic to have the first black president. They just love the idea of it."[64] Others brought up the supposed Democratic "war" on whites. Conservative Representative Mo Brooks claimed that this was an intentional tactic Obama employed in 2008 and 2012—wherein "he divides us all on race, on sex, creed, envy, class warfare, all those kinds of things."[65] Additionally, during the 2012 campaign, and often since, white conservatives have regularly asserted that "their country" is being taken over by Americans of color. One conservative group's email fearfully emphasized the end of the "white Anglo-Saxon Protestant" race because of significant growth in the population of color.[66] Such racially framed assertions are themselves very ironic, since even arch-conservative white Americans are today often multiethnic—that is, they include white groups that are not northern European or Protestant.

Hostility toward Obama and his legislative programs continued to the end of his administration. As we see many times in this book, the phrase "the American Dream" is commonly used by whites to play up the United States as a land of opportunity and downplay racial and class inequalities. Not long ago, Republican Governor Scott Walker openly opposed "Obamacare's" elective Medicaid extension in order to purportedly safeguard this mythical American Dream. He insisted that low-income people (i.e., people of color) must be pressed to get into the labor force so that they could live the Dream—implying the old "culture of poverty" notion long held by white conservatives. The major problem with his argument is that hundreds of thousands of *hard-working* but low-wage cashiers, cooks, nurses' aides, restaurant staff, and caretakers—the majority of them workers of color— were excluded from Medicaid health assistance because of its rejection by state Republican lawmakers like Walker. These low-wage working people were those the Medicaid program was originally envisioned to help.[67]

The white Mississippi state Representative Gene Alday told a reporter: "I come from a town where all the blacks are getting food stamps and what I call 'welfare crazy checks.' They don't work."[68] When his wild racist generalizations were made public, Alday maintained he was not racist and that his remarks had been taken out of context. Alday probably expected his racially framed remarks to remain private. Interestingly, social scientists Leslie Picca and Joe Feagin examined the differential racial commentaries of white college students in both public multiracial settings and private all-white settings. These mostly young whites' racial commentaries in the private settings were often more overtly racist and less restrained. Differential racist performances in public "frontstage" and private "backstage" settings seem to take place among influential whites like Alday as well.[69]

Yet other white conservatives utilized various types of white racist framing for their own political purposes. Michigan Representative Pete Hoekstra, a Republican, sought to unseat Democratic Senator Debbie Stabenow in Michigan. One Hoekstra ad used aggressive white framing. Reflecting Hoekstra's attacks on Stabenow's supposed "big-spending" policies and alleged support of a "growing dependence on China," the ad began with the sound of a gong and included clichéd Asian music. The ad featured the 2012 Miss Napa Valley riding a bicycle beside a rice paddy, and she thanked Senator "Debbie Spenditnow" in a mock Chinese accent.[70] The ad included a link to a campaign website that read "The Great Wall of Debt" with Chinese flags. After much protest, Hoekstra denied the ad was racist, and in a bizarre political move accused Stabenow, who is white, of "playing the race card."[71]

Political Impacts of White Racist Framing

The highly racialized context that President Obama faced during his elections and presidential terms apparently forced him to restrain his public condemnation of the country's systemic racism. Recall from Chapter 2 that in speeches he often catered to white racial opinion in discussing racial matters, such as by accenting blacks' responsibility for life difficulties much more than the systemic racism that creates many such difficulties. In the elite-white-male dominance system it is very difficult for any political official, especially one who is not white, to stray far from a framing of society that is acceptable to most elite and ordinary whites.

Additionally, the public and private racial framing of Obama by a majority of whites doubtless played out in the minority of white votes he garnered in the 2008 and 2012 elections. In 2012 he secured just 39 percent of the white vote nationally. The white southern electorate, which currently votes overwhelmingly Republican, was important in lowering Obama's vote total.[72] One reason for this voting pattern is that a great many white voters still hold to a racist framing of African Americans and other Americans of color. As noted previously, many doubtless fear that more significant advancements in economic and political power for Americans of color will reduce their white power and privilege.

This contemporary white frame is rooted in the oppressive realities of slavery and Jim Crow, eras making up most of U.S. history. Unsurprisingly, one political science study found that the "larger the number of slaves in his or her county of residence in 1860, the greater the probability that a white Southerner today will identify as a Republican, express opposition to race-coded policies such as affirmative action and express greater racial resentment towards African Americans."[73] This finding of many white voters' racial framing and resentment of the black population holds up for the number of black Americans in the county during the Jim Crow era and, indeed, for the number today. The long history of white racial oppression, of whites' unjust enrichment and blacks unjust impoverishment, helps to explain the continuing reality of this country's systemic racism, including persisting and racialized voting patterns.

Acolytes of Elite Men: More White Framing

As we documented previously, the ruling elite does include modest numbers of white women and men and women of color. Even so, these members of the elite have to mostly conform to the normative expectations of leading white men in order to be allowed substantially into the elite sphere. As a rule, they can only move into the mostly lower reaches of the elite by means of powerful white male sponsors who provide them access to critical educational and other social networks. As sociologist Sean Elias has argued from his research, the relatively rare

> black socio-economic power operates in the institutions and social and economic systems long ago created by the white power elite. . . . Subsequently, a racial hierarchy of the elite exists, with the power, capital, etc., of the white power elite far outweighing the power, capital, etc., of the black elite.[74]

Unsurprisingly, an aggressive and comprehensive white racial framing of society among people of color is much less common than such framing by whites, but buying into significant elements of that white frame is nonetheless commonplace. Prevailing white views on important matters remain normative for most Americans; much white historical mythology has been learned even by Americans of color. Elements of the dominant white frame are, indeed must be, accepted by youth of all backgrounds as they are socialized and seek jobs and other positions in white-dominated institutions. Moreover, since the white elite has made white racial framing a global phenomenon through U.S. economic, political, and media hegemony, many immigrants to the United States are operating out of significant elements of this framing before their arrival. The great impact of U.S. media overseas often means that immigrants have a preconceived racial framing of African Americans and other Americans of color.[75]

Alejandro Castellanos and Lloyd Marcus

We can illustrate some of these points by briefly examining the views of two men of color, Alejandro Castellanos and Lloyd Marcus. Operating to a significant degree from a version of that white racial framing, they can be viewed as enablers for more powerful whites. Witness the similarities between how they and elite whites downplay and mythologize U.S. racial history. Like these whites, they seem to have difficulty assessing accurately the contemporary realities of unjust enrichment and unjust impoverishment that follows racial lines. They too rely on the dominant white frame to rationalize much enduring racial discrimination and inequality, as well as to legitimate the ways in which they and whites contribute to and benefit from such racial injustice. Indeed, they are often indispensable to sustaining and perpetuating the overarching elite-white-male dominance system.

Some commentators have expressed amazement that the mind behind the aforementioned "white hands" attack ad of Senator Jesse Helms was that of the Latino (Cuban American) Alejandro Castellanos. Though most commentators agree that the ad was a blatant appeal to the racial biases of whites, expectedly Castellanos described his intended message rather differently: "[N]obody should get a job, or be denied a job because of the color of their skin."[76] Proud of the ad's data-less statement about a threat to white jobs, he said that he felt a personal connection to this fabricated and racialized message:

> My son is named Castellanos . . . one day he could get a job or he could get some deal because he is of some ethnic minority. . . . I hope he never does. I think that lessens you when you do that. . . . The vast majority of Americans believe that. And if it's wrong for us to discriminate that way it's wrong for our government to discriminate that way. Again, it's freedom. . . . when a conservative Republican says the same words that Martin Luther King says, somehow he's racist. . . . I think you're proscribed from talking about quotas and things like that because you're a . . . white guy.[77]

Observe how Castellanos tried to equate the message behind the "white hands" ad to Dr. King's calls for black freedom from centuries of extensive white discrimination. He also implied, inaccurately, that this large-scale discrimination had ended. Clearly, a conventional white-generated colorblind framing informed his defense not only of the racialized ad, but also of the modest government policies seeking to reduce centuries-old anti-black discrimination. Much like leading white conservatives, Castellanos made repeated use of colorblind rhetoric in this and other statements that attempt to cover up the extensive reality of continuing discrimination against African Americans and other Americans of color. Moreover, in a more recent ad against President Obama's health reform program, prepared for the white-run U.S. Chamber of Commerce, Castellanos again drew on racial imagery and conformed to the racial preferences of many white business decision-makers. In that ad a black worker gazes into the camera as a white worker is fired. Commenting on this imagery, a spokesperson for labor unions that favored Obama's health legislation noted that in the ad Castellanos was "trying to use race and class to scare [white] working people about a health care bill."[78]

Consider too Lloyd Marcus, a prominent African American member of the conservative "Tea Party" movement. As with white conservatives, Obama has been a target of much criticism for the relatively few black conservatives like Marcus. Addressing a comment made by Obama that slavery and Jim Crow were justified "all too often" in the name of Christian religion, Marcus has countered with this deflective comment: "how about mentioning that white Christian abolitionists risked their lives helping blacks escape slavery via the Underground Railroad? . . . Over 600,000 (mostly whites) died in the civil war which purged our nation of slavery."[79]

In his reaction Marcus ignored Obama's main point, and he also left out key parts of the Civil War story. It is true that in that war over 600,000 men, on both sides together and a majority white, had been killed. However, this figure includes 258,000 Confederate men who died to support a nation of slavery. And it is also true that by war's end some 210,000 black soldiers and sailors, mostly volunteers and formerly enslaved, had only belatedly been allowed by white racist officials to serve in U.S. military forces, yet they still fought hard to end the slavery system, with a higher rate of casualties than whites.[80] Moreover, in his retort to Obama's slavery comment Marcus perpetuated the familiar lore about the positive contributions of whites to the famous Underground Railroad, the geographical paths that enslaved black Americans followed to freedom before and during the Civil War. This escape system and the associated abolition movement were the first occurrence in U.S. history of a large-scale interracial partnership and did include the courageous involvement of white Quakers and other Christians. However, Marcus left out a major part of the story. The Underground Railroad was mainly operated by free northern blacks, especially in the early years.[81]

Like many white conservatives, Marcus has promoted white virtuousness, including exaggeration of the contributions of whites to real liberty, justice, and democracy, especially for Americans of color. He has also lamented the trials that white men face: "Who is out there giving rich white men props for their many positive contributions to society?"[82] Lost on Marcus here and in his other commentaries, as on many whites at all class levels, is just how dominant and destructive these rich white men have always been across all major institutions. U.S. history is usually told from a perspective acceptable to them, and their real and imagined contributions are accented in mainstream media and textbooks. In contrast, as we document throughout this book, their many *negative* contributions have long been intentionally softened and covered up.

More Racist and Sexist Framing

Let us note a few more examples from the 2014 political season that also illustrate aspects of the dominant white frame. That electoral period saw continuing race-baiting demagoguery from some in the white elite. One political image regularly targets black men as prime examples of criminality. For example, in 2014 the National Republican Congressional Committee paid for a "Willie Horton" type ad attacking the former Nebraska state senator Brad Ashford, a Democrat then running for a U.S. House seat. The ad told the tale of an African American who committed murders after release from prison under the state's "good time" law, one similar to those in other states. Linking the Democrat Ashford to him, the ad's narrator says: "Brad Ashford supported the good time law, and still defends it, allowing criminals . . . to be released early."[83] The deceptive ad mirrored the earlier conservative Horton ad in its appeal to white racial fears. A Democratic campaign committee responded by admonishing Republicans to "be ashamed that they have resorted to divisive rhetoric, playing up racial stereotypes and fear-mongering to save their sinking candidate."[84] However, the fact that some Democratic candidates have also relied, albeit it much less often, on racist framing seemed lost on this Democratic committee.

In this era, as earlier and since, prominent political conservatives have frequently articulated their class, gender, and racial framing of the poor and the latter's supposed "poverty culture." In 2014 the influential Speaker of the House, Paul Ryan, notoriously remarked that "We have got this tailspin of culture, in our inner cities in particular, of men not working and just generations of men not even thinking about working or learning the value and the culture of work."[85] Much social science research strongly contradicts such exaggerated notions about impoverished men not trying to get work. Similarly, when discussing the legalization of marijuana, the television conservative Bill O'Reilly claimed that such drugs were a distinctive part of "black culture," even though whites use such drugs as much or more than blacks do. Frequently, as in these cases, a key part of the contemporary conservative perspective on U.S. society involves ignoring social science research on such important societal issues.[86]

Conclusion

White racial virtue and virtuous western manhood have never been more forthrightly celebrated than in the contemporary era. Such perspectives have shaped much contemporary political discourse and actions, especially from white conservatives. From constitution-violating national security controls and imperialistic militarism overseas to highly racialized executive, legislative, and judicial responses to undocumented immigration from

Mexico and to crime in cities, many white voters, especially men, have sought presidential and legislative candidates who will wield very aggressive state-sanctioned policing and military actions. This often racist and masculinist orientation is defended as necessary for unproven national security reasons or for the sake of U.S. corporate interests. We return to these issues in Chapter 8.[87]

In these presidential administrations, and others discussed in this book, powerful whites and their acolytes often demonstrated a general belief in white superiority over people of color, in the mythical framing of a readily achievable American Dream, and in an emergent post-racial society. Operating out of a self-assured white frame, they declare that the past and present differences in material resources and possessions between Americans of color and white Americans are evidence of superior white virtue, values, and effort. Those who flourish, the morally superior whites and certain white-vetted people of color, deserve the often unearned privilege, security, and comfort they and/or their ancestors have secured. Those who do not thrive deserve their lot in life because of their racial and class inferiority and lack of virtue.

Whites in the power elite have, over more than a century now, indefatigably worked to convince a majority of whites that poor people of color are mainly responsible for their impoverished conditions. This has been particularly useful in buttressing neoliberal austerity attacks on government social programs in the United States and elsewhere. Increasingly over recent decades, a huge rift between the mostly white Republican Party and the much more racially diverse Democratic Party concerns how their members view the role of government in dealing with racial and economic inequality and other serious social problems. For instance, backing among Republicans for government social programs for low-income Americans has significantly declined. In 1987, in a Pew Research Center poll, some 62 percent of Republicans and 79 percent of Democrats agreed "government should take care of people who can't take care of themselves." Twenty-five years later, just 40 percent of Republicans agreed. This decline compared with the still substantial 75 percent of Democrats agreeing with that perspective on impoverished citizens.[88]

Most elite whites and their supporting cast do not understand, or suppress their knowledge of, the centuries-old racial history of great unjust enrichment for whites and of large-scale unjust impoverishment for the many who are not white. Reflecting on the political-economic rise of Europe more than a century ago, W. E. B. Du Bois assessed the fiction of superior white European virtue, values, and knowledge as compared with such in non-European societies:

What is that breath of life, thought to be so indispensable to a great European nation? Manifestly it is expansion overseas. . . . How many of us today fully realize the current theory of colonial expansion, of the relation of Europe which is white, to the world which is black and brown and yellow? Bluntly put, that theory is this: It is the duty of white Europe to divide up the darker world and administer it for Europe's good. This Europe has largely done.[89]

Working in similar fashion, white Americans of European descent have long participated in the process of building up their own prosperity and wealth by stealing the labor and exploiting the labor of many people of color, both within the United States and abroad.

7

Seeking the American Dream
The Case of African Americans

In this chapter we extend our arguments about systemic racism in previous chapters by examining in more detail one central and revealing case about how white Americans, elite and ordinary whites, have racially framed and organized U.S. society—and thereby often taken action to prevent access to real liberty and socioeconomic advancement for a great many Americans. Our specific example of this systemic discrimination by elite white men involves one of the country's oldest, largest, and most oppressed communities of color—African Americans. Our historical and contemporary examples in this chapter underscore the centrality of white-on-black oppression to the past and present development of U.S. society.

At the same time, we highlight here the substantial reality and impact of African American *agency* and *resistance* to this white racial oppression, especially over recent decades. That recurring African American pushback against the elite-white-male dominance system has involved great effort, much creativity, and substantial contributions by African Americans, who have thereby made this still racially oppressive country more just, freer, and more democratic than it otherwise would have been.

Resisting Racism: The Black Liberty-and-Justice Dream

In April 1963, Dr. Martin Luther King Jr. was confined to a jail cell in Birmingham, Alabama, having been arrested for anti-segregation demonstrations. At this time most members of the white male elite in the South and the North, as well as most ordinary whites, were *strongly opposed* to the civil rights movement in which King was a prominent leader. This was conspicuous in a major letter signed and published by prominent white clergy, all of them male and including powerful bishops, that paternalistically admonished blacks to withdraw support from civil rights leaders like Dr. King (termed "outsiders"). These mostly elite white clergy provided a clear statement of the commonplace and arrogant white racial framing of society, one where a majority of whites and their legal system were virtuous and where protesting blacks were unvirtuous and unwise.

The famous letter accused Dr. King of using "extreme measures" that provoke "hatred and violence," claiming that civil rights demonstrations were "unwise and untimely" and that racial issues should only be "properly pursued in the courts." Soon, in response, King wrote his prescient *Letter from the Birmingham Jail* in which he pressed these powerful white men to live by their own religious ideals and speak out for racial equality and social justice. He talked about the "shattered dreams" of black Americans, asserting that the chief obstacle to racial justice was Birmingham's ossified white power structure and the rigid segregationist system it controlled, which left oppressed black citizens with no alternative but to actively protest. King's perceptive letter was not only a potent moral defense of nonviolent action against racist laws, but an unwavering challenge to the dominant white framing of whites as virtuous and blacks an unvirtuous. This was more than King's individual vision; he congealed in the eloquent letter a point-by-point counter-framing of systemic white racism that was drawn from the *collective* understandings of African Americans developed over long centuries of racial oppression. In the letter he thus takes time to contextualize the black movement for liberty and eloquently underscores a key reason for the black demonstrations in Birmingham: "Injustice anywhere is a threat to justice everywhere."[1]

A few months later, Dr. King gave his legendary speech at the March on Washington for Jobs and Freedom. Most people are familiar with brief quotations from it, the most publicized of which is the "I have a dream" refrain. This is frequently cited as King's optimism regarding the U.S. racial future. Indeed, King's critical *Letter* has been contrasted, especially by white analysts, with his "I have a dream" speech—the latter often being described as a more optimistic "appeal to people in the uplifting spirit of hope and keeping dreams alive."[2] Today, such white framing and sanitizing of King's views about white racism and racial change is still widespread, yet his views were far more complex and radical than the simplifications white analysts have imposed to make him an inoffensive civil rights icon.

If we consider King's celebrated "dream" refrain in the context of that *entire* Washington speech, his view is significantly less optimistic. His optimism was consistently tempered by his understanding of the foundational and systemic reality of white racial oppression then taking the form of Jim Crow segregation. To foreground the old white-crafted liberty rhetoric that blacks sought to make reality, his speech included references to Abraham Lincoln's Gettysburg Address, the Declaration of Independence, the Emancipation Proclamation, the U.S. Constitution, and the Bible. Thus, King's legendary speech was a fervent example of forceful black counter-framing in an extensively white-normed social context. King was defiant of the superior white virtuousness at the epicenter of conventional white framing. He demanded a serious implementation of the liberty-and-justice rhetoric in the form of redressing of systemic oppression targeting African Americans.[3]

King's strong focus there on human *freedom* reflects a key concept long found in the writings and activism of African Americans. This is more than the freedom of conventional white rhetoric. Their *counter-framed* view accents *real* freedom from racist coercion, and for choosing individual and group life courses. The conventional white American Dream of material security (decent job, house, retirement) is wrapped up in the meritocratic "work hard and you'll get ahead" philosophy. Yet King had a much broader Dream, one that accented social justice. For King, as with most African Americans then and now, the *true* American Dream has been one of major racial change involving *racial justice and equality,* including economic and political equality that comes from eliminating racial barriers.[4] Undeniably, the dominant version of the white American Dream has *never* been concerned with actual liberty and justice for all.

Societal oppression has often bred resistance. Human beings have a distinctive ability to reflect on oppressive conditions and counter them with a collective consciousness and counter-framing that generates social change efforts. Early on, especially powerful white men put African Americans at the *center* of the profitable capitalistic system—and at the heart of that exploitative system's legitimating white racial framing. By the 18th century the racist thinking of white Americans—i.e., a developed white racial frame—was substantially crafted in response to rationalizing this black oppression. Because of their great importance in this oppressive system, African Americans have long been the *prototypical* example of inferior "minorities" and unvirtuous "nonwhites" that are deeply imbedded in almost all white minds.[5]

Unsurprisingly, thus, black protest consciousness and counter-framing has frequently produced black efforts that challenge in fundamental ways the country's still foundational and systemic racism, with its rationalizing white frame. Since the early days of slavery African Americans have been active theorists of their oppressive experiences, and they have made their counter-framing very clear in a long history of anti-oppression manifestos and protests such as those of the 1950s–1960s civil rights movement. Over several centuries of protest and white retaliation, they have produced what is perhaps the most fully developed and proclaimed anti-racist counter-frame of any subordinated U.S. group.

White Recalcitrance and Resistance to Change

Why has the country's *rhetorical* liberty-and-justice-for-all ideal never been realized? The answer has always lain in the large-scale benefits of systemic racism for most whites. The answer to the related question of why a majority of whites do not try to live by their liberty-and-justice ideals in regard to Americans of color is that most view these as applying only to those who are fully human and virtuous. Black Americans and numerous other Americans of color are typically framed as not as fully human or as generally deserving as more virtuous whites. Most whites believe in or passively accept a racially hierarchical society with privileged and virtuous whites at the top. As President Woodrow Wilson put it in a 1909 speech to teachers,

> We want one class of persons to have a liberal education, and we want another class of persons, a very much larger class, of necessity, in every society, to forego the privileges of a liberal education and fit themselves to perform specific difficult manual tasks. You cannot train them for both in the time that you have at your disposal.[6]

Undoubtedly, in his white framing—he was a committed supporter of Jim Crow segregation—that first and privileged class was only white.

Let us now examine some major racial barriers to socioeconomic mobility— the defining attribute of the conventional white American Dream. If not for many white-framed societal norms and social policies, most imbedded in systemic racism, there would be far more socioeconomic mobility and success for African Americans and other Americans of color than there has been, in both the past and present. And they would be much more likely to achieve this traditional American Dream.[7]

Racial Segregation in Education: Whites Resisting Change

For centuries a great many African American activists have made clear that the achievement of full legal rights for all Americans is only one of their major societal goals. Their efforts have certainly been essential to bringing down slavery and, more recently, legal segregation across numerous states, yet they have also sought other critical changes in the system of racial oppression to the present day. These have included sharply improved economic and housing conditions for *all* Americans, as well as greatly expanded educational opportunities and other access to asset-generating societal resources. Just prior to his 1968 assassination, Dr. King spoke strongly about the need for another rights revolution that would finally bring these broad socioeconomic and related political changes that were necessary in the elite-white-male dominance system, especially in its systemic racism and classism.[8]

Over the decades since the 1950s emergence of the modern civil rights movement much research has documented the failure of the white American Dream to fully include Americans of color—the systemic racial flaw in this country of which Dr. King and other rights reformers have often spoken. One major aspect of this failure lies in the area of providing first-rate public education facilities like those long provided for most whites.

Unsurprisingly, a key Supreme Court decision both reflecting and propelling the contemporary civil rights movement was a major 1954 school case. The *Brown v. Board of Education of Topeka* ruling by nine white male judges officially mandated the racial desegregation of some public school systems. Its ruling was believed by many to set a general precedent. This ongoing struggle for authentic racial desegregation, explains scholar Gary Orfield, did not occur because black Americans desired to sit next to white Americans in schools. "It was, however, based on a belief that the dominant group would keep control of the most successful schools and that the only way to get full range of opportunities for a minority child was to get access to those schools."[9]

In fact, it was the assertive black struggle for desegregation of societal resources, the decades-long civil rights movement, that *forced* this *Brown* decision by the white male elite, as well as other concessions to expanding civil rights in this era. Historically, as in the present, major changes in patterns of discrimination have come, not from whites suddenly becoming racially progressive, but from organized resistance and associated antiracist counter-framing by African Americans and other Americans of color. Resistance actions have long forced at least some powerful whites (mostly men) to take some legal, political, and economic actions that expanded actual social freedom and justice. One reason for the elite's reform response in the *Brown* decision was the concern of its moderate faction for maintaining societal order—the interest convergence discussed previously in connection with the belated civil rights actions of powerful whites such as Lyndon Johnson in the 1960s (Chapter 6).

As part of this long civil rights tradition, in 1951 black students at Moton High School in Prince Edward County (Virginia) united their classmates, their community, and the National Association for the Advancement of Colored People (NAACP) in opposition to the area's extensive white-imposed segregation of public schools. This student strike is deemed by many historians to signify the beginning of the national desegregation movement; black protests there resulted in a major court case that was subsequently bundled with others into the Supreme Court's famous *Brown* decision.[10] Also note that the courageous Moton students demonstrated the unrelenting *agency* that black Americans in search of authentic liberty and justice have long shown. Even in the face of white violence, they demanded an end to the old segregation laws, then central to the country's systemic racism.

Nonetheless, most white southerners, including in the white elite, *opposed* such progressive educational change. A white federal judge ruled against the students and their parents, reaffirming the elite's commitment to segregation and challenging NAACP arguments about the injurious consequences of racially segregated education. He accepted the old white view that blacks were intellectually inferior. Unmistakably, that old white racial framing of black Americans served as a primary motivation for his decision. With substantial effort, NAACP attorneys appealed to the Supreme Court and won desegregation as part of the 1954 *Brown* decision.[11] Recall that this legal victory was possible because certain more moderate (mostly northern) elements of the white elite supported some racial desegregation, especially for interest convergence reasons.

The Aftermath of Brown: More White Supremacist Resistance

Still, the powerful conservative faction of that white elite, especially its southern members, had no intention of implementing *Brown*. Since the 1950s they, together with most ordinary whites, have fought to keep white students from having to go to racially integrated schools. For example, in Virginia powerful whites such as Senator Harry Byrd (1933–1965) impeded the implementation of *Brown* with a policy of state resistance. Rather than integrate, white supremacist officials closed schools in various counties. For example, in 1959, operating out of an extreme racist frame, the white male decision-makers of Prince Edward County axed their public school system in favor of a whites-only private school financed by state-approved tuition grants and donations from white segregationists.[12] When this massive resistance was belatedly ruled unconstitutional by the Supreme Court in 1964, such government grants to private education became unlawful. Nonetheless, elite and ordinary white southerners continued to do immeasurable damage to a generation of black students deprived of a fully resourced public education.[13] This massive resistance in Prince Edward County (and elsewhere) left the task of educating thousands of black students to the courageous efforts of mostly black adults, who ensured that as many as possible could attend temporary schools in church basements and neighboring communities. Strong segregationist tactics, employed by elite and non-elite whites here and many other areas, were mostly successful—by the end of racial desegregation's first decade a mere 2.3 percent of black children attended racially integrated schools in the Deep South.[14]

Despite these injustices, undeniable in these early years of the civil rights movement is the unyielding *agency* of Virginia's black population. They should be celebrated in the annals of what is freedom-generating in human history. Their efforts reveal the ingenuity and vision of a people who have been forced to participate in an unending struggle to survive the systemic racism imposed by elite and other whites for generations. Even while the audacity and ingenuity displayed in this resistance to oppression remains concealed or superficially treated in white-framed textbooks and media discussions, their dedication to a genuine liberty-and-justice *dream* is hard to miss to those open to the empirical evidence.[15] Likewise, the dominant white framing of U.S. history, and current racial segregation, often conceals the great destructive lengths to which elite and non-elite whites have been willing to go to prevent real racial liberty and justice for this society.

Belatedly, in 2003, some government officials in Virginia apologized for these extraordinary school closures. Even so, those whites responsible for denying education to black students were not suddenly enlightened. Over the ensuing decades after *legal* public school segregation was ended in the 1960s, a modestly modified white framing has allowed whites to continue to view themselves as not racist and as virtuous and well-meaning people— despite the fact that they still protect the country's extensive de facto racial segregation in schools. Nowhere is evidence of the white frame's *myths* more unsettling than in the reactions of some whites to a 1999 symposium on school integration at a Virginia college. Robert Taylor, a white leader who helped build a private whites-only school, refused to attend. Maintaining that the private educational system was not about racial segregation, he claimed that the issue that led to the closing of the Virginia school system long ago was mythical "states' rights" to decide such human rights matters. The passage of time has not convinced Taylor and many other powerful and ordinary whites that they have anything racially horrific for which to atone and remedy.[16]

Ray Moore, a white physician who served on the all-white Moton school board during the school closings, initially cautioned that one speaker at this 1999 symposium, Willie Shepperson, who partook in the protests as a student, might provoke violence there. However, during his address, Shepperson took Moore's hand and told the crowd at the college that whites and blacks had a *moral duty* to ensure racial justice: "I welcome Dr. Moore as a brother in this community and I hope he welcomes me as a brother." Moore replied: "I am a changed person. . . . I was converted when I heard the eloquence of [Shepperson's] words on this platform and the commendable distance that he placed between himself and what I know is a dark anger still hidden deep in his soul."[17] In Shepperson's actions, we catch echoes of King's optimism and are reminded that the chief obstacle to justice and equality is the white power structure that leaves Americans of color with no alternative but to actively protest. Like King, Shepperson's spirited structural analysis was rooted in a centuries-old African American counter-frame that not only critically challenges the white frame, but also forms a truly just and moral framing of the structural changes needed in this still racially immoral society.

Moore on the other hand, despite his words, appeared to be mostly operating out of a contemporary version of that white racial frame. For one, this reunion resulted from Shepperson's initiative. Initially, Moore could not see past the dangerous black male stereotype. Moore's original racialized reaction indicates he was unable to recognize that *moral outrage* by black Americans regarding injustice is reasonable. Like Moore, most whites today do not have the inclination to understand the realities of the country's still systemic racism from a black viewpoint. As the African American writer Ralph Ellison long ago explained: A black person must often

> experience a sensation that he does not exist in the real world at all. He seems rather to exist in the nightmarish fantasy of the white American mind as a phantom that the white mind seeks unceasingly, by means both crude and subtle, to lay to rest.[18]

Ellison's perceptive words shed light on why in the 1950s and 1960s many thousands of black Americans risked their lives to protest racial injustice, whereas many powerful white men very actively stood in the way of their securing genuine justice.

Ongoing School Segregation Today

Given that education remains a central component in reducing social inequality and increasing socioeconomic mobility, the ongoing racial segregation of black students and other students of color remains highly unjust. Recently, researchers tracked a representative sample of 8,258 adults. The study confirms that African Americans who attended public schools integrated by court order were more likely to graduate, attend college, earn a degree, and have better incomes than those who attended segregated schools. No negative impacts from this desegregation on the educations of white students were found. Other researchers have found that whites who attended racially integrated schools are more likely to live in integrated communities as adults and to send their children to racially diverse schools.[19] One key here is that racially integrated schools often provide much better educational facilities than racially segregated schools for students of color.

Nonetheless, in many areas today, racial segregation of public schools is at least as severe as in the legal segregation era. The average white student currently attends a school that is nearly three-fourths white, and less than one quarter students of color. The average black student currently attends a school that is 49 percent black (and 72 percent students of color). Similarly, the average Latino student attends a school in which the student body is about 57 percent Latino (and 75 percent students of color). Generally, this means most black and Latino students are very segregated from whites, and vice versa. Resource inequality is still a key issue in this de facto segregation. Schools with 90 percent or more students of color spend $733 less annually per student than schools with mostly white students.[20] Unsurprisingly, those who make most critical decisions that shape this racial segregation today are still very disproportionately elite whites and their acolytes who are not committed to a truly desegregated and thus "free" society.

For instance, during the George W. Bush presidential administration the actions of top Republican officials routinely had negative impacts on the education of students of color. About 380 school districts nationally, including many in the North, were no longer under (still necessary) court-ordered desegregation by the end of his presidential terms, a dramatic decrease from the 595 school districts under court-ordered desegregation when he came into office. Like powerful white decision-makers before them, Bush and his administrative acolytes demonstrated a strong white framing of racial segregation as unnecessary to eliminate. Demand from powerful white officials in local school districts had kept the pressure on. This pattern of taking segregated school districts out from under important government supervision did decelerate significantly under President Barack Obama (2009–2017), but did not end. In 2014, about 340 districts remained under court order.[21] While the commitment of top officials to meaningful desegregation improved significantly in the Obama era, especially with the appointment of some officials of color, it was not enough of a federal priority to resume major pressures on local districts to end racial segregation in schools, and thus in the school resources critical to socioeconomic mobility. Indeed, the concerns of the African American students of Prince Edward County in the 1950s remain alive today, as the American Dream of educational mobility continues to be out of reach for many Americans of color.

Racial Segregation in Housing: Whites Resisting Change

Contrary to views of the U.S. housing situation that reproduce the mythology of all Americans now having full access to the traditional American Dream, where one lives is often *not* just a matter of personal taste, preference, or merit. Racially segregated residential patterns persist substantially because of centuries of slavery, legal segregation, and contemporary housing-related discrimination. For most of U.S. history, segregated geographical patterns have been fashioned by elite and ordinary white decision-makers, with dire socioeconomic and other consequences for a majority of Americans of color. As with educational discrimination, this white killing of much African American access to adequate housing has been both unjust and largely *intentional*.[22]

Systemic racism's harsh reality, kept in place by white actions out of the dominant anti-black frame, ensured for many decades, up until the 1970s, that white-dominated living spaces were mostly off-limits to African Americans and many other Americans of color. To a significant degree in many geographical areas, whites still actively resist more than token residential segregation, sometimes with violence. Beginning in the 1930s, powerful white male officials in the federal government established a nationwide housing appraisal system wherein skin color officially became a significant consideration for assessing home values and making home loans. Leading Federal Housing Association (FHA) officials cautioned powerful white (male) lenders making home loans that the presence of just one or two families of color could greatly reduce real estate prices in historically white neighborhoods. Accordingly, officials in mortgage institutions implemented official discriminatory policies to keep families of color out of historically white neighborhoods.[23]

With its low-cost mortgages, the 1944 Servicemen's Readjustment Act (nicknamed the "G.I. Bill") ensured that returning white World War II veterans and their families would again profit from being racially privileged. The act provided favorable mortgages to a great many veterans, thereby creating much *white* suburbanization across the country. Between 1934 and 1962, federal government programs like the G.I. Bill financed $120 billion in new housing, with less than 2 percent of that allotted to Americans of color.[24] Even after fighting racist regimes in Europe, returning African American veterans did not benefit much from this federal home loan effort, again because of actively enforced white discrimination. Even today, most whites are unaware of this and other large-scale postwar government programs ("white affirmative action") that greatly helped to create the contemporary white middle class and their relative affluence.

In the era after World War II there were other government programs being operated by powerful white male officials that also made securing housing more difficult for many African Americans and other Americans of color. Consider the federal program referred to as "urban renewal." This program was created by 1949 and 1954 federal housing legislation. The African American essayist James Baldwin referred to these renewal efforts in cities as "Negro Removal" because their top white decision-makers frequently targeted black working class urban communities (often designated "slums"). Federal funds were available to mostly white-male-run city governments to cover the cost of destroying older housing in these areas to make the land profitable for white real estate and allied government decision-makers. Most displaced people were black and Latino, who for the most part did not benefit from white officials' false promises of city "renewal."[25]

In 1968 President Lyndon Johnson signed the Fair Housing Act, the last of the major 1960s civil rights laws. Segregationist language was deleted from federal housing policy; families of color began moving into traditionally white communities in larger numbers. This housing act was supposed to eliminate discrimination in leasing and purchasing of housing. However, over ensuing decades white real estate agents still regularly induced white homeowners to sell homes for less than market value by playing on their racist framing of families of color who might consider moving into their neighborhoods. With resulting white flight, property values depreciated according to calculations of (mostly white) real estate evaluators who viewed desegregating situations negatively from the white racial frame. In contrast, white suburban homes were under demand, and most appreciated. Indeed, mainly because of this important housing asset—the appreciating value of a home—the net worth of a great many white families has increased significantly since World War II.[26]

Today, there is still large-scale racial segregation in virtually all U.S. towns and cities. Demographers John Logan and Brian Stults emphasize major reasons for this:

> Part of the answer is that systematic discrimination in the housing market has not ended, and for the most part it is not prosecuted. . . . studies that track the experience of minority persons in the rental or homeowner market continue to find that they are treated differently than comparable whites.[27]

A National Commission report found that laws banning discrimination in rental and sales housing are at best weakly enforced.[28] Intentional discrimination by powerful white decision-makers and their employees is a major cause of this discrimination. Agents of current housing discrimination include mostly white landlords, bankers, realtors, and government housing officials. For example, studies show significant discrimination by lending institutions against black Americans seeking housing loans. We have previously noted the large-scale discrimination, in the form of subprime loans, by mostly white finance industry executives and their employees against black homeowners prior to the Great Recession. Indeed, these executives *worked with* George W. Bush administration officials to expand these loans to black families they knew would have trouble repaying them.[29]

Studies also show, unsurprisingly, that white homeowners play a central part in the persisting housing discrimination. One survey found a significant proportion of whites openly supporting the view that laws should permit a (white) homeowner to discriminate against African Americans. Many others likely would express such views in private.[30] Over recent decades housing audit studies, using white testers and testers of color, have repeatedly revealed racial discrimination by white homeowners, landlords, and realtors in rental and purchased housing markets across the country.[31] Today, there is no federal organization that proactively and persistently seeks out and punishes the still widespread housing discrimination that is one buttress of the country's continuing systemic racism.

Segregated neighborhoods usually mean major racial inequalities in public services. The historically segregated and racialized neighborhoods of black Americans and other Americans of color generally have *not* received the equitable government investments necessary for good schools, public safety, and transportation infrastructure—investments taken for granted in white communities. If these public investments were made, growing up in racially segregated areas would not diminish upward mobility as much as it does. Major public resources have sometimes been put by top white government officials into communities of color, but too often into programs like racialized policing and other aspects of the prison-industrial complex that overwhelmingly target Americans of color. Over time, this too creates even greater structural socioeconomic disadvantages across the color line.[32]

Occupational Discrimination and the White American Dream

As we documented previously (Chapter 2), occupational segregation along racial lines has long been a key aspect of the country's systemic racism. This segregation has very often not been a matter of choice or of abstract factors like merit, but is the result of explicitly discriminatory actions in the past and in the present by white decision-makers, including top business executives and their implementing managers and supervisors. Recall, for instance, our discussion of the lack of diversity in better-paying jobs in numerous high-tech firms on the West Coast. Black and Latino workers are relatively rare in such jobs. In contrast, about 41 percent of security guards, 72 percent of janitorial cleaners, and 76 percent of maintenance workers are black and Latino.[33] Discriminatory practices are not unique to this industry, for the mostly white managements in a great many workplaces operate out of the dominant racial frame to bar, segregate, and/or subordinate a great many workers of color.

To make matters worse, many white managements further discriminate against women workers of color, using various means to restrict their entry into better-paying job tracks with significant mobility opportunity. This is a societal reality that sociologist Adia Harvey Wingfield terms *systemic gendered racism*.[34] These employers frequently make use of practices imbedding overt and covert racial and gender framing that has long been central in U.S. labor practices. Note, once again, how systemic racism and systemic sexism are closely intertwined and coreproductive of each other within the context of profit-seeking capitalism.

Consider too these centuries of white profitability. For 240-plus years of U.S. slavery, white slaveholders, merchants, and other employers regularly stole much more of the economic value of the substantial labor of black female and male workers than that of comparable white workers. This massive discrimination persisted during the long Jim Crow era; since Jim Crow's official end in 1969 many black workers have continued to receive a lower wage or salary and other less desirable working conditions than comparable whites. Many have been driven by white decision-makers into more or less segregated job classifications for which they are often overqualified, but that guarantee less pay than for similarly qualified white workers. In today's economy a majority of black male workers are employed in unskilled, semi-skilled, service, or other comparatively low-paid jobs; are in professional and managerial positions disproportionately serving black consumers; or are unemployed or in part-time positions and seeking full-time employment. Their black female counterparts frequently face similar employment problems, and they also frequently encounter much gendered-racist discrimination in white-dominated workplaces and other settings. Indeed, in numerous low-wage workplace settings black male and female workers do not get a living wage—defined as the minimum needed to meet basic needs. Not surprisingly, some research indicates that black workers today lose more than $120 billion in wages annually from white-imposed employment discrimination, which usually means increases in the incomes of top white executives and other whites in many workplaces.[35]

Racialized job screening often begins at the hiring stage, while other employment mistreatment is encountered later. Researchers have found that job applicants with "white-sounding" names are much more likely to be sought out by employers than those with "black-sounding" names. In one study black job applicants with white-Anglicized names got more favorable pre-interview evaluations from white sales professionals than did black applicants with black "ethnic names."[36] In addition, research using white testers and testers of color has found white applicants are frequently favored over applicants of color. Beyond the hiring stage black employees face additional workplace discrimination. White workers are frequently given better access than black workers to good job assignments and promotions, as well as to the educational training or mentoring programs assisting moves up the job ladder. Consider too that, in contrast to whites, over the course of their work lives most black employees *repeatedly* face white-imposed discrimination.[37]

As we discussed previously (Chapter 1), white workers benefit from this anti-black racial discrimination. Over centuries, the white capitalistic elite has labored to secure white workers' acceptance of the country's class and racial hierarchies by offering them a "psychological wage of whiteness." As a result, white workers as a group have long had many more economic and other societal privileges and opportunities than black workers and other workers of color; most whites treasure these racial privileges even when it harms their ability to organize with workers of color to better their class position versus capitalistic employers.

One of these significant white privileges is access to whites-only employment and other valuable social networks. Sociologist Nancy DiTomaso has documented the essential white networks that remain central to the reproduction of systemic racial inequalities in jobs and other economic resources. In more than 200 white interviews, she found constant descriptions of the white social networks that her research participants had used to find *most* jobs they secured over a lifetime of employment. They were thus mostly sheltered from truly open competition in U.S. job markets. While these whites also denounced overt job discrimination, few recognized their great built-in white advantages. Most inaccurately attributed their job market successes just to their hard work and other personal virtues.[38]

An omnipresent white racial framing legitimates, rationalizes, and shapes this abiding white confidence in white virtue, including the white work ethic and meritorious qualifications. The notion that a person gets ahead just on the basis of this work ethic and personal merit is central to the unjustified white claim that the United States has long been meritocratic, fair, and democratic. However, this is an ahistorical racial framing in which the systemic forces that advantage white Americans over Americans of color are denied or downplayed. Unsurprisingly, in opinion surveys whites agree at nearly twice the rate of any other racial or ethnic group that *individual initiative* is still the central explanation for persisting U.S. racial inequalities.[39]

Notably, too, most white Americans remain illiterate about U.S. racial history and thus continue to ignore the centuries-long labor history of African American workers, frequently portraying them and their families as indolent and weak. Ironically, as the African American entrepreneur Claud Anderson has emphasized, over several centuries up to the 1960s, black American workers were in fact the *model*, even among many whites, "for doing the hardest, dirtiest, most dangerous and backbreaking work." Reflecting on the black enslavement era, he adds, if nonblacks had been the better workers "why would supposedly bright [white] businessmen spend 250 years traveling half way around the world to kidnap [millions of] innocent, but lazy blacks, then knowingly bring them to America to do work that other ethnic groups could do better?"[40] Constantly, systemic racism was closely intertwined with capitalistic development. Centuries of enslaved and Jim-Crowed black labor played a central role not only in creating the surplus capital that was the basis of much of this country's capitalistic economic development and expansion, but also in creating much prosperity and wealth for generations of white individuals and families— and, most especially, for the white male elite.

Wealth Inequality and the American Dream

Well-Institutionalized Wealth Inequality

In early North American colonies, the wealthiest tenth of the population, virtually all white, owned at least half the inventoried property wealth. Between the American Revolution and the Civil War, great wealth concentration persisted in the hands of the top 10 percent, with only a small drop in wealth concentration in the decades after that war. By the third decade of the 20th century, wealth concentration increased, then declined a bit in the 1930s–1940s, then rose again since the 1950s.[41] Nonetheless, it has always remained high.

More recently, ever more Americans have come to recognize that the conventional rags-to-riches narrative, the most optimistic version of the conventional American Dream, is the stuff of elite class framing and Hollywood fiction. Even being better off than one's parents is becoming more difficult to achieve. In terms of earnings, contemporary U.S. adults do average a bit more than their parents earned at their age. Yet this does not necessarily mean they have more *wealth* (total financial assets less debt). Today, in terms of wealth, only half of adults are better off than their parents were at their age. In one recent survey the median wealth of adults is about $39,000, which puts the United States only 27th among countries internationally. Significantly, between the 1970s and the 1990s the share of wealth owned by the richest 1 percent of families more than doubled; this trend toward greater inequality has continued since.[42]

Central to this reality is that dramatic differences in wealth persist among the largest racial groups. The median white person's wealth is 18 times that of the median Latino American and 20 times that of the median African American. One major reason that whites typically amass more wealth during their lifetimes than blacks or Latinos is because of the greater wealth-generating social and socioeconomic resources they have typically *inherited* over generations from white ancestors (see below). Racial inequality in income is thus only part of the contemporary inequality story. The racialized wealth gap is much larger and is key to understanding the lesser socioeconomic mobility across numerous recent generations of black Americans and other Americans of color.[43]

Currently, mostly white men and their families sit at the top of the U.S. income and wealth hierarchies. They have often more than achieved the "get rich" version of the American Dream. There are roughly 120 million households, approximately 83 million white and the rest households of color. About 96 percent of the top 1 percent of households (in terms of income) are white, and only 1.4 percent are black. Even then, the latter are on average much less rich than the whites therein. Centuries of enslavement, Jim Crow segregation, and contemporary discrimination have prevented most black Americans from amassing the kind of wealth that whites in top socioeconomic ranks of U.S. society currently possess.[44] This wealth picture remains true even though in the United States the average black family's ancestors go back at least as far as the average white family's ancestors. Unjust enrichment for white families over some 20 generations of this country's development is paralleled directly by intentional and unjust impoverishment for black families over those 20 generations.

As we detailed previously, the mostly white Americans at the top of the socioeconomic hierarchy, most especially those in the very top 0.1 percent (upper tenth of the 1 percent, averaging $20 million in net worth), control this country's economy at the top. They include owners and top managers of major corporations who oversee who gets hired and have much other corporate control of workplaces and the larger economy. As we see throughout this book, this mostly white male elite and its implementing acolytes also influence key decisions in U.S. political and other noneconomic institutions as well. They routinely *take action*, such as by lobbying for important laws and subsidizing major political candidates who support their political-economic interests. They donate to institutions of higher learning and thereby often shape the country's information and learning processes. In short, the framing and actions of this ultra-wealthy and very powerful white 0.1 percent regularly reproduce the racial, class, and gender hierarchies and inequalities across all major sectors of U.S. society.

Bank Exploitation of Americans of Color

The discriminatory actions of leading executives and their employees in white-run corporations have long played a central role in ensuring that black Americans and other Americans of color have difficulties in gaining and passing along significant economic resources and assets. This includes the aforementioned white-generated housing discrimination limiting the build-up of significant housing equities over generations. Consider, too, recent top executives' and their acolytes' roles in creating the racial differential in asset losses to U.S. families during the 2007–2009 Great Recession (Chapter 5). The consequences of this major recession fell much more heavily on black families (31 percent reduction in wealth) and Latino families (44 percent reduction) than on white families (11 percent reduction).[45]

Recall that one main reason for this dramatic difference is that, compared to whites, many black and Latino families were disproportionately channeled into costly and often discriminatory subprime housing loans made by mostly white-run financial institutions. White-elite-operated banks and other financial institutions accumulated billions in profits from these discriminatory home loans to Americans of color. An estimated *$71–92 billion* was misappropriated from black individuals and families alone. Note, especially, that such discrimination reduced their housing equity wealth, which would likely have been passed along to later generations as it has been for a great many whites. The assets built up by years of saving efforts were pilfered through the unscrupulous discriminatory actions of mostly white-controlled financial institutions. A report by United for a Fair Economy concluded that the racist framing of borrowers of color had led banking officials to intentionally try to increase profits by unscrupulously pursuing people of color with defective loan products.[46]

Yet again, significant resources, privileges, and power were unjustly gained by whites and structured into the dominant racialized institutions. In addition, substantial racial inequalities are here, as elsewhere, maintained by intergenerational reproduction mechanisms. For instance, white elite banking officials made billions of dollars off the backs of black and Latino borrowers, who in many instances later lost homes via bank foreclosures during the Great Recession. Discriminatory home loan profits brought higher salaries for the mostly white officials in many such financial institutions, some of which was doubtless passed along to their children. That illustrates one important way that whites' unjust enrichment has been central to the creation and perpetuation of society's persisting and great racial inequalities. The subprime home loan discrimination also illustrates certain racist stereotypes and narratives from the dominant white racial frame. For example, this was clear in white officials conceptualizing blacks as "mud people" and their profitable subprime lending as "ghetto loans."[47]

Unsurprisingly, mainstream journalistic and academic accounts almost never called out by name and analyzed, even in part, the powerful white men who ran these exploitative banks, and seldom have they been taken to task for their central role in the subprime catastrophe. Instead, culpability has usually been fixed on vaguely described factors, including the failure of regulatory agencies, unwise appraisers, imprudent credit rating agencies, and poorly informed consumers of color.[48] Vague talk of the "loss" of billions of black and Latino assets implies an accidental loss or the failure of blacks and Latinos to use money properly, as if they were primarily responsible. In fact, it was numerous powerful white men and their employees in important financial institutions who calculatingly exploited and appropriated billions from black and Latino individuals and their families.

The Social Reproduction of Racial Inequality

Much data in this and previous chapters demonstrate the old fictions of unique white virtue and the white American Dream. "Meritorious" whites are regularly portrayed as exemplars of hard work and thus as being able to pass on significant economic resources, whereas the majority of African Americans and many other Americans of color are portrayed as much less virtuous and are systemically barred from doing the same by much direct and indirect discrimination in the past and present. Most elite and nonelite whites, purposely or otherwise, ignore the fact that the great and many positive rewards of centuries of racial discrimination targeting just African Americans—socioeconomic rewards during slavery, during Jim Crow, and from contemporary discrimination—have carried across many white generations into the lives of a majority of contemporary white Americans.

Consider the great wealth generated by African Americans' excruciating work and life sacrifice, wealth that they never received. Using repeated individual and collective violence (actual and threatened), whites at several class levels seized hundreds of millions of unpaid hours of African Americans' work. Economic losses to black individuals and families from this extensive white oppression in the form of centuries of slavery and Jim Crow segregation are estimated by researchers to be much more than the U.S. gross national product (currently, about $17 trillion). Then add in the huge physical and psychological costs from the pain, suffering, and death also resulting from slavery and Jim Crow, and massive community reparations for African Americans today are *the least* in the way of a serious solution for these massive racial oppressions that a truly just and humanistic society should provide. Moreover, continuing racial discrimination and its material, physical, and psychological costs would need to be figured into the sum total of these contemporary reparations.[49]

Consider too that these huge economic and other losses for African Americans have meant significant gains, directly or indirectly, for a great many whites over centuries. The comprehensive, essentially totalitarian, subordination of black Americans under slavery and Jim Crow conditions—most of U.S. history—contributed significantly to the creation, growth, and maintenance of whites' unjust enrichment and other unjust advantages, including much of that enjoyed by the white elite and middle class. Centuries of black labor and property stolen by many millions of whites frequently became income and wealth for even more millions of whites later on; earlier unjust enrichment was usually passed along over many white generations. Central to how this racially inegalitarian society has operated are these often hidden social inheritance mechanisms that ensure that most whites in each new generation, to the present day, inherit wealth-generating racial privileges and resources. Recent research by sociologist Jennifer Mueller on white families and families of color dramatically demonstrates the enormous scale of these socioeconomic and government resources that have been passed along to many white generations. Comparing generational data for white families and families of color, she found great racial inequalities favoring whites in the procurement and intergenerational transfer of monies, housing equities, businesses, land, and other economic assets.[50]

Unsurprisingly, this intergenerational reproduction of significant assets across numerous white generations has generally been buttressed by the previously noted array of "white affirmative action" programs provided by state and federal governments. These extensive programs have included not only the federal government's homestead land acts that from the 1860s to the 1930s gave away 246 million acres of federal lands (formerly Native American lands) to mostly white homesteading families, as well as the various veterans' educational and housing programs after World War II that seriously discriminated against black applicants. To a substantial degree, the white middle class was further developed and expanded by these post-war federal programs and many other federal programs more recently—and not just on the work ethic so exaggerated in the common meritocratic framing of whites' achieving the American Dream.

Conclusion

Indeed, in each major period of overt collective struggle by African Americans against systemic racism, their renewed development of an antiracist counter-framing that openly asserts authentic liberty-and-justice goals has been viewed by a majority of white Americans with great alarm. Thus, majority white resistance to substantial changes in systemic racism was quite evident during the 1960s protest era, and has been ever since. In 1960s opinion polls the now heralded efforts and actions of African American civil rights activists and organizations, especially in regard to full desegregation, were strongly *rejected* by a large majority of whites. Even into the 1980s, the conservative President Ronald Reagan opposed a federal holiday in Dr. Martin Luther King's honor, and he and many other whites viewed King as nothing close to the celebrated civil rights saint of the current era. Indeed, since the 1960s a majority of whites have fought against more substantial desegregation of public schools, workplaces, and other U.S. institutions.[51]

More recently, and prior to his election as the 44th president, Barack Obama, openly critiqued the centuries-old white racist framing of society in his autobiography, *The Audacity of Hope: Thoughts on Reclaiming the American Dream*. There he declared that his personal success should not obscure the harsh fact that white racist framing and discriminatory actions had for centuries placed huge barriers in the way of significant socioeconomic opportunities for a great many Americans of color. He recognized that pervasive white racial framing limits access to the traditional American Dream of material success—e.g., a good job, good housing, financial security—for a majority of African Americans and many other Americans of color.[52] Nonetheless, despite his accent on racial discrimination and critique of the white-proclaimed American Dream, in the wake of his 2008 election white media commentators and leading politicians aggressively urged him to take the *leading role* in exposing what they saw as the "fiction" of white racism and thereby affirm the attainability of the (white) American Dream for all Americans today.[53]

In denying white demands for this unique personal responsibility, Obama went some way in contradicting the dominant white frame as it is used to defend the countless range of privileges and resources amassed and passed along the generations by whites, the group still firmly at the top of the racial hierarchy. Even so, elite white politicians, media commentators, corporate executives, and their supporters continue to fill the airwaves with aggressive talk about how if a person of color "works hard enough, they can overcome anything." The meaning of this stern mythology is that if you are still poor, you just have not worked hard enough (i.e., are not virtuous). There are always a few convenient examples of successful people of color that are seized upon by white propagandists to sustain the believability of this illusionary individualism. They do this in spite of the fact that successful people of color like Obama regularly emphasize the age-old realities of major white-racist barriers to their groups' socioeconomic success.[54]

Undeniably, for centuries, elite-white-male policymakers and their associates have routinely hindered the social, economic, and political mobility of most Americans of color, all the while proclaiming the common racialized mythology of American individualism with its strong accent on individual effort bringing opportunity and material success. The cruelty of this white deceit is only matched by its great social injustice. This traditional American Dream is mostly a *white lie*, and not in the meaning of a minor falsehood. It is the one of the biggest and most malignant white lies about U.S. society, one that tries to cover up centuries of extreme racial oppression.

8
Systemic Sexism, Racism, and Classism
A Troubled Present and Future

U.S. politics regularly demonstrates the gender, racial, and class themes about the elite-white-male dominance system we have emphasized in this book. Let us first consider in this conclusion some dramatic events of the turbulent 2016 election season that illustrate how central these elite white men and their acolytes have been to the development and control of this country's major institutions.

In that election, the capitalistic developer Donald Trump, the Republican nominee for president with no prior electoral or government experience, received much support, especially from white voters, and won the presidency. Yet he is no "man of the people." Indeed, he is one of the world's wealthiest people, a man who has long been enamored of friendly networking with others in the white ruling class.[1] His elitist world is radically different from the world of his ordinary white supporters. One columnist has described his privileged life, quoting the tycoon and television star on his distinctive lifestyle, "I live in the building where I work. I take an elevator from my bedroom to my office. The rest of the time, I'm either in my stretch limousine, my private jet, my helicopter, or my private club in Palm Beach Florida."[2]

Contrary to statements made by many Republican officials and Trump rally supporters, Trump has much in common with those elite officials and their orientation to contemporary oligopolistic capitalism, as well as in regard to their roles in systemic racism and sexism. Trump's capitalist endeavors have put him in league with other white male capitalist Republicans as a longtime member of the corporate-based establishment. Consider his billion-dollar resort project in Scotland, which reportedly brought devastation to an environment many deemed of unique scientific interest. Scots organized and assertively voiced concerns about the resort's influences on wildlife.[3]

Significant elements of systemic racism and systemic sexism could be observed throughout the 2016 U.S. presidential campaign. Trump, as the winning presidential candidate, politically benefited from long-problematical Republican strategies, including Richard Nixon's white southern strategy and organized conservative conspiracies like the Obama-targeted "birther" movement. But more than this, Trump fit into the exclusive world of powerful white male decision-makers. *The Donald*, a moniker his first wife gave him that conjures up images of strong white alpha-males, has referred to women as "ballbreakers" and "far worse than men, far more aggressive" and advised that "If someone screws you . . . screw them back."[4]

During the 2016 campaign Trump became famous for male-sexist commentary that is central to systemic sexism. He once remarked that "When you're a star . . . you can do anything [to women]. Grab 'em by the pussy."[5] Indeed, as a member of the white male elite, he has had great power over numerous non-elites. But this sense of entitlement goes way beyond any one powerful white man. Some mainstream media commentators have suggested that numerous Republican policies involving women's issues (e.g., extreme anti-abortion policies) arise just from paternalistic concern and have nothing to do with male sexist framing of women. Yet, Trump's male-sexist commentary above was not the aberration this conservative political elite and their acolytes would have us believe it to be.[6] Via policy and action, numerous white male members of the political elite, especially but not entirely in its conservative wing, have treated people of color and non-elite white women as lesser than them. Historically and contemporarily, they have mostly gotten away with it politically.

In fact, in recent decades many in the elite's conservative wing have tried to rid U.S. institutions of some modest democracy and fairness that remain. A case in point are the laws that have replaced much of the U.S. civil jury system, giving well-off Americans yet more power and control. Tort reforms, for instance, have produced indescribable anguish and economic destitution for ordinary people due to monetary "caps" on lawsuits that ordinary citizens have a constitutional right to bring against major corporations and other powerful entities for the serious harm they have caused.[7]

As we demonstrated previously, there seems to be little that distinguishes now President Donald Trump in his influential framing and powerful actions from most others who control the country's elite-white-male dominance system, including its sexist, racist, classist subsystems. For this reason, in this final chapter we will examine Trump's effort to become the Republican presidential candidate, and then U.S. president, and numerous related actions and events across the course of the 2016 presidential election in order to underscore our earlier arguments about the continuing centrality and everyday operation of this elite-white-male system.

Donald Trump: Exemplifying White Male Dominance

The 2016 Republican primary race was notable for its battle between two somewhat different capitalistic blocs. Trump often tried to represent the national capitalistic bloc and was initially opposed by many in the international corporate bloc of the Republican Party. Recall from Chapter 2 that the U.S. economy has periodically changed in terms of which major business blocs have had the greatest economic and political influence. A substantially U.S.-oriented capitalistic developer like Donald Trump, with less interest than many multinational corporate capitalists in expanding overseas manufacturing of products to import to the United States, was free to condemn policies that shifted manufacturing jobs overseas. Unlike his more internationalist rivals, such as Jeb Bush (brother of George W. Bush), Trump was at liberty to denounce U.S. imperialistic wars, including the latter Bush's invasion of Iraq.

Racist Political Framing: Reprising the Past

Donald Trump's ascent to the presidential pinnacle using some xenophobic framing should not have been mystifying. He was born into white male privilege, the son of a wealthy conservative real estate entrepreneur. After his election, he demonstrated well these long-existing connections by nominating a very wealthy collection of appointees to his cabinet and other top political positions. One CNN analysis of thirty-five people named by Trump for his cabinet and other top appointments found that almost all were multimillionaires or very well-off, and 94 percent were white. Some 80 percent were white men, and only 6 percent (two people) were men or women of color. For the most part those chosen were arch-conservatives, and several seemed hostile in their previous commentaries and actions to the high U.S. administrative posts for which they were chosen—including an education secretary weakly committed to public schools and firmly committed to private schools and school choice, a secretary of health and human services antagonistic towards the Affordable Care Act, an Environmental Protection Agency head who denied climate change science, and a labor secretary unfalteringly opposed to increases to the minimum wage.[8]

Moreover, Trump seemed rather conventional in much of his white framing during and after the presidential campaign, including in stereotyped framing of many Mexicans and Muslims he sought to exclude from the United States. In his view the country "has become a dumping ground for everybody else's problems. When Mexico sends its people, they're not sending their best. . . . They're bringing drugs. They're bringing crime. They're rapists."[9] He reiterated these spurious charges frequently in speeches. Again the research evidence strongly contradicts this stereotyped imagery, for most documented and undocumented Mexican immigrants are ordinary Mexicans seeking better life opportunities, with no criminal backgrounds. Trump also generalized about Muslim immigrants, suggesting that all should be excluded from the

United States for some time. He regularly played into white voters' racial framing, including stereotyped fears of immigrants who are not white.[10]

A national survey found that more than three-quarters of Trump's supporters were disturbed by the country's growing racial diversity. More than three-quarters felt immigrants were a "burden" on the country, that Islam contradicted "America's values," and that anti-white discrimination was now as serious as discrimination against people of color. Nearly three-quarters said the country needs an autocratic leader "who is willing to *break* some rules to set things right."[11]

Contrary to much publicity he got about being a "populist," Trump would find himself at ease among current and previous elite white leaders. His appeals to racial, gender, and class framing have long been part of electoral politics and public commentary that are essential to perpetuating the important aspects of the elite-white-male dominance system. For instance, in the 18th century Benjamin Franklin, a revered diplomat and liberal founder, was very alarmed over German immigrants sullying the U.S. scene. Franklin publicly fêted his strongly anti-immigrant xenophobia. Calling political opponents offensive names is also something Trump and other presidents and presidential candidates have had in common. Ulysses S. Grant (the 18th president) remarked that James Garfield (the 20th president) was "not possessed of the backbone of an angleworm."[12] "Baboon" was among the derogatory terms used by political enemies to describe Abraham Lincoln. Moreover, beginning in the Reconstruction period after the Civil War, white male executives and their agents actively quashed white workers' demands for economic redistribution and greater enfranchisement by appealing to their white racist framing and accenting their "public and psychological wage of whiteness."[13] Thus, because of the persistence into the present of these old white racial and male sexist frames, like his predecessors Trump used language that connected him well with the majority of white voters, and especially with white men.

Other Republicans seeking the 2016 GOP nomination were similar to Trump in some of their words and deeds. While touting the virtues of earned success, Jeb Bush claimed that black people did expect "free stuff" from whites.[14] Such an assertion by the son and brother of two presidents was not only racially framed but ludicrous on its face. The virtually boundless "free stuff" that Bush himself had received throughout his life owing to his white male elite status is immeasurable.[15] Indeed, the "white man's republic" that was long the United States, and within which the Bush dynasty ascended, was built on the backs of people of color, including enslaved and Jim-Crowed African Americans. This slavery-centered world of Europe and North America gave birth, or shaped substantially, much of what we think of as the "modern world" within which dominant white families have thrived.

The xenophobic and racist framing and rhetoric of various conservative politicians during this 2016 election season had many negative impacts. For example, in spring 2016 the Southern Poverty Law Center did a nonrandom online survey of 2,000 teachers (grades K–12) about the impact of the election. Over half indicated their students were engaging in more uncivil comments; one-third had seen an increase in anti-immigrant and anti-Muslim comments. Many teachers cited Donald Trump's comments in this regard as one factor. More than two-thirds said students—especially immigrant students, children of immigrants, and Muslims—were very concerned about the impact of the presidential election's results on their own families. Four in ten of the teachers even feared discussing the election in their classrooms. These fears among Americans of color, young and old, have continued since Trump was elected U.S. president in November 2016.[16]

Angry White Voters and White Christian Nationalism

So many ordinary white Americans applauded Trump's anti-immigrant nativism, white-centric racial framing, and male sexist framing that he easily won his 2015–2016 primary battle against the Republican establishment and its preferred candidates. Soon thereafter, he then won the presidency with the support of ordinary whites as well. As one news article explained, "Rank-and-file conservatives, after decades of deferring to party elites, are trying to stage what is effectively a people's coup by selecting a standard-bearer who is not the preferred candidate of wealthy donors and elected officials."[17] In accord with Trump's political perspective, many ordinary white voters were clearly worried about undocumented immigration, declining wages and work conditions, international trade deals, and coming-white-minority demographics. However, most conventional Republican leaders were much more committed to international free trade and, often, to continuing use of undocumented immigrant labor in many corporate enterprises. These views of ordinary Americans were evident in much opinion polling during the primaries and later presidential campaign. A majority of Americans agreed that government trade deals had more impact on declining U.S. jobs than natural economic changes. In addition, a substantial majority agreed with the view that the economy was "rigged" in favor of particular groups, a vague theme Trump emphasized.[18]

While in the 2016 presidential election Donald Trump did not gain a majority of all voters, he did win voters in enough key states to win the undemocratic electoral college. He succeeded in gaining a substantial majority of white voters (about 58 percent) to a significant degree because of his expression of white nativist and nationalist themes. Since the 2016 election, a number of these themes have strongly persisted. One key reason is the deep and extensive white racial framing of these issues in the minds of a substantial majority of white Americans. One recent survey by social scientist Justin Gest found that two-thirds of whites said they would support a hypothetical new nationalistic and nativistic *political party* that was committed to "stopping mass immigration, providing American jobs to American workers, preserving America's Christian heritage, and stopping the threat of Islam." Those more likely to support this hypothetical party were white men, especially those with less education, and whites under 40 years of age.[19] This survey and much other data indicate that white nativistic, Christian nationalism will continue to be a critical problem for the United States for years to come.

Previously, we noted Michael Kimmel's interview data (Introduction). They too demonstrate the contemporary anger of ordinary white men in the working class. The effective end of aggressive government-assisted expansion of economic security for the white working class and middle class over recent decades has fortified many ordinary white men's sense of anger over their, or their children's, declining socioeconomic opportunities. By the late 1990s many white men, especially those who were not college graduates, were no longer so easily able to provide their families with the guarantee of good economic stability and advancement they had long regarded as their birthright. Their conviction that they deserve decent-paying jobs and a serious social safety net is certainly more than reasonable. Unfortunately, many of them believe that they are mostly or the only ones *truly deserving* of numerous such government interventions, supports, and entitlements.[20]

This white birthright sense is tied to the dominant white racial and male sexist frames. From cradle to grave, the synthesis of white privilege and masculine privilege—of hegemonic white manhood—is fed to almost all white men. They have long accepted the elite's "con" of the public and psychological wage of whiteness, and of white maleness—the reward they receive for siding with the mostly white male elite on pivotal societal issues. A majority have allowed themselves to be adeptly manipulated by the elite that generally controls the economy, politics, and mainstream media. Additionally, these powerful whites have assisted ordinary white men in accenting scapegoats for their socioeconomic problems, especially Americans of color (and sometimes white women). This old divide-and-conquer strategy successfully separates many white workers and their families from workers of color and their families.

Consequently, the general resentment and anger of white men is often misdirected to the wrong targets. The white male corporate elite is mainly responsible for the deindustrialization, automation, and export of jobs overseas that have generated most of the decline in many traditional blue-collar and some white-collar jobs. Yet, even critical analysts often do not specifically call out and intensively analyze the actual implementers of this massive unemployment and underemployment process. One historian has argued:

> The U.S. has done a terrible job of figuring out what happens to working-class people when their jobs go away. . . . unfettered capital mobility is at the center of inequality in the United States and abroad. We need to place this issue at the center of our agenda to fix American economic problems and our agenda to stop the exploitation of the global poor by western companies.[21]

One problem in most such analyses, however, is the vague abstractions that foreground the "United States" or "western companies" as the vague actors, when in fact this great loss of good jobs for ordinary Americans is substantially the result of recurring and specific profit-oriented decisions by mostly white male capitalists. These destructive actors, like the proverbial "Wizard of Oz," usually remain *hidden* from public understanding and systematic critiques by a seldom-opened societal curtain.

In addition, the weakening of important government services, like unemployment benefits that ordinary whites rely on, is also the result of government legislative, judicial, and executive decisions of mostly elite white men or political officials substantially under their control. The latter decisions are major sources of the diminishing economic security for ordinary white and other Americans. Meanwhile, the ruling white elite pretends that "they are on the side of the very people they are disenfranchising, even at the very moment they are disenfranchising them."[22]

An example of who the average white voter ought to direct anger at is the Silicon Valley corporate elite. These mostly white capitalists represent a more tech-savvy bloc of the usually hidden ruling elite, but still operate in ways similar to their counterparts in other economic sectors. This conclusion is backed by data on modest diversity among better-paid tech company employees and on the Silicon Valley elite's attitudes toward capitalistic and white-male-normed organizational cultures (see Chapter 2). For instance, investor Paul Graham's views unmistakably run parallel to many earlier and contemporary white men with economic power. He has acknowledged being responsible for escalating class inequality. "I've become an expert on how to increase economic inequality," he explained, "and I've spent the past decade working hard to do it. . . . Eliminating great variations in wealth would mean eliminating startups."[23] Most men in the Silicon Valley elite may not so openly admit such evident truths about social class and other social oppression, but some research has shown that their outlooks are frequently similar. As one reporter noted from interviews with them, they generally consider a vague "equality of opportunity" central to an evenhanded and strong economy (the old individualistic theme), while viewing a concrete and government-fostered "equality of outcome" as "economically paralyzing."[24]

While a huge class schism between moneyed white men like the Silicon Valley titans and nonmoneyed white men exists, the white male brotherhood thrives across class lines. This manhood bond is firmly planted and legitimated by the pervasive white racial and male sexist frames. As a result, most ordinary white men do not openly resent or actively organize (e.g., in new assertive and racially integrated unions) against those elite decision-makers who are often most to blame for the socioeconomic problems they and their families face. For instance, the white male elite has automated or exported millions of good jobs, but few ordinary white men call out against them by name for such actions. Other non-elites, such as non-elite people of color and white women, are certainly not responsible for major employment and other economic decisions. Regardless, and even while the majority of non-elite white men are much better off in many ways than most people of color and most non-elite white women, their much discussed "white male anger" is nonetheless usually targeted at these other average Americans.

Women Politicians: Threats to White Masculinity

Donald Trump's commentaries and actions in the long 2016 presidential campaign, as well as those of many of his supporters, constantly highlighted significant aspects of the persisting and systemic sexism that is central to the elite-white-male dominance system. He or his supporters regularly demonstrated male sexist framing and white hyper-masculinity generally, including in regard to competitors inside and outside of the Republican Party. For instance, he constantly described male rivals for the Replublication nomination as weak, often implying their lack of true (white) masculinity.

Journalist Jonathan Chait noted both Trump's many anti-woman comments and other assertive masculine gestures:

> The restoration of male authority threatened by social change is a central theme of Trump's candidacy. His business ventures had long ago identified specifically masculine luxuries—golf, steaks—as ripe for identification with the Trump brand. During the campaign, Trump has called for the statue of Joe Paterno, the legendary, disgraced Penn State coach who ignored evidence his defensive coordinator had serially raped young boys, to be restored to the place of honor from which it had been removed.[25]

This is just one of many examples in a long history of white men accenting a forceful white manhood framing to win political contests. Recall our discussion of President Andrew Jackson, who cultivated an image of white hyper-masculinity, much of that derived from "Indian-killing" and other military actions. Other striking examples include Theodore Roosevelt's attempts to demonstrate he was a virile president ruling in a manly way (see Chapter 1).

In recent decades numerous politicians and media commentators have regularly operated from a self-assured white manhood perspective. Many commentators have accented how the "manly" Republican Ronald Reagan beat out "weak" male Democratic presidential candidates in the 1980s. Reagan cultivated a hyper-masculine image as a tough guy in movies he made before entering politics, an image that has persisted to the present.[26] In 2000, conservative Republican journalist Peggy Noonan, who also celebrated the white manliness of John Wayne, criticized international decisions of then President Bill Clinton as not being tough enough, in contrast to those of Reagan "who was a *man*."[27] Later, George W. Bush was said by many conservatives to be the manly candidate that badly needed to be elected president.

Bush soon reinforced his image of white manliness in photos at his Texas "ranch" using a chainsaw and riding a trail bike, and in a military-like pose with a "Mission Accomplished" banner on a Navy warship. The latter pose got him praised for his "testosterone" and "virility" in the media.[28] As one journalist put it, "For Bush-era Republicans, manliness was an essential trait in public life. Republicans mocked Al Gore as a girlie-man who loved earth tones, and John Edwards who 'looked like the Breck Girl.'"[29] Additionally, in 2003 the *Wall Street Journal* highlighted a broad hyper-masculine theme in an op-ed titled "Political Virility, Real Men Vote Republican." The op-ed also celebrated Bush's manliness as a "daddy politician" characterized by "tough talk, tough action, toughness in a tough job."[30]

Contemporary Sexist Framing: The Case of Hillary Clinton

The dominant male sexist frame justifies and enforces the gender and patriarchal hierarchization of western societies. It too could be observed in full-mode operation during the 2016 presidential campaign, not only in regard to other male politicians but also in regard to women politicians like Hillary Clinton. Famously, Donald Trump claimed that if Clinton were male, she would not secure even a mere "5 percent of the vote," implying a male sexist framing of Clinton and women voters. Hearing this, the columnist Kathleen Parker raised the question, "What if Trump were a woman? Imagine a Donna Trump running as a Republican."[31]

Parker then discussed *the Donald*'s various male privileges, debacles, and framing as she tried to imagine such a *Donna* Trump. This Donna Trump got started in business with much million-dollar help from her dad. She went on to risky business ventures that increased that to billions, but not before several bankruptcies and other commercial fiascoes. Donna said that if abortion were to be banned, women having the procedure should be punished. As a political candidate, Donna uniquely refused to divulge her tax returns. Donna regularly mangled the names of foreign countries and defended not knowing the names of leaders of terrorist groups that had declared the United States to be an enemy.[32] She boasted about sexual conquests, including affairs with married men. Donna racially slammed Mexican immigrants and Muslims and garnered the open support of former Klan leader David Duke.[33] After an even longer litany of an imagined Donna Trump's outrageous, racially framed, and gendered antics, based on things the actual Trump had done or said, Parker concludes that U.S. voters would certainly not consider Donna equipped to run the federal government.[34]

That Donna and not Donald Trump would be judged unqualified for the presidency is linked to the historic reality of the office. The presidency has long been exemplified by a supposedly strong white heterosexual male. The 2016 candidacy of Hillary Clinton fundamentally threatened the long-lasting centrality of white men seeking and serving in that role, just as the eight-year presidency of Barack Obama had done. A great many male politicians and voters alike have long played into the desire to have a "strict father" run the country assertively and without women's interference. Trump's commentaries regularly played on white male fears of racial and patriarchal change in U.S. society.[35]

More Overt Sexism: Various Political Campaigns

Much overt sexism, including masculinist posturing and misogyny, was evident during the 2016 primaries and election season. The male sexist framing of society and other elements of systemic sexism were constantly on display. For example, Trump accused Hillary Clinton of playing the "woman's card," to which she retorted, "Well, if fighting for women's health care and paid family leave and equal pay is playing the woman card, then deal me in."[36] In Republican primary debates, candidates Trump and Marco Rubio got into hyper-masculine posturing, including implied commentaries about the size of Trump's penis. Previously, Trump had baited Ted Cruz with the putdown "pussy," insinuating he was insufficiently masculine. (Researchers find that words like "pussy" are far more often used in exchanges between men than among women.)[37]

Trump regularly demonstrated an aggressive male sexist perspective. He "claimed that Carly Fiorina was too ugly to be President."[38] He admitted to being disgusted by certain physical functions of the female body, including breast-feeding. Trump was not alone among male politicians in this overt male sexist framing. Candidate Ted Cruz said that Hillary Clinton should be "spanked," and candidate Chris Christie vowed to "beat" her "rear end."[39]

Trump has also referred to women as "dogs" or "fat pigs." Again, and contrary to many media commentators, he was *not* unusual. During the course of western history women and other oppressed human groups have been assigned negatively regarded characteristics of nonhuman creatures by their male oppressors. For centuries, elite white men, including founders Thomas Jefferson and William Byrd II, viewed women as *dangerous* and *corrupting*. Slaveholding founders like George Washington had viewed enslaved blacks as their "livestock." In the 1930s and 1940s Jews were likened to "rats" and "mice," and called "beasts," not only by their German Nazi oppressors but also by white gentile Americans. Indeed, Jewish Americans still are characterized that way on contemporary white supremacist websites.[40]

The only Republican woman contending for the 2016 presidential nomination was former corporate executive Carly Fiorina. She too made headlines for attacking Democratic candidate Hillary Clinton as a failed wife: "Unlike another woman in this race, I actually love spending time with my husband."[41] Remarks like these can do considerable damage to women candidates' abilities to gather votes. Fiorina did not problematize the modest time that many male candidates devote to their spouses, even though in a recording posted by Ted Cruz's campaign his wife recounts how their daughter once mistook Cruz for a houseguest. This male politician had been away from his family for too long.[42]

Sadly Clinton is not the only female politician to have faced blatant double standards and recurring pain from systemic sexism and frequent male misogyny. Women seeking political office have often been compared to sex-trade workers (e.g., "high-class prostitutes") and judged just on their looks (e.g., "the hottest member" of the Senate).[43] Just as men are not alone in drawing on the dominant male sexist frame in berating women candidates for office—even though they more commonly do so—conservative Republicans do not have the patent on such tactics either. For instance, one male Democrat remarked that his female rival's awareness of health issues was the result of "pillow talk" with her husband who was also a doctor, yet he won and served for decades in Congress.[44]

Additionally, women politicians are often criticized for venturing into public without makeup or for daring to wear "unfeminine" clothing.[45] The *Washington Post* even ran a serious article just about Hillary Clinton's pantsuits. A *Time* magazine editor complained about her pantsuits, while a fashion expert remarked that Clinton's choice to wear pants meant she was "confused about her gender."[46]

Clinton was dubbed a "stereotypical bitch" by prominent white male conservative media commentators, who claimed that no one wanted to "watch a woman get older before their eyes on a daily basis."[47] According to contradictory statements by conservative white commentators and politicians, she was too "emotional" (male sexist code for "hysterical") or not emotional enough (male sexist code for "unfeminine" and "non-maternal") for the top job.[48] Her supposed onslaught against the right of white heterosexual men to hold the Oval Office took the form of sexist imagery in 2007 and 2016. The "Hillary Nutcracker" (misogynistic symbol), with the tagline "no more nuts in the White House," could be readily purchased. Additionally, many men jeered with slogans like "iron my shirt" and "Trump the Bitch" at political rallies.[49] More generally, research on the media coverage of the 2016 political campaigns found that Clinton got far more negative coverage than either Trump or her primary opponent Senator Bernie Sanders.[50]

Clearly, the U.S. president has long been characterized as necessarily a strong white man, a symbol of a privileged and emphasized white icon. The longstanding image of a strong (white) masculine president was one reason for the very hostile reactions to Clinton's presidential bid from many white men. This conventional white male image also likely accounted for widespread white (especially male) anger in regard to Barack Obama's lengthy presidency. Indeed, a white backlash against Obama's presidency likely helped to fuel the election of Donald Trump as president.[51] White voters resoundingly supported his bid for the White House. As one major paper put it immediately following Trump's win:

> Far from being purely a revolt by poorer whites left behind by globalization . . . Trump's victory also relied on the support of the middle-class, the better-educated and the well-off. . . . What appears to have made the biggest difference . . . was the turnout for Trump of white voters across the board—of both sexes, almost all ages and education levels, and from mid- and higher income levels.[52]

Among other important issues, this election was also centrally about protecting and increasing white privilege and power.

Fighting to Preserve Sexism and Dominant Masculinity

In recent decades the economic decline and other challenges for ordinary white men have generated an increase in especially assertive and aggressive male sexist framing. As with white racial framing, much male sexist framing is not only full of stereotypes, images, and narratives—both pro-male and anti-female—but also highly emotional in the loadings given to these elements. As we saw above, a term often given for the more negative emotional loading is *misogyny*—a phrase to denote male dislike of and contempt for women and girls. We have already noted the long history of this misogyny and other male sexist framing. Indeed, it is extensively present in the views of numerous white men often termed "founding fathers" (see Chapter 1).

Men's Rights Groups

In contemporary North America, many books have been published with misogynistic and related sexist themes. Among other exhortations, they urge men to be more manly, to return to a supposedly dominant prehistoric masculinity, to accent greater risk-taking for societal progress, and to reject what is seen as harmful feminism and a gender-egalitarian society. For example, according to a major book by the distinguished Harvard political scientist Harvey Mansfield, traditional assertive manliness is still substantially *good* for U.S. society. For him the good part of this manliness is the great "quality of spiritedness, shared by humans and animals that induces humans, and especially manly men, to risk their lives in order to save their lives." In his view such an aggressive spirit of risk-taking is necessary and distinctive in male history. Considering recently expanded opportunities for women in society, he argues that unfortunately women are now seen as equal to men, but they are in fact *not* equal in important human abilities. They are indeed "the weaker sex" whose bodies are designed to attract men. He speaks against those who critique the recent male backlash against developing a gender-egalitarian society. He says he sees no male backlash, but then proceeds to describe one: There is only a male "reluctance, a residual, bodily, behavioral unwillingness on the part of men to do their share in the upkeep of gender neutrality."[53]

Mansfield is uninformed here, for there are a large number of contemporary "men's rights" groups and conferences that have developed as part of a backlash against a few decades of women activists trying to reduce the discrimination and other barriers of systemic sexism. Numerous men's groups have been created to deal with what their members view as challenges to their conception of justifiable male privilege and/or real masculinity. Unsurprisingly, the members of the majority of major groups are mostly white men seeking to accent even more of the country's dominant white masculinity. They frequently blame "feminism" (most viciously, "feminazis") for their troubles and take a traditional masculine approach to gender issues. As one commentator who tracks online misogyny has put it, these men's rights groups are generally reacting to an alleged "cultural dethroning of male entitlement," which they view as the result of unfair societal changes sought by too-assertive contemporary women, especially feminist activists. Even modest changes benefitting women seem to agitate those in these men's groups.[54]

One U.S. group that has aggressively asserted their view of traditional white manhood is named A Voice for Men. The white founder told a woman critic that "We are coming for you and . . . all the liars out there that have been ruining people's lives with impunity."[55] Officially, however, the group claims to support nonviolent protests. Its stated mission is more than just buttressing the current systemically sexist society. It is to "denounce the institution of marriage as unsafe and unsuitable for modern men," "educate men and boys about the threats they face in feminist governance," and put a stop to "rape hysteria." The group has even established an "offenders' registry" in order to call out and scare those deemed feminist "bigots" — including recognizable feminist bloggers and students photographed at feminist protests against sexism.[56]

Another North American group, Men's Rights Canada, has continually made headlines with offensive poster campaigns, including a snide response to a progressive Canadian campaign against the major problem of sexual assault called "Don't be that guy." The men's group responded by placing mocking posters around cities that read "Don't be that girl. . . . Women can stop baby dumping." These words appeared under dumpsters and falsely insinuated that women who commit infanticide are insufficiently punished. The same group courted earlier controversy with a sequence of other "don't be that girl" posters suggesting that many women make false rape accusations.[57]

The Southern Poverty Law Center, which tracks U.S. hate groups, has found that most men's rights organizations tend to attract men who embrace very overt misogynistic framing, and some that sanction violence against women. Misogynistic and other sexist actions of men in certain "men's rights" groups, as well as in informal groups of men, are regularly seen online. Consider a few examples. One group of men targeted a woman blogger with many online misogynistic comments after she posted a video in which she protested getting hit on by a man in an elevator. Another female writer, after she tweeted a sexist joke at a tech forum, aroused the online wrath of numerous misogynists in the high-tech sector. Another feminist writer endured unrelenting online abuse, including death threats, after debuting a video series critiquing the very extensive sexism in many popular video games. Clearly, too, there is much data showing that well beyond the Internet there is extensive male abuse, including substantial violence, targeting a great many women, not only in their homes but also as they attempt to speak out against everyday sexism.[58]

Recently, the group A Voice for Men held what it dubbed the first International Conference on Men's Issues. Warren Farrell, one white intellectual father of the "men's rights" movement, was a keynote speaker at this Michigan gathering. In his male sexist framing, virtuous men are being dispossessed of many rights, and are now the lesser sex. He described what he saw as erroneous beliefs about (white) men sitting atop the power structure who "made all the rules" and get "all the rights" and accordingly have only themselves to blame for their alleged disempowerment.[59] However, he had to ignore the real-world data showing that elite white men do mostly control the U.S. Congress and the major corporations, as well as other major institutions. He claimed too that many people ignore the "real" problems faced by men today—that is, fathers are often divided from their children by the court system, there are no men's studies departments on campuses, and men drop out of college and commit suicide at higher rates than women.[60]

Such advocates of traditional sexism and patriarchy ignore not only the continuing reality of (especially white) male dominance in most institutions, but also the way that systemic sexism, which favors most men most of the time, necessarily creates some of the supposed disadvantages. Men's disadvantages are usually the *result of their own or other men's advantages* from that systemic sexism. As anthropologist R. W. Connell puts it,

> Men cannot hold state power without having become, collectively, the agents of violence. Men cannot be the beneficiaries of domestic labour and emotion work without losing intimate connections. . . . Men cannot have predominance in the capitalist economy without being subject to economic stress and paying for most of the social services.[61]

Additionally, within the male gender group, those who suffer somewhat from systemic sexism are usually not the same ones who benefit the most. Members of the mostly white male elite get the greatest array of benefits from systemic sexism, including running society's major institutions, while working class men, and especially men of color, pay the greatest price for doing the dangerous work (such as mining) that is often reserved for male workers. Indeed, powerful white male capitalists usually control those workplaces and their employment rules for these male workers. It seems to us, that if ordinary (white) men really wish change in most of these negative workplace conditions, they need to organize "class rights" groups for significant changes in the society's classist patterns usually dominated or shaped by the most powerful white men.[62]

Women in Major Sports: Perceived Threats to Male Dominance

Only recently in U.S. history have women been allowed or encouraged to participate in traditionally male sports. For most of that sports history barriers to women were vigorously rationalized as ensuring "real" women's femininity. This too was overtly a part of keeping systemic sexism firmly in place. As we noted in Chapter 1, as amateur sports spread dramatically in the late 19th and early 20th centuries, it became clear that "sporting ideals were underpinned by concerns about [white] masculinity and its importance to capitalist society" and that (white) male sports amateurs could not show any signs of subordinate femininity, for they were part of a truly "masculine kingdom."[63]

Thus, a little later on, in 1952 white male Olympic officials eliminated the women's 800 meters track event because they felt women lacked the necessary physical abilities. One official argued for eliminating *all* women's Olympic track and field events because of the "unaesthetic spectacle of women" competing in ways similar to men. In this era, too, the prize-winning white sports columnist Arthur Daley argued that eliminating "girls" from the Olympics was good because they were unattractive "with beads of perspiration." For many decades this enduring male framing of the acceptable female body did not include participation in traditionally male sports.[64]

Interestingly, in a more recent (1991) article on "Why Men Fear Women's Teams," Kate Rounds contended that the physical training advantage of men has historically given them an edge in traditionally male sports, but that in recent decades men have become *afraid* of losing to women who are now successfully doing similar diligent physical training. Many men fear physically strong women, and thus often stereotype and stigmatize them out of the male sexist frame as lesbian or "masculine women." This is not just a matter of an economic threat, but also about male heterosexist framing of women and a male homophobic fear of being seen as weak and gay.[65] Even in the 21st century there is great fear among male athletes in both the amateur and professional sports of football, basketball, and baseball, of being seen as playing "like a girl" or being gay.[66]

Over many decades now, and into the present, many football, basketball, baseball, and hockey coaches in school, college, and professional settings have emphasized a lasting version of dominant (white) manhood framing. Recently, for instance, former National Football League coach and current top college coach Jim Harbaugh has insisted that football is the "last bastion of hope for toughness in America in men, in males."[67] Like many white men in and outside of such sports, he suggests that the dominant (white) manhood standard is in danger of disappearing. In a recent article on "Why Football Matters," Harbaugh insists that U.S. football is unfairly "under attack," for it is one of very few places where "a young man is held to a higher standard. Football is hard. It's tough. . . . It builds character. . . . It literally challenges his physical courage." He argues that football coaches often "serve as a father figure to their players" and asks, rhetorically, "How many mothers look to the coaches of their son's football team as the last best hope to show their son what it means to become a man—a real man?"[68]

Rather explicitly stated, becoming a "real man" involves getting a strong father figure who can teach that manly framing and values. Numerous male commentators assert, explicitly or implicitly, that mothers and other women are too soft and thus a threat to manliness. Across the United States, male coaches in football and other sports frequently urge their players to be very manly, play or hit hard, suffer pain without complaint, and especially to not "play like girls" or "fags." Similar dominant discourses accenting the "real men" framing, including much homophobic, anti-feminist, and racist language (e.g., on bumper stickers), can be found in yet other sports, such as among the predominantly white fans at NASCAR auto races.[69]

Indeed, since at least the late 19th century the emphasis on strong and active manliness has been constantly reinforced by an invigorated homophobia and explicit condemnation of a distinctive type of "homosexual" man considered weak, inferior, and dangerous.[70] As sports scholar Tony Collins underscores, in the present day the "able-bodied, and heterosexual, male still remains the paradigm athlete. Sport's idealisation of the body, its privileging of physical activity over the intellectual, its fetishisation of blind courage means that the male body is the standard against which everything else is measured."[71]

Note too the routine use of strong military metaphors in descriptions of U.S. football and other sports actions, which help to reinforce the dominant framing of real-man masculinity. Comedian George Carlin suggested how large this array of military metaphors is. The football quarterback is called the "field general" and has "to be on target with his aerial assault . . . in spite of the blitz." He uses "the shotgun," "bullet passes," or "long bombs." He may use an "aerial assault" or "ground attack" to attack his "enemy's defensive line."[72] Explicit in such commonplace metaphorical language, language often used without conscious reflection, is also the legitimacy of a highly masculinized military system, one long used for imperialistic interventions overseas.

More Patriarchal-Sexist Discrimination

Recall from an earlier chapter that the 1848 Seneca Falls women's rights conference issued a Declaration of Sentiments asserting that "because women do feel themselves aggrieved, oppressed, and fraudulently deprived . . . we insist that they have immediate admission to all the rights and privileges which belong to them as citizens."[73] Today, however, women still face a fundamentally sexist system and do not have all the rights and privileges that men have in the United States. One reason for this is that over the years attempts to secure an "Equal Rights Amendment" for the U.S. Constitution have failed—mostly because a majority of male legislators in various states still operate out of some version of a male sexist framing society (see Chapter 2). The United States is currently *atypical* in this regard; 80 percent of the world's countries do constitutionally guarantee gender equality. Ironically, in surveys most Americans think we do have that constitutional provision, and 96 percent say that they believe women should have equal rights.[74] At the time of the major attempt at such an amendment in the 1970s there were relatively few women in state and federal legislatures, and women are still seriously underrepresented in most state legislatures today.

Contemporary male gender discrimination, and resulting inequalities, are still regularly rationalized by the dominant male sexist frame.

Over time, women have been agents of change and organized and gained significantly expanded rights, including voting rights and much more control of their own resources and bodies, but to this day they still suffer from discriminatory state laws and substantial formal and informal discrimination in an array of major institutions.

Persisting Discrimination: Male Violence

Today, one still observes numerous examples of men—and at the top of the society, powerful white men—greatly controlling women's bodies and body choices. Currently a majority of women report facing significant sexual harassment, rape, and/or stalking over their lives. They face violence inside and outside the home, with much of that perpetrated with impunity. Indeed, surveys vary but demonstrate that between one-fifth and one-half of women were victims of sexual abuse as children.[75] In recent years the United States has had a very high rape rate per 100,000 people (27 in 2010), and substantially more than that of France, Germany, or England. About 90 percent of victims are women, with at least one in six having been raped over their lifetimes—the latter figure contradicting the arguments of many in men's rights groups. The rape rates are usually higher for women of color. In addition, these and other sexual assault rates are very likely to be underestimates of the actual rates because many girls and women are afraid, for various reasons, to report them.[76]

Indeed, women who have sued for sexual and other violence by men have frequently found (mostly male) prosecutors or judges unsympathetic or discovered that current law does not actually protect them against such discrimination. Others have had their proof of discriminatory pay for equal work or of being fired just because they became pregnant also turned down by prosecutors or judges. Indeed, many cases of gender discrimination in the workplace are difficult to get redress under current U.S. laws.[77] Such discrimination has long-term consequences for women's lives, as well as for their families. As one analyst notes, "Victims of domestic violence are less likely to leave if they can't stand on their own feet financially. And a lifetime of wage discrimination means women and their families also pay a price later when it comes to Social Security benefits."[78]

Furthermore, in recent years many state legislatures dominated by white conservatives have passed laws reducing the control women have over their bodies. These laws, together with conservative court decisions, have placed severe restrictions on legal abortions and even on health insurance coverage for contraception. As the late conservative Supreme Court justice Antonin Scalia once put it: "Certainly the Constitution does not require discrimination on the basis of sex. The only issue is whether it prohibits it. *It doesn't.*[79] This legal perspective helps to buttress the country's systemic sexism and the larger elite-white-male dominance system.

Workplace Discrimination and Systemic Sexism Today

In a recent year full-time women workers in the United States still earned about 79 percent of male workers. While this gap is less than in the 1960s, much of the change has come from women becoming better educated and because of a decline in some men's wages. Today, still, there is a significant gender pay gap at all educational levels and in many occupations. As a summary of a recent scholarly panel put it, over her lifetime this "gender pay gap costs the average woman worker more than $530,000 in lost wages. The lifetime wage losses are even greater for college-educated women, averaging close to $800,000."[80] The disparity has changed little in recent decades, and at the current rate of change it will take more than a century to equalize. In addition, African American, Latino, and Native American women have lower median earnings than white women, and thus much lower than white men.[81] In this latter case we see again evidence of both sexism and gendered racism.

Over the centuries, up to the present day, male employers and workers have maintained several types of gendered discrimination in most capitalistic workplaces, including lower-status job positions and lower wages for women as compared with comparably qualified men. These male decision-makers often operate out of the traditional male sexist framing of men and women that is reinforced in the normative cultures of most employment settings. This sexist framing impacts the employment opportunities and wages of women workers through several different avenues. For instance, in many workplaces this framing routinely results in blatantly sexist discrimination on the part of both elite executives and ordinary male workers. Recall the study cited in Chapter 2 that found few women in better-paying jobs on Wall Street because of the male-centric workplace cultures where overtly sexist framing was commonplace and normative.

Another avenue of expression of male sexist framing takes the form of traditional job segregation. On average, men (especially whites) have significantly greater occupational opportunities than women. These job opportunities tend to be gender-segregated, with male workers getting higher pay for many jobs that are no more skilled or important to society than those women are regularly channeled into. To the present day, women have been concentrated in a smaller number of occupations than men—occupational settings such as domestic worker, fast food worker, nurse, librarian, clerical worker, retail sales worker, and schoolteacher. One issue that can be seen in this list is that women workers often enter caregiving occupations that are essential for healthy communities, but which are frequently devalued and underpaid in this male-dominated society.[82] Moreover, while the proportion of women in certain historically male job categories (e.g., physicians, lawyers) has significantly increased in recent decades, changes in many historically male job categories have been modest or internal job segregation has developed, such as women physicians dominating pediatrics and male physicians dominating surgery, again with significant income differentials. The movement of male workers into certain traditionally female jobs (e.g., nursing) has often exceeded the increase of female workers in comparably skilled male jobs, and these male workers often make higher salaries there. And when women have moved in large numbers into certain male-dominated fields, such as parks and recreation jobs, the pay has frequently declined.[83]

Today, the proportions of women remain low in such occupations as engineers and craft and transport workers and in the most senior positions in many government agencies. As we have noted previously, women also hold relatively few top-level corporate management positions and major directorships. In addition, an invisible "glass ceiling" is regularly found for women in many corporate professional and managerial settings. Those who do make their way into traditionally male jobs there frequently face discrimination in promotions and/or end up earning considerably less than their male counterparts.[84]

Recall too the problem of widespread sexual harassment that makes job success much more difficult for women workers. For many men in managerial and other supervisory positions, work success is a prize they give to women employees who permit some type of sexual harassment. These and other male workers in a diverse array of workplaces operate out of a male sexist frame that regards women as sex objects. Lin Farley summarizes this reality: Sexual harassment is "unsolicited nonreciprocal male behavior that asserts a woman's sex role over her function as a worker."[85] The sexist behavior of both male workers and employers often creates difficult work climates for women workers in many occupations and all areas of the country.

Today, too, many women in moderate-income families, and disproportionately women of color, have the major responsibility for economically supporting their families. For the most part, the capitalistic business world has not adjusted to the everyday needs of these workers, as well as for many women workers in higher-income families. For example, the 1993 Family and Medical Leave Act requires larger companies to allow workers 12 weeks of unpaid leave per year for family issues, but that does not help those who need a *paid* leave or work for smaller firms. The failure of U.S. laws to require employers to provide paid family leave—rare among western countries— has a great impact on women workers, who are much more likely than male workers to have to make employment and career decisions based on their gendered family responsibilities.[86] In this and other ways, the evidence makes clear, women workers often "face penalties" throughout their lives "for having children or caring for family members."[87]

Women workers of color frequently encounter the more difficult or dangerous occupational positions and workplace settings. Consider the conditions faced by many workers in agribusiness food processing factories. The overwhelming majority are working-class women and men of color, including immigrants. Dorothy McKenzie, who worked in southern chicken processing factories for more than a decade, has poignantly captured connections between the ways in which chickens are processed and the ways the largely gendered and racialized work force is treated. Both workers and chickens, she notes, have limited freedom of movement. During a 12-hour work day, she could use the washroom only three times, and the repetitious drudgery of the job produced chronic body pain. When workers complained, managers advised them to consume "less water." They protested and were fired for insubordination.[88] It took the efforts of the Retail, Wholesale and Department Store Union to get their jobs back. Moreover, one researcher who worked in a processing plant described such workplaces as "plantation capitalism" because they are mostly owned by white men and staffed overwhelmingly by working-class women and men of color who earn low wages.[89]

Meanwhile, the mostly white male owners of such large agribusiness firms rake in billions in profits. Just five corporations control more than half of what some term the "meat-industrial-complex." One animal rights researcher, David Nibert, has assessed this stark capitalistic reality. A small number of corporations have benefitted from the brutal treatment of many thousands of human workers and the killings of "billions of other animals" solely because "their exploitation furthered the accumulation of private profit."[90]

Internalizing Gender Oppression

We should note briefly some ways in which women in workplaces and other settings collude in their oppression, especially by internalizing a male sexist framing of women and men. As one feminist analysis puts it, "It is common for women to comport themselves in a feminine fashion, to scale down their aspirations, and to embrace gender-compliant goals." The sexist assumptions, norms, and narratives become part of the "cognitive, emotional, and conative structure of the self," thereby shaping a woman's desires. Meanwhile, the male "homo economicus can safely accept his desires as *given* and proceed without ado to orchestrate a plan to satisfy them."[91] Note too that numerous women collude in the perpetuation of the systemic sexism, and thus the encompassing elite-white-male dominance system, by joining groups with names like Women Against Feminism. Recently under that specific name in the social media, these mostly white and reasonably well-off women have attacked what they misunderstand to be contemporary feminist thought, with their rather negative view influenced by the dominant male sexist framing. For instance, they complain about feminism for supposedly engaging in "man-hating" and for portraying women as "just victims."[92] However, one feminist analyst, Fay Francis, surveyed a large set of Twitter commentaries from Women Against Feminism and concluded they were "overwhelmingly, those who have *benefitted* from it the most. Western white women. Middle class, well-educated women. Women without disabilities. Cisgender, heterosexual women."[93]

Unsurprisingly, significant funding for several of these anti-feminist women's groups has come from powerful white male conservatives. Arch-conservative radio host Rush Limbaugh has contributed heavily to the conservative Independent Women's Forum, as have major white conservative foundations like the Scaife Foundation, the Bradley Foundation, and the Koch brothers' Lambe Foundation.[94] Nothing illustrates the powerful shaping influence of the elite-white-male dominance system better than these relatively privileged white women in anti-feminist groups who parrot the male sexist framing, and by the reality that these groups often get substantial funding from white male conservatives' foundations.

Popular Culture and Media: More Sexist Framing

Today, popular cultural realities contradict any notion that elite or ordinary men are greatly declining in power or that systemic sexism is collapsing. As one young online blogger has underscored, this sexist system is fully operational today, including for supposedly liberated millennials. This is obvious in most types of mainstream media:

> You see it in almost every prime-time drama, reality-show, and all of the pop-media platforms, such as videogames, movies, and comic-books. Girls are the love-interest, the side-kick, or the villain. The love-interests are the damsels in distress, prizes to be won by the conquering hero, subservient and supportive, indebted to the male due to their need to be rescued and disposable. . . . The *villains* are the strong women, the ambitious women, the women with any kind of power that can threaten the hero, be it magical, political, or otherwise, and who aren't afraid to challenge the hero and prove their equality, even superiority, to him.[95]

In a great many settings across the United States, including in many traditional media and new social media, both girls and women are still shown in very conventional ways, and constantly from some version of the male sexist framing of society. Indeed, this gendered reality in the mainstream media is frequently intertwined with a white racial framing that, implicitly or explicitly, foregrounds the bodies and lives of white girls or women.

One also sees a related type of male sexist framing of women in many forms of contemporary advertising. Advertising is a multibillion dollar U.S. industry that is essential to modern consumer capitalism. Conventionally male-sexist ads are everywhere in print and online magazines and newspapers, on billboards, and on most television channels. In these venues, the ads targeting girls and women repeatedly emphasize beauty, clothing, parenting, cooking, and cleaning. Frequently there is a focus on girl's or women's physical appearance and attractiveness, thereby mirroring the dominant sexist framing of this male-dominated society and encouraging viewers to judge women in such terms. In contrast, boys and men are more likely to be portrayed in ads, as they are usually judged in the larger society, in terms of such things as their achievements, and not usually on their physical appearance.[96]

Note too that these mainstream media outlets often teach boys and men to buy into the dominant (white) manhood imagery. This includes accenting certain masculinity-producing aspects of everyday life that the mainstream media, politicians, and ordinary people rarely think critically about. This includes things such as male-oriented athletics. It also includes less obvious examples. For instance, researchers have established a link between the society's dominant masculinity and the commonplace consumption of nonhuman animals, such as the "muscle meat" commonly called and advertised as "steak." In one recent study, research participants mostly from the United States and Great Britain tended to rank men who were vegetarians as *less masculine* than meat-eating men. The researchers concluded:

> To the strong, traditional, macho, bicep-flexing, All-American male, red meat is a strong, traditional, macho, bicep-flexing, All-American food. . . . Soy is not. To eat it, they would have to give up a food they saw as strong and powerful like themselves for a food they saw as weak and wimpy.[97]

Globalizing Systemic Sexism, Racism, and Classism

While we focus in this book on the extraordinarily important implementers of widespread global oppression, elite white men, they are certainly not the only important agents of contemporary patriarchal-sexist and heterosexist control, as the latter types of control can be seen in numerous other areas. Indeed, social oppression targeting women, gay and lesbian people, and certain ethnic groups has long been commonplace in many countries, including in Africa, Asia, and the Middle East.[98] Indeed, in recent years the extremist group Islamic State (i.e., IS) in the Middle East and the extremist group Boko Haram in some African countries have implemented violent religious versions of masculinist and heterosexist oppression.

Nonetheless, the consequences of white hegemonic masculinity and associated oligopolistic capitalism are arguably more enduring and potent, even catastrophic, for the planet in general than those of these local despotic non-western actors. Actually, the development of many such non-western leaders has been greatly shaped by white male imperialists and colonizers from western countries. Recall the discussion of the 1916 Sykes-Picot Agreement, for example. It entrenched white British and French colonial rule in the Middle East, redrew societal boundaries, and became a source of countless major conflicts there to the present. Into the early 21st century, numerous Middle Eastern and North African regimes were autocracies whose legitimacy rested on satisfying their European and American supporters.[99] This was the western colonial residue. However, the U.S.-led invasion of Iraq in 2003 and the Arab Spring in the 2010s helped to undermine this mixture of European influence and local dictatorial rule on which the 1916 agreement hinged.[100] Unsurprisingly, certain sectarian, often religious factions have filled the existing power vacuum as the colonially imposed borders are no longer secured. Today, as journalist Fareed Zakaria underscores, no amount of U.S. militarized masculinity and intervention there "can put Humpty Dumpty back together."[101]

In western countries both white men and women, but especially the most powerful white men, have benefitted greatly for centuries from the racialized capitalistic theft of global resources, including from highly exploited low-wage female and male labor (usually workers of color) producing consumer items for them. Wealth resulting from centuries of this global exploitation, and new technologies assisted by it, sustain numerous symbols of (white) western hegemonic masculinity, such as large pickup trucks and "muscle" cars. Great western wealth also generates and sustains technologically sophisticated and hyper-masculinized military forces that use violence across the globe to uphold western political-economic dominance. For many decades, western multinational executives, media moguls, soldiers, missionaries, and government officials have aggressively, often violently, exported and maintained many elements of the western racial, gender, and class order to across much of the world.[102]

During the colonialism era and today's supposedly post-colonialism era we have experienced much global interconnecting, especially the spread and dominance of large multinational corporations—with their usually tiered sexist, racist, and classist global divisions of labor. For instance, social scientist R. W. Connell has emphasized the reality of a *world gender order*—the "structure of relationships" connecting the "gender orders of local societies on a world scale."[103] Most western multinational corporations are shaped by a white masculinized culture, including in the upper management ranks and much corporate decision-making. Consider how western media executives aggressively circulate sexist and racist meanings globally. The export of white male sexist framing and white racial framing is observable constantly in the mass media and social media of a great many countries—e.g., in the blond, thin, and light-skinned women celebrated as feminine exemplars in the media of Latin American and Asian countries.[104] The large media corporations and other western multinational corporations are central to contemporary oligopolistic capitalism and have created global markets that often have a sexist and racist structuring in terms of the production and consumption of material goods.

In addition, numerous major international agencies (e.g., World Bank) have been run mostly or very disproportionately by elite whites, especially elite white men. This reality signals that the world gender order is constantly interrelated with, and coreproductive of, the world racial order (global systemic racism), as well as of global oligopolistic capitalism. There are local hierarchical social systems, but a majority of these have developed at least some western racial, gender, or class elements because of the spread of western transnational corporations and the development of western-shaped local and national economic, political, and media institutions.

Given this globalized reality of the elite-white-male dominance system, a great many geopolitical crises that have threatened the world's countries for many decades have had roots in this powerful system of exploitation and oppression. This worldwide reality has deeply disturbing ramifications for the prospect of authentic peace, security, liberty, and justice—indeed, for the very survival of humanity. Unsurprisingly, this western-based oppression has repeatedly seen great and regular pushback from oppressed people everywhere. As W. E. B. Du Bois once forecast, powerful white men cannot have peace solely for themselves and other whites: "We shall not drive war from this world until we treat [people of color] as free and equal citizens in a world democracy of all races and nations."[105]

Philanthro-Capitalism: One Elite Strategy

We are thus wary of the white western elite's purported concern for non-elites at home or abroad, especially the most vulnerable populations. Take for example the rise of "philanthro-capitalism," which involves mostly white-elite-sponsored nonprofit foundations that apply the "business logic of profit-making institutions to philanthropic activities."[106] In pursuit of elite interests in shaping broad national and international social policies, numerous billion-dollar philanthropic foundations in western countries have over recent decades been built up by the most powerful members of the capitalistic class, again mostly white men. The foundations often provide the elite with important tax write-offs. Even more importantly, they can offer avenues to sidestep more democratic decision-making entities like the UN, as well as national governments, in targeting an array of important national health and welfare issues. Their actions have brought some major and necessary health and welfare program changes for the world's population, but these actions frequently exclude alternative health and welfare possibilities and concentrate supposedly philanthropic decisions in elite-controlled hands without substantial local democratic input and decision-making.

The leading philanthropic foundations hold hundreds of billions in assets; most are currently based in the United States. This is very significant for democratic decision-making about planet Earth, currently and in the future. Philanthro-capitalism tells us much about what to expect, as the disproportionately white elite is aggressively using it as one more important strategy enabling them to hold onto their undemocratic and hegemonic political-economic power globally. For example, La Via Campesina, an international movement that manages democratic peasant organizations around the globe, has criticized the Bill and Melinda Gates Foundation for its global philanthro-capitalism. They acquired shares of the company Monsanto, which is oriented to agribusiness multinationals' control of agricultural chemicals and seeds globally. The acquisition was justly seen as evidence of the foundation's commercial interests over real humanitarian concerns. Similarly, Facebook CEO Mark Zuckerberg and his wife Priscilla Chan announced that they would eventually give away 99 percent of their wealth, but this turned out to be less altruistic than it seemed. The "giveaway" involved transferring their funds into a personal limited liability company (LLC), a type of organization lacking in transparency and providing Zuckerberg and Chan with continuing control of these assets and tax write-offs for their "donations."[107] Their stated goal is impressive: to "advance human potential and promote equality in areas such as health, education, scientific research and energy."[108] However, whatever its direction, it will be yet one more undemocratic, elite-controlled effort to deal with broad national and global social problems.

Challenges to Elite Control

For the foreseeable future the United States will doubtless be marked by comprehensive economic inequality and economic and political oligarchy, as the mostly white male corporate capitalists retain major societal control. To protect their racialized, gendered, and capitalistic interests, this elite will predictably continue to accent a distinctive brand of conservative market capitalism and thus seek smaller government (e.g., deregulation), privatization of public goods, and reduced taxation (especially for those well-off). Nonetheless, there are broad trends in society that will make this elite dominance highly problematical, and at least suggest the possibility of a more just and democratic future for western societies like the United States.

Will New Technologies Bring Solutions?

Numerous commentators have suggested that new technologies, such as intelligent robots and other artificial intelligence innovations, may reduce the boring or arduous (blue collar and white collar) work that humans do, thereby liberating them for more interesting work or leisure activities. In this perspective automation is seen as a beneficent force. However, the dominant elite's power is unlikely to be displaced just by the societal imbedding of these technologies. The leading astrophysicist Stephen Hawking has made a pessimistic forecast for what this future of technologies probably means for non-elites and society generally:

> If machines produce everything we need, the outcome will depend on how things are distributed. Everyone can enjoy a life of luxurious leisure if the machine-produced wealth is shared, or most people can end up miserably poor if the machine-owners successfully lobby against wealth redistribution. So far, the trend seems to be toward the second option, with technology driving ever-increasing inequality.[109]

Recently, Robert McChesney and John Nichols have provided a more detailed view of this troubled reality of capitalistic control of potentially liberating technologies:

> If we the people are going to make the future that is now our own, then we must begin a knowing, conscious *fight* for shared prosperity, genuine opportunity, and the full realization of the promise of new technologies. . . . The oppressive prospects of technology—to spy on us, to profit off our desperation and misery, to make us work harder for less, to control rather than to free us—are only beginning to be fully realized.[110]

At best, even these critical analysts only vaguely mention the dominant elite, including the machine-makers, lying behind the likely calamitous effects of technological change. As we have repeatedly seen, *they* need to be called out much more explicitly. These elite, mostly white and male technology owners and controllers are the real threat, not the new technologies. Most North Americans and Europeans do not understand how powerful white capitalists have controlled technologies substantially in their own interest—to the point, for example, that much technological automation is being used to get rid of jobs that ordinary workers need and thereby to greatly increase their long-term unemployment or underemployment.

McChesney and Nichols do underscore the only reasonable remedy for these dire circumstances:

> There is no app that will achieve the better and more humane life that is possible. . . . We the people are the only force that can make a future worthy of our hopes and our humanity. . . . the only tool that has ever taken the power to define the future away from the elites and given it to the whole of humanity: *democracy*.[111]

We would add to this view that this democratic force of ordinary people must be *well informed* about how these elites and this society actually operate—that is, they must become engaged in deframing and reframing away from their own racist, sexist, and classist framing of society (see below). And they also must be willing to organize extensively and democratically over a very long period of time. It took centuries to create the contemporary elite-white-male dominance system, and it will certainly take many years to undo that system and restructure this society in truly democratic ways.

Changing Demographics: Whites No Longer the Majority

Another trend that many have viewed as a sign of optimism for a more democratic U.S. future involves current and expected demographic changes. If U.S. birth and immigration rates persist at current levels, by the 2040s half the population will be Americans of color. White Americans are now just over 60 percent of the population, down significantly in recent decades. As of the 2010 census, whites were a demographic minority in California, Texas, New Mexico, and Hawai'i. Soon, a majority of elementary and secondary school students will be African, Latino, Asian, and Native American. Other things being equal, they and their parents will increasingly demand greater input in the operation of currently white-dominated school systems. Similar demands for greater input in major economic (and political) decision-making will likely increase from American workers of color, who by the 2030s will make up more than half the working-age population.[112]

Currently, a majority of whites appear to view these demographic changes in negative ways, and mainly through the prevailing white racial frame. Back in the 1990s, journalist Dale Maharidge's book *The Coming White Minority* assessed white Californians' reactions to this major demographic change already taking place there. He argued that whites there had credible fears: "Whites dread the unknown and not-so-distant tomorrow," he wrote, "when a statistical turning point will be reached that could have very bad consequences for them. . . . They fear losing not only their jobs but also their culture."[113]

Today, influential conservatives, especially in the mainstream media, regularly promote such white fears by emphasizing that their being a statistical minority has undesirable implications for the future of "western civilization." Previously, we documented the distress among elite whites in corporate and government worlds in regard to "threats" they have long perceived as coming from people of color globally. These views have long been articulated by prominent white analysts such as Samuel Huntington, a Harvard professor who argued that multiculturalism and demographic diversity were destroying the United States, indeed threatening to dump it "on the ash heap of history."[114] Earlier in U.S. history, he argued, nativists' concerns about immigrant assimilation were unjustified because immigrants were white Europeans, but current immigrant groups of color

> feel discriminated against if they are not allowed to remain apart from the mainstream. The ideologies of multiculturalism and diversity . . . deny the existence of a common culture in the United States, denounce assimilation, and promote the primacy of racial, ethnic, and other subnational cultural identities and groupings.[115]

Huntington is not alone. In their many nativistic writings, speeches, and other commentaries a great many white intellectuals, corporate executives, policymakers, and politicians have made it clear that they most fear the culture and population impacts of immigrants of color from Latin America, Asia, Africa, and the Middle East.

For example, in one study researchers asked many elite white men about their views of Americans of color, including the significant numbers of immigrants coming into the country. Assessing the multiracial future of the United States, one powerful corporate executive gave a reply typical of many. He argued that the impact of immigrants would be negative because

> the strength of the country and the economy is driven by the Anglo-Saxon work ethic heritage which will be gradually destroyed because these other groups don't have that heritage. . . . Because if you look at the historical integration of the black people into the country and the Hispanic, they have always, very few of them have been able to operate on a sophisticated income producing level. [Interviewer: But don't you think that that's the problem of the white people who subjugate them?] I think that is true up until about 1960, 1965 but I don't think this is true in the last 20, 25 years.[116]

Here we see a common feature of the white framing of people of color that we have often observed previously. Today most whites no longer openly cite a biological explanation for racial inequalities, but they do publicly and frequently accent this cultural deficiency view, one that downplays *current* racial discrimination. Again, too, we observe the notion of a superior white Anglo-Saxon society supposedly being in great danger from "these other groups."

In spite of this extensive white fear-mongering, the immediate future of the United States will likely be striking for its continuing racial, class, and gender inequalities and for persisting and substantial control by a white, disproportionately male elite including corporate capitalists and allied top government officials. (They will probably have a greater number of conforming acolytes from subordinated groups.) The country's undemocratic economic organization and undemocratic political institutions—e.g., an unelected Supreme Court, unrepresentative Senate, and unrepresentative House of Representatives—will undoubtedly play a central role in that future. These key political institutions will likely continue to be shaped by the white elite via their well-institutionalized control of corporations and other major organizations.

Still, barring a great elite repression of dissent, there will doubtless be significant positive and democratizing impacts from these major demographic changes. A more diverse Democratic Party will probably become the major political party in numerous legislative bodies at all levels. Still, in many cases liberal politicians of color will likely supplant white liberals, with less net change in liberal political-economic policies probably being the result. At the local and state levels, we expect to see significant political change, with many places having majorities of voters of color and greater representation of their perspectives. At the local, state, and national levels, we also anticipate increased conflict between voters of color seeking greater representation and government services, and disproportionately older white voters (led by the white elite) fighting to preserve white economic and political interests and power. A large segment of the white elite will likely continue to accent government privatization, deregulation, and lower taxes so as to protect their racialized political-economic interests.

Short of a truly democratic revolution, the racial, class, and gender inequalities are likely to remain substantial. For instance, a strong sign of continuing racial inequality can today be observed in the extensive racial segregation in housing and schooling patterns across U.S. towns and cities. As demographer William Frey has emphasized recently, racial "segregation levels for black and Hispanic children are *higher* than for their adult counterparts."[117] That is, in these very important cases there is no trend toward desegregation. Currently, most whites and most people of color live substantially separate lives in schools and neighborhoods. Even the supposedly desegregated workforce remains significantly divided. As we showed previously, disproportionate numbers of workers of color are in lower-paying job categories or facing chronic unemployment, while disproportionate numbers of whites dominate most better-paying, relatively more secure job categories.

Contemporary People's Movements

Pressing for Major Change

Virtually all societies have resistance movements that regularly challenge their ruling elite. Elsewhere we have written in detail about people's movements that try to change the elite-white-male dominance system in the United States,[118] but here we only have space to emphasize a few important points about them. Many ordinary women and men—among them people of color, LGBTQ people, people with disabilities, and animal rights advocates—continue to engage in substantial informal and organized efforts to make the United States more just and democratic. They are able to generate protest movements because there are in society numerous critical counter-frames, home cultures, and local community organizations that are relatively independent of elite control and that can provide significant resources, including experienced leaders, effective organization, funding, and, most importantly, human beings willing to risk their lives for societal change. These influential community organizations, such as the many churches essential to African American civil rights movements in the past and present, periodically offer significant pushback against the overarching elite dominance system, as similar people's protests for centuries now have done.[119]

Consider, for example, one recent movement and organization that developed with the assistance of social media and has been named Black Lives Matter (BLM). Currently with numerous U.S. and Canadian chapters and with localized nonhierarchical leadership, this movement emerged in 2013 in connection with large street protests over the killings of black people in Missouri, Florida, and other states. Over the years since then, scores of BLM-associated marches, rallies, and other demonstrations against systemic racism have taken place, especially over police killings of, and other brutality toward, black urbanites. A great many local black (and other) residents, including many unaffiliated with BLM chapters, have participated in these assertive protests. Many activists have been critical of established black leaders, for selling out or not being aggressive enough. In 2016, some of these black activists confronted the 2016 presidential candidates in regard to their positions on racialized policing and other white racism issues.[120]

In the midst of a still white-framed and white-normed society, this black movement has made important use of a strong black counter-framing of society, one with a focus on ending white racism in policing and other major societal areas. Reverberations of earlier African American resistance movements are clear in the valiant efforts of these current protest groups, as they endeavor to actualize the other American Dream of real liberty and justice. For the most part, African Americans and many other Americans of color have not bought so heavily as white Americans into the elite's insincere rhetoric about liberty and democracy.

Consider too the class-oriented Occupy Wall Street movement (2011–2012). This anti-capitalist movement inspired much international dialogue about the power of the large national and international financial institutions (termed the "1 percent"). Many ordinary people (from the 99 percent) weighed in on the unethical and illegal acts of Wall Street's top decision-makers, even giving rise to new rights laws like the California Homeowner Bill of Rights. Additionally, focusing on the student indebtedness crisis in imaginative ways, the Strike Debt effort emerged as an outgrowth of the Occupy movement. Student loan reforms thereby became matters for more serious political debate. Occupy activists also became part of Million Hoodie marches to remonstrate against police killings of unarmed black people. And the Occupy movement also served as a partial catalyst for the Canadian indigenous peoples' movement Idle No More. In turn, Idle No More inspired additional Native activism and several environmental movements. Additionally, yet other major protest movements have emerged from indigenous groups in the United States and Canada, including the large-scale 2016 protests against oil pipeline construction in North Dakota.[121]

Interestingly, increased protest to the elite's neoliberal financial dominance has had some modest positive effects. As an illustration, Lawrence Summers, one architect of globalizing capitalism and a past U.S. Treasury Secretary discussed in Chapter 5, is part of the elite's more liberal faction. Describing non-elite opposition to global economic integration as not entirely unjustified, he described this global capitalistic project as "carried out by elites for elites, with little consideration for the interests of ordinary people." He asserted that non-elites accurately believe that current "free trade" globalization gives the rich unfair economic advantages. They understand its impacts, for local communities "suffer when major employers lose out to foreign competitors."[122] Notable too are Summers' recent suggestions for a better elite approach: Fostering "international harmonization agreements" as opposed to just international trade agreements; making "labor rights and environmental protection" of utmost concern and "empowering foreign producers" less of a priority; allocating the same political effort to capturing the "trillions of dollars that escape taxation or evade regulation through cross-border capital flows" as for the usual corporation-oriented trade agreements; and actually ensuring that working-class and middle-class parents can realistically secure a better life for their children.[123]

Deframing Oppressive Frames: The Example of Anti-Racist Efforts

Dominant conceptual systems such as the white racial frame, the male sexist frame, and the classist frame are frequently unconscious or barely conscious, and they are neurally fixed. As a result, major conceptual change, while necessary for creating a just society, is difficult. Most people operate from these long-held socially gained frames, and usually emotionally. That makes it hard to challenge their framing just by presenting the empirical facts.[124] The constitutional scholar Derrick Bell long ago emphasized how whites' racial framing, with its racialized emotions, makes a change-the-law model of racial progress problematical:

> Traditional civil rights laws . . . assume that most citizens will obey the law. . . . But the law enforcement model for civil rights breaks down when a great number of whites are willing—because of convenience, habit, distaste, fear or simple preference—to violate the law. It then becomes almost impossible to enforce, because so many whites, though not discriminating themselves, identify more easily with those who do than with their victims.[125]

Central to how the dominant racial, class, and gender frames operate today is "social alexithymia"—the learned and habitual *inability* of a great many in the dominant groups to understand where those subordinated are coming from and what their experiences with oppression are like. Such social alexithymia involves a severe lack of cross-group understanding. For instance, psychological researchers recently interviewed white college students and found that most "expressed some level of distortion and denial of race, racism, or white privilege. [Even] students who demonstrated higher levels of racial awareness also expressed some distortion and/or denial of racism."[126] *Only one student* was strongly antiracist and empathetic toward African Americans. These data suggest the intensity and extent of most whites' socialization into the dominant white racial frame, as well as the difficulty of societal change in this regard.

One difficult but vital lesson for all in the dominant white group is to be brought to a clear understanding of the social justice counter-frames long developed in communities of color dealing with oppression. One important example is the strong antiracist counter-frame developed by African Americans over centuries. This includes a robust critique of white oppression, an aggressive countering of anti-black framing, and a positive assertion of the full humanity of all people and of their right to social justice. This experience-honed perspective on current systemic racism challenges key aspects of the old white racial frame. Social justice educators and activists desiring to break down that dominant racial frame have often created educational programs focused on key aspects of the racist frames of white Americans and of the antiracist frames of African Americans and other Americans of color. Assertively teaching the experience-based understandings of white racism in these antiracist counter-frames can have a significant destabilizing effect on the dominance of that white racial frame in the minds of many whites and others. Certainly, such educational efforts are only a first step and, if substantial structural change is to come, must be expanded to include major antidiscrimination and other antiracist *organization* and *action* across all societal institutions.[127]

Still, major efforts to change white racial framing must be made if systemic change is to happen in this society. The linguist George Lakoff has suggested some steps that can be taken to bring a shift in a population toward a more progressive moral system:

> It begins by strengthening the framing for the progressive moral system and for the progressive view of democracy based around empathy and the responsibility flowing from that empathy. . . . we have to care about others—fellow citizens of the world we have never met and never will meet.[128]

As we see it, deframing for change in the direction of real liberty and democracy for all must involve consciously and critically analyzing major elements of the dominant racist, sexist, and classist frames. Those in the dominant white group, most especially elite white men, and many others must somehow be made much more aware of the fact that the dominant racist, sexist, and classist frames are deeply imbedded in their minds, then be taught the great importance of deframing them, and also be encouraged to reframe away from them to a *real* action-oriented, liberty-and-justice framing of this unjust society.

Consider, as one final example, the efforts of numerous antiracism groups across the country that currently demonstrate the validity of these assertions. For instance, note the successful Antiracism Study Dialogue Circles Metamorphosis (ASDIC) activists in Minnesota. Over just a few years, they have developed more than 150 well-crafted and effective workshops and dialogue groups to stimulate greater local awareness of white racist framing and discrimination, and thereby to stimulate numerous racial-change efforts in local communities. A multiracial group, the ASDIC activists have educated and empowered local people of diverse racial backgrounds to speak out forcefully on patterns of local and national racism; to increase their transformative resistance practices aimed at a just and democratic society; to explore the actual formation via the white racial frame of "raced" persons in systemic racism; to develop the emotional and spiritual dispositions necessary to confront everyday racism and its negative impacts; to rehumanize by counter-framing the U.S.-origin stories underlying much white racism; and to provide the resources and relationships necessary to the creation of personal anti-racism and healthy anti-racist communities. ASDIC has successfully facilitated workshops and dialogue circles with more than 2,000 community participants about antiracist activism, including teachers, students, nonprofit and government staff, and members of religious organizations. Currently, the ASDIC activists and supporters are further developing their anti-racism curriculum models, expanding group facilitator training, and growing their organizational outreach to take their racial change programs beyond Minnesota. These are important first steps to bring change in regard to systemic racism in the United States, if only the first steps.[129]

Elite Pushback: Ongoing Struggles for Human Liberation

These aggressive educational efforts aimed at major deframing and reframing in regard to systemic racism, sexism, and classism are essential to bringing significant structural changes. However, constant collective *vigilance* and progressive *organization* are also very necessary because the white male elite has the power, resources, and supporters to mount devastating private and government pushbacks against serious deframing and reframing efforts and much other anti-oppression organization. They act to protect their powerful individual and group interests in preserving the elite-white-male dominance system.

Repeatedly, this elite pushback has targeted a large array of recent rights movements. Activists of all kinds are frequently belittled and attacked, often with large militarized police forces. For example, in response to the Occupy movement, the white elite put large repressive resources into controlling these activists, who were viewed as seriously challenging their elite class interests. The New York City police department maintained an unnecessarily substantial force at Occupy encampments, and millions of tax dollars were allocated to this over-policing and other active repression of the peaceful protesters. Black demonstrations against police brutality in many cities and Native American protests over land and water issues in the Midwest have been countered by officials with large militarized policing forces, including in some cases the National Guard. Consider, too, less well-known movements, such as the contemporary animal rights movement. In recent years these rights advocates have been callously mocked and otherwise attacked by the mainstream media. They are portrayed as anti-human, and even as a threat to western civilization. This portrayal is in keeping with the dominant capitalistic ethic, which ensures that the capitalistic class's interests in exploiting human and nonhuman animals, as well as the planetary environment, are placed first. By curbing media information about and criticism of global problems like animal exploitation, global climate change, and eco-logical destruction for profit, the arrogant and mostly white capitalistic elite can reduce public awareness of the nature of the high social and environmental costs of profit-driven capitalistic enterprises. By purposefully framing justice-seeking activists as "radicals," the country's elite can generate significant social panic and fears, which proves useful in advancing undemocratic private and government policies, such as anti-terror legislation that curtails democratic constitutional rights.[130]

Central to countering this elite, today as in the past, is building *effective coalitions* across several oppressed groups. As sociologist Domhoff puts it, the power elite wins

> far more often than not against their many opponents, who have never been able to negotiate the compromises and alliances among themselves that would be needed in order to make full use of the power bases they actually have. In fact, figuring out how these disparate oppositional forces might become united enough to take advantage of the divisions within the power elite would be a worthy challenge for all those who share the egalitarian vision [of U.S. society].[131]

Concluding Summary: The Overarching Elite-White-Male Dominance System

In our emphasis mostly on the prevailing white racial frame and the male sexist frame in this chapter, we have continued to render visible powerful white men and the oppressive structures that they routinely create, cultivate, and defend. In the examples of their resistance to progressive change of many kinds, we witness how much national and global control these mostly white and male U.S. decision-makers—a tiny percent of the world's population—still wield over most everyone else. They are indeed central among the world's elites, and they operate today with the often servile assistance of elite white women and elites of color across the globe. Throughout history, this group of very powerful white men has aggressively worked against real global equality and authentic democracy.

We have also provided recent examples of the modus operandi of this elite, including their sexist brotherhood with ordinary white men. Clearly, the substantial majority of ordinary white men desperately need a reframing away from their dominant white masculinity framing, for the latter is a key element in their famous white male anger. This anger and its accent on white male privilege creates long-lasting barriers to the achievement of *real* liberty and justice for all. We have documented the numerous "men's rights" groups and informal male networks that, among other things, target bold women who organize and speak out against systemic sexism.

Importantly, we have shown that advocates of traditional white manhood and associated sexist practices ignore or downplay the societal reality of continuing white male *dominance*—the age-old systemic sexism that still strongly favors (white) men. Ironically, this systemic sexism created and maintained by men also generates most of the gender disadvantages that men complain about. Clearly, the sexist system is still fully operational in its oppression of women today. In this chapter we also briefly explored why a majority of white men found a sense of belonging inside Donald Trump's political domain during the 2016 electoral season, and why many of them seemed to fear the rise of the first woman presidential candidate. We have considered what these and other social changes mean for the future of the white male power structure, and thus of U.S. and global society.

Throughout this book we have examined the large-scale resources used, usually successfully, to punish those who push back substantially against the elite-white-male dominance system. We caution readers that optimism concerning a much more democratic and egalitarian future must be constrained by the reality of a rather small white male minority that has sustained its economic and political power and rule against *all* challengers for centuries—and might well be able to muster these resources to do so repeatedly for much time to come. Sadly, as Paul Kivel has underscored, there is still most centrally in the contemporary U.S. a "ruling class concept of democracy"—which, among other things, has meant an ability to vote in most major elections between candidates who are, or have been vetted by, powerful white men.[132]

We wrote this book because the dominant racial, class, and gender framing and actions of elite white men have yet to be fully problematized and deeply probed. This seems strange considering that for centuries they have so greatly shaped western and global economic, social, and political systems. It is long past time to call out and critically assess these elite men who have long exploited and subordinated ordinary working people, people of color, and women, as well as other smaller groups in society. For centuries they have created empires for capitalistic and racist exploitation, launched endless military invasions to preserve or extend capitalistic empires, built undemocratic political systems, led assaults on the natural environment, and rationalized with their dominant racial, class, and gender framing the oppression of massive numbers of people. Clearly, "we the people" can no longer afford to ignore and allow the domination of the powerful white men at the center of much social oppression, nationally and globally.

The many social costs of systemic racism, classism, and sexism are not just undesirable side effects of these systems, but are substantially the intrinsic and central aspects to their everyday operation. These social costs are great, deep, and broad. Racial, class, and gender subordination creates in any society not only great life and health costs for those groups and individuals who are subordinated, but also a great loss of present and future human abilities and knowledge for a society likely to need those human resources far into its future. In times of societal crisis, which are increasingly frequent in the United States and across the world, such limitations on human abilities and resources create great immediate and long-term problems for all involved.

Large-scale racial, class, and gender subordination has also cost U.S. society in that the widely asserted liberty-and-justice morality is abandoned and made meaningless in everyday practice. That is, the societal benefits that go to the socially dominant groups, especially elite white men, still involve massive violations of *fundamental human rights*. Individual human beings have been routinely sacrificed to the interests and actions of the dominant white male group and its highly organized structures of racial, class, and gender oppression. Unjust impoverishment is a central feature of these centuries-old systems of unjust enrichment, and it is essential for the elite in a society with such systemic oppressions to hide the close and direct connections between their great power and wealth and the lesser socioeconomic conditions of the majority of people. Understanding this fundamental social connectivity and the ways in which it is socially reproduced over generations are important ways for us to begin to free ourselves from a society riven with highly asymmetrical human oppressions. Systemic racial, class, and gender oppressions connect people within a societal nest of complex, interlinked, and cumulative interdependencies. As suggested previously, most people need to see and better understand these great social and intergenerational interconnections as a first step in dealing with major human oppressions.

Epilogue
Making Real "Liberty and Justice for All"

One great historical irony is that in the 18th century the powerful white male founders in the emerging United States vigorously insisted, in struggles with British officials, on their own human and civil rights as they created one of the West's most celebrated rebellions against autocratic authority. In summer 1776 they crafted a Declaration of Independence that famously stated the "self-evident" truth that "all men are created equal" and are endowed with the "unalienable Rights" of "Life, Liberty and the pursuit of Happiness." They further asserted that governments are created "to secure these rights" and derive "their just powers from the consent of the governed." Then they insist that, if "any Form of Government becomes destructive of these ends, it is the Right of the People to alter or to abolish it, and to institute new Government . . . to effect their Safety and Happiness." Although most of the white men who proclaimed these views did *not* deem the relatively radical Declaration as encompassing much more than the rights of propertied white men like themselves, this was an early western statement of broad *human rights*, one that has influenced hundreds of independence movements and human rights documents and speeches ever since. The latter have included the 1789 French "Declaration of the Rights of Man and the Citizen"; the 1848 Seneca Falls women's rights convention's "Declaration of Sentiments"; Abraham Lincoln's 1863 Gettysburg Address; declarations of numerous U.S. workers', women's, civil rights, and environmental groups; and national declarations of independence for Haiti, Mexico, Vietnam, Liberia, and numerous other countries.[1]

Unmistakably, many people across the globe have seen a great need to extend the reality of human rights far beyond what the U.S. founders envisioned. Especially after the Nazi Holocaust and anti-colonialism uprisings of the World War II era, the struggle for expanded human rights led to pathbreaking international actions and documents, including the dramatic and powerful 1948 Universal Declaration of Human Rights (UDHR). Crafted by relatively diverse drafting and vetting committees, and adopted by a multinational and multiracial United Nations General Assembly, that pathbreaking document asserts in Article 1 that "All human beings are born free and equal in dignity and rights. They are endowed with reason and conscience and should act towards one another in a spirit of brotherhood." Further, Article 21 adds that "The will of the people shall be the basis of the authority of government; this will shall be expressed in periodic and genuine elections which shall be by universal and equal suffrage." Article 25 proclaims that "Everyone has the right to a standard of living adequate for the health and well-being of himself and his family, including food, clothing, housing." Article 29 emphasizes that

> Everyone has duties to the community in which alone the free and full development of his personality is possible. . . . everyone shall be subject only to such limitations as are determined by law solely for the purpose of securing due recognition and respect for the rights and freedoms of others and of meeting the just requirements of morality, public order and the general welfare in a democratic society.

Many other human rights are likewise stated clearly in this remarkable and influential human rights document.[2]

Significantly, by the end of the UDHR's drafting period, representatives of many nations and cultural traditions had examined and vetted it. While western human rights concepts greatly influenced the declaration, major ethical and communal rights concepts from Asia, the Middle East, Africa, and Latin America were significant in shaping its stated principles. For example, the Chinese delegate, scholar-diplomat P. C. Chang, imbedded in it Asian (especially Confucian) understandings of humanity and human rights and duties. Together with other non-westerners, he made the UDHR globally relevant in accenting the collective spirit of brotherhood, human moral growth, pluralistic tolerance of ideas, the "will of the people" as governments' basis, and community duties balancing individual rights.[3] In addition, this group accented the right to *self-determination* of all people, a radical view given then pervasive western colonialism and imperialism led by elite white men. In the declaration's radical opening, the stated principles are asserted to be

> a common standard of achievement for all peoples and all nations, to the end that every individual and every organ of society . . . shall strive by teaching and education to promote respect for these rights and freedoms . . . [and] to secure their universal and effective recognition and observance, both among the peoples of Member States themselves and among the peoples of territories under their jurisdiction.

This "territories" phrase critically referenced imperialistic western colonialism.

In the era since its adoption, the UDHR has been used in crafting many international agreements and has become central to much international law. It has been called the "foundational international instrument of the human rights movement."[4] Moreover, since 1948, several enacting covenants on economic, social, and political rights have been signed by most United Nations members. These provide international support for concrete enactment of the UDHR principles. By the 1970s these implementation agreements included the International Covenant on Civil and Political Rights (ICCPR); this was approved by many countries and, when added to the UDHR, created an International Bill of Human Rights.

However, the mostly white male U.S. Senate only ratified this ICCPR in 1992, and with so many official "reservations" that it is essentially invalid for the United States. Despite continuing rhetoric about supporting global liberty and democracy, for decades the elite white, mostly male U.S. leaders have openly rejected implementing a number of the important United Nations' human rights covenants within the United States. Periodically, too, they have rejected explicit United Nations' critiques of continuing U.S. systemic racism, global economic exploitation, political imperialism, and military interventions.

In spite of rejection of full implementation by several western elites, these powerful UN rights covenants nonetheless represent major international concerns about and human rights responses to, as one human rights group puts it, "genocide, oppressive labor practices, the antiapartheid movement, national independence movements, liberation movements of colonized people, and atrocities committed against civilians" and to the "civil rights movement in America, the feminist movement, and the newly empowered voices of indigenous groups and landless peasants."[5] Even without substantial U.S. participation, these agreements signal a major pushback by the world's majority of peoples of color to the international and undemocratic dominance of the western white elite—and, thus, signal an increasing international consensus on the human rights and responsibilities necessary for truly just and democratic societies in the near future of planet Earth.

Recall that much of the framing of societies like the United States by the dominant groups has, for many centuries, defined them in terms of a hierarchical great chain of being in which those in the dominant class, racial, and gender groups routinely have the highest positions and most control of valued resources. In our view, a much more important concept today is the one signaled in these United Nations' efforts to expand the concept and reality of real human rights. This concept might be called a nonhierarchical "great chain of humanity"—full human rights and equitable interconnectedness for all of humanity. That new reality is essential to the survival of human beings, and indeed of all planetary species and the planet itself.

A large number of Americans, especially younger Americans, may be moving already in the direction of believing in societal expansion of class equality and justice, at least in regard to reducing the control of society by the "rich and powerful" and corporations, and to make sure government provides "equal access to basic necessities and public goods." In one 2016 poll of just Democratic Party voters a conservative polling firm explicitly defined capitalism for these respondents in the usual conservative free-market, no-government-intervention terms. Then they followed up by defining socialism as a different political-economic system for those who believe "corporations have too much control and that the capitalist system is set up to favor the rich and powerful" and who believe that "the only way to police corporations and protect the citizens is for the government to take a larger role in managing the economy to make sure that every individual has equal access to basic necessities and public goods, even if that means that some people have to transfer their wealth to others."[6] A *majority* of those who expressed a clear view preferred this democratic socialism. About 40 percent preferred this type of democratic control over corporate capitalism, as compared with 25 percent who preferred traditional corporate capitalism (the rest said both, neither, or undecided). In the opinion poll the Democratic Party voters 45 years and under preferred this type of government control even more strongly (46 percent to 19 percent). Additionally, 57 percent of these voters agreed that this type of government control of capitalism approach would have a "positive impact" on societies like the United States.

This poll did not include Republicans or independents. Interestingly, however, a later poll of Americans of all political persuasions did find that *over half* of younger Americans (18–29 years old) of all political inclinations had a favorable view of socialism, as compared to only a substantial minority (35 percent) of Americans of all ages.[7] It seems likely that the majority of these younger Americans too were reporting a favorable view of what presidential candidate Senator Bernie Sanders was then calling "democratic socialism." A clear majority in both polls had a favorable view of this type of socialism, one in which there was substantial government control of corporations and "every individual has equal access to basic necessities and public goods." In addition, in other polls much larger percentages of black and Latino Americans than of whites have signaled a favorable view of this socialism.[8] Thus, a great many Americans of all backgrounds, and especially younger Americans, seem to be developing a critical recognition that oligopolistic capitalism in the United States is very problematical and in great need of humanitarian reform.

Internationally, too, there is a widespread recognition of and opposition to the exploitation and oppression of the oligopolistic capitalism run by western and other elites. As one analyst of capitalistic imperialism, John

Smith, has underscored, there are now many worker movements globally that are creating "conditions for a rebirth of an international working class movement."[9] There are miners' strikes in South Africa, electronic workers' strikes in China, and textile and garment workers' strikes from Egypt to Bangladesh to Cambodia. Smith stresses the interconnectedness today of the world's workers. While the workers in these low-wage countries have often been the first victims of globalized capitalistic production, many better-off workers and their families in western countries have recently faced renewed capitalistic austerity and oppression—that is, declining job opportunities, exploitative workplaces, and declining economic conditions. As a result, if the latter are to prosper again they will have to join together with the super-exploited workers in other countries to, as Smith puts it metaphorically, finally dig "the grave in which to bury capitalism and thereby secure the future of human civilization."[10]

Let us conclude by underscoring the perceptive analyses of two great contemporary scholar-activists working against not only class oppression, but also the gender and racial oppression examined throughout this book. In the great European scholar-activist Maria Mies' view, a truly liberated society must create "non-exploitative, non-hierarchical, reciprocal relationships between . . . people and nature; women and men; different sections and classes of one society; different peoples."[11]

Certainly, attaining the goals of real liberty, equality, and justice for all will require many more coalition-building efforts among the world's non-elite peoples. The great African American scholar-activist Angela Davis has underscored such efforts in a recent speech on the Occupy movement: Activist groups like Occupy today are saying "no to global capitalism" and are working hard on "how to incorporate opposition to racism, class exploitation, homophobia, xenophobia, ableism, violence done to the environment and transphobia" into organized resistance by the world's 99 percent majority against the ruling elites. Then she concludes, like many resistance leaders over the centuries, that activists for liberatory change will "have to learn how to imagine a new world, one where peace is not simply the absence of war, but rather, a creative refashioning of global social relations."[12]

Notes

Introduction: Elite White Men: The 21st Century Problem

1 The top elite is regularly assisted in exercising great power by acolytes in the near-elite rank just below them. In some cases we draw on data on the "elite" that includes their immediate subordinates.

2 Soraya Chemaly, "Why Aren't We Talking about How Boys and Men Feel about a Woman President?" *RoleReboot*, February 26, 2016, http://rolereboot.org/culture-and-politics/details/2016-02-arent-talking-boys-men-feel-woman-president/ (accessed August 18, 2016).

3 Haeyoun Park, Josh Keller, and Josh Williams, "The Faces of American Power, Nearly as White as the Oscar Nominees," *New York Times*, February 26, 2016, http://www.nytimes.com/interactive/2016/02/26/us/race-of-american-power.html?_r=2 (accessed August 18, 2016).

4 Chemaly, "Why Aren't We Talking about How Boys and Men Feel about a Woman President?"

5 In its modern sense the term "sexism" likely arose first in U.S. English in the 1930s, while social "gender" arose in the 1940s, apparently in academic writings. Social science understandings of institutional sexism and social gender are relatively recent. See "Gender" and "Sexism," *OED Online*, Oxford University Press, note 3 (accessed November 12, 2015).

6 See, for example, David L. Featherman and Robert M. Hauser, *Opportunity and Change* (New York: Academic Press, 1978).

7 William K. Carroll, *Critical Strategies for Social Research* (Toronto: Canadian Scholars' Press, 2004), p. 18.

8 James Burnham, *The Managerial Revolution: What Is Happening in the World* (New York: John Day Co., 1941).

9 Floyd Hunter, *Community Power Structure: A Study of Decision-Makers* (Chapel Hill, NC: University of North Carolina Press, 1953); C. Wright Mills, *The Power Elite* (New York: Oxford University Press, 1959). Thomas R. Dye provides critical updates on Mills in *Who's Running America?*, 8th edn. (New York: Routledge, 2016).

10 Elmer Schattschneider, *The Semisovereign People: A Realist's View of Democracy in America* (New York: Holt, Rinehart and Winston, 1960).

11 G. William Domhoff, "C. Wright Mills, Floyd Hunter, and 50 Years of Power Structure Research," address to Michigan Sociological Association, 2006, http://www2.ucsc.edu/whorulesamerica/theory/mills_address.html (accessed December 7, 2016); G. William Domhoff, *Who Rules America? The Triumph of the Corporate Rich*, 7th ed. (New York: McGraw-Hill, 2013); and Philip Burch, *Elites in American History: The Federalist Years to the Civil War* (New York: Holmes & Meier, 1981).

12 Oliver C. Cox, *Caste, Class, and Race: A Study in Social Dynamics* (Garden City, NY: Doubleday, 1948), p. 344.

13 Oliver C. Cox, *Caste, Class, & Race: A Study in Social Dynamics* (Seattle, WA: Amazon, 2015), Kindle loc. 8883–8891.

14 Kwame Ture [Stokely Carmichael] and Charles V. Hamilton, *Black Power: The Politics of Liberation in America* (New York: Vintage, 1967). On other early sources, see Joe R. Feagin and Clairece B. Feagin, *Discrimination American Style: Institutional Racism and Sexism* (Englewood Cliffs, NJ: Prentice-Hall, 1978).

15 Michael Kimmel, *Angry White Men: American Masculinity at the End of an Era* (New York: Nation Books, 2013), p. 281.

16 Patricia Hill Collins, *Black Feminist Thought: Knowledge, Consciousness, and the Politics of Empowerment* (Boston: Unwin Hyman, 1990), p. 225; see also Patricia Hill Collins, "No Guarantees," in "Symposium on Black Feminist Thought," *Ethnic and Racial Studies* 38 (2015): 2349–2354.

17 bell hooks, *Feminist Theory: From Margin to Center* (Boston, MA: South End Press, 1994); Media Education Foundation, *bell hooks Cultural Criticism & Transformation* (Northampton, MA: Media Education Foundation, 1997).

18 Catharine A. MacKinnon, *Toward a Feminist Theory of the State* (Cambridge, MA: Harvard University Press, 1989), p. 63.

1 The Elite-White-Male Dominance System

1 Arthur O. Lovejoy, *The Great Chain of Being: A Study of the History of an Idea* (Cambridge, MA: Harvard University Press, 1973 [1936]), p. 59ff.

2 We draw on Joe R. Feagin, *The White Racial Frame*, 2nd edn. (New York: Routledge, 2013), chapter 3; and Helena Woodard, *African-British Writings in the Eighteenth Century* (Westport, CT: Greenwood Press, 1999), pp. xv–xviii.

3 See Germain N'Guessan Kouadio, *The Dynamics of Politics and Didacticism in Frances E. W. Harper's Writing* (Paris: Publibook, 2011).

4 Kimberlé Crenshaw, "Demarginalizing the Intersection of Race and Sex: A Black Feminist Critique of Antidiscrimination Doctrine, Feminist Theory and Antiracist Politics," *University of Chicago Legal Forum 140* (1989): 139–167; Angela Davis, "Reflections on the Black Woman's Role in the Community of Slaves," *Black Scholar 3* (December 1971): 2–15; Philomena Essed, *Understanding Everyday Racism* (Newbury Park, CA: Sage, 1991).

5 Patricia Hill Collins, *Black Feminist Thought: Knowledge, Consciousness, and the Politics of Empowerment*, 2nd edn. (New York: Routledge, 2000); Patricia Hill Collins, *Black Sexual Politics: African Americans, Gender, and the New Racism* (New York: Routledge, 2005).

6 Zillah R. Eisenstein, "Developing a Theory of Capitalist Patriarchy and Socialist Feminism," in *Capitalist Patriarchy and the Case for Social Feminism*, ed. Zillah R. Eisenstein (New York: Monthly Review Press, 1979), pp. 5–40.

7 Heidi I. Hartmann, "The Unhappy Marriage of Marxism and Feminism: Towards a More Progressive Union," *Review 2* (Summer 1978): 11. Italics added.

8 Ibid.

9 Michael Albert et alia, *Liberating Theory* (Boston, MA: South End Press, 1986), pp. 104–105.

10 Ibid., pp. 77–80.

11 Kimberlé Williams Crenshaw, "Mapping the Margins: Intersectionality, Identity Politics, and Violence against Women of Color," in *Critical Race Theory: The Key Writings That Formed the Movement*, eds. Kimberlé Crenshaw, Neil Gotanda, Garry Peller, and Kendall Thomas (New York: The New Press, 1995), p. 375.

12 James Madison, *Federalist*, November 10, 1787, http://www.constitution.org/fed/fed era00.htm (accessed August 5, 2010); and Kenneth F. Dolbeare and Linda Medcalf, "The Dark Side of the Constitution," in *The Case against the Constitution*, eds. J. F. Manley and K. M. Dolbeare (Armonk, NY: M. E. Sharpe, 1987), pp. 122–126.

13 Jeffrey A. Winters and Benjamin I. Page, "Oligarchy in the United States?" *Perspectives on Politics 7* (December 2009): 743–744.

14 See Joe R. Feagin, *White Party, White Government: Race, Class, and U.S. Politics* (New York: Routledge, 2012), chapter 1.

15 R.W. Connell, *Masculinities*, 2nd edn. (Berkeley, CA: University of California Press, 2005), p. 215.

16 See Herbert Aptheker, *Early Years of the Republic: From the End of the Revolution to the First Administration of Washington (1783–1793)* (New York: International Publishers, 1976), pp. 74–95.

17 Jack Holland, *A Brief History of Misogyny: The World's Oldest Prejudice* (New York: Little, Brown, 2012), Kindle loc. 236–244.

18 Silvia Federici, *Caliban and the Witch: Women, the Body, and Primitive Accumulation* (New York: Autonomedia, 2004), p. 170. We draw here on the review of, and quotes from, Federici's book in Alex Knight, "Who Were the Witches?—Patriarchal Terror and the Creation of Capitalism," November 5, 2009, https://endofcapitalism.com/2009/11/05/who-were-the-witches-patriarchal-terror-and-the-creation-of-capitalism/ (accessed July 25, 2016).

19 Federici, *Caliban and the Witch*, p. 164.

20 Connell, *Masculinities*, pp. 187–189.

21 Kathleen M. Brown, *Good Wives, Nasty Wenches, and Anxious Patriarchs* (Chapel Hill, NC: University of North Carolina Press, 1996), p. 14.

22 R. Todd Romero, *Making War and Minting Christians: Masculinity, Religion, and Colonialism in Early New England* (Amherst, MA: University of Massachusetts Press, 2011), p. 31.

23 Ibid., p. 36; see Cotton Mather, *Manly Christianity* (London: Ralph Smith, 1711).

24 Romero, *Making War and Minting Christians*, p. 20.

25 Ibid., p. 36; Gordon J. Schochet, *The Authoritarian Family and Political Attitudes in 17th Century England* (New Brunswick, NJ: Transaction Books, 1998), pp. xiii–xiv, 5–90.

26 Romero, *Making War and Minting Christians*, pp. 10, 12.

27 Mrinalini Sinha, "Colonial and Imperial Masculinities," in *International Encyclopedia of Men and Masculinities*, eds. Michael Flood, Judith K. Gardiner, Bob Pease, and Keith Pringle (New York: Routledge, 2013), p. 73.

28 See Collins, *Black Feminist Thought*; Judith Lorber, *Gender Inequality: Feminist Theories and Politics*, 5th edn. (New York: Oxford University Press, 2012); Joe Feagin and Clairece Booher Feagin, *Discrimination American Style: Institutional Racism and Sexism* (Englewood Cliffs, NJ: Prentice-Hall, 1978). See also Nijole Benokraitis and Joe Feagin, *Modern Sexism: Blatant, Subtle and Covert Discrimination* (Englewood Cliffs, NJ: Prentice Hall, 1986).

29 Gerda Lerner, *The Creation of Patriarchy* (New York: Oxford University Press, 1986), pp. 238–239.

30 Karl Mannheim, *Ideology and Utopia* (New York: Harcourt Harvest Books, 1936), p. 3.

31 In a recent online search we found that the phrase "male sexist frame" did not appear on the billions of indexed websites. "Male sexist ideology" appeared a dozen times. Dictionary definitions of "sexism" accent an individualistic perspective foregrounding individual "prejudice," not institutional sexism.

32 Jessica Bennett, "Why Do People Still Use the Word 'Mistress'? A Reporter Reflects," *New York Times*, June 7, 2016, http://www.nytimes.com/2016/06/08/insider/why-do-people-still-use-the-word-mistress-a-reporter-reflects.html?emc=eta1&_r=0 (accessed August 18, 2016).

33 Lisa Wade, "The Virgin/Whore Dichotomy," *The Society Pages*, April 10, 2008, https://thesocietypages.org/socimages/2008/04/10/the-virginwhore-dichotomy-2/ (accessed August 15, 2016).

34 Sylvester A. Johnson, "The Bible, Slavery, and the Problem of Authority," in *Beyond Slavery: Overcoming Its Religious and Sexual Legacies*, ed. Bernadette Brooten (New York: Palgrave Macmillan, 2010), chapter 13, n.p.; Larry R. Morrison, "Religious Defense of American Slavery before 1830," *Journal of Religious Thought* 37 (1981): 18–19.

35 Quoted in Anthony S. Parent, Jr., *Foul Means: The Formation of a Slave Society in Virginia, 1660–1740* (Chapel Hill, NC: University of North Carolina Press, 2003), p. 201.

36 Brown, *Good Wives, Nasty Wenches, and Anxious Patriarchs*, p. 370.

37 Johnson, "The Bible, Slavery, and the Problem of Authority," chapter 13, n.p.; Morrison, "Religious Defense of American Slavery before 1830," 18–19.

38 Keri Leigh Merritt, "Men without Pants: Masculinity and the Enslaved," *AAIHS*, September 11, 2016, http://www.aaihs.org/men-without-pants-masculinity-and-the-en slaved/?utm_content=buffer7c7c8&utm_medium=social&utm_source=twitter. com&utm_campaign=buffer (accessed December 7, 2016).

39 Kenneth A. Lockridge, *On the Sources of Patriarchal Rage: The Commonplace Books of William Byrd and Thomas Jefferson and the Gendering of Power in the Eighteenth Century* (New York: New York University Press, 1992), pp. 37ff; Mark E. Kann, *The Gendering of American Politics* (Westport, CT: Praeger, 1999), p. 6.

40 "The American Gay Rights Movement," *Civil Liberty*, http://civilliberty.about.com/od/ gendersexuality/tp/History-Gay-Rights-Movement.htm (accessed August 18, 2016).

41 Franklin, as quoted in Kann, *The Gendering of American Politics*, p. 6. Italics added.

42 Kann, *The Gendering of American Politics*, p. 23.

43 Annette Gordon-Reed, "Thomas Jefferson and the Empire of Imagination," http:// humanitiesnebraska.org/annette-gordon-reed-with-peter-onuf-on-thomas-jefferson- and-the-empire-of-imagination/ (accessed August 18, 2016). See also Roger G. Kennedy, *Mr. Jefferson's Lost Cause: Land, Farmers, Slavery, and the Louisiana Purchase* (New York: Oxford University Press, 2003), chapter 1.

44 Kann, *The Gendering of American Politics*, p. 98.

45 See George Lakoff, "The Palin Choice: The Reality of the Political Mind," *CommonDreams*, September 2, 2008, http://www.commondreams.org/view/2008/09/02 (accessed April 26, 2011).

46 Eliane Luthi Poirier, "'Boys Will Be Boys': And Other Language That Rigidifies Our Conceptions of Masculinity," *Gender across Borders*, March 30, 2011, http://www.gen deracrossborders.com/2011/05/30/boys-will-be-boys-and-other-language-that-rigidi fies-our-conceptions-of-masculinity-3/ (accessed August 18, 2016). Our italics.

47 Robert A. Williams Jr., *Like a Loaded Weapon: The Rehnquist Court, Indian Rights, and the Legal History of Racism in America* (Minneapolis, MN: University of Minnesota Press, 2005), Kindle loc. 307.

48 Dana D. Nelson, *National Manhood: Capitalist Citizenship and the Imagined Fraternity of White Men* (Durham, NC: Duke University Press, 1998), Kindle loc. 47; and "Uncle Sam," http://www.britannica.com/topic/Uncle-Sam (accessed August 18, 2016).

49 Nelson, *National Manhood*, Kindle loc. 47, 57.

50 Ibid.

51 Ibid.; see also W. E. B. Du Bois, *Black Reconstruction in America 1860–1880* (New York: Atheneum, 1992 [1935]), p. 700.

52 Thomas Winter, "Whiteness," in *American Masculinities: A Historical Encyclopedia*, ed. Bret E. Carroll (Thousand Oaks, CA: Sage, 2003), pp. 491–494.

53 Caryn E. Neumann, "Andrew Jackson," in *American Masculinities: A Historical Encyclopedia*, ed. Bret E. Carroll (Thousand Oaks, CA: Sage, 2003), p. 245.

54 E. H. Chapin, *Christianity: The Perfection of True Manliness* (New York: H. Lyon, 1856); J. B. Figgis, *Manliness, Womanliness, Godliness* (London: S.W. Partridge and Co., 1885); T. Hughes, *True Manliness* (Boston: D. Lothrop and Co., 1880). We draw on Anthony J. Weems and John N. Singer, "Racial Barriers in Eurocentric Sport(ing) Institutions: Countering the White Racial Frame," in *Systemic Racism: Making Liberty, Justice, and Democracy Real*, eds. Ruth Thompson-Miller and Kimberley Ducey (New York: Routledge, forthcoming).

55 Figgis, *Manliness, Womanliness, Godliness*, pp. 5–6. Italics added.

56 Tony Collins, *Sport in Capitalist Society* (Florence, GB: Routledge, 2013), p. 38. Italics added.

57 Dudley A. Sargent, "Are Athletics Making Girls Masculine? A Practical Answer to a Question Every Girl Asks," *Ladies' Home Journal* 29 (March 1912): 11, 71–73. We are indebted to Anthony Weems for suggestions.

58 Elizabeth Cady Stanton, *A History of Woman Suffrage*, vol. 1 (Rochester, NY: Fowler and Wells, 1889), pp. 70–71. We draw on the Fordham University website: http://legacy. fordham.edu/halsall/mod/senecafalls.asp (accessed August 16, 2016). Italics added.

59 "Who Has the Wealth in America?" *Business Week*, August 5, 1972, pp. 55–57; Thomas R. Dye, *Who's Running America?* 5th edn. (Englewood Cliffs, NJ: Prentice Hall, 1990),

pp. 52–62; Corporate Data Exchange, *Stock Ownership Directory: Energy* (New York: Corporate Data Exchange, 1980). See the report summary by Robert Sherrill, "Where Is the Cry of Protest?" *Nation* (October 25, 1980): 413–414.

60 G. William Domhoff, "C. Wright Mills, Floyd Hunter, and 50 Years of Power Structure Research," Address to Michigan Sociological Association, 2006, http://www2.ucsc.edu/whorulesamerica/theory/mills_address.html (accessed December 7, 2016).

61 See Erik O. Wright, *Class Structure and Income Determination* (New York: Academic Press, 1979).

62 Derek Thompson, "America's Monopoly Problem," *The Atlantic*, October 2016, http://www.theatlantic.com/magazine/archive/2016/10/americas-monopoly-problem/497549/ (accessed December 8, 2016).

63 Joel Kovel, *White Racism: A Psychohistory* (New York: Columbia University Press, 1984), p. 113.

64 For details, see Joe R. Feagin, Clairece Feagin, and David Baker, *Social Problems*, 6th edn. (Upper Saddle River, NJ: Prentice-Hall, 2005), chapter 5.

65 Rafael Tammariello, "The Slave Trade," *Las Vegas Review-Journal* (February 8, 1998): 1E.

66 Karl Marx, *Capital*, Vol. I, trans. Ben Fowkes (New York: Vintage Books, 1977), pp. 915, 926.

67 Federici, *Caliban and the Witch*, p. 17. Our italics.

68 Maria Mies, *Patriarchy and Accumulation on a World Scale* (London: Zed Books, [1986] 2014), p. 31.

69 Roxanne Dunbar-Ortiz, *An Indigenous Peoples' History of the United States* (Boston, MA: Beacon Press, 2014), p. 6.

70 Ibid.

71 Francis Jennings, *The Invasion of America: Indians, Colonialism, and the Cant of Conquest* (New York: W.W. Norton, 1976), p. 15.

72 Dunbar-Ortiz, *An Indigenous Peoples' History of the United States*, p. 80.

73 Jennings, *Invasion of America*, pp. 327–328. We discovered the Jennings quotations in Dunbar-Ortiz, *An Indigenous Peoples' History of the United States*.

74 John Winthrop, "A Modell of Christian Charity (1630)," *Collections of the Massachusetts Historical Society*, 3rd series 7 (Boston, 1838): 31–48, http://history.hanover.edu/texts/winthmod.html (accessed November 30, 2010). We modernize the spelling.

75 Deborah Madsen, *American Exceptionalism* (Jackson, MS: The University Press of Mississippi, 1998), pp. 8–9. See Feagin, *White Party, White Government*, chapter 2.

76 Oliver C. Cox, *Caste, Class, and Race* (Garden City, NY: Doubleday, 1948), pp. 332–333. Our italics.

77 Joe R. Feagin, *How Blacks Built America: Labor, Culture, Freedom, and Democracy* (New York: Routledge, 2016), p. 5; Joe R. Feagin, *Systemic Racism: A Theory of Oppression* (New York: Routledge, 2006), pp. 16–45.

78 We are influenced by George Lakoff, *The ALL NEW Don't Think of an Elephant!: Know Your Values and Frame the Debate*, 2nd edn. (White River Junction, VT: Chelsea Green Publishing, 2014), p. 38.

79 Quoted in Reginald Horsman, *Race and Manifest Destiny: The Origins of American Racial Anglo-Saxonism* (Cambridge, MA: Harvard University Press, 1986), p. 209.

80 W.E.B. Du Bois, *Darkwater: Voices from within the Veil* (New York: Harcourt, Brace & Co., 1920), Kindle loc. 302.

81 Andrew Goatly, *Washing the Brain: Metaphor and Hidden Ideology* (Amsterdam, The Netherlands: Benjamins Publishing Company, 2007), p. 46.

82 Ibid., p. 194.

83 F. Nwabueze Okoye, "Chattel Slavery as the Nightmare of the American Revolutionaries," *William and Mary Quarterly* 37 (January 1980): 13.

84 John Dickinson, *Letters from a Farmer in Pennsylvania to the Inhabitants of the British Colonies* (Philadelphia, 1768), p. 38, quoted in Okoye, "Chattel Slavery as the Nightmare of the American Revolutionaries," p. 3.

85 Greg Grandin, "Capitalism and Slavery," http://www.thenation.com/article/capitalism-and-slavery (accessed August 18, 2016). Our italics.

86 Quoted in David E. Stannard, *American Holocaust: Columbus and the Conquest of the New World* (New York: Oxford University Press, 1992), pp. 245–246.

87 William Appleman Williams, "Expansion, Continental and Overseas," in *The Reader's Companion to American History*, eds. Eric Foner and John Arthur Garraty (Boston, MA: Houghton Mifflin Harcourt, 1991), p. 365. We draw on Feagin, *White Party, White Government*, passim.

88 Sinha, "Colonial and Imperial Masculinities," pp. 74–75.

89 Theodore Roosevelt, *The Strenuous Life: Essays and Addresses* (New York: Century Co., 1900), pp. 11–12. See Katie Zezima, "How Teddy Roosevelt Helped Save Football," *Washington Post*, May 29, 2014, https://www.washingtonpost.com/news/the-fix/wp/2014/05/29/teddy-roosevelt-helped-save-football-with-a-white-house-meeting-in-1905/ (accessed August 18, 2016).

90 Connell, *Masculinities*, p. 193.

91 W. J. Cash, *The Mind of the South* (New York: Vintage Books, 1941), pp. 44–46.

92 Winter, "Whiteness," p. 492. See also pp. 491–501.

93 Guy Mount, "Capitalism and Slavery: Reflections on the Williams Thesis," http://www.aaihs.org/capitalism-and-slavery-reflections-on-the-williams-thesis/ (accessed March 25, 2016).

94 Seth Rockman, *Scraping By: Wage Labor, Slavery, and Survival in Early Baltimore* (Baltimore, MD: Johns Hopkins University Press, 2011), Kindle loc. 213–230.

95 *Dred Scott v. John F.A. Sandford*, 60 U.S. 393, 403–408 (1857).

96 Robin L. Einhorn, "Slavery," *Enterprise & Society 9* (September 2008): 494–495, 500.

97 Nancy MacLean, *Freedom Is Not Enough: The Opening of the American Workplace* (New York: Russell Sage Foundation and Harvard University Press, 2006), pp. 20–21, 31.

98 Karen Brodkin, "1998 AES Keynote Address: Global Capitalism: What's Race Got to Do with It?" *American Ethnologist 27* (May, 2000): 243.

99 Elizabeth Esch and David Roediger, "One Symptom of Originality: Race and the Management of Labour in the History of the United States," *Historical Materialism 17* (2009): 1, 19–39.

100 See Max Weber, *The Protestant Ethic and the Spirit of Capitalism*, trans. T. Parsons (New York: Scribner, 1958).

101 Jeffrey Klein, "Shall the Elite Inherit the Earth?" *Mother Jones*, March/April 1996, http://www.motherjones.com/politics/1996/03/shall-elite-inherit-earth (accessed December 7, 2016).

102 Connell, *Masculinities*, pp. 212–213.

2 Elite White Male Dominance: A Contemporary Overview

1 Joseph J. Ellis, "The Indispensable Man," *New York Times*, February 18, 1996, http://www.nytimes.com/1996/02/18/books/the-indispensable-man.html (accessed March 29, 2015).

2 Alan E. Reed, "New Vision and Facilities Transform Washington's Mount Vernon Estate," *Virginia Review*, November/December 2006, http://www.gwwoinc.com/pdf/Virginia_Review_Nov-Dec_2006_Mount_Vernon.pdf (accessed June 26, 2015).

3 Ibid.

4 Ronald T. Takaki, *Iron Cages: Race and Culture in 19th Century America* (New York: Oxford University Press, 1990), pp. 43–55; William H. Calhoun, "Review of *His Excellency: George Washington; Washington's Crossing; An Imperfect God: George Washington, His Slaves and the Creation of America*," *Naval War College Review 58* (2005): 154–160.

5 Calhoun, "Review of *His Excellency: George Washington; Washington's Crossing; An Imperfect God*."

6 Henry Wiencek, *An Imperfect God: George Washington, His Slaves and the Creation of America* (New York: Farrar, Straus and Giroux, 2003), p. 135.

7 Marcia [no last name], "*An Imperfect God: George Washington, His Slaves and the Creation of America* by Henry Wiencek," *What Would the Founders Think?* http://www.

whatwouldthefoundersthink.com/an-imperfect-god-george-washington-his-slaves-and-the-creation-of-america-by-henry-wiencek (accessed March 28, 2015).

8 Lincoln Caplan, "The White-Supremacist Lineage of a Yale College," *The Atlantic*, October 5, 2015, http://www.theatlantic.com/politics/archive/2015/10/the-cause-to-rename-calhoun-college/408682/ (accessed October 10, 2015).

9 Matthew Yglesias, "Rep Trent Franks: Blacks Were Better Off under Slavery," *Think Progress*, February 26, 2010, http://thinkprogress.org/yglesias/2010/02/26/196320/rep-trent-franks-blacks-were-better-off-under-slavery/ (accessed October 9, 2015); Ryan Grimm, "GOP Rep: Blacks Worse Off Now Than under Slavery," *Huffington Post*, April 28, 2010, http://www.huffingtonpost.com/2010/02/26/gop-rep-blacks-worse-off_n_478744.html (accessed October 9, 2015).

10 Pat Buchanan, "A Brief for Whitey," *Buchanan Website*, March 21, 2008, http://buchanan.org/blog/pjb-a-brief-for-whitey-969 (accessed October 9, 2015).

11 Susan A. Basow, *Sex-Role Stereotypes* (Monterey, CA: Brooks/Cole, 1980), p. 286.

12 See, for example, Herb Goldberg, *The Hazards of Being Male* (New York: Signet Books, 1976), pp. 172–179.

13 See Nijole Benokraitis and Joe Feagin, *Modern Sexism: Blatant, Subtle and Covert Discrimination*, 2nd edn. (Englewood Cliffs, NJ: Prentice Hall, 1995).

14 Elizabeth Plank, "We Asked Men to Draw Men to Prove an Important Point," *Identities.Mic*, December 22, 2014, http://mic.com/articles/106974/we-asked-men-to-draw-vaginas-to-prove-an-important-point#.K7I4C8BPC (accessed January 1, 2016).

15 Victoria A. Brownworth, "Op-ed: Violence against Lesbians on the Rise, but Prosecutions Aren't," *shewired.com*, March 14, 2014, http://www.shewired.com/opinion/2014/03/14/op-ed-violence-against-lesbians-rise-prosecutions-aren%E2%80%99t (accessed December 30, 2015).

16 Dreama Moon, "White Enculturation and Bourgeois Ideology: The Discursive Production of 'Good (White) Girls,'" in *Whiteness: The Social Communication of Social Identity*, eds. Thomas K. Nakayama and Judith M. Martin (Thousand Oaks, CA: Sage, 1999), p. 181; Eric Berkowitz, *Sex and Punishment: Four Thousand Years of Judging Desire* (Berkeley, CA: Counterpoint, 2013).

17 Katerina Deliovsky, *White Femininity: Race, Gender, and Power* (Blackpoint, NS: Fernwood Press, 2010), pp. 56, 62.

18 See Ibid., p. 66.

19 Trudier Harris, ed. *Selected Works of Ida B. Wells-Barnett* (New York: Oxford University Press, 1991).

20 Chauncey DeVega, "The Plague of Angry White Men: How Racism, Gun Culture & Toxic Masculinity Are Poisoning America," *Salon*, July 7, 2015, http://www.salon.com/2015/07/07/the_plague_of_angry_white_men_how_racism_gun_culture_toxic_masculinity_are_poisoning_america_in_tandem/ (accessed October 4, 2015).

21 Chauncey DeVega, "Dear White America: Your Toxic Masculinity Is Killing You," *Salon*, August 2, 2015, http://www.salon.com/2015/08/02/dear_white_america_your_toxic_masculinity_is_killing_you/ (accessed October 4, 2015).

22 Josh Harkinson, "Fully Loaded," *Mother Jones*, http://www.motherjones.com/politics/2016/04/fully-loaded-ten-biggest-gun-manufacturers-america (accessed August 18, 2016). Our italics.

23 Sam Polk, "How Wall Street Bro Talk Keeps Women Down," *New York Times*, July 7, 2016, http://www.nytimes.com/2016/07/10/opinion/sunday/how-wall-street-bro-talk-keeps-women-down.html (accessed July 14, 2016).

24 "The American Gay Rights Movement," http://civilliberty.about.com/od/gendersexuality/tp/History-Gay-Rights-Movement.htm (accessed March 18, 2016).

25 Carol S. Walther and David G.T. Embrick, "White Trash and White Supremacy: An Analysis of the James Byrd Jr. and Matthew Shepard Hate Crimes," in *Systemic Racism: Making Liberty, Justice, and Democracy Real*, eds. Ruth Thompson-Miller and Kimberley Ducey (New York: Routledge, forthcoming).

26 Soraya Chemaly, "Why Aren't We Talking about How Boys and Men Feel about a Woman President?" *RoleReboot*, February 26, 2016, http://rolereboot.org/culture-and-politics/

details/2016-02-arent-talking-boys-men-feel-woman-president/ (accessed August 18, 2016); Crosby Burns, Kimberly Barton, and Sophia Kerby, *The State of Diversity in Today's Workforce* (Washington, DC: Center for American Progress, 2012), p. 4; Jesse Washington, "Study: Networking Hinders Black Women Executives," *Associated Press*, January 7, 2009, www.foxnews.com/wires/2009Jan07/0,4670,BlackWomenExecutives, 00.html (accessed March 19, 2009); Bryce Covert, "Only White, Male CEOs Make the Big Bucks," *Think Progress*, October 22, 2013, http://thinkprogress.org/economy/2013/10/22/2816041/white-men-ceos/ (accessed October 4, 2015).

27 Chemaly, "Why Aren't We Talking about How Boys and Men Feel about a Woman President?"

28 Barb Darrow, "IBM CEOs through the Ages," *Gigaom*, October 28, 2011, https://gigaom.com/2011/10/28/ibm-ceos-through-the-ages/ (accessed October 4, 2015).

29 Larry Schwartz, "35 Mind-Blowing Facts about Inequality," *Alternet*, July 13, 2015, http://www.alternet.org/economy/35-mind-blowing-facts-about-inequality (accessed August 9, 2015).

30 United for a Fair Economy, *Born on Third Base: What the Forbes 400 Really Says about Economic Equality & Opportunity in America* (Boston, MA: United for a Fair Economy, 2012), pp. 14–15; Josh Harkinson, "America's 100 Richest People Control More Wealth Than the Entire Black Population," *Mother Jones*, December 2, 2015, http://www.motherjones.com/mojo/2015/12/report-100-people-more-wealth-african-american-population (accessed August 18, 2016); Chloe Sorvino, "America's Richest Women 2015," *Forbes*, September 29, 2015, http://www.forbes.com/sites/chloesorvino/2015/09/29/americas-richest-women-2015/#2f85f13f3e79 (accessed August 18, 2016); Chuck Collins and Josh Hoxie, *Billionaire Bonanza Report: The Forbes 400 and the Rest of Us* (Washington, DC: Institute for Policy Studies, 2015), p. 6.

31 R.W. Connell, *Masculinities*, 2nd edn. (Berkeley, CA: University of California Press, 2005), p. 202.

32 Robert Frank "The Shortage of Women Billionaires," *CNBC News*, http://www.cnbc.com/id/47567609 (accessed July 14, 2016).

33 Andrew Ward, "Black CEOs Lead Just 1% of Fortune 500 Companies," *Daily Finance*, February 20, 2015, http://www.dailyfinance.com/2015/02/20/black-ceos-fortune-500-companies/ (accessed March 28, 2015); see also Richard L. Zweigenhaft and G. William Domhoff, "Trends at the Top: The New CEOs Revisited," April 8, 2014, http://thesocietypages.org/specials/new-ceos-revisited/ (accessed March 21, 2015); Sylvia Ann Hewlett, Melinda Marshall, and Laura Sherbin, "How Diversity Can Drive Innovation," *Harvard Business Review*, December 2013, https://hbr.org/2013/12/how-diversity-can-drive-innovation (accessed March 27, 2015). See also Jillian Berman, "Soon, Not Even 1 Percent of Fortune 500 Companies Will Have Black CEOs," *Huffington Post*, January 29, 2015, http://www.huffingtonpost.com/2015/01/29/black-ceos-fortune-500_n_6572074.html (accessed March 27, 2015).

34 Alliance for Board Diversity, "Missing Pieces: Women and Minorities on Fortune 500 Boards," 2013, http://theabd.org/Reports.html (accessed August 18, 2016).

35 Berman, "Soon, Not Even 1 Percent of Fortune 500 Companies Will Have Black CEOs."

36 Ibid.; and Gregory Wallace, "Only 5 Black CEOs at 500 Biggest Companies," *CNN*, http://money.cnn.com/2015/01/29/news/economy/mcdonalds-ceo-diversity/ (accessed March 28, 2015); Hewlett, Marshall, and Sherbin, "How Diversity Can Drive Innovation."

37 S. Alexander Haslam and Michelle K. Ryan, "The Road to the Glass Cliff," *The Leadership Quarterly 19* (October 2008): 530–546. See also Jillian Berman, "Why We Hire Women and Minorities to Clean Up Our Messes," *Huffington Post*, July 8, 2014, http://www.huffingtonpost.com/2014/06/27/mary-barra-glass-cliff_n_5538167.html (accessed March 27, 2015); Bryce Covert, "Condolences. You're Hired!" *Slate*, March 25, 2014, http://www.slate.com/articles/business/moneybox/2014/03/general_motors_recall_is_mary_barra_the_latest_victim_of_the_glass_cliff.html (accessed March 27, 2015); Jim Axelrod, "GM CEO Mary Barra Apologizes for Recall Delay," *CBS News*, March 18, 2014, http://www.cbsnews.com/news/gm-ceo-mary-barra-apologizes-for-recall-delay/ (accessed March 29, 2015).

38 Berman, "Why We Hire Women and Minorities to Clean Up Our Messes"; Alison Cook and Christy Glass, "Above the Glass Ceiling: When Are Women and Racial/Ethnic Minorities Promoted to CEO?" *Strategic Management Journal 35* (2014): 1080–1089; Michelle K. Ryan and S. Alexander Haslam, "The Glass Cliff: Evidence that Women are Over-Represented in Precarious Leadership Positions," *British Journal of Management 16* (2005): 81–90; Mark Mulcahy and Carol Linehan "Females and Precarious Board Positions: Further Evidence of the Glass Cliff," *British Journal of Management 25* (2014): 425–438.

39 Alison Cook and Christy Glass, "Above the Glass Ceiling: When Are Women and Racial/ Ethnic Minorities Promoted to CEO?," pp. 1080–1089.

40 Berman, "Why We Hire Women and Minorities to Clean Up Our Messes"; Covert, "Condolences. You're Hired!"; Axelrod, "GM CEO Mary Barra Apologizes for Recall Delay."

41 See Richard L. Zweigenhaft and G. William Domhoff, "Trends at the Top: The New CEOs Revisited."

42 Richard L. Zweigenhaft and G. William Domhoff, "Diversity and the New CEOs," *The Society Pages*, July 5, 2012, http://thesocietypages.org/papers/new-ceos/ (accessed June 26, 2015).

43 Alexis Kleinman, "Most Outrageous Things CEOs Said in 2012," *Huffington Post*, December 8, 2012, http://www.huffingtonpost.com/2012/12/07/most-outrageous-ceos-2012_n_2257358.html?slideshow=true#gallery/268115/7 (accessed May 26, 2016).

44 Akin Oyedele, "9 Outrageous Things CEOs Said and Later Regretted," *CEO.com*, October 15, 2014, http://www.ceo.com/flink/?lnk=http%3A%2F%2Fwww.businessinsider.com%2Fceo-outrageous-remarks-and-apologies-2014-10 (accessed May 26, 2016).

45 Kurt Eichenwald, "Texaco Executives, on Tape, Discussed Impeding a Bias Suit," *New York Times* (November 4, 1996): A1; Bari-Ellen Roberts, *Roberts v. Texaco: A True Story of Race and Corporate America* (New York: Avon Books, 1998), pp. 1, 283; Kurt Eichenwald, "The Two Faces of Texaco," *New York Times* (November 10, 1996), Section 3, p. 1.

46 Maureen Ryan, "Les Moonves on 'Big Brother' Racism: 'I Find Some of the Behavior Absolutely Appalling,'" *Huffington Post*, July 29, 2013, http://www.huffingtonpost.com/2013/07/29/les-moonves-big-brother-racism_n_3671480.html (accessed March 25, 2015); Greg Braxton, "'Big Brother' furor: CBS reveals a double standard?," *Los Angeles Times*, July 10, 2013, http://www.latimes.com/entertainment/tv/showtracker/la-et-st-big-brother-furor-cbs-reveals-a-double-standard-20130710-story.html (accessed March 28, 2015). Our italics.

47 Greg Braxton, "'Big Brother' Furor: CBS Reveals a Double Standard?" *Los Angeles Times*, July 10, 2013, http://www.latimes.com/entertainment/tv/showtracker/la-et-st-big-brother-furor-cbs-reveals-a-double-standard-20130710-story.html (accessed March 27, 2015).

48 "'Big Brother' Racism Proves to Be a Ratings Goldmine," *Inquisitr*, July 11, 2013, http://www.inquisitr.com/842210/big-brother-racism-ratings/ (accessed March 27, 2015); "Top 10 Highest Paid CEOs 2015," *Richest Lifestyle*, January 8, 2015, http://www.richestlifestyle.com/highest-paid-ceos/ (accessed March 25, 2015).

49 Joe R. Feagin and Eileen O'Brien, *White Men on Race* (Boston, MA: Beacon, 2003), p. 200.

50 See, for example, Nathan Glazer, *Affirmative Discrimination* (New York: Basic Books, 1976).

51 Oyedele, "9 Outrageous Things CEOs Said and Later Regretted."

52 Margaret Heffernan, "Female Execs Horrified by Former GE CEO's Comments," *Aol. FINANCE*, May 7, 2012, http://www.aol.com/article/2012/05/07/female-execs-horrified-by-speech-by-ge-ex-ceo/20233094/?jwp=1 (accessed May 26, 2016).

53 Amanda Terkel and Ryan Grim, "Jamie Dimon Wants to Mansplain Banking to Elizabeth Warren," *Huffington Post*, June 10, 2015, http://www.huffingtonpost.com/2015/06/10/jamie-dimon-elizabeth-warren_n_7555204.html (accessed May 26, 2016).

54 Jessica Goldstein, "Leaked Email from Marvel CEO Is a Listicle about Why Women Can't Be Superheroes," *Think Progress*, May 5, 2015, http://thinkprogress.org/culture/2015/05/05/3654649/leaked-email-marvel-ceo-listicle-women-cant-superheroes/ (accessed June 26, 2015). Italics in original.

55 Mary Elizabeth Williams, "Adios, Dov Charney and George Will!" *Salon*, June 19, 2014, http://www.salon.com/2014/06/19/adios_dov_charney_and_george_will/ (accessed May 26, 2016).

56 "Tell Sony to Fire Amy Pascal," *Color of Change*, December 16, 2014, http://colorof-change.org/campaign/sony-fire-amy-pascal/ (accessed March 24, 2015); Matthew Zeitlin, "Scott Rudin on Obama's Favorite Movies: 'I Bet He Likes Kevin Hart,'" *BuzzFeed News*, December 10, 2014, http://www.buzzfeed.com/matthewzeitlin/scott-rudin-on-obama-i-bet-he-likes-kevin-hart#.ajpYngjlO (accessed March 24, 2015).

57 See also Rebecca Fortner, "Cracking the Plexi-Glass Ceiling," *RiseUp*, February 9, 2011, Riseup.com (accessed May 11, 2011).

58 Dominic Rushe, "Twitter's Diversity Report: White, Male and Just Like the Rest of Silicon Valley," *Guardian*, July 25, 2014, http://www.theguardian.com/technology/2014/jul/25/twitter-diversity-white-men-facebook-silicon-valley (accessed March 23, 2015).

59 Alexia Tsotsis, "Ellen Pao Says Silicon Valley Isn't a Meritocracy. It's Not," *Tech Crunch News*, May 27, 2015, http://techcrunch.com/2015/05/27/just-look-at-the-numbers/#.pteiz9:kq4b (accessed June 26, 2015).

60 Connell, *Masculinities*, p. 166; for more detail see Joe R. Feagin, Clairece Feagin, and David Baker, *Social Problems*, 6th edn. (Upper Saddle River, NJ: Prentice-Hall, 2005), chapter 5.

61 Julianne Pepitone, "Black, Female, and a Silicon Valley 'Trade Secret,'" *CNN*, March 18, 2013, http://money.cnn.com/2013/03/17/technology/diversity-silicon-valley/?iid=EL (accessed March 28, 2015); "Diversity in Silicon Valley: The Fight to Uncover Data," *CNN*, http://money.cnn.com/interactive/technology/diversity-tech/?iid=EL (accessed March 28, 2015).

62 Maxine Williams, "Building a More Diverse Facebook," *Facebook News Room*, June 25, 2014, http://newsroom.fb.com/news/2014/06/building-a-more-diverse-facebook (accessed March 23, 2015).

63 Ibid.

64 Rushe, "Twitter's Diversity Report."

65 Ibid.

66 "Getting to Work on Diversity at Google," May 28, 2014, http://googleblog.blogspot.ca/2014/05/getting-to-work-on-diversity-at-google.html (accessed March 23, 2015); Rushe, "Twitter's Diversity Report"; David Goldman, "Few Female Engineers and Execs at Google," *CNN*, May 30, 2014, http://money.cnn.com/2014/05/29/technology/google-women/?iid=EL (accessed March 28, 2015); Chris Isidore, "Google: Overwhelmingly White and Male," *CNN*, May 30, 2014, http://money.cnn.com/2014/05/29/technology/google-white-males/index.html?iid=EL (accessed March 28, 2015).

67 James O'Toole, "Apple: Mostly Men, Mostly White," *CNN*, August 12, 2014, http://money.cnn.com/2014/08/12/technology/apple-diversity/index.html?iid=EL (accessed March 28, 2015).

68 Howard Husock, "Tim Cook's $800 Million Giving Pledge: Why It's So Important," *Forbes*, March 29 2015, http://www.forbes.com/sites/howardhusock/2015/03/29/tim-cooks-800-million-giving-pledge-why-its-so-important/ (accessed March 30, 2015); "Current Pledgers," *The Giving Pledge*, http://givingpledge.org/ (accessed March 30, 2015); The Giving Pledge, "Frequently Asked Questions," http://givingpledge.org/faq.aspx (accessed March 30, 2015).

69 Rushe, "Twitter's Diversity Report."

70 Vivek Wadhwa, "My Response to Dick Costolo: Twitter Must Lead Silicon Valley on Diversity," *Crunch Network*, October 6, 2013, http://techcrunch.com/2013/10/06/my-response-to-dickc-twitter-must-lead-silicon-valley-on-diversity/ (accessed March 23, 2015); Claire Cain Miller, "Curtain Is Rising on a Tech Premiere with (as Usual) a Mostly Male Cast," *New York Times*, October 4, 2013, http://www.nytimes.com/2013/10/05/technology/as-tech-start-ups-surge-ahead-women-seem-to-be-left-behind.html (accessed March 23, 2015).

71 Rory Carroll, "Sexism in Silicon Valley: Tinder, the 'Dave Rule' and Tech's Glass Ceiling," *Guardian*, July 2, 2014, http://www.theguardian.com/technology/2014/jul/02/silicon-valley-sexism-tinder-culture-women-ageism (accessed March 23, 2015); Stuart

Dredge, "Dating App Tinder Facing Sexual Harassment Lawsuit from Co-founder," *Guardian*, July 1, 2014, http://www.theguardian.com/technology/2014/jul/01/tinder-sexual-harassment-lawsuit-whitney-wolfe (accessed March 23, 2015); Collen Kriel, "Twitter Faces Gender Discrimination Lawsuit, Follows in Facebook's Steps," *siliconAN-GLE*, March 23, 2015, http://siliconangle.com/blog/2015/03/23/twitter-faces-gender-discrimination-lawsuit-follows-in-facebooks-steps/ (accessed March 23, 2015); Jessica Valenti, "Tinder's Sexual Harassment Scandal Is Not a Surprise. It's Another Wake-Up Call," *Guardian*, July 2, 2014, http://www.theguardian.com/commentisfree/2014/jul/02/tinder-sexual-harassment-silicon-valley-sexism (accessed March 23, 2015).

72 Wadhwa, "My Response to Dick Costolo"; Claire Cain Miller, "Curtain Is Rising on a Tech Premiere with (as Usual) a Mostly Male Cast."; "Defiant Twitter CEO Dick Costolo Fires Back at 'All-Boys Tech Club' Remark," *Tottenham News*, 2013, http://www.totten hamnews.org/sci-tech-3/defiant-twitter-ceo-dick-costolo-fires-back-at-all-boys-tech-club-remark-343.html (accessed March 23, 2015).

73 "People Get Ready," *Amazon Summary*, http://www.amazon.com/People-Get-Ready-Citizenless-Democracy/dp/1568585217/ref=sr_1_2_twi_har_1?s=books&ie=UTF8 &qid=1456421144&sr=1-2&refinements=p_27%3ARobert+W.+McChesney (accessed March 1, 2016).

74 David Rotman, "How Technology Is Destroying Jobs," *MIT Technology Review*, June 12, 2013, https://www.technologyreview.com/s/515926/how-technology-is-destroying-jobs/ (accessed August 18, 2016).

75 G. William Domhoff, *The Myth of Liberal Ascendancy: Corporate Dominance from the Great Depression to the Great Recession* (Boulder, CO: Paradigm Publishers, 2013), passim.

76 Ira Katznelson, *When Affirmative Action Was White* (New York: Norton, 2005), pp. 19–109.

77 Kim Phillips-Fein, *Invisible Hands: The Making of the Conservative Movement from the New Deal to Reagan* (New York: W.W. Norton, 2009), Kindle loc. 296–314. See also Joe R. Feagin, *White Party, White Government: Race, Class, and U.S. Politics* (New York: Routledge, 2012), chapter 4.

78 Thomas Ferguson and Joel Rogers, *Right Turn: The Decline of the Democrats and the Future of American Politics* (New York: Hill and Wang, 1986), p. 79.

79 James Srodes, "The Rule Makers," *Financial World* (March 5, 1991): 40.

80 Ferguson and Rogers, *Right Turn*, p. 79.

81 See Philip H. Burch, *Elites in American History: The Federalist Years to the Civil War* (New York: Holmes and Meier, 1981); G. William Domhoff, *Who Rules America? Challenges to Corporate and Class Dominance*, 6th edn. (New York: McGraw-Hill, 2009). We draw here on Joe R. Feagin, *White Party, White Government*.

82 Robert Caro, *The Years of Lyndon Johnson: Master of The Senate* (New York: Knopf, 2002), p. 9.

83 Jeffrey A. Winters and Benjamin I. Page, "Oligarchy in the United States?" *Perspectives on Politics 7* (December 2009): 743–744. We also draw on Feagin, *White Party, White Government*, chapter 3.

84 Winters and Page, "Oligarchy in the United States?," pp. 743–744.

85 Nicholas Confessore, Sarah Cohen, and Karen Yourish, "Buying Power," October 10, 2015, http://www.nytimes.com/interactive/2015/10/11/us/politics/2016-presidential-election-super-pac-donors.html?smid=tw-share&_r=0 (accessed July 10, 2016).

86 Philip Bump, "The New Congress Is 80 Percent White, 80 Percent Male and 92 Percent Christian," *Washington Post*, January 5, 2015, http://www.washingtonpost.com/blogs/the-fix/wp/2015/01/05/the-new-congress-is-80-percent-white-80-percent-male-and-92-percent-christian/ (accessed March 22, 2015); Emily Baxter and Jamie Keene, "The Excessive Political Power of White Men in the United States, in One Chart," *Think-Progress*, October 10, 2014, http://thinkprogress.org/justice/2014/10/10/3578399/survey-finds-white-men-have-eight-times-as-much-political-power-as-women-of-color/ (accessed March 24, 2015); Reflective Democracy Campaign, "Do America's Elected Officials Reflect Our Population?" http://wholeads.us/ (accessed March 24, 2015);

Chemaly, "Why Aren't We Talking about How Boys and Men Feel about a Woman President?"; Tracey E. George and Albert H. Yoon, "The Gavel Gap: Who Sits in Judgment on State Courts?" http://gavelgap.org/ (accessed August 18, 2016).

87 Eric Lipton, "Half of Congress Members Are Millionaires, Report Says," *New York Times*, January 9, 2014, http://www.nytimes.com/2014/01/10/us/politics/more-than-half-the-members-of-congress-are-millionaires-analysis-finds.html?_r=0 (accessed March 22, 2015); Russ Choma, "Millionaires' Club: For First Time, Most Lawmakers are Worth $1 Million-Plus," *OpenSecrets.org*, January 9, 2014, https://www.opensecrets.org/news/2014/01/millionaires-club-for-first-time-most-lawmakers-are-worth-1-million-plus/ (accessed March 22, 2015).

88 Choma, "One Member of Congress = 18 American Households: Lawmakers' Personal Finances Far from Average," *OpenSecrets.org*, January 12, 2015, https://www.opensecrets.org/news/2015/01/one-member-of-congress-18-american-households-lawmakers-personal-finances-far-from-average (accessed January 10, 2017).

89 Ibid.

90 Domhoff, *Who Rules America?*, chapters 7–8.

91 Quoted in Chris Hedges, "The Obama Deception: Why Cornel West Went Ballistic," *TruthDig*, May 16, 2011, http://www.truthdig.com/report/item/the_obama_deception_why_cornel_west_went_ballistic_20 (accessed May 18, 2011).

92 Michael Eric Dyson, *The Black Presidency* (New York: Houghton Mifflin Harcourt, 2016).

93 Schwartz, "35 Mind-Blowing Facts about Inequality."

94 Anna Palmer and Matthew Murray, "For Black Lobbyists, Progress Is Real but Big Challenges Remain," *Roll Call*, June 9, 2009, http://www.rollcall.com/issues/54_142/-35651-1.html (accessed May 10, 2011); Erika Lovley, "Hill Lags in Hiring Hispanics," *Roll Call*, February 4, 2010, http://www.hispaniclobbyists.org/node/102 (accessed May 10, 2011); Marcus Stern and Jennifer LaFleur, "Leadership PACs: Let the Good Times Roll," September 26, 2009, http://www.propublica.org/article/leadership-pacs-let-the-good-times-roll-925 (accessed October 22, 2010).

95 "Banking on Connections," Center for Responsive Politics, *citizen.org*, June 3, 2010, (accessed October 22, 2010). For detail see Feagin, *White Party, White Government*.

96 Sidney Blumenthal, *The Rise of the Counter-Establishment* (New York: Times Books, 1986), pp. 4–11, 133–170; Peter Steinfels, *The Neoconservatives: The Men Who Are Changing America's Politics* (New York: Touchstone, 1979), pp. 214–277.

97 Emily Bazelon, "Kamala Harris, a 'Top Cop' in the Era of Black Lives Matter," *New York Times Magazine*, May 25, 2016, http://www.nytimes.com/2016/05/29/magazine/kamala-harris-a-top-cop-in-the-era-of-black-lives-matter.html?_r=1 (accessed June 14, 2016).

98 See Burch, *Elites in American History*, pp. 85–159; Feagin, *White Party, White Government*.

99 Ferguson and Rogers, *Right Turn*, p. 78ff.

100 "Washington Post-ABC News Poll," *Washington Post*, April 18, 2011, http://www.washingtonpost.com/wp-srv/politics/polls/postpoll_04172011.html (accessed April 24, 2011). We draw on Feagin, *White Party, White Government*, passim.

101 Larry M. Bartels, "Economic Inequality and Political Representation," Princeton University, August 2005, http://www.princeton.edu/~bartels/economic.pdf (accessed April 24, 2011).

102 Benjamin I. Page, Larry M. Bartels, and Jason Seawright, "Democracy and the Policy Preferences of Wealthy Americans," *Perspectives on Politics 11* (March 2013): 51–73. See Lee Drutman, "What Do Rich Political Donors Get for Their Contributions?" *Sunlight Foundation*, August 15, 2012, http://sunlightfoundation.com/blog/2012/08/15/what-do-rich-political-donors-get-for-their-contributions/ (accessed March 26, 2015).

103 Paul Blumenthal, "It's Time to Name the 2014 Midterms the Dark Money Election," September 4, 2014, *Huffington Post*, http://www.huffingtonpost.com/2014/09/04/dark-money-2014_n_5761774.html (accessed March 27, 2015); JUSTIA US, Supreme Court's "Citizens United v. Federal Election Comm'n 558 U.S. ___ (2010)," https://supreme.justia.com/cases/federal/us/558/08-205/ (accessed March 26, 2015); Lee Drutman, "The

Political 1% of the 1%," *Sunlight Foundation*, June 24, 2013, http://sunlightfoundation.com/blog/2013/06/24/1pct_of_the_1pct/ (accessed March 25, 2015).

104 Naureen Khan, "Donors Freed by McCutcheon Decision: Mostly Wealthy, White Men," *Al Jazeera America*, http://thoughtsandpolitics.blogspot.ca/2014/04/donors-freed-by-mccutcheon.html (accessed March 27, 2015).

105 Ibid.; Luke Stangel, "How Silicon Valley's Top 10 Billionaires Voted with Their Political Cash," *Silicon Valley Business Journal*, July 2, 2013, http://www.bizjournals.com/sanjose/news/2013/07/02/how-silicon-valleys-10-biggest.html?page=all (accessed March 25, 2015).

106 Drutman, "The Political 1% of the 1%."

107 Ibid.; Benjamin Page, Larry Bartels, and Jason Seawright, "Democracy and the Policy Preferences of Wealthy Americans," *Perspectives on Politics* 11 (2013): 51–73; Lee Drutman, "What Do Rich Political Donors Get for Their Contributions?" *Sunlight Foundation*, August 15, 2012, http://sunlightfoundation.com/blog/2012/08/15/what-do-rich-political-donors-get-for-their-contributions/ (accessed March 26, 2015); Martin Gilens, "Under the Influence," *Boston Review*, July 1, 2012, http://www.bostonreview.net/forum/lead-essay-under-influence-martin-gilens (accessed March 25, 2015).

108 Lindsay Young, "A Sketch of the Stealthy Wealthy," *Sunlight Foundation*, October 22, 2015, http://sunlightfoundation.com/blog/2012/10/22/sketch-stealthy-wealthy/ (accessed March 26, 2015); Blumenthal, "It's Time to Name the 2014 Midterms the Dark Money Election."

109 "The World's Billionaires," *Forbes*, March 26, 2015, http://www.forbes.com/profile/sheldon-adelson/ (accessed March 26, 2015); Khan, "Donors Freed by McCutcheon Decision."

110 Drutman, "The Political 1% of the 1%"; Bill Allison, "Stealthy Wealthy: How Harold Simmons' Political Giving Has Benefited His Business Empire," *Sunlight Foundation*, March 13, 2012, http://sunlightfoundation.com/blog/2012/03/13/simmons/ (accessed March 26, 2015); "The World's Billionaires."

111 Blumenthal, "It's Time to Name the 2014 Midterms the Dark Money Election"; Robert Maguire, "Dark Money Hits $50 Million, Most Still to Come," *OpenSecrets.org*, August 28, 2014, http://www.opensecrets.org/news/2014/08/dark-money-hits-50-million-most-still-to-come/ (accessed March 27, 2015); Ben Piven, "Dark Money: Despite $4 Billion Spent, Midterms Hinge on Hidden Funding," *Aljazeera America*, October 31, 2014, http://america.aljazeera.com/watch/shows/midterms/articles/2014/10/31/dark-money-4-billionelection.html (accessed March 28, 2015); Andy Kroll, "5 Signs the Dark-Money Apocalypse Is Upon Us," *Mother Jones*, September 19, 2014, http://www.motherjones.com/politics/2014/09/dark-money-2014-elections-house-senate (accessed March 28, 2015); Robert Maguire, "Dark Money Hits $100 Million with Help from Single-Candidate Groups," *OpenSecrets.org*, October 9, 2014, http://www.opensecrets.org/news/2014/10/dark-money-hits-100-million-with-help-from-single-candidate-groups/ (accessed March 28, 2015).

112 Editorial Board, "Dark Money Helped Win the Senate," *New York Times*, November 8, 2014, http://www.nytimes.com/2014/11/09/opinion/sunday/dark-money-helped-win-the-senate.html?_r=0 (accessed March 27, 2015).

113 Khan, "Donors Freed by McCutcheon Decision."

114 Robert A. Dahl, *How Democratic Is the American Constitution?* (New Haven, CT: Yale University Press, 2001), pp. 54–55. See Joe Feagin, "Heeding Black Voices: The Court, Brown, and Challenges in Building a Multiracial Democracy," *University of Pittsburgh Law Review* 66 (Fall 2004): 57–81; and *Marbury v. Madison* 5 U.S. 137 (1803).

115 Richard Kluger, *Simple Justice: The History of Brown v. Board of Education and Black America's Struggle for Equality*, Vol. 1 (New York: Knopf, 1975), p. 65; J. Allen Smith, *The Spirit of American Government: A Study of the Constitution, Its Origin, Influence, and Relation to Democracy* (Chautauqua, NY: Chautauqua/Macmillan, 1907), Kindle loc. 966–973. Here we also draw on Feagin, *White Party, White Government*, chapter 3.

116 For details, see Nathan Newman and J.J. Gass, "A New Birth of Freedom: The Forgotten History of the 13th, 14th, and 15th Amendments," *Judicial Independence Series, Brennan Center for Justice, New York University Law School*, 2004, pp. 1–3.

117 See Joe R. Feagin, *The White Racial Frame: Centuries of Racial Framing and Counter-Framing*, 2nd edn. (New York: Routledge, 2013), chapter 8.
118 Peter Dreier, "Nine Battleground States That Could Flip the Senate—and the Supreme Court," *The American Prospect*, February 14, 2016, http://prospect.org/article/nine-bat tleground-states-could-flip-senate-and-supreme-court (accessed April 4, 2016).
119 Ibid.
120 Ibid.; Peter Schuler, "Law Professor Reveals Another Side to Oliver Wendell Holmes Jr. in New Book on Former Supreme Court Justice," *The University of Chicago Chronicle* 20, no. 12 (March 15, 2001); http://chronicle.uchicago.edu/010315/alschuler-holmes. shtml (accessed April 4, 2016); C-SPAN Staff, "Life and Career of Frank Easterbrook," March 20, 1989, http://www.c-span.org/video/?7038-1/life-career-frank-easterbrook (accessed April 4, 2016).
121 *Citizens United v. Federal Election Commission*, 558 U.S. 08–205 (2010).
122 Glenn Bracey, "A White Supremacist Century," *RacismReview*, January 24, 2010, http:// www.racismreview.com/blog/2010/01/24/a-white-supremacist-century-supreme- court-as-white-oligarchical-power/ (accessed April 12, 2011).
123 Dreier, "Nine Battleground States That Could Flip the Senate—and the Supreme Court."
124 Joan Biskupic, Janet Roberts, and John Shiffman, "Special Report: At U.S. Court of Last Resort, Handful of Lawyers Dominate Docket," *Reuters*, December 8, 2014, http:// www.reuters.com/article/2014/12/08/us-scotus-elites-special-report-idUSKBN0JM0 ZX20141208 (accessed March 25, 2015).
125 Mark Sherman, "U.S. Supreme Court Justices Have Only Been Addressed by One African-American Lawyer All Term," *Huffington Post*, May 12, 2013, http://www. huffingtonpost.com/2013/05/12/us-supreme-court-justices-african-american-law yer_n_3262462.html (accessed June 26, 2015); Biskupic, Roberts, and Shiffman, "Special Report: At U.S. Court of Last Resort, Handful of Lawyers Dominate Docket"; Hogan Lovells International LLP, "Neal Katyal," http://www.hoganlovells.com/neal-katyal/ (accessed March 25, 2015).
126 Biskupic, Roberts, and Shiffman, "Special Report: At U.S. Court of Last Resort, Handful of Lawyers Dominate Docket."
127 Ibid.
128 Ibid.
129 Ted Nace, *Gangs of America: The Rise of Corporate Power and the Disabling of Democracy* (Berkeley, CA: Berrett-Koehler Publishers), pp. 22, 25.
130 Ibid., pp. 24–25, 101. Our italics.
131 See Kevin Philips, *Wealth and Democracy: A Political History of the American Rich* (New York: Broadway Books, 2002), p. 214; James O'Connor, *The Fiscal Crisis of the State* (New York: St. Martin's Press, 1973); and Feagin, *White Party, White Government*, passim.
132 Democracy Now, "Headlines," July 7, 2015, http://www.democracynow.org/2015/7/7/ headlines#7710 (accessed October 4, 2015); Nicholas Fandos, "A Study Documents the Paucity of Black Elected Prosecutors: Zero in Most States," *New York Times*, July 7, 2015, http://www.nytimes.com/2015/07/07/us/a-study-documents-the-paucity-of-black- elected-prosecutors-zero-in-most-states.html?_r=0 (accessed October 4, 2015).
133 See, for example, Candace Idlebird, "Racist Framing in the Criminal Justice System: Powerful White Officials," Dissertation, Texas A&M University, 2016.
134 Here we summarize Feagin, *White Party, White Government*, chapter 3.
135 Aziz Rana, *The Two Faces of American Freedom* (Cambridge, MA: Harvard University Press, 2010), pp. 326–327.
136 See O'Connor, *The Fiscal Crisis of the State*; John Scott, *Corporate Business and Capitalist Classes*, 3rd edn. (New York: Oxford University Press, 1997).
137 Bryan J. Cook, "The American College President Study: Key Findings and Takeaways," *Spring Supplement 2012*, http://www.acenet.edu/the-presidency/columns-and-features/ Pages/The-American-College-President-Study.aspx (accessed March 21, 2015).
138 Jack Stripling, "Survey Finds a Drop in Minority Presidents Leading Colleges," March 12, 2012, http://chronicle.com/article/Who-Are-College-Presidents-/131138/ (accessed March 21, 2015); ACE, "Study Finds Higher Education Presidential Pipeline Is Slow to

Change," March 4, 2013, http://www.acenet.edu/news-room/Pages/Study-Finds-High er-Ed-Presidential-Pipeline-Slow-Change.aspx (accessed March 21, 2015). We are also indebted to Bryan Cook for information here.

139 National Center for Education Statistics, "Characteristics of Postsecondary Faculty," May 2014, https://nces.ed.gov/programs/coe/indicator_cuf.asp (accessed March 21, 2015).

140 Emma Harris and Joseph Zappa, "Faculty Whiteness Complicates the Classroom," *The Brown Daily Herald*, December 4, 2014, http://www.browndailyherald.com/2014/12/04/faculty-whiteness-complicates-classroom/ (accessed June 26, 2015).

141 Email correspondence to authors (2015).

142 Anna Merlan, "Black Professor Saida Grundy Criticized for Tweets on White Masculinity," *Jezebel*, May 11, 2015, http://jezebel.com/black-professor-saida-grundy-criticized-for-tweets-on-w-1703719773 (accessed May 17, 2015).

143 Alex Bommarito, "Petition to Terminate Boston University's Racist Professor Saida Grundy," *iPetitions*, http://www.ipetitions.com/petition/petition-to-terminate-boston-saidagrundy-racist (accessed May 17, 2015); Meghan Tinsley, "Stand in Solidarity with Professor Saida Grundy," *change.org*, https://www.change.org/p/robert-a-brown-president-of-boston-university-stand-in-solidarity-with-professor-saida-grundy (accessed May 17, 2015).

144 Tinsley, "Stand in Solidarity with Professor Saida Grundy."

145 Scott Jaschik, "Study: Gay Professors Face Discrimination from Students," *USA Today*, June 29, 2011, http://usatoday30.usatoday.com/news/education/2011-06-29-gay-lesbian-college-professors_n.htm (accessed April 15, 2016); Roxanna Harlow, "Teaching as Emotional Labor: The Effects of Professors' Race and Gender on the Emotional Demands of the Undergraduate College Classroom," Ph.D. dissertation, Indiana University, Bloomington, IN, 2002.

146 Eliza Gray, "Racist Video Not the First Scandal for Troubled Fraternity," *Time*, March 9, 2015, http://time.com/3737668/sigma-alpha-epsilon-frat-video-university-oklahoma/ (accessed June 16, 2015); Allen G. Breed, "SAE Fraternity Has Long Racial Past with Roots in 'Dixie Land,'" *thegrio*, March 11, 2015, http://thegrio.com/2015/03/11/sae-racial-past-dixie/ (accessed June 26, 2015); Justin Moyer, "University of Oklahoma Fraternity Closed after Racist Chant," *Washington Post*, March 9, 2015, http://www.washingtonpost.com/news/morning-mix/wp/2015/03/09/university-of-oklahoma-fraternity-suspended-after-racist-chant/ (accessed March 30, 2015); Joey Stipek and Richard Perez-Pena, "Oklahoma Inquiry Traces Racist Song to National Gathering of Fraternity," *New York Times*, March 27, 2015, http://www.nytimes.com/2015/03/28/us/oklahoma-inquiry-traces-racist-song-to-national-gathering-of-fraternity.html (accessed March 30, 2015).

147 Breed, "SAE Fraternity Has Long Racial Past with Roots in 'Dixie Land.'"

148 Ibid.

149 Jessica Holden Sherwood, *Wealth, Whiteness, and the Matrix of Privilege: The View from the Country Club* (Lanham, MD: Lexington Books, 2010).

150 Kris Hundley, "Billionaire's Role in Hiring Decisions at Florida State University Raises Questions," *Tampa Bay Times*, May 9, 2011, http://www.tampabay.com/news/business/billionaires-role-in-hiring-decisions-at-florida-state-university-raises/1168680 (accessed June 25, 2015); Dave Levinthal, "Inside the Koch Brothers' Campus Crusade," March 27, 2014, *Center for Public Integrity*, http://www.publicintegrity.org/2014/03/27/14497/inside-koch-brothers-campus-crusade (accessed March 30, 2015).

151 Hundley, "Billionaire's Role in Hiring Decisions at Florida State University Raises Questions"; Levinthal, "Inside the Koch Brothers' Campus Crusade."

152 Jason Stanley, *How Propaganda Works* (Princeton, NJ: Princeton University Press, 2015), Kindle loc. 4044. See also loc. 4075.

153 *2015 Hollywood Diversity Report* (Los Angeles, CA: UCLA Bunche Center, 2015), p. 2; Chemaly, "Why Aren't We Talking about How Boys and Men Feel about a Woman President?"

154 "Noam Chomsky Interviewed by Various Interviewers," 1992, http://www.chomsky.info/interviews/ (accessed October 4, 2015).
155 Stanley, *How Propaganda Works*, Kindle loc. 4225. Our italics.
156 Blackwaterdog (blogger), "The Arrogance of Being President While Being Black," Daily Kos, February 27, 2010, http://www.dailykos.com/story/2010/02/27/841263/-The-arrogance-of-being-president-while-being-black (accessed May 9, 2011).
157 Feagin, *The White Racial Frame*, p. 10.
158 Ibid., pp. 9–10, 19.
159 Thomas Jefferson, *Notes on the State of Virginia*, ed. Frank Shuffelton (New York: Penguin Books, 1999 [1785]), especially Query 14.
160 Edward T. Hall, *Beyond Culture* (New York: Anchor Books, 1976), p. 42.
161 Richard Morin, "Misperceptions Cloud Whites' View of Blacks," *Washington Post*, July 11, 2001, p. A01.
162 The surveys are in "Race and Ethnicity," www.pollingreport.com/race.htm (accessed February 27, 2009).
163 bell hooks, *All about Love: New Visions* (New York: William Morrow, 2001), pp. 194–195.
164 Sarah Seltzer, "The Numbers Don't Lie: White Men Still Dominate the Media," *Rewire*, https://rewire.news/article/2014/02/24/numbers-dont-lie-white-men-still-dominate-media/ (accessed August 19, 2016).
165 Terrell Jermaine Starr, "Dear White People: Here Are 5 Reasons Why You Can't Really Feel Black Pain," *AlterNet*, December 4, 2014, http://www.alternet.org/dear-white-people-here-are-5-reasons-why-you-cant-really-feel-black-pain (accessed August 9, 2015).
166 Ibid.
167 Adam Peck, "If It's Sunday, It's Meet the Republican White Men," *ThinkProgress*, April 19, 2012, http://thinkprogress.org/media/2012/04/19/467647/sunday-shows-white-men-gop/ (accessed March 23, 2015).
168 Faiz Shakir and Adam Peck, "Report: By a Nearly 2 to 1 Margin, Cable Networks Call on Men Over Women to Comment on Birth Control," *ThinkProgress*, February 10, 2012, http://thinkprogress.org/media/2012/02/10/423211/cable-report-birth-control-men-women/ (accessed June 26, 2015).
169 FAIR, "Study: Cable News, a White Man's World," July 16, 2014, http://fair.org/press-release/study-cable-news-a-white-mans-world/ (accessed March 23, 2015).
170 Edward Herman, "The Propaganda Model Revisited," *Monthly Review 48* (July 1996): 115; Blumenthal, *The Rise of the Counter-Establishment*, pp. 4–11, 133–170; Steinfels, *The Neoconservatives*, pp. 214–277; Feagin, *The White Racial Frame*, chapter 3.
171 Eduardo Galeano, "Media in the Americas," *NACLA Report on the Americas 37* (January/February 2004): 14.
172 Robin Pogrebin, "New York City Plans to Study the Diversity of Its Cultural Groups," *New York Times*, March 3, 2015, http://www.nytimes.com/2015/03/04/arts/new-york-city-plans-to-study-the-diversity-of-its-cultural-groups.html (accessed March 30, 2015).

3 White Imperialism, Racism, and Masculinity: 1890s–1940s

1 W.E.B. Du Bois, *Darkwater: Voices from within the Veil* (New York: Harcourt, Brace & Co., 1920), Kindle loc. 302.
2 Stephen Kinzer, *Overthrow: America's Century of Regime Change from Hawaii to Iraq* (New York: Times Books, 2007).
3 Maria Mies, *Patriarchy and Accumulation on a World Scale* (London: Zed Books, [1986] 2014), Kindle loc. 313, 327.
4 Du Bois, *Darkwater*, Kindle loc. 487.
5 Ibid., Kindle loc. 531.
6 Ibid., Kindle loc. 412.
7 W. E. B. Du Bois, "The African Roots of War," in *W. E. B. Du Bois: A Reader*, ed. Meyer Weinberg (New York: Harper & Row Publishers, [1915] 1970), pp. 413–424.

8 "The Trusteeship Council—The Mandate System of the League of Nations," *Encyclopedia of the Nations*, http://www.nationsencyclopedia.com/United-Nations/The-Trusteeship-Council-the-mandate-system-of-the-league-of-nations.html (accessed June 12, 2015).

9 Ibid.

10 Du Bois, *Darkwater*, p. 28.

11 History Channel Staff, "1920 League of Nations Instituted," http://www.history.com/this-day-in-history/league-of-nations-instituted (accessed June 12, 2015).

12 Howard Zinn, "Chapter 16: A People's War," from *A People's History of the United States. 1492--Present*, "History Is a Weapon" website, http://www.historyisaweapon.com/defcon1/zinnpeopleswar.html (accessed May 18, 2015).

13 Robert Gilpin, *The Political Economy of International Relations* (Princeton, NJ: Princeton University Press, 1987), p. 39.

14 Interview with Donny Gluckstein, *New Left Project*, https://plutopress.wordpress.com (accessed December 25, 2015).

15 Ibid. Our italics.

16 Ibid. Our italics.

17 Richard Rubottom and Carter Murphey, *Spain and the United States: Since World War II* (Santa Barbara, CA: Praeger Publishers Inc., 1984); Oscar Calvo-Gonzalez, "Neither a Carrot nor a Stick: American Foreign Aid and Economic Policymaking in Spain during the 1950s," *Diplomatic History 30* (June 2006): 409–438; Renwick McLean, "Spain's Dilemma: To Toast Franco or Banish His Ghost?" *New York Times*, October 8, 2006, http://www.nytimes.com/2006/10/08/world/europe/08spain.html?_r=0 (accessed May 23, 2015); Elaine Sciolino and Emma Daly, "Spaniards at Last Confront the Ghost of Franco," *New York Times*, November 11, 2002, http://www.nytimes.com/2002/11/11/world/spaniards-at-last-confront-the-ghost-of-franco.html (accessed May 23, 2015); Fiona Govan, "Spanish Judge to Investigate Human Rights Abuses of Spanish Civil War," *Telegraph*, September 2, 2008, http://www.telegraph.co.uk/news/worldnews/europe/spain/2668651/Spanish-judge-to-investigate-human-rights-abuses-of-Spanish-Civil-War.html (accessed May 23, 2015).

18 Adam Tooze, *The Wages of Destruction: The Making and Breaking of the Nazi Economy* (New York: Penguin Books, 2008), preface. Our italics.

19 See, for example, Jeffrey Record, *Japan's Decision for War in 1941: Some Enduring Lessons* (Sevenoaks, UK: Pickle Partners Publishing, 2015).

20 Harry Elmer Barnes, *Perpetual War for Perpetual Peace: A Critical Examination of the Foreign Policy of Franklin Delano Roosevelt and Its Aftermath* (Caldwell, ID: Caxton Printers, 1953), pp. 682–683; Robert B. Stinnett, *Day of Deceit: The Truth about FDR and Pearl Harbor* (New York: Free Press, 2000).

21 Thomas A. Bailey, *Theodore Roosevelt and the Japanese American Crisis* (Redwood City, CA: Stanford University Press,1964); Bruce Russet, *No Clear and Present Danger: A Skeptical View of the United States Entry into World War*, Anniversary edn. (Boulder, CO: Westview Press, 1997); Richard H. Minear, *Victors' Justice: Tokyo War Crimes Trial* (Princeton: Princeton University Press, [1971] 2015); Norimitsu Onishi, "Decades after War Trials, Japan Still Honors a Dissenting Judge," *New York Times*, August 31, 2007, http://www.nytimes.com/2007/08/31/world/asia/31memo.html (accessed May 19, 2015); Nariaki Nakazato, *Neonationalist Mythology in Postwar Japan: Pal's Dissenting Judgment at the Tokyo War Crimes Tribunal. AsiaWorld Series* (Lanham, MD: Lexington Books, 2016); Ryuho Okawa, *The Truth about WWII: Justice Pal Speaks on the Tokyo Trials: Spiritual Interview Series* (Mumbai: IRH Press Company Limited, 2015).

22 Onishi, "Decades after War Trials, Japan Still Honors a Dissenting Judge."

23 Retirement Think Tank Staff, "MetLife Does What Allianz Could Not Do," *Retirement Think Tank*, August 24, 2011, http://www.retirementthinktank.com/metlife-does-what-allianz-could-not-do/ (accessed December 25, 2015); Marc Engels, "H-Net Book Review," February 2004, http://www.h-net.org/reviews/showrev.php?id=8841 (accessed December 25, 2015); Gerald D. Feldman, *Allianz and the German Insurance Business, 1933–1945* (Cambridge: Cambridge University Press, 2001); Sam Greenspan,

"11 Companies That Surprisingly Collaborated with the Nazis," *11 Points*, http://www.11points.com/News-Politics/11_Companies_That_Surprisingly_Collaborated_With_the_Nazis (accessed December 25, 2015); New York Times Staff, "Hugo Boss Acknowledges Link to Nazi Regime," *New York Times*, August 15, 1997, http://www.nytimes.com/1997/08/15/business/hugo-boss-acknowledges-link-to-nazi-regime.html (accessed December 25, 2015); Vera Sharav, "Auschwitz: 60 Year Anniversary—the Role of IG Farben-Bayer," *Alliance for Human Research Protection*, October 26, 2006, http://ahrp.org/auschwitz60-year-anniversary-the-role-of-ig-farben-bayer/ (accessed December 25, 2015); BBC Staff, "UK Siemens Retreats over Nazi Name," *BBC News World Edition*, September 5, 2002, http://news.bbc.co.uk/2/hi/business/2233890.stm (accessed December 25, 2015); "A People's History of the United States," *The Thistle 13*, no. 2 (December 2000/January 2001), http://web.mit.edu/thistle/www/v13/3/oil.html (accessed December 25, 2015); Timothy L. O'Brien, "Chase Reviews Nazi-Era Role," *New York Times*, November 7, 1998, http://www.nytimes.com/1998/11/07/world/chase-reviews-nazi-era-role.html (accessed December 25, 2015); ADL Press Release, "ADL Calls Dictionary's Added Definition of 'Nazi' Offensive; Urges Random House to 'Rethink Your Decision,'" 1997, http://archive.adl.org/presrele/holna_52/2881_52.html (accessed December 25, 2015); Julian Crowley, "10 Global Businesses That Worked with the Nazis," *Business Pundit*, June 13, 2011, http://www.businesspundit.com/10-global-businesses-that-worked-with-the-nazis/ (accessed December 25, 2015).

24 Edwin Black, *IBM and the Holocaust: The Strategic Alliance between Nazi Germany and America's Most Powerful Corporation* (Oshkosh, WI: Dialog Press, 2008).

25 Edwin Black, "IBM's Role in the Holocaust—What the New Documents Reveal," *World Post*, February 27, 2012, http://www.huffingtonpost.com/edwin-black/ibm-holocaust_b_1301691.html (accessed October 4, 2015). Italics omitted.

26 Rafael Medoff, "What FDR Said about Jews in Private," *Los Angeles Times*, April 7, 2013, http://articles.latimes.com/2013/apr/07/opinion/la-oe-medoff-roosevelt-holocaust-20130407 (accessed January 27, 2017).

27 Goldstein, Eric L., *The Price of Whiteness: Jews, Race, and American Identity* (Princeton, NJ: Princeton University Press, 2006), pp. 126, 129; Leonard Dinnerstein, *Anti-Semitism in America* (New York: Oxford University Press, 1994), pp. 109, 119. We are indebted to suggestions from Thaddeus Atzmon.

28 Dinnerstein, *Anti-Semitism in America*, p. 116.

29 Frederic C. Jaher, *The Jews and the Nation: Revolution, Emancipation, State Formation, and the Liberal Paradigm in America and France* (Princeton, NJ: Princeton University Press, 2002), pp. 230ff; Frank E. Smitha, "Roosevelt and Approaching War: The Economy, Politics and Questions of War, 1937–38," http://www.fsmitha.com/h2/ch20b.html (accessed August 18, 2016).

30 Lawrence Baron, "Imaginary Witness: Hollywood and the Holocaust (review)," *Film & History: An Interdisciplinary Journal of Film and Television Studies 35*, no. 1 (Fall 2005): 72–74; Ronnie Scheib, "Review: 'Imaginary Witness: Hollywood and the Holocaust,'" *Variety*, June 9, 2004, http://variety.com/2004/film/reviews/imaginary-witness-hollywood-and-the-holocaust-1200532897/ (accessed May 18, 2015); Paul Buhle and Dave Wagner, *Radical Hollywood: The Untold Story Behind America's Favorite Movies* (New York: The New Press, 2002), p. 211; Alexander McGregor, "Hollywood Walk of Shame," *The I.B. Tauris Blogs*, February 27, 2012, http://theibtaurisblog.com/2012/02/27/walk-of-shame-hollywood-and-anti-semitism/ (accessed May 25, 2015); Shirley Temple Black, *Child Star: An Autobiography* (New York: Warner Books, 1989), pp. 252–253; Associated Press, "Ex-Rep. Martin Dies, 71, Is Dead; Led Un-American Activities Unit," *New York Times*, November 15, 1972, http://query.nytimes.com/gst/abstract.html?res=9D02E3D6143EE63ABC4D52DFB7678389669EDE (accessed May 25, 2015).

31 Ronnie Scheib, "Review: 'Imaginary Witness: Hollywood and the Holocaust'"; *Imaginary Witness, Hollywood and the Holocaust*, directed by Daniel Aker (New York: Anker Productions Inc., 2004); Edward Helmore, "Hollywood and Hitler: Did the Studio Bosses Bow to Nazi Wishes?" *Guardian*, June 29, 2013, http://www.theguardian.com/film/2013/jun/29/historian-says-hollywood-collaborated-with-nazis (accessed May 20, 2015).

32 Black, *Child Star*, pp. 252–253; Associated Press, "Ex-Rep. Martin Dies."
33 David Oshinsky, "Review of Richard Breitman and Allan J. Lichtman, *FDR and the Jews*" (Cambridge, MA: Belknap Press of Harvard University Press, 2013)," *New York Times*, April 5, 2013, http://www.nytimes.com/2013/04/07/books/review/fdr-and-the-jews-by-richard-breitman-and-allan-j-lichtman.html (accessed June 15, 2015).
34 Ibid.
35 Ibid.; Henry Feingold, *The Politics of Rescue: The Roosevelt Administration and the Holocaust, 1938–1945* (New Brunswick, NJ: Rutgers University Press, 1970); "The Evian Conference," United States Holocaust Memorial Museum, Washington, DC, *The Holocaust: A Learning Site for Students*, http://www.ushmm.org/outreach/en/article.php?ModuleId=10007698 (accessed May 25, 2015).
36 U.S. Department of State Archive, "The Casablanca Conference, 1943," http://2001-2009.state.gov/r/pa/ho/time/wwii/88778.htm (accessed June 15, 2015).
37 David Woolner, "African Americans and the New Deal: A Look Back in History," Roosevelt Institute, http://www.rooseveltinstitute.org/new-roosevelt/african-americans-and-new-deal-look-back-history (accessed May 25, 2015).
38 Ibid.
39 Kenneth O'Reilly, *Nixon's Piano: Presidents and Racial Politics from Washington to Clinton* (New York: Free Press, 1995); William P. Jones, *The March on Washington: Jobs, Freedom, and the Forgotten History of Civil Rights*, 1st edn. (New York: W.W. Norton & Company, 2013); John B. Kirby, *Black Americans in the Roosevelt Era: Liberalism and Race* (Knoxville, TN: University of Tennessee Press, 1980); Robin D.G. Kelley and Earl Lewis, *To Make Our World Anew: A History of African Americans* (New York: Oxford University Press, 2000).
40 Hillary Mayell, "New Film *Hart's War* Highlights World War II Bigotry," *National Geographic News*, February 28, 2002, http://news.nationalgeographic.com/news/2002/02/0227_0228_tuskegee_2.html (accessed May 25, 2015).
41 Ira Katznelson, *Fear Itself: The New Deal and the Origins of Our Time* (New York: W.W. Norton & Co., 2013), p. 283.
42 Edwin Black, "Hitler's Debt to America," *Guardian*, February 6, 2004, http://www.theguardian.com/uk/2004/feb/06/race.usa (accessed December 24, 2015); Theodore Cross, *Black Power Imperative: Racial Inequality and the Politics of Nonviolence* (New York: Faulkner, 1984), p. 157.
43 Judith Goldstein, "The Presence of the Past: Confronting the Nazi State and Jim Crow," *Humanity in Action*, 2014, http://www.humanityinaction.org/knowledgebase/332-the-presence-of-the-past-confronting-the-nazi-state-and-jim-crow (accessed December 24, 2015).
44 Robert Vitalis, *White World Order, Black Power Politics: The Birth of American International Relations* (Ithaca, NY: Cornell University Press, 2015).
45 Ron Walters, "Racial Justice in Foreign Affairs," in *African Americans in Global Affairs*, ed. Michael L. Clemons (Boston, MA: Northeastern University Press, 2010), pp. 3–8.
46 James G. Thompson, "Letter to the Pittsburgh Courier," in *Key Readings in Journalism*, eds. Elliot King and Jane Chapman (New York: Taylor & Francis, 2012), p. 56.
47 Devon Carbado and Donald Weiss, eds., *Time on Two Crosses: The Collected Writings of Bayard Rustin* (San Francisco, CA: Cleis Press, 2003), Kindle loc. 107–109.
48 William P. Jones, *The March on Washington*; Louis Ruchames, *Race, Jobs, and Politics: The Story of FEPC*, 1st edn. (Santa Barbara, CA: Greenwood Press, 1971); Andrew Kersten, *Race, Jobs, and the War*, 1st edn. (Santa Barbara, CA: University of Illinois Press, 2007).
49 Marc Gallicchio, *The African American Encounter with Japan and China: Black Internationalism in Asia, 1895–1945* (Chapel Hill, NC: University of North Carolina Press, 2000), pp. 110–120.
50 Yukiko Koshiro, "Beyond an Alliance of Color: The African American Impact on Modern Japan," *Positions: East Asia Cultures Critique 11* (2003): 185.
51 Gallicchio, *The African American Encounter with Japan and China*, pp. 110–120. In this section we draw on Joe R. Feagin, *How Blacks Built America: Labor, Culture, Freedom, and Democracy* (New York: Routledge, 2016).

52 PBS Staff, "Japanese Americans," *PBS.org*, 2007, http://www.pbs.org/thewar/at_home_civil_rights_minorities.htm (accessed May 25, 2015); Harry S. Truman Library and Museum, "Letter from R. R. Wright," July 18, 1946, http://www.trumanlibrary.org/whistlestop/study_collections/desegregation/large/lessons/wright.html (accessed May 21, 2015).

53 W. E. B. Du Bois et al., "Appeal to the World: A Statement on the Denial of Human Rights to Minorities in the Case of Citizens of the United States of America and an Appeal to the United Nations for Redress, 1947," quoted in *Cold War Civil Rights: Race and the Image of American Democracy*, ed. Mary L. Dudziak (Princeton, NJ: Princeton University Press, 2011), p. 45; Library of Congress, "NAACP: A Century in the Fight for Freedom. World War II and the Post War Years," http://www.loc.gov/exhibits/naacp/world-war-ii-and-the-post-war-years.html (accessed May 21, 2015); Walter Francis White, *A Rising Wind* (Garden City, NY: Doubleday, Doran and Company, Inc., 1945).

54 Harry S. Truman Library and Museum, "Letter from A. Philip Randolph," June 29, 1948, http://www.trumanlibrary.org/whistlestop/study_collections/desegregation/large/documents/index.php?pagenumber=5&documentid=1-5&documentdate=1948-07-07&studycollectionid=coldwar&groupid= (accessed May 21, 2015); Harry S. Truman Library and Museum, "Executive Order 9981," July 26, 1948, http://www.trumanlibrary.org/whistlestop/study_collections/desegregation/large/lessons/dseg (accessed May 21, 2015); Robert Caro, *The Years of Lyndon Johnson: Master of the Senate* (New York: Knopf, 2002), pp. 97, 100; President's Committee on Civil Rights, "*To Secure These Rights*," U.S. government printing office, 1947; "Agency History," *Truman Presidential Library*, http://www.trumanlibrary.org/hstpaper/pccr.htm (accessed July 6, 2011).

55 Jed S. Serrano, "The X Factor: How Malcolm X Internationalized the Civil Rights Movement," *Student Pulse*, 2010, http://www.studentpulse.com/articles/231/2/the-xfactor-how-malcolm-x-internationalized-the-civil-rights-movement (accessed July 3, 2014).

56 Marilyn Lake and Henry Reynolds, *Drawing the Global Color Line: White Men's Countries and the International Challenge of Racial Equality* (Cambridge: Cambridge University Press, 2008).

57 Edward K. Strong, Jr., *The Second-Generation Japanese Problem* (Stanford, CA: Stanford University Press, 1934), p. 133.

58 Roger Daniels, *Guarding the Golden Door* (New York: Hill and Wang, 2004), p. 55; John Higham, *Strangers in the Land* (New York: Atheneum, 1963), pp. 96–152.

59 Medoff, "What FDR Said about Jews in Private."

60 Paul Hirsch, "Transcript of American Culture during World War II," *Prezi*, April 28, 2011, https://prezi.com/i0bwybbwsiyp/american-culture-during-world-war-ii/ (accessed May 21, 2015).

61 Bill Ritter and Charles Gibson, "World War II Italian American Internment," *ABC Good Morning America* (October 30, 1997); Stephen Fox, *The Unknown Internment: An Oral History of the Relocation of Italian Americans during World War II* (Boston, MA: Twayne Publishers, 1990).

62 Dorothy Swaine Thomas and Richard S. Nishimoto, *The Spoilage* (Berkeley, CA: University of California Press, 1946), pp. 8–16; Jacobus tenBroek, Edward N. Barnhart, and Floyd W. Matson, *Prejudice, War, and the Constitution* (Berkeley, CA: University of California Press, 1968), pp. 118–120.

63 Mark Weber, "The Japanese Camps in California: World War II West Coast Camps for Japanese-Americans," *Institute for Historical Review*, http://www.ihr.org/jhr/v02/v02p-45_Weber.html (accessed June 15, 2015). See also Mark Weber, "The Japanese Camps in California. World War II West Coast Camps for Japanese-Americans," *The Journal of Historical Review 2*, no. 1 (Spring 1981): 45–58.

64 Quoted in "A More Perfect Union. Japanese Americans & the U.S. Constitution," *Smithsonian Institution Asian Pacific American Program*, http://amhistory.si.edu/perfectunion/non-flash/removal_crisis.html (accessed June 15, 2015). See also Dillon S. Myer, *Uprooted Americans: The Japanese Americans and the War Relocation Authority during World War II* (Tucson, AZ: University of Arizona Press, 1971), p. 327; Audrie Girdner

and Anne Loftis, *The Great Betrayal: The Evacuation of the Japanese-Americans during World War II* (London: MacMillan, 1969), p. 462.

65 Mark Ridley-Thomas, "Internment Resolution," *Huffington Post's the Blog*, June 6, 2012, http://www.huffingtonpost.com/mark-ridleythomas/japanese-internment-resolution_b_1575965.html (accessed May 22, 2015); Michi Nishiura Weglyn, *Years of Infamy: The Untold Story of America's Concentration Camps*, updated edn. (Seattle, WA: University of Washington Press, 1996).

66 Quoted in Zinn, "Chapter 16: A People's War."

67 PBS Staff, "Japanese Americans."

68 "A More Perfect Union. Japanese Americans & the U.S. Constitution," *Smithsonian Institution Asian Pacific American Program.*

69 Jerry Isaacs, "US Congressman Defends WWII Internment of Japanese-Americans," *World Socialist Web Site*, February 11, 2003, http://www.wsws.org/en/articles/2003/02/cong-f11.html (accessed May 20, 2015).

70 Ibid.; Mark Ridley-Thomas, "Internment Resolution."

71 Michelle Malkin, "About *In Defense of Internment*," *MichelleMalkin.com*, February 6, 2006, http://web.archive.org/web/20060206033611/http://michellemalkin.com/aboutidoi.htm (accessed May 23, 2015).

72 Eric Muller, "So Let Me Get This Straight: Michelle Malkin Claims to Have Rewritten the History of Japanese Internment in Just 16 Months?" *George Mason University History News Network*, September 7, 2004, http://historynewsnetwork.org/article/7094 (accessed May 23, 2015); Isaacs, "US Congressman Defends."

73 Yale Law School Staff, "The Atlantic Charter," *The Avalon Project*, 2008, Lillian Goldman Law Library, http://avalon.law.yale.edu/wwii/atlantic.asp (accessed June 15, 2015).

74 Christopher D. O'Sullivan, *Sumner Welles, Postwar Planning, and the Quest for a New World Order, 1937–1943* (New York: Columbia University Press, 2007); Irwin F. Gellman, *Secret Affairs: Franklin Roosevelt, Cordell Hull, and Sumner Welles* (Baltimore, MD: Johns Hopkins University Press, 1995); Benjamin Welles, *Sumner Welles: FDR's Global Strategist: A Biography*, Franklin and Eleanor Roosevelt Institute Series on Diplomatic and Economic History (New York: St. Martin's Press, 1997); Michael Beschloss, *The Conquerors: Roosevelt, Truman and the Destruction of Hitler's Germany, 1941–1945* (New York: Simon & Schuster, 2002).

75 Yale Law School Staff, "The Atlantic Charter"; Beschloss, *The Conquerors*; Harvey O'Connor, *World Crisis in Oil* (New York: Monthly Review Press, 1962), pp. 271–365; Michael B. Stoff, *Oil War, and American Security: The Search for a National Policy on Foreign Oil, 1941–1947* (New Haven, CT: Yale University Press, 1980), p. 197ff; Anthony Sampson, *The Seven Sisters: The Great Oil Companies and the World They Shaped* (New York: Viking, 1975), p. 101ff.

76 Zinn, "Chapter 16: A People's War." Our italics.

77 Donald Markwell, *John Maynard Keynes and International Relations: Economic Paths to War and Peace* (Oxford: Oxford University Press, 2006); Bretton Woods Project, "What Are the Main Concerns and Criticism about the World Bank and IMF?" August 23, 2005, http://www.brettonwoodsproject.org/2005/08/art-320869/ (accessed May 20, 2015); Kourosh Ziabari, "The United Nations Security Council: An Organization for Injustice" *Global Research*, January 20, 2011, http://www.globalresearch.ca/the-united-nations-security-council-an-organization-for-injustice/22875 (accessed May 20, 2015).

78 Janet Creery, "Read the Fine Print First: Some Questions Raised at the Science for Peace Conference on UN Reform," *Peace Magazine*, January–February 1994, http://archive.peacemagazine.org/v10n1p20.htm (accessed September 30, 2016), p. 20; Stanley Meisler, *United Nations: The First Fifty Years*, 1st edn. (New York: Atlantic Monthly Press, 1997); Ziabari, "The United Nations Security Council."

79 Thomas Ferguson, *Golden Rule: The Investment Theory of Party Competition and the Logic of Money-Driven Political Systems* (Chicago, IL: University of Chicago Press, 1995); Michael C. Munger, "Golden Rule: The Investment Theory of Party Competition and the Logic of Money-Driven Political Systems," *Independent Review*, http://www.independent.org/publications/tir/article.asp?a=487 (accessed May 26, 2015).

80 Ferguson, *Golden Rule*, pp. 79–81, 150–157. See Joe R. Feagin, *White Party, White Government: Race, Class, and U.S. Politics* (New York: Routledge, 2012), chapter 5.

81 Zinn, "Chapter 16: A People's War"; Bruce Catton, *The War Lords of Washington. The Inside Story of Big Business Versus the People in World War II*, 1st edn. (Harcourt, NY: Brace & Co., 1948); G. Williams Domhoff, *The Myth of Liberal Ascendancy: Corporate Dominance from the Great Depression to the Great Recession* (Boulder, CO: Paradigm Publishers); Amity Shlaes, "How Government Unions Became So Powerful," *Council on Foreign Relations*, September 4, 2010, http://www.cfr.org/labor/government-unions-became-so-powerful/p22887 (accessed June 15, 2015).

82 Bureau of Labor Statistics, *Bulletin 878* (1946): 3; Jerome F. Scott and George C. Homans, "Reflections on Wildcat Strikes," *American Sociology Review* (June 1947): 278ff; Bruce R. Morris, "Industrial Relations in the Automobile Industry," in *Labor in Post War America*, ed. Colston F. Warne (Brooklyn, NY: Remsen Press, 1949), p. 416; Joel Seidman, *American Labor from Defense to Reconversion* (Chicago, IL: University of Chicago Press, 1953), pp. 91–92; Art Preis, *Labor's Giant Step: Twenty Years of the CIO* (New York: Pioneer Publishers, 1964), p. 236.

83 Brandon T. Locke, "The Military-Masculinity Complex: Hegemonic Masculinity and the United States Armed Forces, 1940–1963," *Dissertations, Theses, & Student Research*, Department of History, University of Nebraska, DigitalCommons@University of Nebraska-Lincoln, August, 2013.

84 Gordon Adams, *The Politics of Defense Contractors: The Iron Triangle* (New Brunswick, NJ: Transaction Books, 1982).

85 "Just the Facts," *Common Cause*, January/February/March 1992, p. 4; Maryellen Kelley and Todd A. Watkins, "In from the Cold: Prospects for the Conversion of the Defense Industrial Base," *Science 268*, April 28, 1995, http://science.sciencemag.org/content/268/5210/525, p. 525; Jeff Erlich, "Loan Support Will Not Boost U.S. Arms Sales," *Defense News* (February 27, 1995/March 5, 1995): 26; C. Wright Mills, *The Causes of World War Three* (Westport, CT: Greenwood Press, 1976).

86 Charlotte Hooper, "Masculinities, IR and the 'Gender Variable': A Cost-Benefit Analysis for (Sympathetic) Gender Sceptics," *Review of International Studies 25*, no. 2 (1999): 475–480; Charlotte Hooper, *Manly States: Masculinities, International Relations, and Gender Politics* (New York: Columbia University Press, 2001).

87 Zachary Keck, "Ghosts of Imperialism Past: How Colonialism Still Haunts the World Today," *The National Interest*, February 4, 2015, http://nationalinterest.org/blog/the-buzz/ghosts-imperialism-past-how-colonialism-still-haunts-the-12185 (accessed November 22, 2015).

88 W. E. B. Du Bois, *The World and Africa* (New York: International Publishers, [1946] 1965), p. 23. Our italics.

89 Liam O'Ceallaigh, "When You Kill Ten Million Africans You Aren't Called 'Hitler,'" *Diary of a Walking Butterfly*, December 22, 2010, http://www.walkingbutterfly.com/2010/12/22/when-you-kill-ten-million-africans-you-arent-called-hitler/#note-1 (accessed May 14, 2015).

90 See Penny M. Von Eschen, *Race Against Empire: Black Americans and Anticolonialism, 1937–1957* (Ithaca, NY: Cornell University Press, 1997); Brenda Gayle Plummer, *Rising Wind: Black Americans and U.S. Foreign Affairs, 1935–1960* (Chapel Hill, NC: University of North Carolina Press, 1996); Mary L. Dudziak, *Cold War Civil Rights: Race and the Image of American Democracy* (Princeton, NJ: Princeton University Press, 2002); Nick Bryant, *The Bystander: John F. Kennedy and the Struggle for Black Equality* (New York: Basic Books, 2006). pp. 388, 472; Walter Goodman, *The Committee: The Extraordinary Career of the House Committee on Un-American Activities* (New York: Farrar, Strauss & Giroux, 1968).

4 White Imperialism, Racism, and Masculinity: Globalization Since the 1950s

1 Thomas Winter, "Cold War," in *American Masculinities: A Historical Encyclopedia*, ed. Bret E. Carroll (Thousand Oaks, CA: Sage, 2003), p. 100.

2 Stephen Kinzer, *Overthrow: America's Century of Regime Change from Hawaii to Iraq* (New York: Times Books, 2007); Amy Goodman and Juan González, "Part II . . . Overthrow: America's Century of Regime Change from Hawaii to Iraq," *Democracy Now*, May 8, 2006, http://www.democracynow.org/2006/5/8/part_ii_overthrow_americas_century_of (accessed June 10, 2015).

3 Dan Merica and Jason Hanna, "In Declassified Document, CIA Acknowledges Role in '53 Iran Coup," *CNN.com*, August 19, 2013, http://www.cnn.com/2013/08/19/politics/cia-iran-1953-coup/?hpt=po_c2 (accessed June 14, 2015).

4 RT News Staff, "CIA Finally Admits It Masterminded Iran's 1953 Coup," *RT News*, August 19, 2013, http://rt.com/usa/iran-coup-cia-operation-647/ (accessed June 14, 2015); Saeed Kamali Dehghan and Richard Norton-Taylor, "CIA Admits Role in 1953 Iranian Coup," *Guardian*, http://www.theguardian.com/world/2013/aug/19/cia-admits-role-1953-iranian-coup (accessed June 14, 2015).

5 Wolfgang K. Kressin, "Prime Minister Mosaddegh and Ayatullah Kashani from Unity to Enmity: As Viewed from the American Embassy in Tehran, June 1950–August 1953," *The Defense Technical Information Center*, http://www.dtic.mil/dtic/tr/fulltext/u2/a239339.pdf (accessed June 14, 2015); Mark J. Gasiorowski, *U.S. Foreign Policy and the Shah: Building a Client State in Iran* (Ithaca, NY: Cornell University Press, 1991), p. 59; Stephen Kinzer, *All the Shah's Men: An American Coup and the Roots of Middle East Terror*, 2nd edn. (Hoboken, NJ: Wiley, 2008).

6 Abbas Milani, *The Shah*, reprint edn. (New York: Palgrave Macmillan Trade, 2012).

7 Kinzer, *All the Shah's Men*; Arash Norouzi, "9/11: The Terrorists' Motivation Professor Rick Shenkman Peruses Kinzer's 'Red Line' Theory," *The Mossadegh Project*, September 15, 2011, http://www.mohammadmossadegh.com/news/richard-shenkman/ (accessed October 4, 2015).

8 Goodman and González, "Part II . . . Overthrow"; Kinzer, *Overthrow*.

9 Kinzer, *Overthrow*.

10 "Peurifoy's First-Name Diplomacy Succeeded in Hard Assignments; Defeat of Guatemala Reds a High Point in Career—Work in Greece Bolstered Reputation as Trouble Shooter," *New York Times*, August 13, 1955, http://query.nytimes.com/gst/abstract.html?res=9805E5DF1E3EE53BBC4B52DFBE66838E649EDE (accessed October 4, 2015); Fulbright Thailand, "Thailand-U.S. Educational Foundation (Fulbright)'s Newsletter," Issue 28, August 2010, http://www.fulbrightthai.org/data/newsletter/Issue28.pdf (accessed October 4, 2015); David M. Barrett, "Sterilizing a 'Red Infection' Congress, the CIA, and Guatemala, 1954," *Central Intelligence Agency Library*, May 8, 2007, https://www.cia.gov/library/center-for-the-study-of-intelligence/kent-csi/vol44no5/html/v44i5a03p.htm (accessed October 4, 2015).

11 Winter, "Cold War."

12 Quoted in Myra Mendible, "LBJ's War Policies: Post-Vietnam Syndrome: National Identity, War, and the Politics of Humiliation," *Library of Social Science*, http://www.libraryofsocialscience.com/essays/mendible.html (accessed March 21, 2016). Our italics.

13 Fredrik Logevall, as quoted in Richard A. Koenigsberg, "Warfare as a Test of Manliness," *Library of Social Science*, https://www.libraryofsocialscience.com/newsletter/posts/2016/2016-01-13-Mendible1.html (accessed August 18, 2016).

14 Koenigsberg, "Warfare as a Test of Manliness."

15 Goodman and González, "Part II . . . Overthrow"; Kinzer, *Overthrow*; Editors, "Augusto Pinochet President of Chile," *Encyclopedia Britannica Online* http://www.britannica.com/EBchecked/topic/461158/Augusto-Pinochet (accessed June 10, 2015).

16 Florencia Melgar and Sarah Gilbert, "The Coup. Chapter 1," *The Other 9/11*, http://www.sbs.com.au/theother911/ (accessed June 10, 2015).

17 Uri Friedman, "The Other 9/11: A CIA Agent Remembers Chile's Coup," *The Atlantic*, September 11, 2014, http://www.theatlantic.com/international/archive/2014/09/chile-coup-salvador-allende-cia/380082/ (accessed June 10, 2015); Melgar and Gilbert, "The Coup"; Goodman and González, "Part II . . . Overthrow"; Kinzer, *Overthrow*; Editors, "Augusto Pinochet"; Florencia Melgar and Sarah Gilbert, "The Sanctuary," *The Other 9/11*, http://www.sbs.com.au/theother911/ (accessed June 10, 2015).

18 Philip Sherwell, "The World According to Henry Kissinger," *The Telegraph*, May 21, 2011, http://www.telegraph.co.uk/news/worldnews/us-politics/8528270/The-world-accord ing-to-Henry-Kissinger.html (accessed October 4, 2015); William Shawcross, *Sideshow: Kissinger, Nixon and the Destruction of Cambodia* (New York: Simon and Schuster, 1979), p. 395; Ben Kiernan and Taylor Owen, "Roots of U.S. Troubles in Afghanistan: Civilian Bombing Casualties and the Cambodian Precedent," *The Asia-Pacific Journal*, June 28, 2010, http://www.japanfocus.org/-ben-kiernan/3380/article.html (accessed October 4, 2015).

19 Kiernan and Owen, "Roots of U.S. Troubles in Afghanistan."

20 Sherwell, "The World."

21 Ibid.; Burton Feldman, *The Nobel Prize: A History of Genius, Controversy, and Prestige* (New York: Arcade Publishing, 2012), p. 16; The Economist Staff, "The Birth of Bangladesh: Blood Meridian," *The Economist*, September 21, 2013, http://www.economist.com/ news/books-and-arts/21586514-new-history-sheds-fresh-light-shameful-moment-american-foreign-policy-blood (accessed October 4, 2015); Gary Bass, *The Blood Telegram: Nixon, Kissinger and a Forgotten Genocide* (New York: Knopf Publishing Group, 2013).

22 Bass, *The Blood Telegram*.

23 Ibid.

24 Winter, "Cold War."

25 Randy Laist, "The Hyperreal Theme in 1990s American Cinema," *Americana: The Journal of American Popular Culture (1900–present)* 9, no. 1 (Spring 2010), http://www. americanpopularculture.com/journal/articles/spring_2010/laist.htm (accessed November 9, 2015).

26 Anonymous, "Nationalism," in American Masculinities: A Historical Encyclopedia, ed. Bret E. Carroll (Thousand Oaks, CA: Sage, 2003), p. 331; see also Bret E. Carroll, "George Washington," in *American Masculinities: A Historical Encyclopedia*, ed. Bret E. Carroll (Thousand Oaks, CA: Sage, 2003), p. 483.

27 Jonathan Stein and Tim Dickinson, "Lie by Lie: A Timeline of How We Got into Iraq," *Mother Jones*, September/October 2006, http://www.motherjones.com/politics/2011/12/ leadup-iraq-war-timeline (accessed December 27, 2015).

28 Dexter Filkins, "Did George W. Bush Create ISIS?" *The New Yorker*, May 15, 2015, http://www.newyorker.com/news/news-desk/did-george-w-bush-create-isis (accessed December 27, 2015).

29 Walter Pincus and Dana Milbank, "Bush Clings to Dubious Allegations about Iraq," *Washington Post*, March 18, 2003, p. A13, http://www.leadingtowar.com/PDFsources_ claims_yellowcake/2003_03_18_WP.pdf (accessed December 27, 2015); Simon Maloy, "Yes, Bush Lied about Iraq: Why Are We Still Arguing about This?" *Salon*, February 10, 2015, http://www.salon.com/2015/02/10/yes_bush_lied_about_iraq_why_are_we_ still_arguing_about_this/ (accessed December 27, 2015); Stein and Dickinson, "Lie by Lie."

30 Laurence Silberman, "The Dangerous Lie That 'Bush Lied,'" *The Wall Street Journal*, February 8, 2015, http://www.wsj.com/articles/laurence-h-silberman-the-dangerous-lie-that-bush-lied-1423437950 (accessed December 27, 2015); John Glaser, "The Lie That Got Us In: The Bush Administration Knew There Were No WMDs in Iraq," *Anti-War Blog*, March 19, 2013, http://antiwar.com/blog/2013/03/19/the-lie-that-got-us-in-the-bush-administration-knew-there-were-no-wmds-in-iraq/ (accessed December 27, 2015).

31 Lee H. Hamilton, "Let's Defeat ISIS without Destroying Our Values," *World Post* (a partner of *Huffington Post*), December 23, 2015, http://www.huffingtonpost.com/lee-h-hamil ton/lets-defeat-isis-without-destroying-our-values_b_8870398.html (accessed December 27, 2015).

32 Filkins, "Did George W. Bush Create ISIS"; Zack Beauchamp, "Bush Didn't Know Anything about Maliki, but Put Him in Charge of Iraq Anyway," *Vox Topics*, August 12, 2014, http://www.vox.com/2014/8/12/5994749/bush-maliki-iraq (accessed December 27, 2015); Fox News Staff, "Bush Backs Embattled Al-Maliki in Speech to VFW, Says

Only Iraqis Can Decide Who Governs Them," *FoxNews.com*, August 22, 2007, http:// www.foxnews.com/story/2007/08/22/bush-backs-embattled-al-maliki-in-speech-to-vfw-says-only-iraqis-can-decide-who.html (accessed December 27, 2015); "Agreement Between the United States of America and the Republic of Iraq on the Withdrawal of United States Forces from Iraq and the Organization of Their Activities during Their Temporary Presence in Iraq," http://www.state.gov/documents/organization/122074. pdf (accessed December 27, 2015); Herald Sun Staff, "US Troops Complete Their With-drawal from Iraq," *Herald Sun* (Australia), December 18, 2011, http://www.heraldsun. com.au/news/breaking-news/us-troops-complete-their-withdrawal-from-iraq/sto ry-e6frf7jx-1226225154019 (accessed December 27, 2015).

33 Peter Bergen, "Bush's Toxic Legacy in Iraq," *CNN.com*, June 16, 2014, http://www.cnn. com/2014/06/13/opinion/bergen-iraq-isis-bush/index.html (accessed December 27, 2015); Stein and Dickinson, "Lie by Lie."

34 James W. Messerschmidt, *Hegemonic Masculinities and Camouflaged Politics: Unmasking the Bush Dynasty and Its War against Iraq* (London: Paradigm Publishers, 2010).

35 Paul Kivel, "Afterword from *You Call This a Democracy?* Who Benefits, Who Pays, and Who Really Decides," *The Peace and Justice Centre*, http://paulkivel.com/resource/after word-from-you-call-this-a-democracy-who-benefits-who-pays-and-who-really-de cides/ (accessed December 26, 2015).

36 Howard Zinn, "Chapter 16: A People's War," from *A People's History of the United States. 1492-Present*, "History Is a Weapon" website, http://www.historyisaweapon.com/def-con1/zinnpeopleswar.html (accessed December 31, 2015).

37 ABC News Staff, "Colin Powell on Iraq, Race, and Hurricane Relief," *20/20 (ABC News)*, September 8, 2005, http://abcnews.go.com/2020/Politics/story?id=1105979&page=1 (accessed February 4, 2016).

38 Toby Harnden, "Condoleezza Rice Approved 'Torture' Techniques," *The Telegraph* (U.K.), April 23, 2009, http://www.telegraph.co.uk/news/worldnews/northamerica/ usa/5208701/Condoleezza-Rice-approved-torture-techniques.html (accessed January 3, 2016); Associated Press, "As Bush Adviser, Rice Gave OK to Waterboard," *Fox News*, April 22, 2009, www.foxnews.com/politics/2009/04/22/bush-adviser-rice-gave-ok-wa terboard/ (accessed January 3, 2016).

39 Malise Ruthven, "The Map ISIS Hates," *New York Review of Books*, June 25, 2014, http:// www.freerepublic.com/focus/f-news/3172768/posts (accessed December 27, 2015); Timothy McGrath, "Watch This English-Speaking ISIS Fighter Explain How a 98-Year-Old Colonial Map Created Today's Conflict," July 2, 2014, *Los Angeles Daily News* (accessed December 28, 2015).

40 McGrath, "Watch This English-Speaking ISIS Fighter"; Michael Gunter, *The Kurds Ascending: The Evolving Solution to the Kurdish Problem in Iraq and Turkey* (New York: Palgrave Macmillan, 2008); Lee H. Hamilton, "Let's Defeat ISIS without Destroying Our Values"; Malise Ruthven, "The Map ISIS Hates"; Interview with Kamal Abu Jabern (For-mer Foreign Minister of Jordan) in *Lawrence of Arabia: The Battle for the Arab World*, directed by James Hawes (UK: PBS Home Video, October 22, 2003).

41 Stein and Dickinson, "Lie by Lie." Our italics.

42 Ibid.

43 Kivel, "Afterword from *You Call This a Democracy?*"; Fred Barbash, "Bush: Iraq Part of 'Global Democratic Revolution': Liberation of Middle East Portrayed as Continuation of Reagan's Policies," *Washington Post*, November 6, 2003, http://www.washingtonpost. com/wp-dyn/articles/A7991-2003Nov6.html (accessed December 26, 2015); National Endowment for Democracy (NED), "Remarks by President George W. Bush at the 20th Anniversary of the National Endowment for Democracy," *United States Chamber of Commerce*, Washington, DC, November 6, 2003, http://www.ned.org/remarks-by-presi dent-george-w-bush-at-the-20th-anniversary/ (accessed December 26, 2015).

44 McGrath, "Watch This English-Speaking ISIS Fighter."

45 Stephen D. Wrage, "Genocide in Rwanda: Draft Case Study for Teaching Ethics and International Affairs," *Peace and Conflict Monitor*, April 1, 2009, http://www.monitor. upeace.org/innerpg.cfm?id_article=606 (accessed June 1, 2015).

46 Frontline PBS Staff, "100 Days of Slaughter. The Chronology of U.S./U.N. Actions," *WGBH Educational Foundation*, http://www.pbs.org/wgbh/pages/frontline/shows/evil/etc/slaughter.html (accessed June 4, 2015); Adam Jones, "Case Study: Genocide in Rwanda, 1994," *Gendercide Watch 1999–2013*, http://www.gendercide.org/case_rwanda.html (accessed June 1, 2015); Chris McGreal, "French Politicians Accused of Assisting Rwandan Genocide," *Guardian*, August 6, 2008, http://www.theguardian.com/world/2008/aug/06/rwanda.france (accessed May 27, 2015).

47 Roméo Dallaire, "The Media Dichotomy," in *The Media and the Rwanda Genocide*, ed. Allan Thompson, http://www.idrc.ca/EN/Resources/Publications/openebooks/338-0/index.html (accessed June 10, 2015). Italics added.

48 Samantha Power, "Bystanders to Genocide," *The Atlantic*, September 2001, http://www.theatlantic.com/magazine/archive/2001/09/bystanders-to-genocide/304571/ (accessed May 27, 2015); Romain Kabahizi (ETO Survivor), blog, March 28, 2006, http://rwandansurvivors.blogspot.ca/ (accessed June 1, 2015). Italics added.

49 Emily Willard, ed. "The Rwanda Sitreps: Daily Pleas to New York Detail How International Failure Left Peacekeepers Ill-Equipped to Respond to Rising Violence in January 1994," February 4, 2013, *National Security Archive Electronic Briefing Book*, no. 455, http://nsarchive.gwu.edu/NSAEBB/NSAEBB455/ (accessed June 13, 2015).

50 Roméo Dallaire, *Shake Hands with the Devil: The Failure of Humanity in Rwanda* (Boston, MA: Da Capo Press, 2003), p. 513.

51 Ella Baker School Staff, "Ella Baker's Life," *The Ella Baker School at the Julia Richman Education Complex*, April 12, 2011, http://www.ellabakerschool.net/resources/about-ella-baker/ella-bakers-life (accessed June 9, 2015).

52 Power, "Bystanders to Genocide." Italics in original.

53 Kim Ten, "The Rwanda Massacre: Worldwide Complicity," *Free Republic*, April 5, 2004, http://freerepublic.com/tag/vanity-news/index?more=3885605 (accessed June 1, 2015). See facsimile from Major Gen. Roméo Dallaire, "Request for Protection for Informant," *National Security Archive*, January 11, 1994, http://nsarchive.gwu.edu/NSAEBB/NSAEBB53/rw011194.pdf (accessed May 27, 2015); Memorandum from Prudence Bushnell, "Death of Rwanda and Burundian Presidents in Plane Crash Outside Kigali," *National Security Archive*, April 6, 1994, http://nsarchive.gwu.edu/NSAEBB/NSAEBB53/rw040694.pdf (accessed May 27, 2015); Colette Braeckman, *Rwanda: Histoire D'un Genocide* (Paris: Fayard, 1994); Jean-Paul Gouteux, *Un Genocide Secret d'tat: La France et le Rwanda, 1990–1997* (Paris: Editions Sociales, 1998); Gérard Prunier, *The Rwanda Crisis: History of a Genocide* (New York: Columbia University Press, 1995); Francois-Xavier Verschave, *Complicite de Genocide? La Politique de la France au Rwanda* (Paris: Editions La Decouverte, 1994).

54 People's Pundit Daily Staff, "Report: Bill Clinton Was Fully Aware of Rwandan Genocide, and Did Nothing. The Clinton Lie That Might Have Cost 300,000 Lives," *People's Pundit Daily*, April 6, 2015, http://www.peoplespunditdaily.com/news/politics/2015/04/06/report-bill-clinton-was-fully-aware-of-rwandan-genocide-and-did-nothing/ (accessed June 10, 2015).

55 Ibid.

56 Frontline, "Ghosts of Rwanda" (Transcript), *WGBH Educational Foundation*, April 9, 2004, http://www.pbs.org/wgbh/pages/frontline/shows/ghosts/etc/script.html (accessed June 10, 2014).

57 White House, Office of the Press Secretary, "Remarks by the President at U.S. Naval Academy Graduation Ceremony," *U.S. Naval Academy Annapolis, Maryland*, May 25, 1994, http://clinton6.nara.gov/1994/05/1994-05-25-presidents-naval-academy-commencement-speech.html (accessed October 4, 2015). See also Al Carroll, "Bill Clinton and Rwandan Genocide," *Daily Kos*, June 20, 2014, http://www.dailykos.com/story/2014/06/20/1308511/-Bill-Clinton-and-Rwandan-Genocide (accessed June 10, 2015); Colum Lynch, "Rwanda: Genocide under Our Watch," April 18, 2015, http://glykosymoritis.blogspot.ca/2015/04/rwanda-genocide-under-our-watch.html (accessed June 13, 2015).

58 People's Pundit Daily Staff, "Report."

59 Iain Dale, "Rwanda: The Shame of Donald Steinberg," February 24, 2009, http://iain dale.blogspot.ca/2009/02/rwanda-shame-of-donald-steinberg.html (accessed June 13, 2015).
60 Power, "Bystanders to Genocide"; McGreal, "French Politicians Accused of Assisting Rwandan Genocide."
61 Richard Clarke and Susan Rice (from), Tony Lake (to), "Draft Message to General Quesnot on Rwanda Peacekeeping," *Clinton Library MDR* Case no. 2014–0278, October 1, 1994, http://nsarchive.gwu.edu/NSAEBB/NSAEBB511/docs/DOCUMENT%204.pdf (accessed June 13, 2015).
62 Rory Carroll, "US Chose to Ignore Rwandan Genocide," *Guardian*, March 31, 2004, http://www.theguardian.com/world/2004/mar/31/usa.rwanda (accessed May 27, 2015).
63 George Orwell, "Appendix," in *1984* (New York: Signet Classic, 1961).
64 Africa Speaks, "Genocide in Rwanda," May 7, 2004, http://www.africaspeaks.com/reasoning/index.php?topic=9276.0;wap2 (accessed January 10, 2017); Tom Blanton and Emily Willard, eds. "1994 Rwanda Pullout Driven by Clinton White House, U.N. Equivocation," *National Security Archive Electronic Briefing Book No. 511*, April 16, 2015, http://nsarchive.gwu.edu/NSAEBB/NSAEBB511/ (accessed June 13, 2015).
65 Paul Greenberg, "The U.N.: Rot at the Top," *Jewish World Review*, April 7, 2005, http://www.jewishworldreview.com/cols/greenberg040705.asp (accessed June 1, 2015); Ali B. Ali-Dinar, "Rwanda: OAU Report, 07/07/00," *University of Pennsylvania, African Studies Center*, July 8, 2000, http://www.africa.upenn.edu/Urgent_Action/apic-070800.html (accessed June 1, 2015); McGreal, "French Politicians Accused of Assisting Rwandan Genocide."
66 Dallaire, "The Media Dichotomy." Italics added.
67 Frontline, "Ghosts of Rwanda."
68 Ibid.
69 Carl Wilkens, "Oral History Interview, June 7, 2013," *Washington, D.C., The National Security Archive*; Carl Wilkens, *I'm Not Leaving* (Spokane, WA: World Outside My Shoes, 2013); Frontline, "Ghosts of Rwanda."
70 Colum Lynch, "Exclusive: Rwanda Revisited," *Foreign Policy*, April 5, 2015, https://foreignpolicy.com/2015/04/05/rwanda-revisited-genocide-united-states-state-department/ (accessed June 13, 2015).
71 Power, "Bystanders to Genocide."
72 Clint McDuffie, "Review of Ben Carrington," in *Race, Sport and Politics: The Sporting Black Diaspora* (London: Sage, 2010), *Project Muse*, https://muse.jhu.edu/article/477709 (accessed 12 October 2016).
73 "We Charge Genocide," *Petition to the United Nations*, 1951, http://www.blackpast.org/ (accessed May 30, 2015).
74 Jeremiah Wright, "Confusing God and Government," http://en.wikipedia.org/wiki/Jeremiah_Wright_controversy#cite_note-22 (accessed May 14, 2015). For details, see Joe R. Feagin, *The White Racial Frame: Centuries of Racial Framing and Counter-Framing*, 2nd edn. (New York: Routledge, 2013), pp. 180–189.
75 Frontline, "Ghosts of Rwanda."
76 Power, "Bystanders to Genocide."
77 Allan Thompson, "Introduction," in *The Media and the Rwanda Genocide*, ed. Allan Thompson, http://www.idrc.ca/EN/Resources/Publications/openebooks/338-0/index.html (accessed June 10, 2015); Dallaire, "The Media Dichotomy"; PBS Frontline Staff, "Interview Samantha Power," *WGBH Educational Foundation*, http://www.pbs.org/wgbh/pages/frontline/shows/ghosts/interviews/power.html (accessed June 10, 2015).
78 Andrew Woolford, "Making Genocide Unthinkable: Three Guidelines for a Critical Criminology of Genocide," *Critical Criminology 14*, no. 1 (2006): 89. See David Bleich, *The Materiality of Language: Gender, Politics, and the University* (Bloomington, IN: Indiana University Press, 2013), pp. 1–16 and passim.
79 Anne-Marie de Brouwer and Sandra Chu, eds. *The Men Who Killed Me: Rwandan Survivors of Sexual Violence* (Vancouver, BC: Douglas & McIntyre, 2009), pp. 14–15,150–151.
80 Robert Elias, "War Crimes Listing," http://www.the-philosopher.co.uk/whocares/popups/warcrimes.htm (accessed June 3, 2016). He provides the FBI definition.

81 PBS Frontline Staff, "Interview General Roméo Dallaire," *WGBH Educational Foundation*, April 1, 2004, http://www.pbs.org/wgbh/pages/frontline/shows/ghosts/interviews/dallaire.html (accessed June 4, 2015).

82 Laura Seay, "Professor Warns against 'Badvocacy' on Behalf of Africa," *Catholic World News*, March 14, 2011, http://www.ewtn.com/vnews/getstory.asp?number=112091 (accessed May 28, 2015); Wrage, "Genocide in Rwanda."

83 Juan Cole, "War Talk, Jingoism and White Supremacy at GOP Debate," *Informed Comment*, January 19, 2010, http://www.juancole.com/2016/01/war-talk-jingoism-and-white-supremacy-at-gop-debate.html (accessed February 4, 2016). See also W. E. B. Du Bois, "Mexico," in *W. E. B. Du Bois: A Reader*, ed. Meyer Weinberg (New York: Harper & Row Publishers, 1970), pp. 413–424.

5 More Oligopolistic Capitalism: The Current Neoliberal Era

1 YouTube, "Chinese Professor," https://www.youtube.com/watch?v=OTSQozWP-rM (accessed June 22, 2015); John Pomfret, "More Political Ads Paint China as Benefiting from Weak U.S. Economy," *Washington Post*, October 28, 2010, http://www.washingtonpost.com/wp-dyn/content/article/2010/10/28/AR2010102803256.html (accessed June 22, 2015).

2 Nick Wing, "CAGW Campaign Ad Imagines China-Dominated Future (Video)," *Huffington Post*, October 22, 2010, http://www.huffingtonpost.com/2010/10/22/cagw-china-future-ad_n_772623.html (accessed June 27, 2015).

3 Wendy Brown, *Undoing the Demos: Neoliberalism's Stealth Revolution* (New York: Zone Books, 2015); Elias Isquith, "Neoliberalism Poisons Everything: How Free Market Mania Threatens Education—and Democracy," *Salon*, June 15, 2105, http://www.salon.com/2015/06/15/democracy_cannot_survive_why_the_neoliberal_revolution_has_freedom_on_the_ropes/ (accessed August 19, 2015).

4 David Harvey, *A Short History of Neo-Liberalism* (New York: Oxford University Press), pp. 159–164.

5 Daphna Whitmore, "Interview with John Smith, author of *Imperialism in the Twenty-first Century*," *Redline*, June 1, 2016, https://rdln.wordpress.com/2016/06/01/interview-with-john-smith-author-of-imperialism-in-the-twenty-first-century/ (accessed December 30, 2016).

6 George Monbiot, "Sick of This Market-Driven World? You Should Be," *Guardian*, August 5, 2014, http://www.theguardian.com/commentisfree/2014/aug/05/neoliberalism-mental-health-rich-poverty-economy (accessed August 19, 2015).

7 Mark Weisbrot, "The World Has Nothing to Fear from the US Losing Power," *Guardian*, May 3, 2014, http://www.theguardian.com/commentisfree/2014/may/03/world-nothing-fear-us-power-china-economy-democracy (accessed August 19, 2015); Nick Miroff, "Latin America's Political Right in Decline as Leftist Governments Move to Middle," *Guardian*, January 28, 2014 (accessed August 19, 2015); Denis Rogatyuk, "Ecuador: Zombie Neoliberalism Threatens 'Citizen's Revolution,'" *Links International Journal of Socialist Renewal*, August 15, 2015, http://links.org.au/node/4557 (accessed August 19, 2015); Federico Fuentes, "How Rejecting Neoliberalism Rescued Bolivia's Economy," *Green Left Weekly*, August 10, 2015, https://www.greenleft.org.au/node/59730 (accessed August 19, 2015).

8 Maria Mies, *Patriarchy and Accumulation on a World Scale* (London: Zed Books, [1986] 2014), Kindle loc. 346.

9 Ibid.

10 Brandy Jensen and Deirdre Howard-Wagner, "Arizona 2010," in *Unveiling Whiteness in the Twenty-First Century: Global Manifestations, Transdisciplinary Interventions*, eds. Veronica Watson, Deirdre Howard-Wagner, and Lisa Spanierman (Lanham, MD: Lexington Books, 2014), p. 237.

11 David Harvey, "The 'New' Imperialism: Accumulation by Dispossession," *Socialist Register 40* (2004): 75.

12 Ibid., p. 72.
13 George Monbiot, "If You Think We're Done with Neoliberalism, Think Again," *Guardian*, January 14, 2013, http://www.theguardian.com/commentisfree/2013/jan/14/neo liberal-theory-economic-failure (accessed August 19, 2015); Secretariat of the United Nations Conference on Trade and Development, *Trade and Development Report* (New York and Geneva, 2012), http://unctad.org/en/PublicationsLibrary/tdr2012_bn.pdf (accessed August 19, 2015).
14 International Monetary Fund Staff, "IMF Members' Quotas and Voting Power, and IMF Board of Governors," *International Monetary Fund*, August 9, 2015, https://www.imf. org/external/np/sec/memdir/members.aspx (accessed August 9, 2015); George Monbiot, "Greece Is the Latest Battleground in the Financial Elite's War on Democracy," *Guardian*, July 7, 2015, http://www.theguardian.com/commentisfree/2015/jul/07/ greece-financial-elite-democracy-liassez-faire-neoliberalism (accessed August 9, 2015).
15 Mike Davis, *Late Victorian Holocausts: El Niño Famines and the Making of the Third World* (New York: Verso, 2002); Monbiot, "Greece Is the Latest Battleground in the Financial Elite's War on Democracy."
16 Lynn Stuart Parramore, "James Galbraith: Greek Revolt Threatens Entire Neoliberal Project," *AlterNet*, July 9, 2015, http://www.alternet.org/economy/james-galbraith-greek-re volt-threatens-entire-neoliberal-project?sc=tw (accessed August 9, 2015).
17 Gregory J. Krieg, "An Idiot's Guide to the Greek Debt Crisis," *ABC News*, November 4, 2011, http://abcnews.go.com/blogs/headlines/2011/11/an-idiots-guide-to-the-greek-debt-crisis/ (accessed August 9, 2015).
18 Weisbrot, "The World Has Nothing to Fear from the US Losing Power."
19 Ibid.
20 Noël Cazenave, *Conceptualizing Racism: Breaking the Chains of Racially Accommodative Language* (Lanham, MD: Rowman & Littlefield Publishers, 2015).
21 Brown, *Undoing the Demos*.
22 Dana-Ain Davis, "Narrating the Mute: Racializing and Racism in a Neoliberal Moment," *Souls: A Critical Journal of Black Politics, Culture, and Society* 9, no. 4 (2007): 348–349, citing pages 354, 357.
23 Hannah Fingerhut, "In Both Parties, Men and Women Differ over Whether Women Still Face Obstacles to Progress," *Pew Research Center*, August 16, 2016, http://www.pewre search.org/fact-tank/2016/08/16/in-both-parties-men-and-women-differ-over-wheth er-women-still-face-obstacles-to-progress (accessed August 18, 2016).
24 See Joe R. Feagin, *The White Racial Frame: Centuries of Racial Framing and Counter-Framing*, 2nd edn. (New York: Routledge, 2013), p. 10ff.
25 W. E. B. Du Bois, *Black Reconstruction in America: An Essay toward a History of the Part Which Black Folk Played in the Attempt to Reconstruct Democracy in America, 1860–1880* (New York: The Free Press, 1965), p. 700.
26 Randolph Hohle, *Race and the Origins of American Neoliberalism* (New York: Routledge, 2015), p. 4.
27 George Lipsitz, *How Racism Takes Place* (Philadelphia, PA: Temple University Press, 2011), p. 35. Italics added.
28 See R. W. Connell, *Masculinities*, 2nd edn. (Berkeley, CA: University of California Press, 2005), p. 255.
29 Neil Barofsky, *Bailout: An Inside Account of How Washington Abandoned Main Street While Rescuing Wall Street* (New York: Free Press, 2012), pp. 34, 37; Time Magazine Staff, "25 People to Blame for the Financial Crisis," *Time*, http://content.time.com/time/ specials/packages/article/0,28804,1877351_1878509_1878508,00.html (accessed July 5, 2015).
30 Mike McIntire, "Bailout Is a Windfall to Banks, If Not to Borrowers," *New York Times*, January 17, 2009, http://www.nytimes.com/2009/01/18/business/18bank.html?pagewan ted=all (accessed June 27, 2015).
31 U.S. Department of Treasury, "TARP Programs," June 17, 2015, http://www.treasury. gov/initiatives/financial-stability/TARP-Programs/Pages/default.aspx# (accessed July 7, 2015); Paul Kiel and Dan Nguyen, "Bailout Tracker: Tracking Every Dollar and Every

Recipient," *ProPublica*, July 7, 2015, https://projects.propublica.org/bailout/ (accessed July 7, 2015).

32 Amelia Thomson-DeVeaux, "Obama and Romney Spar over the American Dream," *Public Religion Research Institute*, December 8, 2011, http://publicreligion.org/2011/12/obama-and-romney-spar-over-the-american-dream/#.VSzrAJOncaY (accessed April 14, 2015).

33 McIntire, "Bailout Is a Windfall to Banks, If Not to Borrowers"; Julie Creswell, "Storm and Crisis: A Tale of 3 Companies; In New Orleans, the Business Haves and Have-Nots," *New York Times*, September 6, 2005, http://query.nytimes.com/gst/fullpage.html?res=9401E1D91531F935A3575AC0A9639C8B63 (accessed July 7, 2015).

34 McIntire, "Bailout Is a Windfall to Banks, If Not to Borrowers."

35 Ibid.

36 Sarah Burd-Sharps and Rebecca Rasch, "Impact of the US Housing Crisis on the Racial Wealth Gap across Generations," *Social Science Research Council, an Independent Report Commissioned by the American Civil Liberties Union*, June 2015, https://www.aclu.org/files/field_document/discrimlend_final.pdf (accessed July 7, 2015), p. 1.

37 Glenn Greenwald, "Larry Summers, Tim Geithner and Wall Street's Ownership of Government," *Salon*, April 4, 2009, http://www.salon.com/2009/04/04/summers/ (accessed June 29, 2015).

38 Barofsky, *Bailout*, p. 95.

39 "Inside Job" directed by Charles H. Ferguson, 2010 (Culver City, CA: Sony Pictures Classics). Also see the film's official website at http://www.sonyclassics.com/insidejob/ (accessed July 1, 2015); Time Magazine Staff, "25 People to Blame for the Financial Crisis"; Barofsky, *Bailout*, p. 42.

40 "Inside Job," directed by Charles H. Ferguson; Time Magazine Staff, "25 People to Blame for the Financial Crisis"; Barofsky, *Bailout*, p. 42; Michael Mandel, "German and French Banks Got $36 Billion from AIG Bailout," *Bloomberg Business*, March 15, 2009, http://www.businessweek.com/the_thread/economicsunbound/archives/2009/03/german_and_fren.html (accessed June 27, 2015); Bob Herbert, "A Second Opinion?" *New York Times*, September 22, 2008, http://www.nytimes.com/2010/10/09/opinion/09herbert.html (accessed June 27, 2015).

41 Devin Banerjee and Ian Katz, "Tim Geithner to Join Leveraged Buyout Firm Warburg Pincus," *Bloomberg News*, November 16, 2013, http://www.bloomberg.com/news/articles/2013-11-16/tim-geithner-to-join-leveraged-buyout-firm-warburg-pincus (accessed July 1, 2015).

42 Barofsky, *Bailout*, p. 3.

43 Markin, "Bush/Obama and the Bank Bailout," *American Left History*, November 3, 2012, http://markinbookreview.blogspot.ca/2012/11/bushobama-and-bank-bailout.html (accessed April 14, 2015).

44 Barofsky, *Bailout*, p. 29.

45 Ibid., pp. 29, 42.

46 Ibid., pp. 3, 89; Sean McElwee, "Is There an American Dream for Black Children?" September 22, 2014, *Huffington Post*, http://www.huffingtonpost.com/sean-mcelwee/american-dream_b_5858106.html (accessed April 2, 2015); Trevor Delaney, "Subprime Lenders under Fire," *Black Enterprise* (October 2007): 31–32; Vikas Bajaj and Ford Fessenden, "What's Behind the Race Gap?" *New York Times*, November 4, 2007, http://www.nytimes.com/2007/11/04/weekinreview/04bajaj.html (accessed April 14, 2015), p. 16; Kimberly Blanton, "A 'Smoking Gun' on Race, Subprime Loans," *Boston Globe*, March 16, 2007, http://www.boston.com/business/globe/articles/2007/03/16/a_smoking_gun_on_race_subprime_loans/?page=2 (accessed April 14, 2015); Manny Fernandez, "Study Finds Disparities in Mortgages by Race," *New York Times*, October 15, 2007, http://www.nytimes.com/2007/10/15/nyregion/15subprime.html?_r=2&oref=slogin& (accessed April 14, 2015).

47 McElwee, "Is There an American Dream for Black Children?"; Delaney, "Subprime Lenders Under Fire"; Bajaj and Fessenden, "What's Behind the Race Gap?"; Blanton, "A 'Smoking Gun' on Race, Subprime Loans"; Fernandez, "Study Finds Disparities in Mortgages by Race."

48 Michael Powell, "Bank Accused of Pushing Mortgage Deals on Blacks," *New York Times*, June 6, 2009, http://www.nytimes.com/2009/06/07/us/07baltimore.html (accessed April 4, 2015).

49 Barofsky, *Bailout*, pp. xvi, 1, 3, and 19.

50 Jean Swanson, *Poor-Bashing: The Politics of Exclusion* (Toronto, ON: Between the Lions Press, 2003), p. 78. See also Henry A. Giroux, *Against the Terror of Neoliberalism: Politics beyond the Age of Greed* (London: Paradigm Publishers, 2008), pp. 63, 65, 71; SantaFe-Marie, "The 'Dems and Minorities Caused the Subprime Crisis' Smear—Fight Back. Updated 2x," *Daily Kos*, September 29, 2008, http://www.dailykos.com/story/2008/9/28/165119/719/709/613561 (accessed June 6, 2015).

51 Lynn Stuart Parramore, "The New Corrupt Elite That Is Running Our Economy," *AlterNet*, May 5, 2015, http://www.alternet.org/economy/new-corrupt-elite-running-our-economy (accessed June 29, 2015); Victoria Finkle, "The Long Shadow of Robert Rubin," *American Banker*, December 10, 2014, http://www.americanbanker.com/news/law-regulation/the-long-shadow-of-robert-rubin-1071601-1.html (accessed June 29, 2015); Aaron Bartley and Kevin Connor/Eyes on the Ties, "How Robert Rubin's Bright-Eyed Proteges Came to Dominate Wall Street," *Alternet*, March 15, 2009, http://www.alternet.org/story/131568/how_robert_rubin's_bright-eyed_proteges_came_to_dominate_wall_street/ (accessed October 4, 2015).

52 Parramore, "The New Corrupt Elite That Is Running Our Economy"; Rip Empson, "With an IPO on Its Radar, Lending Club Adds Former Treasury Secretary Larry Summers to Its Heavyweight Board," *Tech Crunch*, December 13, 2012, http://techcrunch.com/2012/12/13/with-an-ipo-on-its-radar-lending-club-adds-former-treasury-secretary-larry-summers-to-its-heavyweight-board/ (accessed June 29, 2015); Charles Ferguson, "Larry Summers and the Subversion of Economics," *The Chronicle of Higher Education*, October 3, 2010, http://chronicle.com/article/Larry-Summersthe/124790/ (accessed June 29, 2015); Greenwald, "Larry Summers, Tim Geithner and Wall Street's Ownership of Government"; Evelyn M. Rusli, "Summers Joins Andreessen Horowitz," *New York Times*, June 29, 2011, http://dealbook.nytimes.com/2011/06/29/larry-summers-joins-andreessen-horowitz/?hp (accessed June 29, 2015).

53 Larry Summer, "If We Really Valued Excellence, We Would Single It Out," http://larrysummers.com/2016/04/01/if-we-really-valued-excellence-we-would-single-it-out/ (accessed August 18, 2016).

54 Barofsky, *Bailout*; Banerjee and Katz, "Tim Geithner to Join Leveraged Buyout Firm Warburg Pincus"; Susan Milton, "Treasury Nominee Has Ties to Orleans," *Cape Cod Times*, November 25, 2008, http://www.capecodtimes.com/article//20081125/NEWS/811250313 (accessed June 29, 2015).

55 Brian Knowlton, "Geithner Is Pressed for Bailout Details," *New York Times*, February 11, 2009, http://www.nytimes.com/2009/02/12/business/economy/12treasury.html?gwh=ABC48BD8716A61A663FF07D10ACB1829 (accessed June 27, 2015); Corbett B. Daly, "Nobel Laureate Krugman Slams Geithner Bailout Plan," *Reuters*, March 23, 2009, http://www.reuters.com/article/2009/03/23/us-usa-financial-krugman-sb-idUSTRE52M4SS20090323 (accessed June 27, 2015).

56 Barofsky, *Bailout*, pp. 72, 98.

57 Michael A. Fletcher and Anthony Faiola, "Advisers to Obama Wary of Bonus Tax," *Washington Post*, March 23, 2009, http://www.washingtonpost.com/wp-dyn/content/article/2009/03/22/AR2009032201606.html (accessed June 27, 2015); Neil Barofsky, *Bailout*, pp. 181–182; Markin, "Bush/Obama and the Bank Bailout."

58 Barofsky, *Bailout*, pp. 90–91.

59 Jesse Eisinger, "Why Only One Top Banker Went to Jail for the Financial Crisis," *New York Times Magazine*, April 30, 2014, http://www.nytimes.com/2014/05/04/magazine/only-one-top-banker-jail-financial-crisis.html (accessed June 29, 2015); Gretchen Morgenson and Louise Story, "In Financial Crisis, No Prosecutions of Top Figures," *New York Times*, April 14, 2011, http://www.nytimes.com/2011/04/14/business/14prosecute.html (accessed June 29, 2015); David Dayen, "Eric Holder Didn't Send a Single Banker to Jail for the Mortgage Crisis. Is That Justice?" *Guardian*, September 25, 2014,

http://www.theguardian.com/money/us-money-blog/2014/sep/25/eric-holder-resign-mortgage-abuses-americans (accessed June 29, 2015).

60 Dayen, "Eric Holder Didn't Send a Single Banker to Jail"; Joint State-Federal National Mortgage Servicing Settlements, "About the Settlement," http://www.nationalmortgage settlement.com/about (accessed July 4, 2015); Eric T. Schneiderman, "Bank of America Deal a Victory for New York Families," *Huffington Post*, August 21, 2014, http://www. huffingtonpost.com/eric-t-schneiderman/bank-of-america-deal-a-vi_b_5698608. html (accessed July 4, 2015); Shahien Nasiripour, "Elizabeth Warren Teams with Arch Conservative on Bank Transparency Bill," *Huffington Post*, January 8, 2014, http://www. huffingtonpost.com/2014/01/08/elizabeth-warren-bank-settlements_n_4561584.html (accessed July 4, 2015); Ben Hallman, "'Historic' JP Morgan Settlement Won't Help Most of the Neediest Cases," *Huffington Post*, November 20, 2013, http://www.huffingtonpost. com/2013/11/20/jpmorgan-chase-settlement_n_4309511.html (accessed July 4, 2015).

61 Time Magazine Staff, "25 People to Blame for the Financial Crisis"; David Leonhardt, "Washington's Invisible Hand," *New York Times*, September 26, 2008, http://www. nytimes.com/2008/09/28/magazine/28wwln-reconsider.html (accessed July 5, 2015).

62 Parramore, "The New Corrupt Elite That Is Running Our Economy."

63 Elizabeth Warren, *A Fighting Chance* (New York: Metropolitan Books, 2014), passim; Hillary Chabot, "Harvard Trips on Roots of Elizabeth Warren's Family Tree," *Boston Herald*, April 27, 2012, http://www.bostonherald.com/news_opinion/us_politics/2012/04/ harvard_trips_roots_elizabeth_warren%E2%80%99s_family_tree (accessed October 4, 2015); Sally Jacobs "Elizabeth Warren's Family Has Mixed Memories About Heritage," *Boston Herald*, September 15, 2012, http://www.boston.com/news/politics/2012/ senate/2012/09/15/elizabeth-warren-family-has-mixed-memories-about-heritage/ cPMflfaOlndM1jFbimJ4tM/story.html (accessed October 4, 2015); Touré, "Elizabeth Warren, Scott Brown and the Myth of Race," *Time*, October 5, 2012, http://ideas.time. com/2012/10/05/elizabeth-warren-and-the-myth-of-race/ (accessed October 4, 2015).

64 Nasiripour, "Elizabeth Warren Teams with Arch Conservative"; Warren, *A Fighting Chance*.

65 Lois Beckett, "FDIC Chairwoman: Mortgage Industry 'Didn't Think Borrowers Were Worth Helping,'" *ProPublica*, July 13, 2011, http://www.propublica.org/blog/item/ fdic-chairwoman-mortgage-industry-didnt-think-borrowers-were-worth-helping (accessed June 30, 2015).

66 The Daily Bail Staff, "PBS Frontline: The Warning—How Greenspan, Summers & Rubin Conspired to Silence Derivatives Whistleblower Brooksley Born (Complete Video)," *The Daily Bail*, http://dailybail.com/home/pbs-frontline-the-warning-how-greenspan-sum mers-rubin-conspi.html (accessed June 29, 2015).

67 "2009 Profile in Courage Award Recipients Announced," *John F. Kennedy Presidential Library and Museum*, March 25, 2009, http://www.jfklibrary.org/About-Us/News-and-Press/Press-Releases/2009-Profile-in-Courage-Award-Recipients-Announced.aspx (accessed June 29, 2015).

68 Kevin Dugan, "Fed Whistleblower Quits Wall Street, Weighs Book," *New York Post*, March 20, 2015, http://nypost.com/2015/03/20/fed-whistleblower-quits-wall-street-weighs-book/ (accessed June 29, 2015); Jake Bernstein, "So Who Is Carmen Segarra? A Fed Whistleblower Q&A," *ProPublica*, October 28, 2013, http://www.propublica.org/ article/so-who-is-carmen-segarra-a-fed-whistleblower-qa (accessed June 29, 2015); Parramore, "The New Corrupt Elite That Is Running Our Economy."

69 Patricia Hill Collins, "Learning from the Outsider within: The Sociological Significance of Black Feminist Thought," *Social Problems* 33 (1986): 14–32. See Joe R. Feagin, *White Party, White Government: Race, Class, and U.S. Politics* (New York: Routledge, 2012), chapter 5.

70 Susan C. Strong, "Two American Dreams: Poison or Power?" http://www.opednews. com/articles/Two-American-Dreams--Pois-by-Susan-Strong-America_Anger_ Democracy_Equality-160128-14.html (accessed August 18, 2016).

71 "Transcript: Bill Clinton's Remarks at DNC," *CBS News*, September 6, 2012, http://www. cbsnews.com/news/transcript-bill-clintons-remarks-at-the-dnc/ (accessed April 18, 2015);

Kimberley Ducey, "Former Advisor Axelrod Warns White Racist Hostility to Obama Infects Politics," *RacismReview.com*, March 2, 2015, http://www.racismreview.com/blog/2015/03/02/former-adviser-axelrod-warns-white-racist-hostility-to-obama-infects-politics/ (accessed April 18, 2015).

72 Daniel J. Mitchell, "The American Dream Is Alive," *New York Times*, January 1, 2015, http://www.nytimes.com/roomfordebate/2015/01/01/is-the-modern-american-dream-attainable/the-american-dream-is-alive (accessed April 18, 2015).

73 Richard L. Zweigenhaft and G. William Domhoff, "Diversity and the New CEOs," *The Society Pages*, July 5, 2012, http://thesocietypages.org/papers/new-ceos/ (accessed June 26, 20–15); Nick Gass, "Carly Fiorina: 'Yes, I am Running for President,'" *Politico*, May 4, 2015, http://www.politico.com/story/2015/05/carly-fiorina-2016-presidential-bid-117593.html (accessed July 1, 2015).

74 Carrie Lukas, "Why Carly Fiorina's Feminism Flummoxes Liberals," *New York Post*, June 30, 2015, http://nypost.com/2015/06/30/why-carly-fiorinas-feminism-flummoxes-liberals/ (accessed July 1, 2015). See Carrie Lukas and Sabrina Schaeffer, *Liberty Is No War on Women* (Colorado Springs, CO: CreateSpace Independent Publishing Platform, 2012).

75 Tal Fortgang, "Checking My Privilege: Character as the Basis of Privilege," *The Princeton Tory*, April 2, 2014, http://theprincetontory.com/main/checking-my-privilege-character-as-the-basis-of-privilege/ (accessed April 9, 2015).

76 Fortgang, "Checking My Privilege"; Tal Fortgang, "Why I'll Never Apologize for My White Male Privilege," *Time*, May 2, 2014, http://time.com/85933/why-ill-never-apologize-for-my-white-male-privilege/ (accessed April 9, 2015); Katie McDonough, "'I'll Never Apologize for My White Privilege' Guy Is Basically Most of White America," *Salon*, May 4, 2015, http://www.salon.com/2014/05/04/ill_never_apologize_for_my_white_privilege_guy_is_basically_most_of_white_america/ (accessed April 9, 2015); Eva Epker, "Should Tal Fortgang Be Checking His Privilege?" *The Stanford Review*, May 21, 2014, http://stanfordreview.org/article/should-tal-fortgang-be-checking-his-privilege/ (accessed April 9, 2015); Violet Baudelaire, "To the Princeton Privileged Kid," May 1, 2014, *GroupThink*, http://groupthink.jezebel.com/to-the-princeton-privileged-kid-1570383740 (accessed April 9, 2015); Daniel Gastfriend, "Reflections on Privilege: An Open Letter to Tal Fortgang," *Huffington Post*, May 7, 2014, http://www.huffingtonpost.com/daniel-gastfriend/open-letter-tal-fortgang_b_5281169.html (accessed April 9, 2015); Briana Payton, "Dear Privileged-at-Princeton: You. Are. Privileged. And Meritocracy Is a Myth," *Time*, May 6, 2014, http://time.com/89482/dear-privileged-at-princeton-you-are-privileged-and-meritocracy-is-a-myth/ (accessed April 9, 2015); Michael D. Phillips, "In Response to Tal Fortgang," *The Daily Princetonian*, May 8, 2014, http://dailyprincetonian.com/opinion/2014/05/letter-to-the-editor-dear-tal-fortgang/ (accessed April 9, 2015); Rod Dreher, "Tal Fortgang, Yes!" *The American Conservative*, May 3, 2014, http://www.theamericanconservative.com/dreher/tal-fortgang-yes/ (accessed April 9, 2015); Mary Elizabeth Williams, "We Don't Need Your Apology Princeton Kid," *Salon*, May 5, 2014, http://www.salon.com/2014/05/05/we_dont_need_your_apology_princeton_kid/ (accessed April 9, 2015).

77 Howard Zinn, *You Can't Be Neutral on a Moving Train: A Personal History of Our Times* (Boston, MA: Beacon Press, 2002), p. 165.

78 John Blake, "Return of the Welfare Queen," *CNN*, January 23, 2012, http://www.cnn.com/2012/01/23/politics/weflare-queen/index.html (accessed April 18, 2015).

79 Kenneth J. Neubeck and Noël A. Cazenave, *Welfare Racism: Playing the Race Card against America's Poor* (New York: Routledge Press, 2001). This concept was first accented by Philomena Essed in *Understanding Everyday Racism* (Newbury Park, CA: Sage, 1991).

80 Blake, "Return of the Welfare Queen."

81 Michael Lind, "How the South Skews America: We'd Be Less Violent, More Mobile and in General More Normal If Not for Dixie," *Politico Magazine*, July 3, 2015, http://www.politico.com/magazine/story/2015/07/how-the-south-skews-america-119725_Page2.html (accessed July 5, 2015).

82 Rana Foroohar, *Makers and Takers* (New York: Crown Business, 2016).

83 Jonathan D. Ostry, Prakash Loungani, and Davide Furceri, "Neoliberalism: Oversold?" *Finance & Development 53* (2016), http://www.imf.org/external/pubs/ft/fandd/2016/06/ostry.htm (accessed August 18, 2016).

84 David Colander et alia, "The Financial Crisis and the Systemic Failure of Academic Economics," *Kiel Institute for the World Economy*, https://www.ifw-kiel.de/ (accessed April 12, 2016), p. 2.

85 PWCGlobal, "A Marketplace without Boundaries? Responding to Disruption," *PWC-Global*, http://www.pwc.com/gx/en/ceo-survey/2015/assets/pwc-18th-annual-global-ceo-survey-jan-2015.pdf (accessed August 18, 2016), p. 9.

86 Sharon Beder, *Free Market Missionaries: The Corporate Manipulation of Community Values* (London: Earthscan, 2006), p. 151. See Feagin, *The White Racial Frame*, p. 10.

87 "Three Rich Treasury Secretaries Laugh It Up Over Income Inequality," *Headlines News*, May 9, 2015, https://www.headlines-news.com/2015/09/05/251179/three-rich-treasury-secretaries-laugh-it-up-over-income-inequality (accessed January 27, 2017).

88 Swanson, *Poor-Bashing*, p. 78.

6 The Politics of Systemic Racism: Domestic Change and Reaction

1 "Presidency of the United States of America," *Encyclopedia Britannica Online*, 2010 (accessed December 22, 2010). See Joe R. Feagin, *White Party, White Government: Race, Class, and U.S. Politics* (New York: Routledge, 2012), chapter 3.

2 Quoted in David D. Porter, "What Must Blacks Go Through? An Experiment Will Let You See," *Orlando Sentinel*, September 13, 1989, p. G1. Italics added.

3 Edward Herman, "The Propaganda Model Revisited," *Monthly Review 48* (July 1996): 115; Sidney Blumenthal, *The Rise of the Counter-Establishment* (New York: Times Books, 1986), pp. 4–11, 133–170; Peter Steinfels, *The Neoconservatives: The Men Who Are Changing America's Politics* (New York: Touchstone, 1979), pp. 214–277; Joe R. Feagin, *The White Racial Frame: Centuries of Racial Framing and Counter-Framing*, 2nd edn. (New York: Routledge, 2013), Chapter 3.

4 Ted Glick, "Racism and the Presidential Elections," *The Black Commentator*, Issue 106 (September 23, 2004), http://www.blackcommentator.com/106/106_racewire.html (accessed May 12, 2015).

5 Derrick Bell, "*Brown v. Board of Education* and the Interest Convergence Dilemma," *Harvard Law Review 93* (1980): 518.

6 Ibid., p. 518.

7 Tali Mendelberg, *The Race Card: Campaign Strategy, Implicit Messages, and the Norm of Equality* (Princeton, NJ: Princeton University Press, 2001), p. 13.

8 Stanford University, "February 13, 1964 Richard Nixon Criticizes the Tactics of Civil Rights Leaders," *Martin Luther King Jr. and the Global Freedom Struggle*, http://kingencyclopedia.stanford.edu/encyclopedia/chronologyentry/1964_02_13/ (accessed June 22, 2015).

9 Kevin Phillips, *The Emerging Republican Majority* (New Rochelle, NY: Arlington House, 1969).

10 Ibid., pp. 103–105; Joseph A. Aistrup, *The Southern Strategy Revisited* (Lexington, KY: University Press of Kentucky, 1996), p. 9; and "The Middle Americans," *Time*, January 5, 1970, http://www.time.com/time/subscriber/personoftheyear/archive/stories/1969.html (accessed February 4, 2011).

11 Earl Ofari Hutchinson, "The Nixon Tapes, Racism and The Republicans," *Alternet*, December 18, 2003, http://www.alternet.org/story/17422 (accessed July 7, 2011).

12 Ted Kopell, "Nightline: The Haldeman Diaries," *ABC News*, May 16, 1994, https://tvnews.vanderbilt.edu/broadcasts/647816 (accessed July 7, 2011).

13 Kenneth O'Reilly, *Nixon's Piano: Presidents and Racial Politics from Washington to Clinton* (New York: Free Press, 1995), pp. 6–7. See also Bruce Oudes, ed., *From: The President: President Nixon's Secret Files* (New York: Harper and Row, 1989), p. 451ff.

14 Tim Cox, "Rights Groups Cautious about 'Odd Couple' Appearances," *United Press International*, November 22, 1988.

15 Peter G. Bourne, *Jimmy Carter: A Comprehensive Biography from Plains to Post-Presidency* (New York: Scribner, 1997), pp. 132–140.

16 Ted Glick, "Racism and the Presidential Elections."

17 "Jimmy Carter on Civil Rights President of the U.S., 1977–1981," *On the Issues*, http://www.ontheissues.org/Celeb/Jimmy_Carter_Civil_Rights.htm (accessed June 23, 2015).

18 Robert Hager (Reporter) and Chuck Scarborough (Anchor), "Jimmy Carter Doing Damage Control for 'Ethnic Purity' Remarks," *NBC Today Show*, April 9, 1976, https://archives.nbclearn.com/portal/site/k-12/browse/?cuecard=33592 (accessed September 10, 2015).

19 Christian James, *Civil Rights during the Carter Administration, 1977–1981* (Bethesda, MD: LexisNexis, 2007), pp. vi–viii.

20 Sara Bondioli, "Jimmy Carter: Southern White Men Turn to the GOP Because of 'Race,'" *Huffington Post*, April 10, 2014, http://www.huffingtonpost.com/2014/04/10/jimmy-carter-gop-race_n_5125582.html (accessed June 16, 2015).

21 Bondioli, "Jimmy Carter"; see also Bourne, *Jimmy Carter*, pp. 132–145.

22 Kyle Longley, Jeremy D. Mayer, Michael Schaller, and John W. Sloan, *Deconstructing Reagan: Conservative Mythology and America's Fortieth President* (Armonk, NY: M.E. Sharpe, 2006), p. 78. We also draw on Feagin, *White Party, White Government*, passim.

23 Quoted in Bob Herbert, "The Ugly Side of the G.O.P.," *New York Times*, September 25, 2007, http://www.nytimes.com/2007/09/25/opinion/25herbert.html (accessed June 19, 2011).

24 Steven Neal, "D-e-a-v-e-r Spells Insensitivity," *Chicago Tribune*, May 9, 1985, Zone C, p. 19; Terrel Bell, *The Thirteenth Man* (New York: Free Press, 1988), pp. 104–105.

25 Michelle Alexander, *The New Jim Crow: Mass Incarceration in the Age of Colorblindness* (New York: New Press, 2010), p. 49; and Naomi Murakawa, "The Origins of the Carceral Crisis: Racial Order as 'Law and Order' in Postwar American Politics," in *Race and American Political Development*, eds. Joseph Lowndes, Julie Novkov, and Dorian Warren (New York: Routledge, 2008), pp. 236–248.

26 Nicholas Pell, "The 10 Dumbest, Most Offensive Political Ads in Recent Memory," *Alternet*, December 27, 2011, http://www.alternet.org/story/153584/the_10_dumbest%2C_most_offensive_political_ads_in_recent_memory (accessed June 22, 2015); Susan Faludi, "Hillary Plays the Winning Gender Card," *The Los Angeles Times*, November 9, 2007, http://www.latimes.com/news/la-oe-faludi9nov09-story.html (accessed June 20, 2015).

27 Beth Schwartzapfel and Bill Keller, "Willie Horton Revisited," *The Marshall Project*, May 13, 2013, https://www.themarshallproject.org/2015/05/13/willie-horton-revisited (accessed June 20, 2015); Roger Simon, "How a Murderer and Rapist Became the Bush Campaign's Most Valuable Player," *The Baltimore Sun*, November 11, 1990, http://articles.baltimoresun.com/1990-11-11/features/1990315149_1_willie-horton-fournier-michael-dukakis (accessed June 23, 2015).

28 "Center to Protect Patient Rights Grantees," *Los Angeles Times*, May 27, 2012, http://spreadsheets.latimes.com/cppr-funding/ (accessed September 10, 2015); Peter H. Stone, "Fine Line between Politics and Issues Spending by Secretive 501(c)(4) Groups," *The Center for Public Integrity*, October 31, 2011, http://www.publicintegrity.org/2011/10/31/7205/fine-line-between-politics-and-issues-spending-secretive-501c4-groups (accessed September 10, 2015); Lee Fang, "New Pro-Romney Super PAC Run by Operative Behind Racist Willie Horton, 'Ground Zero Mosque' Ads," *Think Progress*, June 27, 2011, http://thinkprogress.org/politics/2011/06/27/254046/romney-super-pac-racist/ (accessed September 10, 2015).

29 Wisconsin Public Television, "The 30 Second Candidate," *PBS*, http://www.pbs.org/30secondcandidate/timeline/years/1990.html (accessed May 12, 2015); Keli Goff, "7 of History's Most Racist Political Ads," *The Root*, October 2, 2012, http://www.theroot.com/blogs/blogging_the_beltway/2012/10/racist_political_ads_7_top_contenders.html (accessed May 12, 2015).

30 Harvey B. Gantt, "Interview C-0008. Southern Oral History Program Collection (#4007)," Southern Oral History Program Collection, Southern Historical Collection, Wilson Library, University of North Carolina, January 6, 1986.

31 David S. Broder, "Jesse Helms, White Racist," *Washington Post*, July 7, 2008, http://www.washingtonpost.com/wp-dyn/content/article/2008/07/06/AR2008070602321.html (accessed June 22, 2015).

32 Quoted in Kevin Sack, "South's Embrace of G.O.P. Is Near a Turning Point," *New York Times*, March 16, 1998, p. A1.

33 Quoted in "Rap's Sister Souljah Raps Clinton's Rebuke," UPI press release, June 16, 1992; "Sister Souljah: In the Eye of the Storm," *Larry King Live*, June 19, 1992.

34 Joan Vennochi, "Sister Souljah Moments," *Boston Globe*, September 16, 2007, http://www.boston.com/news/nation/articles/2007/09/16/sister_souljah_moments/ (accessed June 16, 2015); Matt Bai, "Jeb and the Myth of the Sister Souljah Moment," *Yahoo News*, January 29, 2015, http://news.yahoo.com/jeb-and-the-myth-of-the-sister-souljah-moment-001041049.html (accessed June 16, 2015); Vennochi, "Sister Souljah Moments."

35 "Sister Souljah," Crier & Company, *CNN*, July 2, 1992.

36 Quoted in Michael Posner, "Jesse Jackson Hints He Might Not Back Clinton," *Reuters Library Report*, June 17, 1992.

37 Glick, "Racism and the Presidential Elections"; New York Times Staff, "The 1992 Campaign: Democrats; Club Where Clinton Has Golfed Retains Ways of Old South," *New York Times*, March 23, 1992, http://www.nytimes.com/1992/03/23/us/1992-campaign-democrats-club-where-clinton-has-golfed-retains-ways-old-south.html (accessed June 20, 2015); Paul Frymer, *Uneasy Alliances: Race and Party Competition in America* (Princeton, NJ: Princeton University Press, 1999), pp. 4–6, 43, 89–99, 137. See Joe R. Feagin, Hernán Vera, and Pinar Batur, *White Racism: The Basics*, 2nd edn. (New York: Routledge, 2000), passim.

38 Bai, "Jeb and the Myth of the Sister Souljah Moment."

39 Charles M. Blow, "War against Whites? I Think Not," *New York Times*, August 6, 2014, http://www.nytimes.com/2014/08/07/opinion/charles-blow-war-against-whites-i-think-not.html (accessed September 11, 2015).

40 See Joe R. Feagin, *How Blacks Built America: Labor, Culture, Freedom, and Democracy* (New York: Routledge, 2016); and Joan Biskupic, "Reagan's Influence Lives on in U.S. Courts," *USA News*, May 12, 2008, http://usatoday30.usatoday.com/news/washington/judicial/2008-05-11-appellate-judges_N.htm (accessed June 22, 2015).

41 Feagin, Vera, and Batur, *White Racism*, pp. 182–185; David Garrow, "Lani Guinier," *The Progressive*, September 1993, p. 28.

42 Ron Christie, *Black in the White House* (Nashville, TN: Nelson Current, 2006), p. 122. Feagin, *White Party, White Government*.

43 Jordan T. Camp, "'We Know This Place': Neoliberal Racial Regimes and the Katrina Circumstance," *American Quarterly* 61 (September 2009): 693–717.

44 Office of Civil Rights Evaluation, U.S. Commission on Civil Rights Redefining Rights in America, "The Civil Rights Record of the George W. Bush Administration, 2001–2004," http://www.thememoryhole.org/pol/usccr_redefining_rights.pdf (accessed April 12, 2005).

45 David Corn, *The Lies of George W. Bush: Mastering the Politics of Deception* (New York: Crown, 2003), p. 66.

46 Chandler Davidson, Tanya Dunlap, Gale Kenny, and Benjamin Wise, "Republican Ballot Security Programs: Vote Protection or Minority Vote Suppression—or Both? A Report to the Center for Voting Rights & Protection," September 2004, http://www.votelaw.com/blog/blogdocs/GOP_Ballot_Security_Programs.pdf (accessed December 30, 2016), pp. 96–106 and passim. See also Feagin, *White Party, White Government*, especially Chapter 7.

47 Faludi, "Hillary Plays the Winning Gender Card."

48 Ibid.

49 Max Blumenthal, *Republican Gomorrah: Inside the Movement That Shattered the Party* (New York: Nation Books, 2010), Kindle loc. 4816–4817; Jim Brunner "Snohomish County GOP Pulls '$3 Bills' Smearing Obama from Fair Booth," *Seattle Times*, August 27, 2008, http://seattletimes.nwsource.com/html/localnews/2008140846_fair27m0.html (accessed April 26, 2011).

50 Ed Pilkington, "Racial Fear Has Infected US Politics and Made Obama's Job Harder, Axelrod Says," *Guardian*, February 10, 2015, http://www.theguardian.com/us-news/2015/feb/10/obama-axelrod-racial-fear-american-politics (accessed June 16, 2015).

51 Ibid.

52 CNN Staff, "Carter Again Cites Racism as Factor in Obama's Treatment," *CNN.com*, September 19, 2009, *CNN*, http://www.cnn.com/2009/POLITICS/09/15/carter.obama/index.html (accessed June 16, 2015); see also Ewen MacAskill, "Jimmy Carter: Animosity towards Barack Obama Is Due to Racism," *Guardian*, September 16, 2009, http://www.theguardian.com/world/2009/sep/16/jimmy-carter-racism-barack-obama (accessed June 16, 2015).

53 Russ Mitchell, "King Announced Bid for Fourth Term," *The Daily Reporter*, March 8, 2008, http://www.spencerdailyreporter.com/story/1316727.html (accessed June 18, 2015). Italics added.

54 Gebe Martinez, "Why Is the GOP Slighting Hispanics?" *Politico*, August 4, 2009, http://www.politico.com/news/stories/0809/25745_Page2.html (accessed June 18, 2015).

55 Jonathan Capehart, "Rep. Mo Brooks Talks 'War on Whites' as the GOP Loses the Battle for Votes," *Washington Post*, August 4, 2014, http://www.washingtonpost.com/blogs/post-partisan/wp/2014/08/04/rep-mo-brooks-talks-war-on-whites-as-the-gop-loses-the-battle-for-votes/ (accessed May 13, 2015).

56 Eric Kleefeld, "Hillary Supporter Cuomo: Obama Tried to 'Shuck and Jive' with Media," *Huffington Post*, March 28, 2008, http://www.huffingtonpost.com/2008/01/10/hillary-supporter-cuomo-o_n_80914.html (accessed June 23, 2015).

57 Roland Martin, "Martin: 'Shucking and Jiving' and the Campaign Trail," *CNN*, January 11, 2008, http://politicalticker.blogs.cnn.com/2008/01/11/martin-shucking-and-jiving-and-the-campaign-trail/ (accessed June 20, 2015).

58 Amelia Thomson-DeVeaux, "Obama and Romney Spar over the American Dream," *Public Religion Research Institute*, December 8, 2011, http://publicreligion.org/2011/12/obama-and-romney-spar-over-the-american-dream/#.VSzrAJOncaY (accessed April 14, 2015).

59 John Blake, "Return of the Welfare Queen," *CNN*, January 23, 2012, http://www.cnn.com/2012/01/23/politics/weflare-queen/index.html (accessed April 18, 2015).

60 Ibid.

61 Ibid. Italics added.

62 Jack White, "The Hot Un-Ghetto Mess!" *The Root*, May 19, 2011, http://www.theroot.com/articles/culture/2011/05/schwarzenegger_gingrich_strausskahn_white_people_behaving_badly.2.html (accessed August 9, 2015).

63 Claudio E. Cabrera, "Judge Admits Sending Racist Email About Obama," *The Root*, March 1, 2012, http://www.theroot.com/racist-obama-emails-judge-richard-cebull (accessed March 2, 2012); Lucy Madison "Orange County GOP Official Refuses to Resign over Racist Email," *Los Angeles Wave, Wire Services*, April 19, 2011, http://www.wavenewspapers.com/news/orange-county-racist-ape-chimp-email-gop-republican-obama-davenport-119993794.html (accessed February 10, 2012).

64 Eric Alterman, "Right-Wing Racism: Past, Present—and Future," *The Nation*, February 29, 2012, http://www.thenation.com/article/166524/right-wing-racism-past-present-and-future# (accessed June 20, 2015).

65 Sam Levine, "GOP Congressman Accuses Democrats of Waging a 'War on Whites,'" *Huffington Post*, August 4, 2014, http://www.huffingtonpost.com/2014/08/04/mo-brooks-war-on-whites_n_5647967.html (accessed May 11, 2015).

66 Devin Burghart, "Tea Party Nation Warns of White Anglo-Saxon Protestant 'Extinction,'" *IREHR*, March 29, 2011, http://www.irehr.org/issue-areas/tea-parties/19-news/76-tea-party-nation-warns-of-white-anglo-saxon-protestant-extinction (accessed April 15, 2011).

67 Tara Culp-Ressler, "Scott Walker: Denying Health Care to Low-Income People Helps Them 'Live the American Dream,'" *ThinkProgress*, November 14, 2014, http://thinkprogress.org/health/2014/11/14/3592511/scott-walker-medicaid-expansion/ (accessed April 2, 2015); Sabrina Tavernise and Robert Gebeloff, "Millions of Poor Are Left

Uncovered by Health Law," *New York Times*, October 2, 2013, http://www.nytimes.com/2013/10/03/health/millions-of-poor-are-left-uncovered-by-health-law.html (accessed April 2, 2015).

68 Chris Hoenig, "'Blacks Don't Work and Get Crazy Welfare Checks' Quote Taken Out of Context?" *DiversityInc*, February 18, 2015, http://www.diversityinc.com/news/blacks-dont-work-get-crazy-welfare-checks-quote-taken-context/ (accessed June 16, 2015).

69 Leslie H. Picca and Joe Feagin, *Two-Faced Racism: Whites in the Backstage and Frontstage* (New York: Routledge, 2007).

70 Jennifer Huffman, "Miss Napa Valley Caught in Super Bowl Ad Debacle," *NapaValleyRegister.com*, February 16, 2012, http://napavalleyregister.com/news/local/miss-napa-valley-caught-in-super-bowl-ad-debacle/article_7a733ab6-586d-11e1-a96f-0019bb2963f4.html (accessed June 18, 2015).

71 Ibid.

72 Michael Lind, "How the South Skews America: We'd Be Less Violent, More Mobile and in General More Normal If Not for Dixie," *Politico Magazine*, July 3, 2015, http://www.politico.com/magazine/story/2015/07/how-the-south-skews-america-119725_Page2.html (accessed July 5, 2015).

73 Quoted in Lind, "How the South Skews America."

74 Sean Elias, email communication, August 18, 2016.

75 See Rosalind S. Chou and Joe R. Feagin, *The Myth of the Model Minority: Asian Americans Facing Racism*, 2nd edn. (New York: Paradigm-Routledge, 2015).

76 Wisconsin Public Television Staff, "Interview with Alex Castellanos (part 1)," *PBS Online*, http://www.pbs.org/30secondcandidate/q_and_a/castellanos1.html (accessed June 16, 2015).

77 Heather Digby Parton, "GOP's Grotesque Racist Ads: Why It Just Can't Escape Its Ugly History," *Salon*, October 22, 2014, http://www.salon.com/2014/10/22/gops_grotesque_new_racist_ad_why_it_just_cant_escape_its_ugly_history/ (accessed June 17, 2015); Eric Boehlert, "Going Negative," *Salon*, March 15, 2004, http://www.salon.com/2004/03/16/castellanos_3/ (accessed June 17, 2015).

78 Ibid.

79 Lloyd Marcus, "The Left's War on White America," *RenewAmerica.com*, February 27, 2015, http://www.renewamerica.com/columns/marcus/150227 (accessed June 17, 2015).

80 PBS Staff, "People & Events: The Civil War and Emancipation 1861–1865," *PBS Online*, http://www.pbs.org/wgbh/aia/part4/4p2967.html (accessed June 21, 2015); "Teaching with Documents: Black Soldiers in the Civil War," *National Archives*, http://www.archives.gov/education/lessons/blacks-civil-war/ (accessed June 17, 2015); Elsie Freeman, Wynell Burroughs Schamel, and Jean West, "The Fight for Equal Rights: A Recruiting Poster for Black Soldiers in the Civil War," *Social Education 56*, no. 2 (February 1992): 118–120.

81 Henry Louis Gates Jr., "Who Really Ran the Underground Railroad?" *The Root*, March 25, 2013, http://www.theroot.com/articles/history/2013/03/who_really_ran_the_underground_railroad.html (accessed June 17, 2015).

82 Lloyd Marcus, "The War on Rich White Men," December 16, 2013, *TeaParty.org*, http://www.teaparty.org/war-rich-white-men-32034/ (accessed May 11, 2015).

83 Alexandra Jaffe and Ben Kamisar, "NRCC Releases Willie Horton-Style Ad in Nebraska House Race," *The Hill*, October 17, 2014, http://thehill.com/blogs/ballot-box/campaign-ads/221063-nrcc-releases-willie-horton-style-ad-in-nebraska-house-race (accessed May 12, 2015).

84 Ibid.

85 M. Blow, "War Against Whites? I Think Not."

86 For social science evidence, see Joe R. Feagin, *Racist America: Roots, Current Realities, and Future Reparations*, 3rd edn. (New York: Routledge, 2014).

87 Jackson Katz, "Politics Is a Contact Sport," in *Media/Cultural Studies: Critical Approaches*, eds. Rhonda Hammer and Douglas Kellner (New York: Peter Lang, 2009), pp. 539, 543, 548.

88 Dan Balz, "Politics Is the Great Divider in United States," *Washington Post*, June 4, 2012, https://www.washingtonpost.com/politics/politics-is-the-great-divider-in-united-states/2012/06/04/gJQALpKSEV_story.html (accessed January 27, 2017).
89 W. E. B. du Bois, *Darkwater: Voices from within the Veil* (New York: Harcourt, Brace & Co., 1920), Kindle loc. 434–458.

7 Seeking the American Dream: The Case of African Americans

1 Martin Luther King Jr., "Letter from a Birmingham Jail," *African Studies Center—University of Pennsylvania*, http://www.africa.upenn.edu/Articles_Gen/Letter_Birmingham.html (accessed April 15, 2015).
2 See for example, Dan Geringer, "King's 'Letter from Birmingham Jail' Contrasts Sharply with More Famous 'Dream' Speech," *Philly.com*, January 21, 2014, http://articles.philly.com/2014-01-21/news/46377839_1_dream-speech-king-birmingham-jail (accessed May 5, 2015).
3 Richard Nordquist, "10 Things You Should Know about Dr. King's 'I Have a Dream' Speech," *About Education*, http://grammar.about.com/od/essaysonstyle/a/Ten-Things-You-Should-Know-About-Dr-King-S-I-Have-A-Dream-Speech.htm (accessed April 15, 2015).
4 Lester Spence, "For Black People, There Is Martin Luther King's Dream," *New York Times*, January 1, 2015, http://www.nytimes.com/roomfordebate/2015/01/01/is-the-modern-american-dream-attainable/for-black-people-there-is-martin-luther-kings-dream (accessed April 18, 2015).
5 See George Lakoff, *Women, Fire, and Dangerous Things: What Categories Reveal about the Mind* (Chicago, IL: University of Chicago Press, 1987), pp. 8–86.
6 Woodrow Wilson, "The Meaning of a Liberal Education," *High School Teachers Association of New York 3* (1908–1909): 19–31.
7 We draw in this chapter on Joe R. Feagin, *The White Racial Frame: Centuries of Racial Framing and Counter-Framing*, 2nd edn. (New York: Routledge, 2013), pp. x, 3–40.
8 See William Henry Chafe, *The Unfinished Journey: America Since World War II* (New York: Oxford University Press, 2003), p. 354.
9 Civil Rights 101, "School Desegregation and Equal Educational Opportunity," *The Leadership Conference*, http://www.civilrights.org/resources/civilrights101/desegregation.html (accessed May 5, 2015).
10 Ronald L. Heinemann, "Moton School Strike and Prince Edward County School Closings," *Encyclopedia Virginia*, http://www.encyclopediavirginia.org/Moton_School_Strike_and_Prince_Edward_County_School_Closings (accessed May 11, 2015).
11 Smithsonian National Museum of History, "Black Students on Strike! Farmville, Virginia," http://americanhistory.si.edu/brown/history/4-five/farmville-virginia-1.html (accessed May 11, 2015).
12 Heinemann, "Moton School Strike and Prince Edward County School Closings."
13 University of Richmond, "Prince Edward Free Schools Association," *History Engine*, 2008–2009, http://historyengine.richmond.edu/episodes/view/4444 (accessed May 6, 2015); Donald P. Baker, "Shame of a Nation, about Brown v. Board of Education," *Race Matters*, March 4, 2001, http://www.racematters.org/shameofanation.htm (accessed May 6, 2015); David Pembroke Neff, "The Defenders of State Sovereignty and Individual Liberties," *Encyclopedia Virginia*, http://www.encyclopediavirginia.org/Defenders_of_State_Sovereignty_and_Individual_Liberties (accessed May 7, 2015).
14 Civil Rights 101, "School Desegregation and Equal Educational Opportunity"; Virginia Historical Society, "The Closing of Prince Edward County's Schools," http://www.vahistorical.org/collections-and-resources/virginia-history-explorer/civil-rights-movement-virginia/closing-prince (accessed May 6, 2015); University of Richmond, "Prince Edward Free Schools Association"; P. Baker, "Shame of a Nation, about Brown v. Board of Education."
15 See Aldon Morris, "A Retrospective on the Civil Rights Movement: Political and Intellectual Landmarks," *Annual Review of Sociology 25* (1999): 538.

16 Baker, "Shame of a Nation, about Brown v. Board of Education."

17 The quotes here are from Baker, "Shame of a Nation, about Brown v. Board of Education."

18 Ralph Ellison, "*An American Dilemma*: A Review," in *The Collected Essays of Ralph Ellison*, ed. J.F. Callahan (New York: Random House, 2011), p. 328.

19 Rucker C. Johnson, "Long-Run Impacts of School Desegregation & School Quality on Adult Attainments," *National Bureau of Economic Research*, Working Paper No. 16664, January 2011, http://www.nber.org/papers/w16664.pdf (accessed April 4, 2015); Nikole Hannah-Jones, "Segregation Now," *ProPublica*, April 16, 2014, http://www.propublica.org/article/segregation-now-full-text (accessed April 4, 2015).

20 Gary Orfield, Erica Frankenberg, Jongyeon Ee, and John Kuscera, "*Brown* at 60: Great Progress, a Long Retreat and an Uncertain Future," *The Civil Rights Project/Proyecto Derechos Civiles*, May 15, 2014, http://civilrightsproject.ucla.edu/research/k-12-education/integration-and-diversity/brown-at-60-great-progress-a-long-retreat-and-an-uncertain-future/Brown-at-60-051814.pdf (accessed April 2, 2015). See especially p. 10. See also Ary Spatig-Amerikaner, "Unequal Education: Federal Loophole Enables Lower Spending on Students of Color," *Center for American Progress*, August 2012, https://cdn.americanprogress.org/wp-content/uploads/2012/08/UnequalEduation.pdf (accessed April 2, 2015). We draw on pp. 2–3, 7.

21 Feagin, *The White Racial Frame*, pp. 84–85; Hannah-Jones, "Segregation Now."

22 Feagin, *The White Racial Frame*, p. 2.

23 California Newsreel, "The House We Live In," *Race—The Power of an Illusion*, http://newsreel.org/transcripts/race3.htm (accessed April 13, 2015).

24 Ibid.; Feagin, *The White Racial Frame*, p. 36.

25 Heber Brown III, "James Baldwin: Urban Renewal Means Negro Removal," *Faith in Action*, http://faithinactiononline.com/2008/01/james-baldwin-urban-renewal-means-negro-removal/ (accessed April 13, 2015); American Experience, "Kenneth Clark Interview with James Baldwin," *PBS.org*, http://www.pbs.org/wgbh/amex/mlk/sfeature/sf_video_pop_04b_tr_qt.html (accessed April 13, 2015); Newsreel, "Episode Three: The House We Live In"; DetroitYES!, "8 Mile Road," http://www.detroityes.com/webisodes/2002/8mile/021106-04-8mile-berlin-wall.php (accessed April 13, 2015).

26 U.S. Department of Housing and Urban Development, "Fair Housing—It's Your Right," *HUD.gov*, http://portal.hud.gov/hudportal/HUD?src=/program_offices/fair_housing_equal_opp/FHLaws/yourrights (accessed April 5, 2015); Newsreel, "Episode Three: The House We Live In."

27 John R. Logan and Brian Stults, *The Persistence of Segregation in the Metropolis: New Findings from the 2010 Census: Census Brief Prepared for Project US2010* (Providence, RI: Brown University, 2011), pp. 2–3.

28 National Commission on Fair Housing and Equal Opportunity, "Report, 2008," as summarized in Gary Orfield, *Reviving the Goal of an Integrated Society: A 21st-Century Challenge* (Los Angeles, CA: UCLA Civil Rights Project, 2009), p. 5.

29 Gregory D. Squires, personal communication; Sunwoong Kim and Gregory D. Squires, "The Color of Money and the People Who Lent It," *Journal of Housing Research 9* (1998): 271–284; Trevor Delaney, "Subprime Lenders under Fire," *Black Enterprise* (October 2007): 31–32; Vikas Bajaj and Ford Fessenden, "What's Behind the Race Gap?" *New York Times*, November 4, 2007, p. 16.

30 Martin D. Abravanel and Mary K. Cunningham, *How Much Do We Know? Public Awareness of the Nation's Fair Housing Laws* (Washington, DC: U.S. Department of Housing and Urban Development, 2002), p. 20.

31 "The Multi-City Study of Urban Inequality," *Russell Sage Foundation Newsletter* (Fall 1999): 2; Shanna L. Smith, National Fair Housing Alliance, "Testimony before the House Financial Services Committee, Subcommittee on Housing and Community Opportunity," February 28, 2006, www.house.gov/financialservices/media/pdf/022806ss.pdf (accessed May 18, 2009); Margery Austin Turner et al., *Housing Discrimination against Racial and Ethnic Minorities 2012* (Washington, DC: U.S. Department of Housing and Urban Development, 2013), pp. 1–5.

32 Robert J. Sampson, *Great American City: Chicago and the Enduring Neighborhood Effect* (Chicago, IL: University of Chicago Press, 2012); Patrick Sharkey, *Stuck in*

Place: Urban Neighborhoods and the End of Progress toward Racial Equality (Chicago, IL: University of Chicago Press, 2013); Richard Florida, "The Persistent Geography of Disadvantage," *The Atlantic, CityLab*, July 23, 2013, http://www.citylab.com/housing/2013/07/persistent-geography-disadvantage/6231/ (accessed April 5, 2015).

33 "From Jim Crow Jobs to Employment Equity: How to Create Quality Jobs for Everyone," *Center for Social Inclusion (CSI)*, October 2011, pp. 1–18, http://www.centerforsocial inclusion.org/wp-content/uploads/2012/07/From_Jim_Crow_Jobs_to_Employment_ Equity.pdf (accessed April 2, 2015); Working Partnerships USA, "Tech's Diversity Problem: More than Meets the Eye," http://wpusa.org/WPUSA_TechsDiversityProblem.pdf (accessed April 2, 2015).

34 Adia Harvey Wingfield, *Doing Business with Beauty: Black Women, Hair Salons, and the Racial Enclave Economy* (Lanham, MD: Rowman and Littlefield, 2008).

35 Joe R. Feagin, *How Blacks Built America* (New York: Routledge, 2016), pp. 16–42; *Racist America: Roots, Current Realities, and Future Reparations*, 3rd edn. (New York: Routledge, 2014), pp. 178–189; Tim Wise, "Commentary," http://academic.udayton.edu/ race/01race/white10.htm (accessed November 24, 2004).

36 Stevie Watson, Osei Appiah, and Corliss G. Thornton, "The Effect of Name on Pre-Interview Impressions and Occupational Stereotypes: The Case of Black Sales Job Applicants," *Journal of Applied Social Psychology* 41 (2011): 2405–2420.

37 Marc Bendick, Jr., "Situation Testing for Employment Discrimination in the United States of America," *Revue Horizons Stratégiques, Centre D'analyse Stratégique* (July 2007): 6–18; Marc Bendick, Jr., Mary Lou Egan, and Suzanne Lofhjelm, "Workforce Diversity Training: From Anti-Discrimination Compliance to Organization Development," *Human Resource Planning* 24 (2001): 10–25.

38 Nancy DiTomaso, *The American Non-Dilemma: Racial Inequality without Racism* (New York: Russell Sage Foundation, 2013); Nancy DiTomaso, "The Great Divide: How Social Networks Drive Black Unemployment," *New York Times*, May 5, 2013, http://opinion ator.blogs.nytimes.com/2013/05/05/how-social-networks-drive-black-unemployment/ (accessed April 2, 2015).

39 Dom Apollon, "Colorlines.com Survey: What Explains Racial Disparities?" *Colorlines*, August 15, 2011, http://colorlines.com/archives/2011/08/poll_unity_on_american_ dream_dissolves_when_explaining_failures.html (accessed April 2, 2015).

40 Claud Anderson, *Black Labor, White Wealth* (Edgewood, MD: Duncan & Duncan, 1994), p. 97. See also Feagin, *How Blacks Built America*, pp. 15–48.

41 Jackson Turner Main, *Social Structure of Revolutionary America* (Princeton: Princeton University Press, 1965), pp. 286–87; Peter H. Lindert and Jeffrey G. Williamson, "Three Centuries of American Inequality," *Institute for Research on Poverty Discussion Papers* (Madison, WI: University of Wisconsin Press, 1976), pp. 18–31.

42 Erin Currier, "The Numbers Show Rags-to-Riches Happens Only in the Movies," *New York Times*, January 1, 2015, http://www.nytimes.com/roomfordebate/2015/01/01/is-the-modern-american-dream-attainable/the-numbers-show-rags-to-riches-happens-only-in-movies (accessed April 18, 2015); Larry Schwartz, "35 Mind-Blowing Facts about Inequality," *Alternet*, July 13, 2015, http://www.alternet.org/economy/35-mind-blowing-facts-about-inequality (accessed August 9, 2015).

43 "Interactive Race Graphic," *Urban Institute*, 2014, http://www.urban.org/changing-wealth-americans/lost-generations-interactive-race.cfm (accessed April 4, 2015); Sean McElwee, "How Thomas Piketty and Elizabeth Warren Demolished the Conventional Wisdom on Debt," *Salon*, May 18, 2014, http://www.salon.com/2014/05/18/ how_thomas_piketty_and_elizabeth_warren_demolished_the_conventional_wisdom_ on_debt/ (accessed April 4, 2015); Insight—Center for Community Economic Development, "The Racial Gap in Debt, Credit and Financial Services," http://www.insightcced.org/uploads/publications/assets/the-racial-gap-in-debt.pdf (accessed April 4, 2015); "From Jim Crow Jobs to Employment Equity."

44 Antonio Moore, "America's Financial Divide: The Racial Breakdown of U.S. Wealth in Black and White," *Huffington Post*, April 13, 2015, http://www.huffingtonpost.com/anto nio-moore/americas-financial-divide_b_7013330.html (accessed April 16, 2015).

45 Sean McElwee, "Is There an American Dream for Black Children?" September 22, 2014, *Huffington Post*, http://www.huffingtonpost.com/sean-mcelwee/american-dream_b_5858106.html (accessed April 2, 2015); Delaney, "Subprime Lenders under Fire"; Bajaj and Fessenden, "What's Behind the Race Gap?," p. 16; Kimberly Blanton, "A 'Smoking Gun' on Race, Subprime Loans," *The Boston Globe*, March 16, 2007, http://www.boston.com/business/globe/articles/2007/03/16/a_smoking_gun_on_race_subprime_loans/ (accessed April 14, 2015); Manny Fernandez, "Study Finds Disparities in Mortgages by Race," *New York Times*, October 15, 2007, http://www.nytimes.com/2007/10/15/nyregion/15subprime.html (accessed April 14, 2015).

46 Amaad Rivera, Brenda Cotto-Escalera, Anisha Desai, Jeannette Huezo, and Dedrick Muhammad, *Foreclosed: State of the Dream 2008* (Boston, MA: United for a Fair Economy, 2008).

47 Michael Powell, "Bank Accused of Pushing Mortgage Deals on Blacks," *The New York Times*, June 6, 2009, http://www.nytimes.com/2009/06/07/us/07baltimore.html?_r=1 (accessed March 16, 2011).

48 Gregory D. Squires, Derek S. Hyra, and Robert N. Renner, "Segregation and the Subprime Lending Crisis," *Economic Policy Institute (EPI)*, November 4, 2009, http://epi.3cdn.net/d1219ac2d8a407a2f5_b3m6b5bkb.pdf (accessed April 4, 2015); Debbie Gruenstein Bocian, Wei Li, Carolina Reid, and Roberto G. Quercia, "Lost Ground, 2011: Disparities in Mortgage Lending and Foreclosures. Executive Summary," *Center for Responsible Lending*, November 2011, http://www.responsiblelending.org/mortgage-lending/research-analysis/Lost-Ground-exec-summary.pdf (accessed April 4, 2015).

49 See Ruth Thompson-Miller, Joe R. Feagin, and Leslie H. Picca, *Jim Crow's Legacy: The Segregation Stress Syndrome* (Lanham, MD: Rowman and Littlefield, 2015); Feagin, *How Blacks Built America*, chapter 2.

50 Jennifer C. Mueller, personal communication, July 11, 2013. See Jennifer Mueller, "The Social Reproduction of Systemic Racial Inequality," unpublished Ph.D. dissertation, Texas A&M University, 2013.

51 See Cornel West and Christa Buschendorf, *Black Prophetic Fire* (Boston, MA: Beacon Press, 2014), Kindle loc. 1076.

52 Deborah F. Atwate, "Senator Barack Obama: The Rhetoric of Hope and the American Dream," *Journal of Black Studies 38*, no. 2 (November 2007): 121–129, 124 and 125; Barack Obama, *The Audacity of Hope: Thoughts on Reclaiming the American Dream* (New York: Three Rivers Press, 2006), pp. 81 and 233; "Text of Obama's Speech: A More Perfect Union," *The Wall Street Journal*, March 18, 2008, http://blogs.wsj.com/washwire/2008/03/18/text-of-obamas-speech-a-more-perfect-union/ (accessed April 2, 2015).

53 See, for example, "President-Elect Obama: The Voters Rebuke Republicans for Economic Failure," *The Wall Street Journal*, November 5, 2008, http://www.wsj.com/articles/SB122586244657800863 (accessed April 15, 2015).

54 See Howard Zinn, *You Can't Be Neutral on a Moving Train: A Personal History of Our Times* (Boston, MA: Beacon Press, 2002), p. 165; Jane Flax, *The American Dream in Black and White: The Clarence Thomas Hearings* (Ithaca, NY: Cornell University Press, 1998), p. 42.

8 Systemic Sexism, Racism, and Classism: A Troubled Present and Future

1 Carlos Lozada, "I Just Binge-Read Eight Books by Donald Trump. Here's What I Learned," *Washington Post*, July 30, 2015, https://www.washingtonpost.com/news/book-party/wp/2015/07/30/i-just-binge-read-eight-books-by-donald-trump-heres-what-i-learned/ (accessed May 25, 2016).

2 Ibid.

3 "Anthony Baxter on Donald Trump's Callous Capitalism," *Moyers & Company*, August 3, 2012, http://billmoyers.com/segment/anthony-baxter-on-donald-trump%E2%80%99s-callous-capitalism/ (accessed May 3, 2016); Abigail Abrams, "Donald Trump Supreme Court Battle: Wind Turbines near Scottish Resort to Be Challenged by Billionaire Presidential

Candidate," *International Business Times*, October 8, 2015, www.ibtimes.com/donald-trump-supreme-court-battle-wind-turbines-near-scottish-resort-be-challenged-2132719 (accessed May 3, 2016).

4 Quoted in Lozada, "I Just Binge-Read Eight Books by Donald Trump"; Amy Argetsinger, "Why Does Everyone Call Donald Trump 'The Donald'? It's an Interesting Story," *Washington Post*, September 1, 2015, https://www.washingtonpost.com/news/arts-and-entertainment/wp/2015/09/01/why-does-everyone-call-donald-trump-the-donald-its-an-interesting-story/ (accessed May 25, 2016).

5 "Transcript: Donald Trump's Taped Comments about Women," *New York Times*, October 8, 2016, http://www.nytimes.com/2016/10/08/us/donald-trump-tape-transcript.html (accessed October 9, 2016).

6 See, for example, Libby Nelson, "Donald Trump's History of Misogyny, Sexism, and Harassment: A Comprehensive Review," *Vox*, October 9, 2016, http://www.vox.com/2016/10/8/13110734/donald-trump-leaked-audio-recording-billy-bush-sexism (accessed October 9, 2016).

7 Joanne Doroshow, "Watch Hot Coffee, a Powerful New Film on HBO June 27," *Huffington Post*, June 26, 2011, http://www.huffingtonpost.com/joanne-doroshow/watch-hot-coffee-a-powerf_b_884318.html (accessed October 9, 2016).

8 CNN Staff, "Who's in Trump's Cabinet?" CNN Politics, January 5, 2017, http://www.cnn.com/interactive/2016/11/politics/new-cabinet/ (accessed January 7, 2017); see also Lauren Gambino and David Smith, "Democrats Target 'Troublesome' Trump Cabinet Nominees," January 5, 2017, https://www.theguardian.com/us-news/2017/jan/05/democrats-prepare-for-confirmation-battle-over-troublesome-trump-cabinet-nominees (accessed January 8, 2017).

9 Kate Stanhope, "NBC: We Disagree with Donald Trump on 'a Number of Issues'." *Hollywood Reporter*, June 25, 2015, https://www.hollywoodreporter.com/live-feed/nbc-we-disagree-donald-trump-805198 (accessed June 26, 2015); David Remnick, "American Demagogue," *New Yorker*, March 14, 2016, http://www.newyorker.com/magazine/2016/03/14/behind-the-trump-phenomenon (accessed May 2, 2016); Chauncey DeVega, "Donald Trump's Racism Is as American as Apple Pie," *Salon*, December 11, 2015, http://www.salon.com/2015/12/11/donald_trumps_racism_is_as_american_as_apple_pie/ (accessed March 8, 2016).

10 John Hecht, "Donald Trump's Anti-Immigrant Remarks Spark Outrage in Mexico," *Hollywood Reporter*, June 26, 2015, http://news.yahoo.com/donald-trumps-anti-immigrant-remarks-spark-outrage-mexico-040007644.html (accessed June 25, 2015).

11 Italics added. The PPRI and the Brookings survey is summarized in Ed Kilgore, "Trump Fans Really Want a Less-Diverse America," *New York Magazine*, June 23, 2016, http://nymag.com/daily/intelligencer/2016/06/trump-fans-really-want-a-less-diverse-america.html (accessed September 19, 2016).

12 DeVega, "Donald Trump's Racism Is as American as Apple Pie"; Lisa Belkin, "7 Ways Donald Trump Is Just Like the Founding Fathers," *YAHOO! News*, April 7, 2016 https://www.yahoo.com/news/7-ways-donald-trump-is-just-1402033286914102.html (accessed May 3, 2016).

13 Heather Cox Richardson, "Killing Reconstruction," *Jacobin 18* (September, 2015), https://www.jacobinmag.com/2015/08/racism-reconstruction-homestead-act-black-suffrage/ (accessed March 23, 2016); Belkin, "7 Ways Donald Trump Is Just Like the Founding Fathers."

14 "Noam Chomsky on Trump: We Should Recognize the Other Candidates Are Not That Different," *Democracy Now*, September 22, 2015, http://www.democracynow.org/2015/9/22/noam_chomsky_on_trump_we_should (accessed May 2, 2016); Megan McArdle, "The Die-Hard Republicans Who Say #NeverTrump," *Bloomberg View*, February 29, 2016, http://www.bloombergview.com/articles/2016-02-29/the-die-hard-republicans-who-say-nevertrump (accessed May 3, 2016); Chauncey DeVega, "Jeb Bush Is Erasing History: Why His Comments about Black Americans Are Even Worse Than You Thought," *Salon*, September 30, 2015, http://www.salon.com/2015/09/30/jeb_bush_is_erasing_history_why_his_comments_about_black_americans_are_even_worse_than_you_thought/ (accessed March 23, 2016).

15 DeVega, "Jeb Bush Is Erasing History."

16 "The Trump Effect: The Impact of the Presidential Campaign on Our Nation's Schools," *Southern Poverty Law Center*, April 13, 2016, https://www.splcenter.org/20160413/ trump-effect-impact-presidential-campaign-our-nations-schools (accessed January 27, 2017); Madeline Will, "The Election Is Over, But for Teachers, Hard Conversations Are Just Beginning," http://blogs.edweek.org/teachers/teaching_now/2016/11/post_elec tion_teaching.html (accessed December 8, 2016).

17 Patrick Healy and Jonathan Martin, "For Republicans, Mounting Fears of Lasting Split," *New York Times*, January 9, 2016, http://www.nytimes.com/2016/01/10/us/politics/for-republicans-mounting-fears-of-lasting-split.html (accessed April 2, 2016).

18 Andrea Seebrook, "America's Anxiety around the Economy Grows," *Market Place*, June 27, 2016, http://www.marketplace.org/2016/06/27/world/americans-uncertainty-around-economy-grows (accessed June 30, 2016).

19 Justin Gest, "Why Trumpism Will Outlast Donald Trump," *politico.com*, August 16, 2016, http://www.politico.com/magazine/story/2016/08/why-trumpism-will-outlast-donald-trump-214166 (accessed January 27, 2017).

20 Gene Demby, "On Who Gets to Be a 'Real American,' and Who Deserves a Helping Hand," *NPR.org*, March 23, 2016, http://www.npr.org/sections/codeswitch/2016/03/23/470908502/ on-who-gets-to-be-a-real-american-and-who-deserves-a-helping-hand (accessed March 8, 2016).

21 Laura Clawson, "Five Questions on Outsourcing and Activism: 'Out of Sight' Author Erik Loomis," *Daily Kos*, http://www.dailykos.com/stories/2016/6/28/1541729/-five-questions-on-outsourcing-and-activism-out-of-sight-author-erik-loomis (accessed August 18, 2016).

22 Michael Kimmel, *Angry White Men: American Masculinity at the End of an Era* (New York: Nation Books, 2013), p. 281.

23 Gregory Ferenstein, "I Quizzed Dozens of Silicon Valley Elites about Inequality: Here's What They Told Me," *Vox Media*, January 9, 2016, http://www.vox.com/2016/ 1/9/10738910/silicon-valley-elites-quiz (accessed April 2, 2016).

24 Ibid.

25 Jonathan Chait, "How Trump Has Revived the Republican Cult of Manliness," *New York Magazine*, May 16, 2016, http://nymag.com/betamale/2016/05/gop-cult-masculini ty-trump.html (accessed May 19, 2016).

26 Michael Rogin, *Ronald Reagan the Movie: And Other Episodes in Political Demonology* (Berkeley, CA: University of California Press, 1988).

27 Peggy Noonan, "Why Did They Do It?" *Wall Street Journal*, April 24, 2000, http://www. wsj.com/articles/SB956526736138049046 (accessed August 18, 2016). Italics added.

28 Cathy Young, "The Cult of 'Manliness,'" *Reason*, July 2006, https://reason.com/ archives/2006/07/01/the-cult-of-manliness (accessed May 19, 2016).

29 Chait, "How Trump Has Revived the Republican Cult of Manliness."

30 Jay Nordlinger, "Political Virility: Real Men Vote Republican," *Wall Street Journal*, September 17, 2003, http://www.wsj.com/articles/SB122729590716548555 (accessed August 18, 2016).

31 Kathleen Parker, "Commentary: Donald Trump in His Own Damning Words," *Chicago Tribune*, April 30, 2016, http://www.chicagotribune.com/news/opinion/commen tary/ct-trump-women-dogs-abortion-clinton-perspec-0502-jm-20160430-story.html (accessed May 1, 2016).

32 Ibid.; and Akbar Shahid Ahmed, "Donald Trump: I Can't Be Expected to Recognize Arab Name After Arab Name," *HuffPost Entertainment*, September 16, 2015, http://www.huffing tonpost.com/entry/donald-trump-republican-debate_us_55fa20b4e4b08820d9175a80 (accessed May 3, 2016); Patrick Caldwell, "Donald Trump Doesn't Know Foreign Groups Because They're Just 'Arab Name, Arab Name,'" *Mother Jones*, September 16, 2015, http://www.motherjones.com/mojo/2015/09/donald-trump-arab-names (accessed May 3, 2016).

33 Parker, "Commentary: Donald Trump in His Own Damning Words"; Jasmine C. Lee and Kevin Quealy, "The 210 People, Places and Things Donald Trump Has Insulted

on Twitter: A Complete List," *New York Times*, April 4, 2016, http://www.nytimes.com/interactive/2016/01/28/upshot/donald-trump-twitter-insults.html (accessed May 3, 2016); McArdle, "The Die-Hard Republicans Who Say #NeverTrump."

34 Parker, "Commentary: Donald Trump in His Own Damning Words"; McArdle, "The Die-Hard Republicans Who Say #NeverTrump."

35 Stephan Richter, "Trump and the Fear of Hillary: A Political Psychogram of the 2016 Race," *The Globalist*, http://www.theglobalist.com/donald-trump-hillary-political-elections/ (accessed August 18, 2016).

36 Quoted in Parker, "Commentary: Donald Trump in His Own Damning Words."

37 Lawrence Simkins and Christine Rinck, "Male and Female Sexual Vocabulary in Different Interpersonal Contexts," *Journal of Sex Research 18* (1982): 160–172.

38 Stephen Marche, "How Toxic Masculinity Poisoned the 2016 Election," *Esquire*, March 9, 2016, http://www.esquire.com/news-politics/news/a42802/toxic-masculine-discourse/ (accessed March 18, 2016).

39 Bonnie Fuller, "GOP Presidential Candidates' Attacks on Hillary Clinton & Megyn Kelly Are War on All Women," *Hollywood Life*, February 5, 2016, http://hollywoodlife.com/2016/02/05/donald-trump-slams-women-hillary-clinton-megyn-kelly-insults-war/ (accessed May 2, 2016); Jennifer G. Uffalussy, "We Need to Talk about Ted Cruz Suggesting Hillary Clinton Deserves a 'Spanking,'" http://fusion.net/story/253438/ted-cruz-hillary-clinton-spanking-sexism/ (accessed August 18, 2016).

40 Janell Ross, "So Which Women Has Donald Trump Called 'Dogs' and 'Fat Pigs'?" *Washington Post*, August 8, 2015, https://www.washingtonpost.com/news/the-fix/wp/2015/08/08/so-which-women-has-donald-trump-called-dogs-and-fat-pigs/ (accessed May 1, 2016); "Roots of Oppression," *Human Liberation, Animal Liberation*, http://human-animal-liberation.blogspot.ca/2009/06/roots-of-oppression.html (accessed March 8, 2016); Charles Patterson, *Eternal Treblinka: Our Treatment of Animals and the Holocaust* (New York: Lantern Books, 2002); Stephen Messenger, "13 Really Good Reasons to Stop Using Animal Names as Insults," *The Dodo*, https://www.thedodo.com/13-reasons-stop-animal-insults-985362019.html (accessed April 19, 2016).

41 Ruth Marcus, "Carly Fiorina's Outrageously Sexist Attack on Hillary Clinton Is the Worst Yet," *Washington Post*, January 15, 2016, https://www.washingtonpost.com/opinions/carly-fiorinas-outrageously-sexist-attack-on-hillary-clinton-is-the-worst-yet/2016/01/15/5ec62f4c-bbb2-11e5-b682-4bb4dd403c7d_story.html (accessed May 2, 2016).

42 Ibid.

43 Susan Page, "Study: Sexist Insults Hurt Female Politicians," *USA Today*, September 23, 2010, http://usatoday30.usatoday.com/news/politics/2010-09-22-sexist-insults-female-politicians_N.htm (accessed May 2, 2016).

44 Nick Baumann and Patrick Caldwell, "Republicans Blew Their Chance to End Hillary Clinton's Career 15 Years Ago: Have They Learned Their Lesson?" *Mother Jones*, March 19, 2015, http://www.motherjones.com/politics/2015/03/hillary-clinton-rick-lazio-2000-senate-sexism (accessed May 2, 2016).

45 Catherine Rampell, "The Sexist Double Standard behind Why Millennials Love Bernie Sanders," *Washington Post*, February 4, 2016, http://www.washingtonmonthly.com/political-animal-a/2016_03/message_to_millennials_bernie059844.php (accessed April 5, 2016); Elizabeth Enochs, "5 Times Hillary Clinton's Style Was Criticized Instead of Her Ideas," *Bustle*, June 3, 2015, http://www.bustle.com/articles/86973-5-times-hillary-clintons-style-was-criticized-instead-of-her-ideas (accessed April 6, 2016).

46 Enochs, "5 Times Hillary Clinton's Style Was Criticized Instead of Her Ideas."

47 Emine Saner, "Top 10 Sexist Moments in Politics: Julia Gillard, Hillary Clinton and More," *Guardian*, June 14, 2013, http://www.theguardian.com/politics/2013/jun/14/top-10-sexist-moments-politics (accessed May 2, 2016).

48 Ibid.

49 See "Official Site, 2016 Hillary Nutcracker," http://www.hillarynutcracker.com/ (accessed May 2, 2016); and Saner, "Top 10 Sexist Moments in Politics."

50 Carter Maness, "Harvard Study Confirms the Media Tore Down Clinton and Built Up Trump and Sanders," http://universepolitics.com/2016/06/18/harvard-study-confirms-the-media-tore-down-clinton-built-up-trump-and-sanders/ (accessed August 18, 2016).

51 Adia Harvey Wingfield and Joe R. Feagin, *Yes We Can: White Racial Framing and the 2008 Presidential Campaign* (New York: Routledge, 2010).

52 Jon Henley, "White and Wealthy Voters Gave Victory to Donald Trump, Exit Polls Show," *The Guardian*, November 9, 2016, https://www.theguardian.com/us-news/2016/nov/09/white-voters-victory-donald-trump-exit-polls (accessed November 11, 2016).

53 Harvey C. Mansfield, *Manliness* (New Haven, CT: Yale University Press, 2006), Kindle loc. 22–34, 161–163.

54 David Futrelle, "White Hot Rage," *The American Prospect*, November 20, 2013, http://prospect.org/article/white-hot-rage (accessed February 5, 2016).

55 Ibid.

56 Ibid. See also, A Voice for Men, "Policies," http://www.avoiceformen.com/policies/ (accessed February 5, 2016).

57 Ishmael N. Daro, "Men's Rights Activist Launch Another Offensive Poster Campaign," *Canada.com*, April 7, 2014, http://o.canada.com/news/mens-rights-posters-dont-be-that-girl-423582 (accessed February 5, 2016).

58 Joel Rose, "For Men's Rights Groups, Feminism Has Come at the Expense of Men," *NPR*, September 2, 2014, http://www.npr.org/2014/09/02/343970601/men-s-rights-movement (accessed February 5, 2016).

59 Ibid.

60 Ibid.

61 R.W. Connell, *Masculinities*, 2nd edn. (Berkeley, CA: University of California press, 2005), p. 248.

62 Ibid., p. 249.

63 Tony Collins, *Sport in Capitalist Society* (Florence, GB: Routledge, 2013), p. 38. Italics added.

64 Quotes are from Dave Zirin, Jeremy Earp, and Chris Boulton, "Not Just a Game: Power, Politics & American Sport" Transcript, *Media Education Foundation*, 2010, http://www.mediaed.org/cgi-bin/commerce.cgi?preadd=action&key=151 (accessed March 10, 2016). See also Caroline Fusco, "Setting the Record Straight: The Experiences of Lesbian Athletes," *Atlantis 23* (Fall/Winter 1998): 70.

65 Kate Rounds, "Why Men Fear Women's Teams," *Ms.*, (January–February 1991): 43–45.

66 Fusco, "Setting the Record Straight: The Experiences of Lesbian Athletes."

67 Kevin Manahan, "Rush Limbaugh Agrees with Michigan's Jim Harbaugh: Football Is Last Hope for Toughness in U.S. Men," http://www.nj.com/giants/index.ssf/2015/04/rush_limbaugh_agrees_with_jim_harbaugh_football_is.html (accessed August 18, 2016).

68 John Harbaugh, "Why Football Matters," April 22, 2015, http://www.baltimoreravens.com/news/article-1/Why-Football-Matters-By-John-Harbaugh-/4aeda6f9-1ade-4a1a-88a5-51ef73e20a9a (accessed August 18, 2016). We are indebted to Anthony Weems for this reference.

69 See Joshua I. Newman and Michael D. Giardina, *Sport, Spectacle, and NASCAR Nation* (New York: Palgrave Macmillan, 2100), pp. 128–132.

70 See Connell, *Masculinities*, p. 196.

71 Collins, *Sport in Capitalist Society*, p. 129.

72 Morris B. Holbrook, *Consumer Research: Introspective Essays on the Study of Consumption* (Los Angeles, CA: Sage, 1995), p. 177.

73 Elizabeth Cady Stanton, *A History of Woman Suffrage*, vol. 1 (Rochester, NY: Fowler and Wells, 1889), pp. 70–71. We draw on the Fordham University website at http://legacy.fordham.edu/halsall/mod/senecafalls.asp (accessed August 18, 2016).

74 Jessica Ravitz, "The New Women Warriors: Reviving the Fight for Equal Rights," *CNN*, April 16, 2015, http://www.cnn.com/2015/04/02/us/new-womens-equal-rights-movement/ (accessed June 1, 2016).

75 Bruce Frankel, "Report: Child Abuse Estimates Low: Federal Data Understate Problem, Gallup Group Says," *USA Today*, December 7, 1995, p. A3.

76 "Victims of Sexual Violence," *RAINN*, https://rainn.org/statistics/victims-sexual-vio lence (accessed August 18, 2016); Barbara Krahe, "Societal Responses to Sexual Violence against Women: Rape Myths and the 'Real Rape' Stereotype," in *Women and Children as Victims and Offenders: Background, Prevention, Reintegration*, eds. H. Kury, S. Redo, and E. Sheapp (Berlin: Springer, 2016), pp. 671–700.

77 Ravitz, "The New Women Warriors."

78 Ibid.

79 See Jessica Neuwirth, *Equal Means Equal: Why the Time for an Equal Rights Amendment Is Now* (New York: The New Press, 2015).

80 Amanda Teuscher, "Why Are There So Many Different Gender Wage Gap Calculations?" *The Prospect Group Blog*, October 27, 2016, http://prospect.org/blog/tapped/why-are-there-so-many-different-gender-wage-gap-calculations (accessed January 27, 2017).

81 AAUW, "The Simple Truth about the Gender Pay Gap," *American Association of University Women*, Fall 2016, http://www.aauw.org/research/the-simple-truth-about-the-gen der-pay-gap/ (accessed August 18, 2016).

82 Teuscher, "Why Are There So Many Different Gender Wage Gap Calculations?"

83 Claire C. Miller, "As Women Take over a Male-Dominated Field, the Pay Drops," *New York Times*, March 18, 2016, http://www.nytimes.com/2016/03/20/upshot/as-women-take-over-a-male-dominated-field-the-pay-drops.html (accessed August 18, 2016); see statistics reports at https://www.dol.gov/wb/stats/stats_data.htm#facts (accessed August 18, 2016).

84 Merida L. Johns, "Breaking the Glass Ceiling: Structural, Cultural, and Organizational Barriers Preventing Women from Achieving Senior and Executive Positions," *Perspectives on Health and Information Management 10* (Winter 2013), http://www.ncbi.nlm. nih.gov/pmc/articles/PMC3544145/ (accessed June 13, 2016).

85 Lin Farley, *Sexual Shakedown* (New York: McGraw-Hill, 1978), p. 14.

86 "Know Who You're Pulling For," *Star Tribune*, October 11, 1992, p. 22A. See also Joe R. Feagin, Clairece Feagin, and David Baker, *Social Problems*, 6th edn. (Upper Saddle River, NJ: Prentice-Hall, 2005), chapter 5.

87 Teuscher, "Why Are There So Many Different Gender Wage Gap Calculations?"

88 David Moberg, "Poultry Giants Fight Organizers," *In These Times*, January 30, 2004, http://inthesetimes.com/article/689/poultry_giants_fight_organizers (accessed March 8, 2016).

89 Angela Stuesse, *Scratching Out a Living: Latinos, Race, and Work in the Deep South* (Berkeley, CA: University of California Press, 2016), p. 127.

90 David Nibert, *Animal Rights/Human Rights: Entanglements of Oppression and Liberation* (Lanham, MD: Rowman & Littlefield Publishers, 2002), pp. 3, 94.

91 "Feminist Perspectives on the Self," *Stanford Encyclopedia of Philosophy*, http://plato. stanford.edu/entries/feminism-self/ (accessed August 18, 2016). See also "In Academia, Women Collaborate Less with Their Same-Sex Juniors," http://www.sciencemag.org/news/ 2014/03/academia-women-collaborate-less-their-same-sex-juniors (accessed August 18, 2016). Italics added.

92 Natalia Borecka, "Entitlement and Apathy, the Case of Women against Feminism," *Lone Wolf Magazine*, August 15, 2014, https://lonewolfmag.com/women-against-feminism/ (accessed July 22, 2016).

93 Fay Francis, "#(White) Women against Feminism," http://www.bad-housekeeping.com/ author/fay-francis/ (accessed August 18, 2016).

94 Eli Clifton, "Guess Which Women's Group Rush Limbaugh Has Donated Hundreds of Thousands of Dollars To?" *Nation*, June 12, 2014, https://www.thenation.com/article/ guess-which-womens-group-rush-limbaugh-has-donated-hundreds-thousands-dollars/ (accessed July 22, 2016); Lee Fang, "How John Birch Society Extremism Never Dies," *Think-Progress*, February 21, 2011; Media Matters, "Independent Women's Forum," http://conser vativetransparency.org/recipient/independent-womens-forum (accessed July 10, 2016).

95 Amanda Boyajian, "Thoughts on Language, Dialog, and Gender," *Daily Kos*, April 25, 2016, http://www.dailykos.com/stories/2016/4/25/1519714/-thoughts-on-language-di alog-and-gender (accessed April 26, 2016). Italics added.

96   See "No Comment," *The Progressive*, October 1992, p. 12; Elayne Rapping, "Gender Politics on the Big Screen," *The Progressive*, October 1992, p. 36.

97   "Meat and Masculinity: Men May Avoid Vegetarian Options over Manly Perception of Meat," *HuffPost Masculinity*, May 17, 2012, http://www.huffingtonpost.com/2012/05/17/meat-men-masculinity_n_1524224.html (accessed May 2, 2016).

98   Victoria A. Brownworth, "Op-ed: Violence against Lesbians on the Rise, but Prosecutions Aren't," *shewired.com*, March 14, 2014, http://www.shewired.com/opinion/2014/03/14/op-ed-violence-against-lesbians-rise-prosecutions-aren%E2%80%99t (accessed December 30, 2015).

99   Fareed Zakaria, "An Enclave Strategy for Iraq," *Washington Post*, June 19, 2014, https://www.washingtonpost.com/opinions/fareed-zakaria-an-enclave-strategy-for-iraq/2014/06/19/e06d8938-f7ea-11e3-a606-946fd632f9f1_story.html (accessed December 28, 2015).

100 Timothy McGrath, "Watch This English-Speaking ISIS Fighter Explain How a 98-Year-Old Colonial Map Created Today's Conflict," July 2, 2014, *Los Angeles Daily News* (accessed December 28, 2015).

101 Zakaria, "An Enclave Strategy for Iraq."

102 Connell, *Masculinities*, p. 199.

103 Ibid., p. xxi.

104 Ibid., p. 199.

105 W. E. B. Du Bois, "The African Roots of War," in *W. E. B. Du Bois: A Reader*, ed. Meyer Weinberg (New York: Harper & Row Publishers 1970), pp. 413–424. The quote is on p. 368.

106 Sarah Lazare, "How Billionaires Use Nonprofits to Bypass Governments and Force Their Agendas on Humanity," *truthout*, March 13, 2016, http://www.truth-out.org/news/item/35189-how-billionaires-use-nonprofits-to-bypass-governments-and-force-their-agendas-on-humanity (accessed May 24, 2016).

107 Ibid.

108 Quoted in ibid.

109 Alexander C. Kaufman, "Stephen Hawking Says We Should Really Be Scared of Capitalism, Not Robots," *Huffington Post*, October 8, 2015, http://www.huffingtonpost.com/entry/stephen-hawking-capitalism-robots_us_5616c20ce4b0dbb8000d9f15 (accessed May 25, 2016).

110 Robert W. McChesney and John Nichols, *People Get Ready: The Fight against a Jobless Economy and a Citizenless Democracy* (New York: Nation Books, 2016), Kindle loc. 257–273.

111 Ibid. Italics added.

112 Steve H. Murdock, *An America Challenged: Population Change and the Future of the United States* (Boulder, CO: Westview Press, 1995), pp. 33–47; and U.S. Census Bureau, "An Older and More Diverse Nation by Midcentury," August 2008, http://www.census.gov/Press-Release/www/releases/archives/population/012496.html (accessed August 18, 2016); William H. Frey, *Melting Pot Cities and Suburbs: Racial and Ethnic Change in Metro America in the 2000s* (Washington, DC: Brookings Institution, 2011).

113 Dale Maharidge, *The Coming White Minority: California's Eruptions and America's Future* (New York: Random House, 1996), p. 11.

114 Samuel P. Huntington, "The Erosion of American National Interests," *Foreign Affairs* (September/October 1997): 28ff.

115 Ibid., p. 33.

116 Joe Feagin and Eileen O'Brien, *White Men on Race* (Boston, MA: Beacon Press, 2003), p. 248.

117 William H. Frey, *America's Diverse Future: Initial Glimpses at the U.S. Child Population from the 2010 Census* (Washington, DC: Brookings Institution, 2011), p. 1. Italics added.

118 See Joe R. Feagin, *Racist America: Roots, Current Realities, and Future Reparations*, 3rd edn. (New York: Routledge, 2014); Feagin, Feagin, and Baker, *Social Problems*, chapter 5.

119 See Aldon Morris, *The Origins of the Civil Rights Movement: Black Communities Organizing for Change* (New York: Free Press, 1984); Joe R. Feagin and Clairece B. Feagin, *Racial and Ethnic Relations*, 6th edn. (Upper Saddle River, NJ: Prentice-Hall, 1999), Chapter 8.

120 Jelani Cobb, "The Matter of Black Lives," *New Yorker*, http://www.newyorker.com/mag azine/2016/03/14/where-is-black-lives-matter-headed (accessed July 21, 2016); "Black Lives Matter," https://en.wikipedia.org/wiki/Black_Lives_Matter (accessed July 21, 2016).

121 Rebecca Solnit, "Why Imperfect Occupy Still Had Lasting Effects," *Mother Jones*, September 16, 2013, http://www.motherjones.com/politics/2013/09/occupy-wall-street-an niversary-effects (accessed April 2, 2016).

122 Lawrence Summers, "What's Behind the Revolt against Global Integration?" *Washington Post*, April 10, 2016, https://www.washingtonpost.com/opinions/whats-behind-the-re volt-against-global-integration/2016/04/10/b4c09cb6-fdbb-11e5-80e4-c381214de1a3_ story.html (accessed May 24, 2016).

123 Ibid.

124 George Lakoff, *The ALL NEW Don't Think of an Elephant!: Know Your Values and Frame the Debate*, 2nd edn. (White River Junction, VT: Chelsea Green Publishing, 2014), p. 23.

125 Derrick Bell, *Faces at the Bottom of the Well* (New York: Basic Books, 1992), p. 55–56.

126 Lisa B. Spanierman et al., "White University Students' Responses to Societal Racism a Qualitative Investigation," *The Counseling Psychologist 36* (November 2008): 860.

127 We draw on Joe R. Feagin, *The White Racial Frame*, 2nd edn. (New York: Routledge, 2013), chapter 9.

128 Lakoff, *The ALL NEW Don't Think of an Elephant!*, p. 82.

129 We draw here on emails and notes from Okogyeamon (Herb Perkins), Bundy Trinz, Margery Otto, and Tim Johnson.

130 John Sorenson, *Constructing Ecoterrorism: Capitalism, Speciesism, and Animal Rights* (Winnipeg, MB: Fernwood Publishing, 2016).

131 G. William Domhoff, "C. Wright Mills, Floyd Hunter, and 50 Years of Power Structure Research," address to Michigan Sociological Association, *Who Rules America*, 2016, http://www2.ucsc.edu/whorulesamerica/theory/mills_address.html (accessed December 8, 2016).

132 Paul Kivel, "Afterword from *You Call This a Democracy?* Who Benefits, Who Pays, and Who Really Decides," http://paulkivel.com/resource/afterword-from-you-call-this-a-democracy-who-benefits-who-pays-and-who-really-decides/ (accessed December 26, 2015).

Epilogue: Making Real "Liberty and Justice for All"

1 "Declaration of Independence," *Library of Congress*, http://www.loc.gov/rr/program/ bib/ourdocs/DeclarInd.html (accessed August 18, 2016).

2 "Universal Declaration of Human Rights," *United for Human Rights* http://www.human rights.com/what-are-human-rights/universal-declaration-of-human-rights/preamble. html (accessed August 18, 2016).

3 "Interview with Lydia H. Chu," *East Asian Institute Newsletter*, http://weai.columbia. edu/professor-lydia-h-liu-on-human-rights-pioneer-and-columbia-alum-p-c-chang/ (accessed August 18, 2016); Sumner B. Twiss, "Confucian Contributions to the Universal Declaration of Human Rights: A Historical and Philosophical Perspective," in *The World's Religions: A Contemporary Reader*, ed. Arvind Sharma (Minneapolis, MN: Fortress Press, 2010), pp. 110–112.

4 Louis Henkin, Sarah H. Cleveland, Laurence R. Helfer, Gerald L. Newman, and Diana F. Orentlicher, *Human Rights* (New York: Foundation Press, 2009), p. 216.

5 Judith Blau and Alberto Moncada, *Human Rights: Beyond the Liberal Vision* (Lanham, MD: Rowman & Littlefield, 2005), p. 63; see also "The Universal Declaration of Human Rights."

6 "National Democrat Primary Survey," *American Action Network*, February 2–4, 2016, http://static.politico.com/e2/b7/4b6f2ac94dfc9a5c21e4c8d20cdf/socialism-final-1.pdf (accessed December 8, 2016).

7 Gallup, "Americans' Views of Socialism, Capitalism Are Little Changed," May 6, 2016, http://www.gallup.com/poll/191354/americans-views-socialism-capitalism-little-changed.aspx (accessed January 27, 2017).

8 Pew Research Center, "December 2011 Poll," *Pew Research Center* http://www.demo craticunderground.com/118741931 (accessed August 26, 2016).

9 "Interview with John Smith," *Redline,* https://rdln.wordpress.com/2016/06/01/inter view-with-john-smith-author-of-imperialism-in-the-twenty-first-century/ (accessed September 19, 2016).

10 John Smith, "Imperialism in the Twenty-First Century," *Monthly Review 67* (July–August 2015), http://monthlyreview.org/2015/07/01/imperialism-in-the-twenty-first-century/ (accessed September 19, 2016).

11 Maria Mies, *Patriarchy and Accumulation on a World Scale* (London: Zed Books, [1986] 2014), pp. 211–212.

12 Angela Davis, "The 99%: A Community of Resistance," https://www.theguardian.com/commentisfree/cifamerica/2011/nov/15/99-percent-community-resistance (accessed December 8, 2016).

Index

Made in the USA
Monee, IL
25 April 2024

57504890R00184